DESIGNING MODERN JAPAN

DESIGNING MODERN JAPAN

Sarah Teasley

REAKTION BOOKS

To all my teachers, past, present and future

Published by
REAKTION BOOKS LTD
Unit 32, Waterside
44–48 Wharf Road
London N1 7UX, UK
www.reaktionbooks.co.uk

First published 2022
Copyright © Sarah Teasley 2022

The publishers would like to thank The Great Britain Sasakawa Foundation
for its support in the publication of this work

Printed and bound in India by Replika Press Pvt. Ltd

A catalogue record for this book is available from the British Library

ISBN 978 1 78023 202 7

Contents

NOTE ON TRANSLITERATION AND DATES

In keeping with Japanese practice, all Japanese names are given with the surname first, then given name, except when the person has chosen a different order and is best known in Japan and overseas by that name. All Japanese names and words are transliterated using the modified Hepburn romanization system, with macrons over long vowels, unless the individual or organization has chosen a different spelling. Korean names are transliterated using the McCune-Reischauer Romanization system. Chinese names are transliterated using pinyin. Tokyo, Osaka, Kyoto and Kyushu are given without macrons, as per standard practice, in the main text; all names of organizations and publications in Japanese provide the macrons. English names of Japanese organizations and publications are the organizations' own translations, when available. Organizations and publications are given first in Japanese with English in parentheses, then referred to subsequently by the English name. Translations are by the author unless indicated.

Birth and death dates are provided, where publicly accessible, upon the first mention of designers, design policymakers, design educators and other key figures in the history of design in modern Japan. Dates are not provided for other historical figures such as prime ministers, or for historical figures who worked primarily outside Japan and whose dates are readily available in other publications. The relative paucity of dates for female designers and other women introduced in the book reflects the structural discrimination that kept women from advancing in professional practice, taking senior roles in organizations or otherwise becoming publicly known as leading figures in their fields.

Butterfly Stool, designed by
Yanagi Sōri for Tendō Mokkō,
1954. This image appeared in
a Tendō Mokkō catalogue in
1960, with graphic design by
Sugiura Kōhei.

Introduction

Early in the autumn of 1991, I walked into a bookshop in Osaka and my world changed forever. I had been in Japan for a few weeks. I had only meant to browse but found myself transfixed by a metres-wide expanse of magazines, all to do with architecture and design. There were achingly beautiful architecture journals like *Shinkenchiku* (New Architecture) and *Architecture and Urbanism* (*a+u*) whose thick, glossy paper and unexpected heft in the hand echoed the expense and restrained luxury of the glass and concrete houses within. Visually energetic graphic design journals like *IDEA* and *Dezain no genba* (Designers' Workshop) showcased the offices of leading graphic designers and illustrators, as well as their typographic and layout techniques. Magazines like *AXIS* proffered the sleek monotone minimalism of Japanese industrial design in its styling heyday. *Sōen* and *Ryūkō tsūshin* (Trend Communication) presented an intoxicating, enchanting riot of fashion. Then there were the shelves of magazines like *Mono* (Things) and *Brutus*, which told young men how to buy and use designed things in a tone that was both didactic and compelling, and auto magazines detailing the latest styling and technical changes in exquisite detail. *Burein* (Brain) and *Kōkoku hihyō* (Advertising Critique) provided sophisticated, forensic analyses of Japan's eye-catching adverts. A few rows over, separate from the architecture and design journals and the men's consumer bibles, sat title after title of fashion, beauty and lifestyle magazines for women, carefully segmented by age and income but again promising an immediate, satisfying life through design.[1]

Coming from 1980s Canada, where design – in my circles at least – was not presented as a career option and architects seemed always in danger of unemployment, I was blown away. In Canada, I had subscribed to a national magazine presenting catwalk looks from Paris and New York and followed the 'before and after' home interiors column in a local monthly. But the design industries seemed hardly acknowledged, at least not for a wide public. The exuberance of design and architecture in this one generalist bookshop in Osaka, on the other hand, not only evidenced the existence of multiple vibrant design industries but seemed to welcome newcomers into their worlds. Design is not something hidden away for those who know how to access it, the magazines seemed to say. Instead, their message was one of democratic capitalism: whether by studying it or buying it, anyone can access the excitement and promise of design.

Less than a year after my bookshop epiphany, the world of Japanese design changed irrevocably. The value of the yen and asset prices in Japan crashed, bringing down corporate clients' capital and budgets for commissioning new work and shrinking the purchasing power of design consumers. All of this brought an end to the frothy exuberance of design and, eventually, to many of the titles on those shelves. But the wealth of Japanese design culture remained: its knowledge, its techniques, its oeuvre and, most importantly, its people.

This book is the story of the care, dedication, often inexplicable passion and sheer hard graft on the part of the people who created and nurtured Japan's design industries in the roughly 150 years before that bookshop encounter. As we will see, Japan had extensive and sophisticated design industries and cultures centuries earlier. They were internationalized, incorporating foreign design trends and technologies and exporting products to far-flung consumers, and they responded ably to, and in many cases created, highly segmented markets at home. In the mid-nineteenth century, after the Japanese government committed to new and extensive trade and diplomatic relations with multiple foreign countries, designers had to weather extreme disruption within the domestic economy. The story of the systems and products they created as old markets shifted and disappeared is part of a much larger story about design within the global movement of capital, knowledge and people. Precisely how people in Japan who cared about design responded to these opportunities and changing conditions, however, is a very local story. This book aims to articulate what they did, how and why they did it, and some of the results of those actions.

In modern Japan – which this book parses as the roughly 150 years between the mid-nineteenth century and the end of the twentieth century, or the *bakumatsu* to early Heisei periods in Japanese period-ization – designers were not the only ones who cared about design.[2] Equally important, for the narrative in this book, are the policymakers and entrepreneurs who saw design and designers as helpful for tilting those historical events and conditions towards their preferred outcomes. So too are the consumers whose actions determined the fates of designers, manufacturers, retailers and whole industries, as demands and tastes changed over time.[3] As a practice and a profession, design never occurs in a vacuum. There is always a user – intended if not always actual – and often, if not always, a client. In late nineteenth- and twentieth-century Japan, the client was often the state, or, more specifically, politicians and civil servants who wanted to encourage particular kinds of economic activity or social behaviour, and who saw promoting design, and supporting mechanisms by which others could promote design, as likely to help realize a desired outcome. More often than not, as we will see, that outcome was economic development through increased export income. From the mid-twentieth century onwards, CEOs and corporate managers increasingly took their place. For some entrepreneurs, too, the design industries' ability to create captivating and compelling products, sometimes improving users' quality of life, made them support design as a tool for increasing profits and market share. And throughout the period, people in Japan and overseas, in their activities as consumers, played an outsized role in shaping the direction of design in Japan. Recognizing user agency and empowering people to take part in designing products and systems intended for their use are integral aspects of design practice today.[4] This book does not suggest that policymakers, entrepreneurs and consumers are inherently designers, but it does place these groups close to the heart of the story, as key actors in the design industries in Japan, whether directly or indirectly.

'Design' is a slippery term. In practice, design often refers to the act of creating a pattern or original that can be used, once or repeatedly, to create something in its image, replicating all or part of the idea set down. Design is also the tangible or intangible model created as part of this process, and the products of those actions and activities. It is also the set of professions and disciplines formed in industry and education to carry out these activities, as a specialist practice, and to train people to do this. These are very abstract, general definitions of design on the one hand. On the other, they are my own definitions of design, formed from my own situated experiences working in academic and professional design milieus in Japan, the United States, Britain and Australia.

But design means different things to different people, at different times and in different places. Rather than applying definitions current in design practice and theory today, this book works from the definitions of design that shaped its practice in the periods explored. In Japan today, *dezain* stands as the noun and, with *suru*, the verb (*dezain suru*), but many other words have represented these practices in Japan, and yet others do today.[5] Designers and others argued about the most appropriate terminology for design's practices, products and industries throughout the period covered here. This book explores those definitions and the implications and impact of their use, including, if briefly, the impact both on people's lived experience and on the subsequent record of what those words and definitions excluded, such as much of women's creative design activity in this period.

This book offers a history of design industries, professions and practice in Japan from the mid-nineteenth to the late twentieth century. It argues that the history of design is incomplete without the social, political, environmental and, particularly, economic story, positioning design history narratives as inseparable from economic and industry narratives.[6] It also offers a partial history of Japan during this period, refracted through the lens of Japan's design industries and the experiences of people within them. As a history of modern Japan, it argues that attention to design as a practice and product can tell us something about how macro narratives were interpreted and – sometimes – experienced.[7]

The book's geographic coverage follows its subject-matter as well: design in Japan, but with the understanding that the boundaries of Japan changed over this period, from the annexation of the Ryūkyū Islands, Ezo (Hokkaidō), Taiwan and Korea in the late nineteenth and early twentieth centuries, to further military expansion into China and Southeast Asia in the 1930s and '40s. But the geography it covers is porous and not limited to national borders, not least because designers who identified or identify as Japanese, and who were or are principally active in Japan, travel and work overseas as well. Things designed in Japan – from lacquerware to cars, and from production processes to video games – themselves travelled and continue to travel overseas, too. The story in this book is also inseparable from that of a globalizing economy and the international flow of ideas and people – and of capital, underneath it – during this period.

As a book written in English, it would be reasonable for readers to expect a particular story: one that emphasizes the products that those of us who grew up with Japanese exports, wherever we lived in the world, remember from this period. Of course, what this history comprises would depend on our own individual and national or regional experience of Japanese design. For me, as a child on the west coast of North America in the 1970s and '80s, this would have meant a history centred first on Little Twin Stars pencils and notebooks, then on images of Detroit autoworkers attacking Japanese cars with sledgehammers. From my teenage years, it would include the fresh pleasures of sushi and Japanese advertising, and eventually the seductive promise of Japan's roaring economy and those magazines. Bubble-era Japan's thick, glossy architectural magazines and the exuberant nightclub interiors and minimalist villas within them offered sensory delights, but also a vision of design as a profession offering joy and expansive potential, rather than one that was predominantly functional and at high risk of unemployment. All of this was viewed first from across the Pacific Ocean and then from within Japan, and filtered through a growing awareness of Japan's wartime aggression, the injustices Nikkei (Japanese diaspora) communities in my countries had experienced during the war, and the unresolved legacies of these actions on both sides of the ocean. This brief account of my own situated experience of design from Japan only underlines the importance of recognizing how the very understanding of design – as well as Japan – is highly contingent.

But individual and subjective experiences of designed products from Japan, experienced outside Japan, are only one aspect of the story. This book attempts to place experiences of Japanese design outside Japan at its periphery, and to centre the story on designers and design in Japan, working in ways generated by economic conditions, social norms and political and personal responses to them.

Overall, the book argues that design is a tool that people, often but not always trained in its use, employ consciously to do certain things, frequently taking advantage of existing conditions to do so. In Japan, from well before the modern period, these were regularly towards political ends: design as a policy lever for economic development, political stability or social cohesion. Design as a tool facilitates commerce and, through it, capitalism. Without markets, and sellers competing for attention from consumers within them, design would be very different and its history much poorer, certainly in modern Japan as in many countries. This book argues, crucially, that people equipped with design tools – mostly but not always men – were able to harness design's usefulness to policy and commerce to creatively explore the discipline's potential and possibilities. Or, to put this differently, the usefulness of design for industrial policy and commerce – themselves predicated on Japan's particular position within East Asia, geographically and historically, and in global geopolitics and economic networks in this period – allowed men, primarily, to develop design as a number of interrelated powerful practices, communities and, eventually, disciplines in Japan. *Designing Modern Japan* sets out this argument. It also explores the various tensions that emerged from this harnessing of design to larger forces, and larger forces to design. These included tensions between design for local sustainability and for national development, and tensions between the developmental state, corporate interest and consumer or citizen well-being. These tensions, explored in the book, raise questions. Who benefits from design policy? Who benefits from the promotion of design? This book names and explores how those elements played out in the context of Japan, and in doing so attempts to contribute to our knowledge both of modern Japan and of design in the modern world.

This is not just a Japanese story. The questions, perspectives and issues raised in this book could be asked of many other locations also entangled, in various ways, in global circuits involving design. Economic development and lifestyle improvement through design is a story from Britain in the 1830s, Canada in the 1950s and China in recent decades, to give only three examples. The impact of consumer demand, resource scarcity or war on design's directions are stories experienced in multiple places around the world. In saying this, the book does not suggest that the story of design in modern Japan simply parallels design's trajectory in other locations and periods. Rather, whether to do with wartime graphic propaganda, community revitalization through design or arguments about design for craft industries or mass production, there are many similarities between what designers and the people around them did in modern Japan, and what was happening overseas. There were deep connections, too. As today, Japanese designers in the twentieth century and to some extent the late nineteenth century were often part of international communities. Sometimes this was directly, through participation in international organizations and events; at other times it was by participating more indirectly in the local reception and reformulation of internationally circulating ideas about design practice and education or, indeed, visual styles and design philosophies, in Japan's design divisions, consultancies, design schools and local government institutes.

Designers in modern Japan were also operating – as designers in Japan do today – in an internationally networked economy and market. Decisions about fabric patterns made in Britain impacted designers in Japan in the 1880s, for example. Decisions made by Japanese ceramics designers and export promoters in the mid-twentieth century affected designers and promoters in Scandinavia, and vice versa. Trade policy, including tariffs and copyright infringement issues, is another common theme throughout the book that imbricates design practice in Japan always within global markets and competition. In this sense, the book works from a global history perspective to tell a national story, with a much wider field than either design or Japan in mind.[8] To tell both the Japanese story and the stories of its many connections, similarities and comparisons, however, would make for a very long book. Rather than trying to do both, the book attempts to tell a Japanese story, with a focus on priorities and concerns from various perspectives in Japan.[9] The intention is that readers familiar with design histories elsewhere will see those connections. For readers less familiar with design's histories in other parts of the world, the book could serve as a prompt for more reading.

Designing Modern Japan is not a celebration of 'good design', nor does it focus on the 'Japaneseness' of things designed, made or used in Japan and the ways they are designed, made or used. While it explores these categorizations and the desires, imperatives and quandaries that prompt people to create and perpetuate them, the book suggests that it is more accurate and useful to understand the 'Japaneseness' of Japanese design as something produced in the process of design itself.[10] As the book recounts, questions about what, precisely, made a design 'Japanese' often preoccupied designers and design's promoters in Japan and led them to make particular decisions that they felt distilled something local, familiar or historically specific and unique into tangible objects or environments.

'Japaneseness' continues to be a useful tool for designers, as well for companies and government departments. However, ideas of

Japaneseness are often applied by others, after the fact. A good example of this is the frequent association, in museum catalogues and design magazines, of the Butterfly Stool, a plywood seat designed by Yanagi Sōri (1915–2011) for the firm Tendō Mokkō, as inherently Japanese. Curators and writers often attribute a sense of Japaneseness to the stool's elegant structural form, its minimalist construction, its visual emphasis on the wood grain of the veneers or its visual resemblance to the *torii* gates that mark the entrance to a Shintō shrine. Such classifications are conveniently easy to make and often popular for their difference, but they can also be inaccurate or at the very least incomplete. In the case of the Butterfly Stool, the manufacturer's expectation that whatever the form, it could be broken down for flatpack distribution, to lower export costs and minimize potential damage during transport, was also a key factor. The curves were the result of years-long experimentation and negotiation between Yanagi and the production team, led by Tendō Mokkō's lead engineer, Inui Saburō (1911–1991), to find a sweet spot between aesthetic pleasure, structural integrity and production efficiency. Concepts of Japaneseness can also assume lives of their own, as the persistent popularity abroad of *wabi-sabi* as a design principle in craft design, architecture and interiors exemplifies. Tea practitioners and scholars have documented the historical and contemporary importance of *wabi* and *sabi* as particular aesthetics guiding tea practitioners' decision-making in the set-up and execution of the tea ceremony from the sixteenth century onwards.[11] But this does not mean that these principles, by virtue of having emerged from specific communities of practice within the Japanese archipelago, define a universal national aesthetic over time.

Inui Saburō, head of the technical division at Tendō Mokkō, with one of the firm's hot presses, c. 1960.

To be sure, it is tempting to look for the 'Japaneseness' of designs from Japan. But doing so can lead us to miss things, and sometimes to misunderstand them.[12] 'Japanese design' as a concept is not the

Designing Modern Japan

same thing as design from or in Japan. *Designing Modern Japan* is a history of design as conceptualized, practised, taught and sold in Japan, as its boundaries expanded and contracted, in the period historians of Japan generally agree to be 'modern': the mid-nineteenth century onwards. Rather than argue for aesthetic categories or labels, it argues that Japaneseness in design in Japan resides in a few very simple categories: was it designed or made in Japan? Did the idea, form or production methods circulate there? Rather than propose a narrative of uniqueness or exceptionalism, the book sets out design in modern Japan as partaking in a common, globally networked set of actors and agendas. Where there is exceptionalism or uniqueness, it is in how those actors and agendas come together; in how actors assign value to some elements over others. When, why and how the Japanese government backed design as a lever for economic development, and when it chose not to, for example, might say something about the specificity of Japan in this period.[13]

As a history of design in modern Japan, this book aims to offer different things to different audiences. For people interested in Japanese design, it argues that objects' aesthetics make them immediately compelling, but that the structural stories behind objects and environments can be even more entrancing, not least because they begin to explain why designs from Japan are as they are, beyond the overall gesture towards 'Japaneseness'. To design historians and people interested in the history of design, it insists that design history misses a trick when we overlook how policy, law and economics structure what is possible in design. Designs come from designers' creativity and imagination, to be sure, but they are shaped by myriad other factors, including product standards, the behaviours and tolerances of materials, taxes and tariffs, supply chains, social hierarchies, geography and – equally if not most importantly – consumers who will pay for some things and not others.

To historians and those interested in history, the book argues that history misses a trick by overlooking design. It suggests that historical narratives and conditions can be understood afresh if viewed from the perspective of how design factored into the creation and experience of those conditions. The story of Japan's post-war economic miracle and the importance of the Ministry of International Trade and Industry (MITI), for example, is well known. *Designing Modern Japan* addresses industrial policy through its interface with design and designers from the 1870s onwards – that is, it looks at how some people were able to harness government agendas to promote design. After investigating how designers experienced, worked with and sometimes shaped the execution of aspects of that policy, it largely confirms general conclusions that others have made, but presents industrial policy from a perspective not often taken.[14] In doing so, the book aims to show that design's histories are inseparable from those more macro histories, and that looking from design can offer something fresh and significant.

Power shapes how people and things relate to each other in that network, and what happens as a result. Design in modern Japan was therefore of course subject to power, not just the expression of indigenous essence or individual genius. Some sections of the book focus on political power in the form of design policy and industrial policy that affected design. In other sections, the book tries to work against power, for example in Chapter One, by presenting artisans' design activities before exploring national-level design promotion by government officials. Where women's activities cannot be identified or makers are anonymous, it points out the privilege enjoyed by the men who can be identified: the ones who are written into documents and who created and ran the institutions that created the archives, and the value systems that structured their archival practices.

The book focuses on social and economic power networks and ideas, but the affordances and capacities of the material environments in which these played out, and of the materials themselves that composed them, are important for telling the history. The book's narrative and interpretation are underpinned by specific methods for design historical thought. First, artefact analysis: what we can learn about history from studying, and studying with, things.[15] Second, history as the experience of people interacting with ideas, artefacts and environments, a perspective drawing on design research and environmental history.[16] Third, the standard history practice of building narrative from close examination of print and archival materials: design magazines, textbooks, yearbooks, economic data, biographies, corporate and public archives, research reports, conference proceedings and other printed and manuscript sources, alongside the products, sketches, prototypes, interiors, interviews and hours spent in design environments that are the material of the design historian. The granular insights into historical actions and decisions afforded by the study of artefacts, environments, interactions and experiences largely sits below the surface in *Designing Modern Japan*, for reasons of length as much as anything else, but were integral in developing the narrative emphases presented here.

History is written partly on consensus; we create new arguments from analyses of primary data and work from and with existing arguments when we assess them to be valid. While the book draws extensively on primary material, it was not feasible to work from primary sources for all points. Sources are indicated; the overall historical narrative presents current consensus – and some debates – on the arc of modern Japanese history.

There are excellent histories of design in modern Japan available in Japanese, both overview histories – many of them by protagonists with first-hand experience of the histories they write – and specialized histories of particular institutions, organizations, designers or places. Much of this research is referred to in the notes for each chapter; *Designing Modern Japan* would not be able to cover such breadth without those scholars' close research and, also, their activism in archiving design materials. Conversely, while this book is written in English, it aims to make particular contributions to the Japanese-language literature and communities of design history practice, through both the particular interpretation of the history of design in modern Japan and the kind of design history it proposes (as requiring integral attention to economics, policy and law, and as a form of history-writing rather than a specialist field concerned with designers and their actions alone).

For years, one of the few comprehensive narratives of design – and particularly design policy – in modern Japan available in English was *Japanese Design: A Survey since 1950*, the catalogue accompanying the Philadelphia Museum of Art's 1994 exhibition of the same name.[17] Since *Designing Modern Japan* was conceived, material on design in modern Japan available in English has increased greatly, both in the form of surveys and specialist research. Again, many of these publications appear in the notes. Among the most significant are publications by Japan-based authors, including translations.[18] This new body of work also represents a shift towards representing Japan as part of an interconnected regional network in East Asia or the Asia-Pacific rather than on its own, concurrent with and reflecting economic and geopolitical change more widely.[19] The book also joins a body of scholarship in the social, cultural and economic history of modern Japan, which, while not being overtly 'about' design, locate the ideas, products and consumers of design activities within modern Japanese history.[20]

It is very easy when compiling histories to focus on those who write them. Social history tells us that written records convey the opinions and actions of the powerful only, creating a limited and partial view of the past. Local and regional history makes it clear that experiences of historical events and conditions vary by place as much as by social class, by age or by gender. And historical evidence like diaries and interviews makes clear that individuals and communities interpret and experience top-down policy and ideas in their own way. A lacquerer following a pattern book may choose to change a pattern for specific effect, for example. Likewise, students do not always do as their teachers tell them. It would be very useful to know more directly what students and apprentices in Meiji Japan, for example, thought about craft, design and making, and how different sorts of people experienced these, but this is incredibly difficult to know. Much of this book explains what a few people, mostly men, made when presented with the opportunity to do so, and discusses what they thought about design and making in relation to society and economy. But it also attempts to incorporate positions and opinions from others, and to consider when history was made not by people but by inanimate objects, environments and things. The point is that how they all interacted produced multiple different experiences of design in modern Japan. This allows us to tell a story. Like the magazines in the bookshop in Osaka in 1991, this book tells only one of many possible stories, but it is a significant one.

Designing Modern Japan

1 'As a practical object it will be profitable': Design, Industry and Internationalization from the Tokugawa to the Meiji Periods

In 1876, dozens of porcelain vases from Japan went on display in Philadelphia. A sepia stereoscopic photograph cannot convey the exuberant decoration, the vases overglazed with colourful motifs and pictorial scenes and encrusted with moulded porcelain plants and animals. Tall bodies swelled under narrow necks before blossoming into wide mouths with extravagantly fluted edges. Vivid palettes – complex pictorial imagery and vegetal patterns rendered in red, green, yellow, black and white, with touches of pink, brown and blue – offered further visual stimulation, especially in the densely packed display. A high level of skill was required to create these objects: to fire them without collapse or warping; to maintain the circular form and symmetry, particularly of the fluted necks; to paint the intricate patterns and images; and to fire the different glazes so neatly, including multiple firings at different temperatures. Together, they appear visually compelling and extremely worked. In the juxtaposition of colours, imagery and impressive scale and form, they invite questions about the different elements and the vases' manufacture.

The vases were designed and made in Arita, a porcelain district in western Japan. Arita had developed as the leading Japanese porcelain district in the early seventeenth century, possibly with Korean artisans kidnapped during Japan's then national leader Toyotomi Hideyoshi's invasion of the Korean peninsula in 1697.[1] The kilns were moved to Arita, in the Hizen domain, to prevent rapid deforestation for kiln firewood in their previous location. In the seventeenth century, Arita developed a specialized industry in highly decorative overglaze porcelains, versatile in Chinese motifs, forms and colours. Their hybrid East Asian style, adapted for European tastes and interiors, allowed

Porcelain vases displayed in front of painted screens, stereoview of the Japanese section, Main Building, Centennial Exposition, Philadelphia, 1876.

them to find a strong market in Europe, along with other kilns in the Hizen domain. Thus, Hizen porcelains had been a desirable luxury for wealthy Europeans for three centuries, competing in the porcelain market with the Chinese and French. In other words, by 1876 Arita makers had already been producing products for a similar market for some generations. Now, by combining their existing design elements in new ways, they were again drawing on available skills, materials, tools, techniques and infrastructure to accommodate their clients' assessment of market demand and tastes.

Designing Modern Japan

The vases were exhibition pieces, made specifically for display at an international exposition to capture the attention and imagination of masses of foreign viewers – not only Americans but the international press and many international visitors. The vases were commissioned by the Japanese government to form part of the Japanese national display at the Centennial Exposition, held to commemorate the one hundredth anniversary of American independence. Exhibition commissioners, appointed from within government departments with a European adviser, established criteria to help the Japanese exhibit win prizes and gain international acclaim for the sophisticated nature of what Japan could manufacture, represented here by products from Japan's highly developed crafts industries.[2] The display comprised hundreds of decorative objects, not least the folding screens (*byōbu*) with patterns of fans and gold-leafed cityscapes that sat immediately behind the plinths. Within the exhibition hall, it competed with similar displays stuffed with highly visual exhibition pieces, all following a standard aesthetic logic and vying with each other for visitor attention.[3]

In this context, design decisions conformed to international ideas, commonly shared among successful Western exhibitors, of what made a good exposition piece: the items were showy, visually complex and massed together at impressive scale in their display. They also combined multiple visual and formal standards associated overseas with Japanese export ceramics of the previous three centuries – including some adopted from Chinese ceramics. The difference between Japanese and Chinese motifs and style and the particular metaphorical, literary or historical associations of each decorative element would be well understood by some Japanese viewers, but for American and other viewers in

Dish for export, 1690–1720, porcelain decorated in underglaze blue and overglaze enamels, diameter 31.4 cm, Arita kilns.

Philadelphia would likely have created an effect of Far Eastern exotica. At the same time, sets of large decorative vases – imported from China or Japan, or fired in France – had been an established trend in European luxury interiors since the eighteenth century, and were adopted in the United States as well. The vases offered an already familiar object – one associated with foreignness, with the foreignness and exoticness visually amplified for visitor impact.

Close examination of any object will reveal the coexistence of local practices and wider connections, both old and new, as an indication of broader historical change and continuity. In this sense, the vases present several key aspects of design and making in mid-nineteenth-century Japan. In 1868, after decades of domestic instability and new foreign pressures, Japan gained a new national government. During the Tokugawa period (1615–1868), the government had attempted to control foreign trade and diplomacy, in part to maintain domestic political stability. The new Meiji government saw increased engagement as inevitable but wanted to retain sovereignty over foreign powers' interactions with Japan. Stronger projection of Japan's image to foreign powers was part of its strategy for accomplishing this. This decision would have profound effects. As the vases suggest, much of its impact was in how people modified their existing resources and arrangements to accommodate the economic and material changes that followed this decision.

This chapter explores the impact of political and economic change in mid- and late nineteenth-century Japan on design and related industries, activities and products. The chapter begins with an overview of design and making in the Tokugawa period to understand the conventions and industries in place. This means treading familiar ground for readers acquainted with early modern and modern Japanese history, particularly the histories of consumption, technology and exhibitions. It then focuses on specific design initiatives launched in direct response to historical events. Their initiators included local politicians and entrepreneurs concerned to mitigate the impact of global events on their own communities; civil servants charged with curating Japan's participation in international expositions; intellectuals interested in articulating Japan's national identity during this time; educators who saw improved design as a way to help manufacturing communities weather change; and designer-makers, themselves concerned to maintain viability. The chapter discusses design practice and products in relation to these ideas and demonstrates how Japan's existing design and making practices adapted to political, economic and material change in the Meiji period (1868–1912).

A principal takeaway from the chapter is the sheer heterogeneity of ideas already in circulation before the emergence of standardized mechanisms and institutions for design promotion. Post-war Japanese design is associated internationally with a strong national design policy and with the central government commitment to design promotion this entails. This was hardly the case in the nineteenth century. As we will see, while makers and their local supporters had recognized the importance of 'good design' in capturing public imagination and market share for several centuries, it would take the successes and failures of product exports for the national government to identify design as relevant for the national good. Chapter Two onwards will trace the arc of a specific set of policies, themselves derived from particular ideas about the power of design. Some policies originated with people in government – national, regional and local – who saw promoting design as a way to support economic development and improve lives. Others came from the commercial world, from entrepreneurs who saw design as a way for firms – and by extension national and local economies – to become more competitive. In this chapter, no such centralized vision or will describes design in the Meiji period. The chapter articulates how different groups of people, all invested in design in some way, thought that design, as a conscious intervention into the making of commodities, could help someone – individuals, communities, regions, even the Japanese nation – thrive during this period. It argues that all of these groups saw design as a mechanism for supporting industries and communities to weather change, and that some also saw design as a lever that could accelerate change. It suggests that these interventions and attitudes were less powerful, ultimately, in shaping design practice, let alone its products or consumer demand, than some had hoped. State intervention impacted some aspects of crafts industries, but other aspects – and some industries – were largely untouched by reforms. These aspects were shaped, the chapter argues, by larger historical developments and by designer-makers' and users' responses to them.

With their riotous juxtaposition of colour, style and motif, the Arita vases indicate the depth of Japanese design skill, technological ability and market maturity in place before the Meiji period. Japan in the mid-nineteenth century was a sophisticated early modern society with a developed market economy, social structures and cultural production.[4] In the centralized political system known as the *bakuhan*, the shogunate passed patrilineally through the ruling family. The Tokugawa *bakufu* oversaw the country from its base in Edo (present-day Tokyo), while the imperial family, formerly the nation's rulers, remained in Kyoto, with the emperor a nominal figurehead only. Hereditary lords known as *daimyō* oversaw each domain or *han*, with an additional civil service infrastructure. Each province was responsible for an annual financial contribution to the *bakufu*'s coffers, generated by a tax on households. As we will see, this led whole villages and regions to develop cottage industries to procure this much-needed income. Interregional competition between *daimyō* became another driver of innovation, as *daimyō* supported the development of local industries and acquisition of imported technical knowledge to increase profits and prestige.[5] *Daimyō* were required to maintain a full residence in Edo, where their families lived permanently, in addition to the provincial seat, and to spend one of every two years in Edo.[6] This system spurred the development of road infrastructure from regions to the capital, as well as land and sea shipping routes for industrial and agricultural products. It also helped the regime to maintain power over the *daimyō* by depleting their finances – in addition to two households, *daimyō* were expected to travel in lavish processions and live well, extending their patronage to luxury goods producers.

The *bakuhan* dictated a formal status hierarchy. Below *daimyo* were samurai, followed by farmers, artisans and merchants, with 'untouchables' and some other groups outside. The behaviour, dress, residential location and occupations of each status group were prescribed by law. For example, sumptuary laws passed in 1628 limited peasants to garments of *asa* (hemp and ramie) and cotton, while allowing village heads to wear silk.[7] A flurry of laws passed in 1683 included at least seven restrictions on townspeople's clothing, including on embroidery, thin silk crepe and dappled tie-dye.[8] The social status system was highly prescriptive but also flouted, particularly as by the nineteenth century wealth distribution no longer mapped onto social structure.⁹ As the Tokugawa period went on, people also began taking on roles and activities outside those prescribed. An annual provincial rice tax, levied on villages and converted into currency on the commodity market in Osaka, the nation's finance and trading centre, supported the operations of the *bakufu*, the domains and the samurai (who undertook a variety of activities, including serving the Tokugawa and domain governments). Commerce made many merchants wealthy, especially in Osaka, leading to new fashions as merchant households found ways to circumvent the sumptuary restrictions. Farmers were expected to make their living from agriculture, but the tax burden prompted households and villages to develop secondary industries, both to produce goods for their own needs and to earn additional income by making products for urban markets.¹⁰ Indeed, a proto-industrial economy developed in many farming villages, with local entrepreneurs, sometimes the village headman, serving as middlemen between urban distributors and farming households.¹¹

Entire villages and regions began to incorporate part-time industrial production into household activities, as farmers discovered that manufacturing – particularly of textiles – could supplant insufficient income from fickle crops. Village production could be divided into two types of goods: those manufactured for local use, within the household or village, and those manufactured for redistribution around Japan. The latter were supplemental for many farm households and served as cottage industries, with products made by hand in the evenings and winters; local merchants contracted with households in a 'putting-out' system, bringing them the raw materials and later purchasing the finished goods to pass on to a wholesaler or directly to shops.¹² Some regions went one step further and established specialized workshops where farm women especially would work to gain extra income. In some cases, these went as far as to compete with the luxury manufacturers in Kyoto.¹³ In the Kiryū district, north of Tokyo, entrepreneurs who had already developed a cotton broadcloth industry were able to prise the technical secrets of high loom silk weaving from the Nishijin weavers of Kyoto and to develop a local industry in printed patterned silks from the mid-eighteenth century.¹⁴

The Kiryū weavers never matched Nishijin in market share or income, but they found a profitable niche in the booming Edo market among both samurai and townspeople, in turn spawning imitators in

neighbouring regions. Such single-product production was common across materials and products and had the added benefit of 'branding' products as from specific villages and regions known for particular goods. Such localized manufacturing was often supported by provincial administrations as part of competition between *daimyō*. The British designer Christopher Dresser (1834–1904) travelled between Kyoto and Nagoya as part of a larger journey around Japan in 1876–7. He noted passing through villages specializing in goods including bamboo flutes, paper-leather, bottle gourds and baskets woven from wisteria vines, to give only some examples.[15] The Kiryū merchants, too, promoted their silks as distinct from those of competitors.

Cities housed both consumers and niche manufacturing areas.[16] Thanks to its dual populations of *daimyō* and artisan households, Edo had over 1 million residents by 1700, making it comfortably the largest city in the world.[17] As the market economy grew, merchants prospered thanks to their roles as middlemen, in shipping, warehousing, distribution and retail. This created a market in cities like Edo and

Utagawa Hiroshige III, *The Cotton Looms of Kawachi*, 1877, woodblock print, Edo (Tokyo). Kawachi, part of present-day Osaka, had access to both cotton and indigo. The image depicts weavers at work and a variety of indigo-dyed Kawachi cotton textiles, sewn into kimono for workers and passers-by.

Designing Modern Japan

especially Osaka, further from central oversight, for luxury products for merchants. The castle towns that became administrative centres for each domain, too, developed luxury and everyday product industries to supply the local *daimyō*'s household and the goods and service providers who clustered around them. A rich and complex network of workshops, distribution guilds and merchants developed to produce goods for these overlapping markets. Cities gained artisans making everything from shop signs to decorative armour, tofu and buckets. Most clustered in specialist neighbourhoods, where proximity offered competitive advantage through local supply chains and closely located sub-specialisms for the breakdown of production for some more complex products. The Arita vases sent to Philadelphia would have been made in one of the many family firms active in the region, with all aspects of production, from design to clay preparation, forming, glaz-

Obi, 1840–80, polychrome figured silk, 450 cm x 33.5 cm. The obi is woven in the style of Nishijin work, but cannot be fully attributed to Nishijin makers.

ing, firing, painting and finishing, conducted in a hierarchical division of labour. Kimono silk, on the other hand, was the combined result of multiple households' work, with cocoons raised and thread spun in peasant households, then the textile woven, dyed and painted in separate household workshops in specialist urban neighbourhoods.[18]

In Kyoto, the centre of luxury goods production thanks to its history as the imperial capital, artisans increasingly supplied a national market, employing the city's prestige and rich networks of skilled artisans and supply chains. Artisans working in silk cloth weaving, dyeing and ceramics occupied entire neighbourhoods. The Kyoto ceramics industry was one of several prestigious regions that competed for the attentions of tea ceremony practitioners, and Kyoto itself contained several distinct ceramics neighbourhoods.[19] Tea and dining ceramics were luxury products with a wider market, including wealthy merchants aspiring to a cultured and elegant life, as well as *daimyō* and samurai.[20] Kyoto was also home to the Nishijin district, the acknowledged leader in silk weaving and dyeing. By the late seventeenth century, merchants specializing in purchasing woven and dyed silk textiles and other Kyoto luxury products for sale to consumers in Edo and Osaka had emerged; these merchants, as epitomized by the Mitsui family's Echigoya, forerunner of today's Mitsukoshi department store, maintained their headquarters in Kyoto but had their principal shop in Nihonbashi, the main commercial area in Edo.

Most luxury products, including silk textiles, lacquerware, decorative metalwork, tea ceramics and cloisonné, were created in dedicated workshops, often family-run and extending over the generations. Batch production and a division of labour were common. In Nishijin, for example, weaving, dyeing and embroidery were separate trades with distinct workshops located in adjacent blocks, allowing for efficient production while enabling craftsmen to gain esteem from peers and patrons as artists in their particular trade.[21] Makers in materials like ceramics and metals created their objects in-house, with artisans taking responsibility for aspects of the technical process that increased in complexity over the course of their careers. Workers joined as

Hasegawa Mitsunobu (illustrations) and Hirase Tessai, *The Nishijin Workshops of Kyoto*, c. 1797, woodblock print, Osaka. Weavers' work depended on gender and seniority as well as skill.

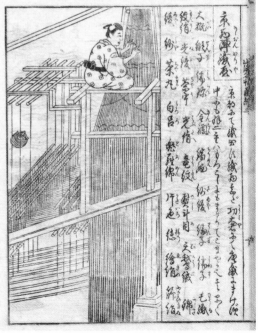

Designing Modern Japan

children and learned their craft through apprenticeships, observing the master and more senior artisans at work.[22] Written manuals, when they existed, were in principle restricted to artisans deemed senior enough to deserve access to this powerful knowledge, and also prized by connoisseurs partly for that sense of exclusivity. While many images of making from the period show women at work, men predominated in artisanal household work and were the named artisans; women participated in household industries and were especially important for weaving and spinning in peasant households.

In castle towns, *daimyō* often sponsored the development of specific industries. Shizuoka, for example, developed lacquerware and woodworking; Yamagata, in northern Japan, metalwork and gilt, wood and lacquer Buddhist altars. These local industries took advantage of location and local materials: Yamagata with forests and mines, and Shizuoka with its forests and fortuitous location between Tokyo and Osaka, for good distribution to multiple markets. Many of the more technically specific crafts were sponsored directly by domains, who also then served as their principal client. Close to the Arita potteries, the Nabeshima clan, *daimyō* of the neighbouring Saga domain, supported workshops producing porcelain specifically for their use.[23] (Nabeshima porcelains were not for sale but rather produced as display pieces and as gifts to the Tokugawa and other important families.) Domainal patronage allowed the potters to engage in extensive research and development into glazes, firing temperatures, kiln shapes and clays for the region's iconic polychrome pieces. The prosperous and powerful Maeda family, rulers of the Kaga domain (in present-day Ishikawa prefecture), were also well known as patrons of multiple luxury crafts industries, from lacquerware, decorative cast metalwork and the local Kutani polychrome-glazed ceramics to Kaga *yūzen* paste resist-dyed silks, used in samurai women's kimono and produced in the castle town of Kanazawa.

Pattern and product design was the domain of the workshop master. Some workshops specialized in particular styles, which they replicated and evolved to maintain brand identity over successive generations. Indeed, a trademark system with distinct logos for makers and shops protected intellectual property and created a prototypical branded landscape in which products and shops alike advertised their brand on the street, in print advertisements and through association with famous individuals. Woodblock prints of kabuki actors and women

who worked in the licensed quarters, adorned in the latest fashions and with fashionable interiors and objects, communicated the latest fashions around Japan as well.[24]

Makers and commissioning merchants alike paid close attention to changing consumer tastes, particularly in woven and dyed silk and cotton textiles, and adapted products to woo customers in the competitive urban markets. While replicating thread production or weaving required detailed technical knowledge, mimicking a popular block-printed pattern was as simple as cutting a new *katagami*, or paper pattern. Talented, highly skilled textile painters could easily learn new motifs. Woodblock-printed books known as *hinagata-bon*, literally 'pattern-books', circulated emergent fashions, sometimes to consumers as well as makers. These could have print runs in the thousands. The application of such patterns was hardly limited to textiles. Many pattern books presented new takes on classical themes and could be applied across media. An artist's stylization of plovers dancing above the waves in the moonlight, for example, a common motif

Utagawa Hiroshige III, *Knife Makers in Sakai, Izumi Province*, 1877, woodblock print, Edo (Tokyo). Sakai, a prosperous merchant town adjacent to Osaka, was known for its metalwork. The shop's name, Izumiya, a reference to its location, appears in phonetic hiragana script and large logo-style Chinese characters on the workshop awning.

Designing Modern Japan

based on a well-loved classical poem, might appear on the hem of a kimono, a ceramic dish and a lacquerware box. Artists' patterns were also popular: the classical painting and calligraphy-inflected designs and ceramics, silk textiles and lacquerware products of Kyoto-based brothers Ogata Kōrin (1658–1716) and Ogata Kenzan (1663–1743), scions of an established Kyoto textile merchant family active in the late seventeenth and early eighteenth centuries, were widely valued and imitated, a style known as Rinpa.[25] Most workshops would not have seen pieces by Kōrin or Kenzan, destined for the hands of elite clients; rather, designs were circulated through their replication in the printed *hinagata-bon*.[26]

The popularity of *hinagata-bon* also testifies to the importance of fashion in early modern Japan. This was directly linked to commercial expansion and urbanization: to increased spending power in cities and also to increasingly effective knowledge circuits – publishing, printing and moving books between cities and the countryside.[27] By the late

Kimono patterns by Nishikawa Sukenobu, in *Rare and Popular Kimono Patterns of the Capital* (Kyoto, 1716), woodblock-printed book.

Katsukawa Shunshō and Kitaoka Shigemasa, illustration from *The Cultivation of Silkworms*, (1786), woodblock print, Edo. The final image of the book, which illustrates the process of raising silkworms and making cloth from the silk, in the style of beautiful women prints (*bijinga*), depicts women perusing *hinagata*, chirimen silk and brocade obi with a representative from the kimono merchant Echigoya.

seventeenth century, well-informed townspeople and prosperous farmers could purchase *hinagata-bon* and ukiyo-e woodblock images of famous actors and courtesans to stay abreast of the latest fashions. Samurai families could order the latest Nishijin silks from merchants like Echigoya, and other families the latest cottons.[28] After purchase, these were sewn into *kosode*, a type of kimono typified by shorter sleeves (*kosode* literally means 'small sleeve'), and matched with woven and

Designing Modern Japan

embroidered obi sashes, and accessories such as decorative woven and braided ties, metal, ivory, lacquer and tortoiseshell hairpins, paper fans and wooden *geta* footwear.[29]

Fashion consumption showed status. By the late seventeenth century, men and women of all status groups wore *kosode*, with status differentiated by pattern, accessories and hairstyle. Wealthy merchants and high-status samurai alike wore silk, while lower-status samurai and the majority of merchants, artisans and farmers – in other words, most people – wore cotton and hemp.[30] Fashion change appeared through textile design rather than tailoring, in contrast with European fashions at this time.[31] *Yūzen* silks, a technique developed in the eighteenth century that combined paste-resist and brush-applied dyeing techniques, were considered the most elegant until the late eighteenth century. The location, size and type of patterns could be varied, allowing wealthy townspeople and samurai alike to demonstrate fashionability through the adoption of new styles. Endemic poverty made purchasing clothes – new or old – difficult for many households, but economic growth during the eighteenth century in Edo, particularly, resulted in new fashionable textiles and new fashion systems for non-elite urban residents as well.[32] By the early nineteenth century, striped woven cottons were popular among men in Edo. Printed silks whose repeat patterns were applied to the fabric with *katagami* paper patterns became fashionable among townspeople. The former in particular showed how Edo had taken over from Kyoto and Osaka as the trend centre, indicating Edo's sheer size, political importance and growing economic clout. It also demonstrates the economic importance of the fashion industry in early modern Japan.

Fashion, and the major economic impact it has, allows us to see how the market economy sometimes trumped the status system in terms of shaping production, and that people had agency to subvert status laws. When sumptuary laws passed in the 1680s prevented wealthy townspeople from wearing *kosode* made with *shibori* tie-dyed silk, for example, townspeople began making and wearing kimono from stencil-dyed silk whose patterns imitated *shibori*. Townspeople could also display their wealth and fashionability through undergarments and accessories.[33] Sumptuary laws did not stop people from wearing fashionable clothes; instead, they prompted innovative new trends as people sought fashionability around them.

Fashion allowed not just the material of textiles but its pattern and decoration to signify taste and fashionability. The rise in popularity

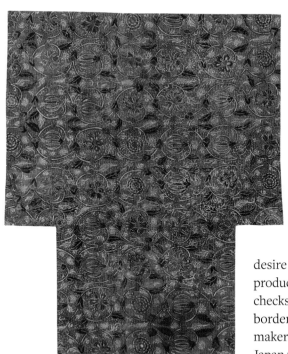

Kimono made from imported sarasa cloth produced on the Coromandel Coast of India for export to Japan, 1700–1750, India, painted mordant-dyed cotton with applied gold leaf.

Utagawa Toyokuni II, *Gust of Wind on a Clear Day*, c. 1830, woodblock print, Edo. The tortoiseshell hair ornaments and European-style glass, like the woman's flower-patterned silk brocade obi and the striped covering, connect imported materials and patterns with urban luxury and fashionability.

of stripes and *sarasa*, or textile patterns derived from block-printed Indian cotton calicos, illustrates this point nicely.[34] Indian textiles – silk yarns, silk and cotton cloth in stripes, checks and chintzes – were imported by Portuguese and then Chinese and Dutch traders from the mid-sixteenth century, alongside Chinese and European cloth. Imports saw a steep rise in the seventeenth century, particularly cotton from the Coromandel Coast of southeast India.[35] Not everyone could access or afford imported textiles, but the novelty of these new patterns created desire for them, eventually resulting in domestic production as well and the diffusion of stripes and checks, particularly, across fashion markets. While borders were controlled by the *bakufu*, designers, makers, retailers and consumers in early modern Japan participated in international fashion trends that spanned the Eurasian continent.

Foreign connections provided markets as well as ideas. After over two centuries of trade and communication with China and Europe between the fifteenth and early seventeenth centuries, the *bakufu* decided to reduce and control international communication. It designated four ports for international trade and diplomacy, including Nagasaki, on Japan's southern tip, which was allocated all trade with Dutch merchants. The Satsuma domain handled trade with the Ryūkyū Kingdom, the archipelago south of Japan, and from there with China, and the Tsushima domain, occupying an island in the sea between Japan and Korea, trade with Korea. Changes in trade policy included commodity categories as well as volume of flow. Sixteenth- and seventeenth-century Japan had exported silver; following controls of silver exports in the eighteenth century, manufactured goods such as tea and ceramics, including Arita porcelains, became major exports.[36] Limited trade opportunities did not stop designers from incorporating imported ideas. The Arita kilns provide a good example here: dishes employed glazes, patterns, motifs and forms from Chinese porcelains. These were themselves amalgams of centuries of experimentation, local materials, technical innovation and market demand in China, Europe, Southeast Asia and the Middle East. Arita products were then tailored further for European demand as mediated by Chinese traders and the Dutch East India Company (voc) from the mid-seventeenth century.

Trade also allowed samurai associated with the *bakufu* as well as *daimyō*, merchants, doctors and other research-minded elites affiliated with Nagasaki and other powerful domains to access foreign knowledge through imported treatises and European and Chinese objects. This knowledge, known as *rangaku*, or Dutch studies, was taught at specialized schools in Nagasaki, Edo and the castle cities of major domains. It was also exported to other provinces, where its proponents competed with sponsors of Chinese and nativist schools, prompting some of the wealthier *daimyō* to sponsor research into areas such

Collection of Sarasa that Arrived in Ancient Times, c. late 18th–early 19th century, woodblock-printed book. Many sarasa pattern manuals were printed in black and white, with the colours to apply indicated by text. This manual printed the suggested colour schemes directly onto the pattern.

Designing Modern Japan

Box from a marriage set, lacquer and gold on wood, 1700–1750, 14.9 x 13.7 cm.

as mechanics, metallurgy, medicine and, by the mid-nineteenth century, photography.[37] This new technical knowledge too fed design innovation.

Luxury crafts had varied markets depending on the rarity of materials, the difficulty and time involved in the manufacturing process, and the intended use of their products. Lacquerware was among the most exclusive of craft industries. The number of layers of lacquer required to create one piece, the time and skill required to apply them, and the preciousness of the lacquer and gold leaf used to make lacquerware made it extremely expensive to make and commission. As such, lacquerware was used predominantly for the dowries of the daughters of the Tokugawa clan and *daimyō*.[38] Sets could run to hundreds of pieces, including combs, mirrors and boxes for cosmetics and hairpins, elbow rests, pillows, games, inkstones and writing boxes, writing desks, shelves and screens. A luxury lacquer workshop could operate for more than two years with one commission alone. Many producers were located in Kyoto, with its reputation for luxury industries, or in Edo, where producers had close access to the *daimyō* market. By the eighteenth century, as the domestic market economy strengthened, wealthy Osaka merchants adopted the lacquerware bridal trousseau tradition on a more limited scale. This diversified lacquer workshops' clientele (and flouted sumptuary laws aimed at suppressing merchant displays of wealth).

Indeed, exquisitely crafted objects from the workshops of renowned artists played an important role in social life, both in everyday interactions and on special occasions. The tea ceremony was an important pastime and part of male sociality among *daimyō* and the more elite samurai, as well as for wealthy merchants in cities like Osaka and Kyoto. The appreciation of the many objects used in the ceremony – including ceramic tea bowls, lacquered wooden tea caddies, bamboo tea scoops and ironware kettles – was an important element of the ceremony itself; one marker of a good host was impeccable taste in the selection of individual objects and the ability to curate the appropriate assembly for the occasion.[39] Guests were expected to recognize the worth of the objects and assembly and to demonstrate due appreciation for them. Christopher Dresser noted the significance of guests performing connoisseurship as the proper and expected behaviour during tea:

> After each of the guests has duly inspected the object, the chief guest shuffles again across the floor and returns it to its place. Object after object is brought, examined, and returned in the same manner.
>
> It is on these occasions that the rare things of the household are used; and the pride which a Japanese manifests in the possession of some little tea jar, a spoon, or a cup by a celebrated maker is something remarkable.[40]

Simply put, things eased social interactions. A meticulously carved sword guard (*tsuba*) with an unusual combination of differently coloured alloys, worn by a male samurai, or a curiously shaped toggle (netsuke), worn by both samurai and wealthy merchants, attracted attention and tacitly conveyed the status of the wearer during informal meetings. They were collectors' items, signs of good taste and – especially in the 'floating worlds' in Edo and Osaka, where fashion was important – if well chosen marked the wearer as a connoisseur (*tsū*) of good design and the good life. Like ceramic tea bowls, lacquered wooden tea caddies and the other objects used in the tea ceremony, fashion accessories like *tsuba* and netsuke could be passed around from person to person during social gatherings for admiration and comment; the ability to recognize an important maker or particularly unusual technique or material was another marker of the *tsū*.[41] Accessories like *tsuba* and netsuke, as well as tea ceremony objects, could be passed on as gifts or tributes; an object's provenance and lineage were often carefully documented, particularly if they came from the workshop of an agreed master or illustrious owner, and were thought to attest to and increase its value. Given the social importance of connoisseurship, *hinagata-bon* aimed specifically at collectors were another lucrative genre for publishers.[42]

The market economy that developed in early modern Japan enabled a sophisticated system of designed products, with luxury and everyday items alike produced in specialist regions and distributed through well-honed channels to urban consumers at a variety of levels.

Designing Modern Japan

In the cities especially, fashionability – knowledge of the latest designs and trends – was crucial for those with the means to access goods; *hinagata-bon* and woodblock prints played an important role in keeping manufacturers, merchants and consumers up to date, and savvy manufacturers and merchants could use trademarked designs by named designers to boost sales, public profile and profit. Both this system and many of the designs, styles and items themselves continued into the early twentieth century, despite the radical, even revolutionary, changes that transformed Japan's economic, political and social landscape after the 1860s. One question to answer is why this was so. Another is why we should expect otherwise.

Local and National Responses to Internationalization

In the early modern period, domestic change had prompted people to start designing and making things in new ways. After the 1850s, Japan's governments engaged in increased international trade and diplomacy, leading to a reorganization of domestic political and social systems. Regime change and subsequent shifts in political power, patronage, social and economic structures and everyday life, alongside exposure to global flows of capital and products, once again required light industry makers, artists and craftspeople to find new income sources, including new markets and new products.

By the 1830s, the growing gap between the ideals of Tokugawa political and social systems and actual conditions had weakened the shogunate's power. The agriculture-based taxation system did not account for rural industrialization and entrepreneurship, increasingly powerful merchants and distribution guilds or the key role played by the Osaka commodity traders. Poor harvests in the 1830s and '40s exacerbated the fall in government income and prompted popular uprisings. The power of central government in relation to the domains had also weakened. Wealthy southern provinces such as Satsuma, Tosa and Chōshū were able to leverage their wealth, distance from the centre and access to imported technological knowledge to act even more independently of the central government.

When naval, whaling and trading ships from the United States, Russia and the United Kingdom began appearing off Japanese shores in the early nineteenth century, this new external pressure exacerbated domestic instability.[43] The Tokugawa regime was aware of the impact of renewed European and American interest in Asia on neighbouring countries, which included Britain's negotiation of unequal treaties with China following the Opium War of 1839–42, Russian interest in expanding eastwards from Siberia, and British, French and Dutch colonies in Southeast Asia. American naval warships appeared in Yokohama Bay in 1853 with a demand from the u.s. president for the opening of trade relations. In March 1854 the *bakufu*, under threat of force, signed a treaty allowing trade and the stationing of an American consul on Japanese soil. Agreements establishing eight extraterritorial treaty ports similar to those created after the Opium Wars in China followed in 1858, of which Yokohama, Kōbe and Nagasaki were the most prominent. The treaty ports were soon populated with European and American diplomats, missionaries and entrepreneurs as well as Chinese and Indian traders. Many samurai saw the presence of 'foreign barbarians' as a threat to national sovereignty and the Tokugawa *bakufu*, in signing the unequal treaties, as having humiliated the nation.

The establishment and activities of treaty ports accelerated economic, social and eventually political change. The treaties bound Japan to accept foreign imports and limited the government's ability to impose tariffs or quantity controls. Japanese consumers' lack of familiarity with foreign products kept imports low at first, but soon imports of all kinds were flooding the market, their value soaring above that of exports. The result was a trade imbalance and an outflow of Japanese gold and silver reserves. It was not until the 1880s that Japanese exports resurged and Japanese production once again challenged imports in the domestic market.[44] Trade also led to fluctuating fortunes for Japanese manufacturers and consumers. Raw silk manufacturers, for example, found markets overseas in the 1850s and '60s as pébrine, a silkworm disease, ravaged the French and Italian silk industries and the Taiping Rebellion disrupted the silk industry in Qing China. Overseas demand tripled prices for silk thread at home, hurting weaving districts. In Nishijin, workshops stopped production for a year. In Kiryū, workshop production fell 64 per cent between 1856 and 1861, to only 361 bolts of silk.[45] At the same time, cheap foreign imports of cotton textiles – their prices guaranteed in the unequal treaties – drove down domestic cotton prices, bankrupting many Japanese cotton thread and cloth producers.[46] Townspeople, samurai and peasants alike responded to economic disruption with often violent public protests. *Daimyō* from Chōshū, Satsuma and other outlying domains recognized the central government's weakness and pressed for the emperor's return to the centre of power. The *bakufu* responded with a succession of political and economic reforms, but these were insufficient. After successive rebellions in the 1860s, Tokugawa Yoshinobu (1837–1913), the last shogun, abdicated, ending the Tokugawa regime. A group of former domain leaders, largely from Satsuma and Chōshū, reinstated the emperor as the head of a new government in 1868.[47]

From the 1870s, a new national government composed of former domain officials sought to reshape Japan for a powerful negotiating position within the world order. The new leaders aimed to create national systems that would strengthen Japan's international standing through industrialization, economic development and a recognizably 'modern' landscape. When increased military strength was added, Japan's leaders hoped this would help renegotiate relations with European powers and the United States and allow the retention of sovereignty. Slogans like 'rich country, strong army' (*fukoku kyōhei*), 'civilization and enlightenment' (*bunmei kaika*) and 'increase production and promote industry' (*shokusan kōgyō*), illustrate this fundamental stance and emphasize the relationship of industry and militarization: militarization required capital, and capital could be gained through trade.

Among other things, international security required domestic stability. Many of the *bakuhan* systems were dismantled. The emperor's residence was relocated to Edo, now renamed Tokyo, and government communications worded to emphasize his will as the ultimate base of all government directions and decisions. *Daimyō* hereditary rights to sovereignty and revenue collection within their domains were removed, and the domains themselves replaced with prefectures led by centrally appointed governors. A basic land tax replaced the former village-based rice levies, making individual farm households responsible for selling grain on the market directly rather than contributing it to domainal coffers. Samurai economic and social privileges were systematically removed, and all Japanese reclassified into three status groups: *kazoku* (nobility, or former *daimyō* families), *shizoku* (higher-ranking samurai) and *heimin* (everyone else). The government repealed sumptuary regulations limiting displays of wealth through fashion, home-building and other forms of conspicuous consumption and abolished restrictions on principal occupation, allowing samurai and farmers to open shops, for example.

Like the expansion in foreign trade, these major changes had a direct impact on design and manufacturing. Lacquerware provides a good example of how crafts industries adapted to the new economic and social situation at home by taking advantage of international connections. Workshops producing roughly finished tableware in red and black lacquer for rural markets were less affected by the period's macroeconomic swings than high-end producers in cities like Kyoto. Once well supported by bridal trousseau orders from *daimyō* families and aspirational merchants, the luxury lacquerware industry had begun to falter several decades before the Meiji Restoration, as *daimyō* families with declining incomes started recycling objects already in the family, rather than ordering new ones.[48] Workshops developed lines in alternative, more mass-market products like *inro*, a small case worn as a fashion accessory by men. But with the disappearance of the *daimyō* system and sinecures altogether in the 1860s and elite men's adoption of Western-style suits – which required accessories such as watches and tobacco pouches, rather than *inro* – lacquerware makers needed a new market. Exporters like the trading houses in Yokohama and Kōbe and foreign consumers proved ready to oblige. Products like *inro*, writing boxes and pieces from dowry sets found popularity with Western collectors. Workshops also explored applying signature techniques and styles to hairbrushes, glove boxes and other Western products.

Economic and social change affected some ways of working. Increased demand led some workshops to lower standards by cutting steps in the process, assigning technically demanding work to less seasoned artisans and using cheaper materials, as the time-consuming techniques made it difficult to fill immediate orders. At the other end of the spectrum, the well-connected painter and lacquerware craftsman Shibata Zeshin (1807–1891) began using lacquer techniques to 'paint' landscapes and still-lifes onto framed pictorial surfaces, similar to the format of Western-style painting.[49] The hybrids of painting and lacquerwork emerging from his workshop demonstrated how traditional motifs, methods and materials

Designing Modern Japan

Shibata Zeshin, *inro* showing silkworm moths and cocoons on mulberry leaves, 1865, gold hiramakie, takamakie and black lacquer on a gold lacquer ground on carved wood with silk cord, 9.2 x 7.2 x 2.2 cm. This *inro* is one of a set of twelve, each featuring seasonal items or items associated with a different month of the year, and made with different lacquer techniques.

could be rethought for the new market at home and abroad. The Tokyo-born and -based Zeshin had studied painting and lacquerware in Kyoto, where he was affiliated with the prominent Maruyama-Shijō school of painting. After the Meiji Restoration, his acknowledged skill, existing patronage network and pictorial style gained his workshop commissions for international expositions and private clients. Zeshin's workshop organization did not change greatly after the Meiji Restoration. His workshop found new clients, for whom it produced new types of objects, but the design process, working methods and organization of work within the studio remained similar to those in the Tokugawa period.

Zeshin's strategy of adapting his workshop's techniques and materials for products catering to a new market appeared in other industries, too, particularly among elite craftsmen with government and export firm patronage. In metalwork, thanks to the ban on samurai

The Namikawa Yasuyuki cloisonné workshop, Kyoto, c. 1904, one image of stereograph. Despite training schools opened in the 1880s, most artisans continued to learn their craft through apprenticeships in workshops.

sword-wearing, both sword-makers and workshops specializing in decorative *tsuba* sword guards lost their main markets virtually overnight. The new government enacted laws that privileged Shintō over Buddhism. These prompted waves of anti-Buddhist sentiment and devastated the cast bronze industry, which had specialized in candlesticks, incense burners and other objects for Buddhist temples and home altars. Metalworkers in towns like Kyoto and Mito, north of Tokyo, reapplied their techniques for finely worked metal to create vases, urns, boxes and articulated animals whose hyperrealism and extreme skill provoked curiosity and purchases abroad.

The gift of a decorative suit of armour to Queen Victoria in 1859, now in the collections of the Victoria and Albert Museum, London, did not spark a craze for armour purchases or displays in British drawing rooms. However, foreign collectors proved keen to acquire altar fittings, swords and *tsuba*. As with *inro*, many major museums now have collections of the latter numbering in the hundreds, including those

Suzuki Chōkichi, vase decorated with chrysanthemums, bamboo and vine with a thrush and butterfly, c. 1880, cast and patinated bronze with applied gold and with shakudo, shibuichi and other patinated copper decoration, 27.2 cm x 29.5 cm.

Designing Modern Japan

donated by former collectors in subsequent decades. Intervention from the international exposition commissioners and the new export firms like the Komai and Ōzeki companies, specialist export manufacturing firms for metalwork, helped the better-connected workshops to apply their skills to new products, too. Elite craftsmen like metal-carvers Kanō Natsuo (1828–1898) and Unno Shōmin (1844–1915) branched out into new products such as 'paintings' made by chiselling alloys. Suzuki Chōkichi (1848–1919), a bronze caster, found a strong following for his immense incense burners with life-sized figures of birds and animals. Suzuki's other innovation was to reference Japanese mythology and history, for example in multi-sectioned encrusted vases based on *usubata*, a kind of vase used in formal flower arrangements, but reimagined with new surface patterns from illustrated woodblock print books of storied warriors in famous battles.

For ceramics, a large industry with more than twenty major production regions, the situation was equally challenging and well demonstrates the important economic role of decorative crafts industries.[50] After domains were abolished in 1871, domain-backed kilns lost their financial and political support.[51] Smaller kilns specializing in tea ceremony ceramics lost their indirect backing, as the samurai and wealthy merchants who had been their principal clients reduced household spending; the number of family-run kilns in the Kiyomizu-Gojōzaka district in Kyoto, for example, halved between 1853 and 1888.[52] Kilns that specialized in everyday use ceramics for customers across the social spectrum were less affected by these specific changes, but also lost income with the end of the *daimyō* and samurai sinecures, as well as inflation in the 1870s and deflation in the 1880s.[53]

Shrinkage in the domestic market was offset partly by government commissions for exposition pieces, then by dealers' purchases to supply the rampant European and American taste for decorative Japanese vases, plates and *objets d'art*. In the early modern period, the Hizen kilns had specialized in export ceramics. Now, other ceramics regions around Japan saw the export market as key to their survival. In 1867, the Satsuma domain displayed gold-and-white porcelains in the Exposition Universelle in Paris. The resulting popularity of Satsuma ware led to explosive sales of 'Satsuma' in Europe – and to the development of 'Satsuma ware' kilns in places like Kyoto and Tokyo, far from Satsuma itself. The boom in Satsuma ware continued through the 1880s in Europe, and until the turn of the century in the United

Kanzan workshop, two-handled vase, one of a pair, 1875, porcelain painted in overglaze enamels and gilt, 37 cm x 16.2 cm, Kyoto. In the 1870s, some Kyoto kilns adopted the decorative style of Satsuma ware, complete with flourishes of form and gilt, to take advantage of the popularity of Satsuma ware in the European and American markets.

States, until foreign collectors gained a more sophisticated knowledge of the actual range of Japanese ceramics and tastes of native connoisseurs. It also prompted potters to experiment with Western technologies like mechanized production and charcoal-fired kilns, important for achieving hard porcelains. Some kilns chose to go head to head with Limoges and Sèvres, rather than relying on the 'exotic' nature of Japanese designs for their sales. Arita potters travelled to Vienna in 1873 for research and in 1875 established Kōransha as a Western-style incorporated company rather than a single family

Designing Modern Japan

enterprise, to this end.[54] After a split in opinion as to whether the Arita kilns should specialize in mechanically produced or hand-painted wares, Kōransha directors in favour of mechanization formed a new company, the Seiji Gaisha. An 8,000-yen loan from the Japanese government allowed them to import machinery from Limoges.[55] However, the new firm's elaborate Western-style porcelains proved too expensive, and its Western-style production system was inefficient and unpopular compared to the established workshop system, leading it to founder; historians suggest that it attempted too much change too soon.[56]

Other Arita makers responded with more incremental forms of design change. In one vase displayed at the 1876 Centennial Exposition in Philadelphia, potters muted their colour palette by removing the red and green but retaining Arita's signature deep cobalt blue and gold on white. They incorporated a geometrical neck and base ring

Tsuji and Hyōchien workshops, pair of vases for the European and American markets, 1875, porcelain with underglaze blue painting in Arita (Tsuji workshop) and overglaze enamelling and gilt (Hyōchien workshop), height 21.3 cm, Arita and Tokyo.

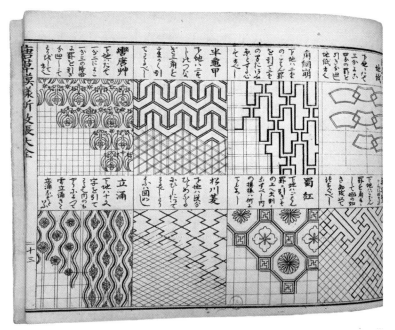

Chinese-style floral geometrical repeat patterns and their underlying grid system, in Murakami Takeji and Maekawa Zenbei (publisher), *Collection of Patterns Antique and Modern: A Book of Peerless Designs for the Common Good* (1885), woodblock-printed book, Osaka.

decoration and precise finish, all characteristics of Arita work. But they also added painted pictorial imagery – lifelike carp and birds in flight – and a milky finish. The result was a vase that was recognizably Arita, yet distinctively new. In style, iconography, colour and finish the animals particularly did not look like Arita ware, and they were not. The vase was formed, fired and underglazed in Arita by the Tsuji workshop under its eleventh-generation head, Tsuji Katsuzō (1847–1929).[57] It was then transported to Tokyo for overglaze enamelling by the Hyōchien decorating workshop, which had been established by Kawahara Noritatsu (1845–1914) in 1873 for the express purpose of decorating export ceramics. The Hyōchien workshop had emerged from the ceramics experimental workshop established to produce work for the 1873 Vienna World's Fair. It specialized in the enamelling of Western-style realist scenes onto ceramics from other Japanese kilns. Significantly, it offered not only new designs but a new production system, to adapt to market demand for novelty.[58]

Arita potters were not the only regional ceramics producers to revamp their product line-ups after the decline of Satsuma's popularity in the 1880s. By the 1890s, many Kyoto kilns were specializing in ceramics with more obviously 'Western' motifs and shapes. Kilns in Seto and Minō, important ceramics districts near Nagoya, began producing

Designing Modern Japan

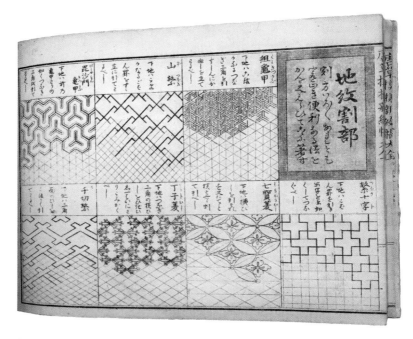

blanks in the shape of Western-style tableware for overglaze finishing at separate factories in Nagoya and eventual export to European and American dining tables.[59] Other Seto and Minō kilns continued to produce inexpensive tableware for Japanese domestic use, and diversified into sanitary ware.

Artisans determined their products' designs in a variety of ways. Some worked from their own workshops' and industries' design heritage. Others used research into European products and consumer tastes and borrowed designs from other popular export arts and crafts areas like woodblock prints. Artists and printers continued to produce *hinagata-bon*, and workshop masters to use them, but the books too reflected broader social change. A set of pattern books published in Osaka in 1885 explained how to draw a variety of contemporary and historical patterns and family crests using geometrical drawing tools such as a compass and ruler, with additional explanation of these tools. Other pages provided block-printed and woven pattern samples, similar to a fabric sample book but printed onto the page. National universal education emerged in the 1870s and helped to prompt a market for textbooks, mass printed by commercial firms; the Ministry of Education included drawing as part of the standard curriculum, including geometrical drawing. These pattern books clearly incorporated the elements and function of *hinagata-bon* and textile sample books into the new textbook format, with content applicable in both industrial and educational contexts; perhaps unsurprisingly, editor Murakami Masatake published a number of drawing textbooks in this period.

Regional patronage for design and craft industries changed as well, with domain patronage replaced by support from entrepreneurs and politicians concerned to maintain their local economic base. Sakurai Tsutomu (1843–1931), a domain official turned politician, co-founded the Eishinsha kiln near Kōbe in 1876 as a vocational centre to train and employ former samurai who had lost their incomes.[60] Eishinsha was very much a sign of the times: Sakurai chose a declining ceramics district, Izuhara, as the location for his project, capitalizing on its existing infrastructure, and hired experts in porcelain from Nabeshima kilns who had lost their domainal sponsorship to supervise and lead the project. Eishinsha potters studied processes and products from Sèvres and developed a reputation for their porcelain 'basketry', fired in white porcelain and imitating openwork reticulated baskets.

Kyoto's economy, as we have seen, depended on the textile industry and other forms of craft manufacturing. Some local industries faced real challenges. Nishijin suffered first from domestic competition after the Kiryū weavers established production in the 1730s, then from changing fashions and from reforms restricting its guild-based system in the 1840s. Foreign competition, the rising cost of silk and the dismantling of the *daimyō* patronage system in the 1850s and '60s meant further economic damage. The district declined precipitously, sliding from 7,000 looms in 1730 to only 3,819 looms by 1864.[61] With Nishijin a major part of Kyoto's social and economic base, the prefectural government sent two weavers to Lyon to study French techniques and acquire looms in 1873, then sponsored other textile artisans to travel to Europe. It opened a specialist weaving and dyeing training centre to disseminate European techniques, including loom use and chemical dyes, in 1874–5.[62] Kyoto's government also sought to boost export sales by inviting foreigners to exhibitions in Kyoto, no mean task given that foreign presence was restricted to treaty ports alone at this time.[63]

Prefectural and municipal governments also identified formal education as a mechanism for strengthening local industries in difficult and changing environments. In 1880, Kyoto prefecture backed a proposal from Kyoto painters for a new painting school. Industry figures

Designing Modern Japan

in Kyoto provided financial support for the school, seeing such training as useful for ensuring that Kyoto products had competitive designs.[64] Bureaucrats in Tokyo created the Tokyo Industrial Workers' School (Tōkyō Shokkō Gakkō) in 1881, to train future shop foremen in woodworking, metalworking, textiles, ceramics and applied chemistry, again technical aspects of industries identified as important for the metropole's economy. Significantly, the school's curriculum identified design drawing as a separate technical discipline. Students – aged from thirteen to 25 and including women in the part-time course – entered the department of drawing, artistic crafts or ordinary crafts, from which they further specialized in areas like historical painting, embroidery, wood sculpture, ceramics and lacquerware. Given the existing tradition of painters providing design sketches, the drawing department may have provided design training. Indeed, one required course taught students to translate motifs for products, which certainly sounds like a continuation of the early modern period design practice of painters creating motifs for crafts and textiles.[65] By 1887, Kanazawa, too, had a similar school, supported by the prefectural government and again with a separate design department.[66]

For civic-minded entrepreneurs, promoting local industry was a way to support the locality to thrive. To give one example, in 1887 alone, cousins Tanaka Gentarō (1853–1922) and Hamaoka Kōtetsu (1853–1936) launched the Kyoto Weaving Company (Kyōto Orimono Gaisha) and Kyoto Ceramics Company (Kyōto Tōki Gaisha), as well as an exporter, the Kansai Trading Company (Kansai Bōeki Gaisha), and a warehousing company to store goods before shipping, the Kyoto Warehousing Company (Kyōto Sōko Gaisha).[67] The cousins were also active in banking, railroads, the Kyoto stock exchange and politics. As the combination of ventures indicates, the cousins' interests lay in taking advantage of new trade and infrastructure possibilities to produce and sell Kyoto products abroad and to import foreign goods. For workshops in traditional industrial regions and cities like Kyoto and Kanazawa, overseas demand offered a way to continue production and retain income; for entrepreneurs, it meant new business opportunities, potentially also spurring the emergence of new crafts regions. For both, exports supported livelihood during a volatile time.

The economic rationale for such investment was significant. Today, objects like lacquerware, ceramics and silk textiles are understood – collected, sold and displayed – as decorative art, or as craft. Japan's textile industries did diversify into a combination of craft workshops and large-scale mechanized production beginning in the 1870s. But crafts were industries, too, and economically significant ones at that. In his account of Japanese manufacturing from the premodern period onwards, published in 1898, the eminent historian Yokoi Tokifuyu listed Japan's significant industries during the Tokugawa period as consisting of ceramics, lacquerware, weaving, dyeing, swords and other craft armaments, bronzes, woodcarving of Noh masks, netsuke and other objects, paper-making, woodblock carving and Western machinery.[68] In the Meiji period, textiles particularly but also ceramics, lacquerware and everyday wood products remained high-volume industrial products, both in the minds of their sponsors and in their economic function. Japan's increased enmeshment in international networks was integral to the important economic status of regional crafts industries. Textiles alone – both woven fabric and silk and cotton thread – accounted for 40 to 50 per cent of Japanese exports between 1874 and 1901.[69]

Local change, led by local entrepreneurs and politicians, took place alongside national projects to modernize major systems and infrastructure. After 1868, the new government embarked on a comprehensive survey of 'best practice' in areas including education, industry, governance, law, transportation, communications and the military in Europe and the United States. At first this continued the Tokugawa period system of studying imported knowledge through print – translations of European and American books – and schools.[70] Elite institutions for learning, however, were now concentrated in Tokyo. The government engineering school in Tokyo, the Kōbu Gakkō, opened to train indigenous engineers and architects in 1871. In 1877, the government converted a Tokugawa school for foreign books and translation into what would become the Imperial University, also in Tokyo. This school trained young men, often from samurai families connected to the domains that formed the new government, in medicine, engineering, natural sciences and other areas deemed nationally important. Education and ideas of knowledge and learning developed also from the *bakufu* and domain schools for Western knowledge, not least since many of the new government leaders and administrators had studied at them.

While the new higher education system included civil engineering and architecture, design for manufacturing had a faint and transient presence in these early national institutions, perhaps unsurprisingly

Designing Modern Japan

This photograph of Tejima Seiichi aged 22 was taken on the occasion of his departure to the United States for study in 1870. Tejima, previously a student at the Tokugawa *bakufu* school in Tokyo, poses sitting on a wooden chair, in kimono and hakama, with the swords and hairstyle befitting his position from an elite samurai family.

since both crafts and commerce had sat far from samurai education. In 1877, the Ministry of Public Works elevated the engineering school to a college, renaming it the Kōbu Daigakkō (Engineering College). The reorganized college included a new art school, the Kōbu Bijutsu Gakkō. Lecturers taught pattern design for products (*zuan*, literally 'image-idea') across departments including woodworking, metalworking and lacquerware, and the school contributed product designs for the 1877 National Industrial Exposition in Tokyo. However, the school soon adopted a purely fine art curriculum, leading one foreign observer, Gottfried Wagener (1831–1892), to comment that Japanese artists had a dislike of industrial design and would not master it.[71] It closed in 1883. As we will see later on in this chapter and in Chapter Two, design education for manufactured products would largely sit at prefectural and municipal level until the turn of the century.

Overseas first-hand experience was important for the new national government as well as for local business leaders and politicians. In 1871–3, fully half of the new government, including a number of key cabinet ministers, embarked on an inspection tour of Europe and North America, named the Iwakura Embassy after leader Count Iwakura Tomomi.[72] The group met with national governments and undertook a comprehensive survey of government and industry throughout the countries visited, from textile mills in Lancashire and schools in Massachusetts to the Berlin opera house. The purpose was to identify effective systems for governance and social services through which to create political stability and economic development. The new government also dispatched bright young men, again often former samurai from domains well represented in the new government, to Europe and the United States to study subjects they had identified as key for development: medicine, law, engineering, education.[73] Former samurai women were sent as well, charged with developing girls' education, for

example Shimoda Utako (1854–1936) and Ōe Sumi (1875–1948), both of whom travelled to Britain to study domestic economy. Ministries expected Japanese returning from overseas study to teach, translate and publish, maximizing the return on their investment by distributing knowledge to a wider pool of people, who could then use it and disseminate it themselves. This system would continue in a similar format for decades, into the post-war years. It would also, as we will see, allow local, regional and national government officials and entrepreneurs to identify the design strategies that contributed to the Lancashire mills' success in international markets, and to propose ways to recreate them back home.

At national level, systems implemented through these studies of European and American systems and technologies included universal education, male conscription and the Gregorian calendar. The government adopted a Prussian-style military and a legal system modelled on France's Napoleonic Code. Investment in new physical infrastructure for transportation and communication was important: the first telegraph lines appeared in 1869, followed by a national postal service

Utagawa Hiroshige III, *The Railroad at Yatsuyamashita*, early 1870s, *nishiki-e* woodblock print, Tokyo. The new railway and telegraph lines between Tokyo's Shinagawa area and Yokohama were a popular subject for woodblock prints in the early 1870s. This image emphasizes the disruptive presence of the steam train through the clouds of billowing grey smoke.

Designing Modern Japan

in 1871 and Japan's first railway in 1872, running between Yokohama and Shimbashi in Tokyo.[74] Other visible effects of infrastructure modernization included gas lighting and Western-style government and commercial buildings in wood as well as brick, mortar and glass, often built by carpenters using traditional tools and techniques to create foreign forms.[75] Urban infrastructure developments became an important subject-matter for woodblock prints, and printmakers took advantage of technological developments for formal experimentation in their medium, most notably the addition of synthetic inks and use of existing natural inks to simulate them.[76] Such infrastructure changes indicate why the Meiji government wanted to build capacity in technical areas like metallurgy, chemistry and engineering: how to fire bricks, how to make steel, how to manage gasworks, and how to do all of this with the level of standard quality required for safe, effective use.

Both physical and social infrastructure required knowledge. But sending people overseas for training took time. For immediate technology transfer, the government contracted European and American educators to teach at the Engineering College and the other elite institutions that would eventually form the Imperial University.[77] These advisers, known as *oyatoi gaikokujin* (hired foreigners), could also be consulted on architecture, engineering works and hardware purchased from abroad. Design for crafts industries was not an obvious area for hiring *oyatoi gaikokujin*, but once in Japan their expertise could serve new purposes. Wagener, the observer who commented on industrial design, arrived in Japan in 1869 to serve as chief chemist for a foreign-owned soap factory in Nagasaki but was soon consulted by the nearby former Nabeshima kilns.[78] His initial engagement with ceramics did not last long. By 1870 he was an instructor in natural sciences and German at the Daigaku Nankō, another predecessor to the Imperial University. In 1872, however, his familiarity with glaze chemistry and more general interest in the applied arts led the Austrian government to recommend him as the right person to lead the new government's international exposition team for the Vienna World's Fair the following year. Promoting crafts industries was not an immediate priority for the *oyatoi gaikokujin* system, but, as we will see, Wagener played an outsize role in doing precisely this. The sideways slip from soap to ceramics also indicates how policy outcomes could be the product of adjacencies, existing networks and chance encounters.

Where did design and making of light industry products sit within the Meiji government vision of modernization? As the appearance and disappearance of design from the Engineering College suggests, in practice this depended largely on politicians' and industrialists' priorities. Throughout the Meiji period, politicians disagreed about which industries most urgently required government support and investment. Some, most prominently Itō Hirobumi and Yamao Yōzō in the Ministry of Public Works, insisted that the priority should be to gain capital in order to purchase steel and armaments for the military, and that the development of new heavy industries – steel, chemicals, shipbuilding – would be more effective to this end.[79] Others, including Ōkubo Toshimichi, finance minister from 1871 to 1873 and minister of the interior from 1873 to 1878, advocated for the modernization of indigenous industries such as silk and lacquerware over imported new ones. Economic historians have argued, however, that ministers' divergent standpoints were ultimately less important for industrial growth than entrepreneurial activity.[80] In the 1880s, entrepreneurs in the textile industry were boosting exports by establishing large-scale cotton-spinning mills in cities and mechanizing smaller-scale silk filatures and weaving firms in rural areas. Largely handmade, workshop-based industrial products – including luxury crafts – would also remain important exports for acquiring foreign capital well into the 1910s. For some of those involved in creating and promoting them, design would be key to doing so successfully.

Design by Committee: Government Design Advising, Luxury Crafts and the International Exposition System

All of these factors combined to put the Arita vases on display in Philadelphia in 1876. The Philadelphia Centennial Exposition was neither the first time that Japanese products had been shown at an international exposition nor a Japanese government's first foray into trade and diplomacy through exposition participation. It did, however, mark the coming together of workshop owners, entrepreneurs and government officials around an emergent roadmap for sovereignty and economic development, supported partially by luxury crafts.

Japan's first appearance in the international exposition system came in 1862, when British consul Rutherford Alcock, newly arrived in Edo, invited the Tokugawa *bakufu* to participate in the Great London

Exposition the same year.[81] When the *bakufu*, unsure of what might be appropriate, appointed Alcock as commissioner, the resulting exhibit become more a collection of available items than a strategic investment in design-fronted diplomacy: the small display consisted of ordinary household objects – teapots, baskets, straw raincoats, paper and lacquer items, along with some antique luxury goods such as ivories, bronzes and woven silk cloth – and more touristic items such as maps and illustrations of Japanese scenes.[82] The products displayed were in fact the fruits of Japanese industry, but exhibition visitors saw craft. Many visitors found the image of Japan presented delightfully exotic; the combination of unusual (to British eyes) materials, techniques and styles such as lacquer and woodblock prints amid the oil paintings, machinery and raw materials of other exhibitors heightened the sense of novelty and difference. It led British designers like Christopher Dresser to begin to explore the aesthetics and materials of Japanese things, while creating an image of Japan as a fairyland of the handmade, untouched by Western industrialization. Dresser's phrasing captures well many British observers' impression of the skill and care applied to crafts production in Japan:

> Each piece of ware is produced entirely by the one man and is to him a sort of child that he loves; he has watched its development through all its stages; he has nursed it tenderly, and he has done all that he could to give to it beauty of form and perfection of character . . . There is much pride in Japan manifested by the maker in completing a little cup, a lacquer box, a sheet of leather-paper, or even a pair of chop-sticks.[83]

One hundred and fifty years later, foreign consumers still see unparalleled skill, attention to detail and devotion to craft in Japanese products, and Japanese manufacturers exploit this image in advertisement taglines for 'highly-skilled Japanese engineering and craft'. But in the 1860s and '70s, the challenge was to find products that seemed modern and sophisticated to foreign consumers, yet different enough to sell.

By the 1867 Exposition Universelle in Paris, political leaders pushing for increased export trade had gained enough information about the international exposition system to organize their own exhibits, all intended to fuel exports. Significantly, there were three exhibitors from Japan: the Tokugawa *bakufu* and two powerful southern domains, Saga, home to the Arita kilns, and Satsuma, their neighbours who were responsible for trade with the Ryūkyū Kingdom.[84] Both were domains to which the *bakufu* had entrusted foreign trade and diplomacy, and both had engaged directly with European naval crews and engineering knowledge for some decades. Familiarity bred results with European buyers and the exposition jury. Saga focused its display on 520 cases of the colourful export porcelains for which Arita was already known, making it legible to collectors and dealers and garnering sales – and income – for Saga.[85] Satsuma presented a rich variety of Satsuma and Ryūkyū wares and was awarded a prize in Class 26, 'Leather, Ivory and Basketry Objects', for 'lacquerware on sculpted ivory; boxes; morocco leather goods with lacquered interiors; cigar cases; tortoiseshell, etc.'[86] The *bakufu*, which requested products from all domains, including those with little experience of Europeans, was awarded a prize in Class 43, 'Agricultural Products (Non-Alimentary) Easy to Conserve', for a 'collection of textile fibres'.[87] At a time when a nation's ability to produce manufactured goods correlated to the extent to which European powers saw it as a sophisticated power, Satsuma's awards clearly outclassed the *bakufu*'s.[88] The *bakufu*'s exhibit had been intended partly to demonstrate its political legitimacy as the national government, but the awards' distribution suggests that the motley assortment of products, many chosen by domain officials unfamiliar with European tastes or international exposition protocol, had the opposite effect.[89]

The 1867 experience directly informed the new government's approach to international expositions. For the 1873 Vienna World's Fair, five years into the new Meiji government, the government appointed Sano Tsunetami (1823–1902), a high-ranking civil servant from Nagasaki who had been part of the Saga delegation in 1867, to organize Japan's contribution.[90] Sano had a pre-Restoration background in *rangaku* and metal refining and previously ran the Saga domain experimental foundry.[91] For Vienna, he assembled a team for the express purpose of preparing the exhibition. In addition to the *oyatoi gaikokujin* Gottfried Wagener, members included Kawahara Noritatsu, founder of the Hyōchien export ceramic enamelling workshop responsible for decorating the vase with carp we encountered earlier.[92] Wagener was charged to showcase Japanese industry, as was standard for international expositions, with their trade-fair-meets-public-amusement

Designing Modern Japan

character. Sano and Wagener understood the exposition aesthetic, as well as what to show and what not to show. Japan in 1870 lacked the large-scale mechanized textile mills, foundries and other heavy industries whose products represented the manufacturing strength of world powers like Britain and France. Wagener and Sano determined that luxury crafts were the manufactures that would best represent Japan's excellence in technological development and aesthetic achievement and might best sell in European markets.

Persuaded by the 1867 jury results and Japonisme's growing grip on European buyers, the team presented Japan as a land of artistic excellence and tradition, embodied in highly technical applied arts objects. International expositions included anything under the sun – rolling stock, umbrellas, paintings, raw materials, even people – but Sano and Wagener emphasized luxury crafts as an area of industry in which Japanese skill and technique could compete. They were also appealing in terms of visual novelty and being easily sellable to museum collections.[93] The 1873 exhibition showed some curiosities and 'ethnographic' objects, located within a miniature Japanese garden and installed by Japanese gardeners and carpenters in traditional costume, to the great fascination of the Viennese. However, the bulk of products displayed were ornaments in lacquer, ceramics, metal and cloisonné: the types of objects that had won Satsuma an award in 1867. Wagener recognized the importance of appealing to European taste and selected objects that would compare in type and display with the towering

Yokoyama Matsusaburō, *Satsuma Vases*, c. 1872–3, albumen print, Tokyo. Yokoyama photographed the items in a preliminary display in Tokyo, prior to their shipment to Vienna. The photographs were collected in the album *Book of Photographs of Products Submitted to the International Exposition in Austria* (1873).

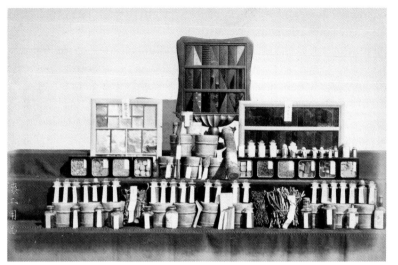

Yokoyama Matsusaburō, *Goods for Lacquer Craft*, c. 1872–3, albumen print, Tokyo. Displays such as this one, showing the materials, techniques, tools and processes of lacquering, accompanied the displays of finished items.

objets d'art commonly exhibited by European nations. These included blue-and-white Arita porcelains, lacquerware sets and massive metal incense burners whose decorative surfaces responded to the late nineteenth-century European love of pattern and conventions of employing national history and myth as motifs.

The size of the incense burners was part of a more general strategy to astonish viewers through contrast. Wagener stressed objects that were particularly large or small, required noticeable technical skill or employed techniques not available in Europe, marking a difference from the European crafts displayed while emphasizing the ingenuity and history of Japanese luxury manufacturing. Japan also exhibited the tools and materials required to make luxury goods, with an emphasis on the highly developed nature of the processes. The result was impressive: Japan's exhibit won 198 prizes and medals, and the Viennese joined the rush to acquire Japanese things and aesthetics.[94] Japonisme boomed, with museums and private collectors across Europe snapping up entire collections. London's South Kensington Museum, now the Victoria and Albert Museum, for example, purchased more than two hundred ceramics pieces from the exhibition, along with lacquers, bronzes and enamels.[95]

A new network of entrepreneurial dealers facilitated purchases. One immediate result of the Vienna exhibition was a state–private joint enterprise, the Kiriū Kōshō Kaisha, a manufacturing and trading firm established in 1874 to supply the growing overseas market with

Designing Modern Japan

Japanese luxury crafts. Tea merchant Matsuo Gisuke (1836–1902) and art dealer Wakai Kenzaburō (1834–1908) led the Kiriū Kōshō Kaisha operation, which included agents in London, Hong Kong and Vienna and advertised itself as trading 'bronzes, lacquered, pottery and porcelain wares, tea, silk, curiosities and other Japanese manufactures'.[96] Alongside its dealing work, the company coordinated crafts acquisitions for the international expositions. After Vienna and Philadelphia, the Japanese government participated in another exposition in Paris, in 1878. The Kiriū Kōshō Kaisha opened shops in New York and Paris to take advantage of the taste for Japanese products fuelled by the expositions and to sell display items that remained unsold after the fairs had ended. Suppliers included many of the workshops mentioned already in this chapter, including the Eishinsha kiln and the metalworker Suzuki Chōkichi. This fact points to the company's influence, in terms of growing businesses at the time, their lasting fame and their presence in museum collections today.

In addition to purchasing completed pieces from its suppliers, the company operated its own workshops and commissioned new pieces based on overseas market research. It transmitted the latter through more than 1,900 design drawings which were circulated to internal and contracted workshops. Many of the company's designs continued to use early modern motifs, particularly bird and flower designs derived from Chinese painting and the asymmetrical composition favoured by Japanese artists and clients. These were applied to Western-style plates and large metal and ceramic vases for drawing rooms, rather than to fans and kimono hems. Designs and commissions also included wooden furniture, metal light fixtures and ceramic salt and pepper shakers. Few records remain about many of the firm's designers, other than that most were based in Tokyo and Kyoto and had trained as painters in well-established and prominent early modern painting lineages such as the Kano and Rinpa schools.[97] This background may explain the predominance of bird and flower motifs in the designs, testifying to the historical lack of any clear divide between 'fine art' and 'decorative' painting in Japan; early modern painters moved freely between collectible media such as handscrolls and decorative installations such as sliding screens and wall panels.[98] The Kiriū Kōshō Kaisha closed in 1891 due to financial shortfall. Despite its short life, it had a significant impact in at least three ways: it offered a model for future luxury crafts exporters; it created a system to conduct products from Japanese manufacturers to the new overseas market; and it conveyed overseas market trends and popular designs to domestic manufacturers through drawings commissioned by artist-designers. For these reasons, historians value it as a prototype or harbinger of later state sponsorship of design exports, and also for the institution of a system of collaboration between consultant designers and manufacturers.

Thanks to exporters and exhibition-makers, the taste for things Japanese soon expanded within North America. Meiji exhibition commissioners continued a similar strategy of foregrounding showy, technically difficult luxury crafts objects in their displays in Philadelphia in 1876, Chicago in 1893 and St Louis in 1904. As the towers of vases at the opening of this chapter begin to suggest, display design in Philadelphia amplified commissioners' adherence to standard international exhibition strategies of creating visual draw through excess, bombast, ornament and scale. Visitors entered the space past chest-high cast bronze incense burners that combined mythological scenes with prodigious casting, with other bronzes of similar scale demarcating the corners of the space. At the centre, visually, the commissioners placed formally ornate ceramics, lacquerware, enamels and metalwork, presented symmetrically on a central dais with further work in cases and free-standing around the perimeter of the space. They framed the exhibit with large woven banners with a chrysanthemum seal, symbol of both the emperor and the nation, overhung by Japanese flags and labelled 'Empire of Japan' in Japanese and English, on a large lacquer and gold plaque. Commissioners complemented the 'art industry' displays with successively ambitious architectural installations – most famously a recreation of Byōdōin, a temple outside Kyoto, on the shore of Lake Michigan in 1893 – and exhibitions of Japanese education, railroads and other requisite elements of a modern nation.[99]

The international expositions fuelled foreign consumption of Japanese luxury crafts. In Europe, Japanese displays at fairs such as the 1885 Nuremberg Metalwork Exhibition and the Paris universal expositions of 1878 and 1889 combined with the promotions of a growing network of dealers – typified by the ambitious Siegfried Bing in Paris, as well as Japanese exporters like Yamanaka & Company, specialists in flamboyantly carved wooden 'Yokohama furniture' – to maintain the high profile and supply of Japanese luxury goods for drawing rooms and museums across Europe and America.[100] Japanese art and crafts' popularity among prominent artists and intellectuals like the Goncourt

Designing Modern Japan

brothers and James Abbott McNeill Whistler helped to show how Japanese products could be integrated into Western interiors, both the dark, heavily furnished interiors popular in the late nineteenth century and the lighter 'artistic' designs that emerged as a reaction to them.

FROM THE EARLY DAYS of exporting such products, entrepreneurs had recognized the importance of design in calibrating product quality and strategically marketing Japanese work. As the economic importance of export crafts industries grew, product design became a concern for bureaucrats in the national government, too. Some members of the Meiji government, well aware of products' economic role, developed design improvement schemes often modelled on European examples to bolster the industry, for both national and regional good. The short-lived design curriculum for the woodworking, lacquerware and metalwork departments in the Engineering College in 1877 was one result.

Another result of the civil servants' experiences at the Vienna World's Fair was a new government Product Design Department, the Seihin-gakari. The department opened in 1876, to prepare for that year's Philadelphia Centennial Exposition; its official mandate was 'to take charge in advising on trends in overseas demand objects, preparing product drawings and supporting and guiding producers in the various crafts areas' for both the government expositions and general exports.[101] It was led by Sano Tsunetami, now a prominent figure in the Ministry of the Interior. (When he became finance minister in 1880, the department moved with him.) Sano staffed the department with young former samurai whom he had earlier involved in the project to organize effective exposition displays. Hirayama Eizō (1855–1914), for example, had travelled to Vienna as part of the 1873 exhibition team, when he was only eighteen, and remained there afterwards to study decorative arts design and production at the national Kunstgewerbeschule from 1874 to 1877, before becoming a key member of the Seihin-gakari.[102] Department members' overseas experience, in particular their experience of products lauded at the 1867 and 1873 exhibitions, would shape their design advising.

As its remit suggests, the Product Design Department's principal activity was to produce and circulate designs for potential exhibition and to export products to producers around Japan, in order to maintain quality and steer production according to overseas market taste. Commissioners compiled designs, which covered ceramics, lacquerware, metalwork, basketry, embroidery, textiles, leather and cloisonné and furniture, into books known as the *Onchi zuroku*, a title derived from a classical Chinese proverb about learning from the past to generate new knowledge (*onkō chishin*; the title combined a contraction of the proverb with 'zuroku' or album).[103] The first volume appeared in 1875; publication spanned 84 volumes and more than 4,000 designs before ending in 1885. Some designs were produced by Seihin-gakari members and affiliated artists in response to specific workshop requests, then lent to the workshops. In other cases, master artisans produced the designs, which the department then compiled for further lending to other workshops. Yet other designs for inclusion were selected from entries to National Industrial Expositions, about which more later.

Workshops with access to the *Onchi zuroku* were not required to reproduce its designs exactly. Rather, the drawings were indicative of types of ornament, forms, materials and objects likely to sell. One pair of bronze vases, presented to u.s. General Ulysses S. Grant by the Japanese government, followed the indicative scale, colour scheme, composition and decorative handles of the *Onchi zuroku* design, but introduced variance within the detail of the decorative bands at foot and neck. An underglazed ceramic flower vase by Kawamoto Masukichi I, fired in 1881 in the style of cut glass (*kiriko*), retained the form and concept of the *Onchi zuroku* design but varied the surface pattern and colour.

The composition of *Onchi zuroku* designs reflected designers' training – often in Tokugawa period techniques, materials and styles – as well as overseas trends. Such popular Tokugawa period motifs as chrysanthemums, plum blossoms and birds were often used; designers also continued the practice of employing classical Chinese patterns as part of Japan's aesthetic heritage.[104] In this way, the *Onchi zuroku* applied the model of the *hinagata-bon* – the Tokugawa period pattern books – in a new economic system: published not as commodities in their own right or as style guides to domestic fashion, but as intermediary objects intended to facilitate the production of commodities that could generate income for the nation. Design had become a policy tool within national government, for some politicians and civil servants at least. This reflects a particular role for luxury craft objects: of obtaining capital for the nation as well as communicating status

– in this instance national status, rather than that of an individual, household or domain.[105]

The particular direction in which civil servants took their design advising soon raised many questions for them. These included the extent to which European design and the Western market's tastes could or should be incorporated into the existing design and production system in Japan; and the extent to which the design and production system needed to adapt itself to the international market. As part of this conundrum, the question of what precisely 'modern Japanese design' should be was at the forefront of the Product Design Department members' concerns and had obvious immediate resonance for exporters. In 1879, department members including Sano and Hirayama joined with Kawase Hideharu (1840–1928), the head of the government's Bureau of Commerce, and influential exporters such as Matsuda Gisuke of the Kiriu Kōshō Kaisha to create a study and discussion group, the Ryūchikai (Dragon Pond Society), to pursue that question. The Ryūchikai analysis coincided with a widespread resurgence of nativist sentiment in Japan in response to the state embrace of Western-style customs in the 1870s. Led by Sano, the Ryūchikai's dual mandate was to promote indigenous crafts and arts production as part of the 'increase production and promote industry' policy, and to protect Japan's premodern artistic heritage at a time when some civil servants and members of the artistic elite had become concerned that Japanese historical objects were being sold off to foreign collectors, depleting the country of necessary referents of its own past.[106] In practice, it functioned as a test bed for generating design ideas and debating what actual 'modern Japanese design' might be, with the idea that conclusions would then be conveyed to manufacturers for their use.[107] To this end, the Ryūchikai sponsored exhibitions as well as a monthly product design competition, published a journal and organized debates and lectures on Japan's artistic heritage. As part of their search for a distinctive design identity in an increasingly globalized market, Ryūchikai members also held study events around art objects from earlier periods such as bronzes and ink paintings, a category newly renamed 'Japanese ancient art' (*Nihon kobijutsu*).

Ryūchikai activities centred around Tokyo, the seat of government, and need to be understood alongside the kinds of crafts promotion activities at local level discussed earlier in this chapter. Like Sano, many influential Ryūchikai members had begun their careers as bright young

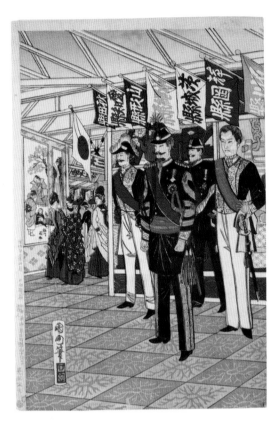

samurai in domains, but by 1879 were committed to strengthening the new national government at home and abroad. Both Ryūchikai members and business leaders and politicians in the regions were concerned to improve products' reception through improved design, and through that to acquire capital and maintain local economic well-being. Moving from public policy to entrepreneurial strategy, we could also compare this to distributors', retailers' and makers' own strategies for responding to market demands. Makers and commissioners had been gauging the right balance to strike of familiarity and novelty since the emergence of competitive domestic markets in the early modern period. Domains had long promoted strong crafts industries in pursuit of political status as well as economic success. Now, it was also an interest for some members of the national government.

Luxury crafts could also be political tools. From this angle, Japan as a nation could not yet demonstrate its position as a modern nation through military might or industrial output. It therefore needed another

Utagawa Kunitoshi, *Views of the Third National Industrial Promotion Exhibition*, 1890, woodblock prints, triptych, Tokyo. Behind the Meiji elite dressed in Western-style clothing, portrayed with the exuberant use of synthetic red inks, the local manufactures of each prefecture are set out, including kettles from Yamagata Prefecture, immense ceramic vases from Nagasaki Prefecture, Western-style clothing from Osaka, fans from Saitama Prefecture and woven textiles from Kyoto.

Designing Modern Japan

medium for demonstrating the sophistication through which it might differentiate itself in Western eyes from neighbours like China, thus keeping the archipelago from the Euro-American colonization and exploitation that had befallen other Asian nations. Japan's leaders saw an appeal to history and technical ability in the form of art as a way of doing so. Given that the unequal treaties would endure until 1899, when Japan renegotiated its treaty with Great Britain, such narratives and the perceptions they might engender mattered.

The narratives around design and making presented through luxury craft exports also reflect changes in popular sentiment in Japan. By the 1890s, historians were conducting a national survey of historical art objects and writing histories of Japanese art and architecture that explained these in the language and concepts of European art history. This included classifying objects and buildings according to a framework of stylistically distinct historical periods: the 'Momoyama', the 'Fujiwara' and so on.[108] In doing this they were mirroring the Eurocentric narratives of unequal development and potential among nations presented in 'world' histories of art, design and architecture by European authors such as James Fergusson (*History of Architecture*, 1865–7). Works like *Ideals of the East* (1903) by Okakura Kakuzō (Tenshin, 1863–1913) explicitly linked artistic and technological achievement to a nation's degree of civilization, with Japan as the culmination of Asian civilizational development.

There was a further geopolitical edge. In the 1880s, the influential intellectual and educator Fukuzawa Yukichi called for Japan to 'leave Asia' (*datsu-a*) and join what he saw as the group of civilized, progressive nations – that is, the imperial powers. His timing was telling. Japan's territorial expansion had begun with the colonization of the northern island of Ezo (Hokkaidō) in 1869, extending to the Ryūkyūs (Okinawa) in the south in 1879. Japan's subsequent acquisitions of Taiwan and the Korean peninsula through the Sino-Japanese and

Russo-Japanese wars in 1894–5 and 1904–5, respectively, revealed an imperial power with colonies gained and maintained through military might, like its chosen competitors in Europe and the USA.

At a time when non-Western nations' art, architecture and design was often discussed by Europeans as lacking historical development over time, proving that Japan 'had history' was an international political strategy. This was not always explicitly in the minds of product designers, of course. For many, applying Japanese or even Chinese motifs could equally have been about differentiating their products from those of French or Austrian competitors taking advantage of current popularity for a particular style; identifying their own work from that of local or regional competitors domestically; selecting styles that they could work effectively within their particular constraints; or even exploring a new technique out of curiosity or for personal challenge. Nor was style necessarily considered as political by shoppers in London, Chicago or Melbourne. Nonetheless, the link in the minds of Ryūchikai members between economic development, industrial promotion and the search for a distinctively Japanese style in the nation's aesthetic past is important for understanding the context in which self-conscious 'design' developed in late nineteenth-century Japan – and for making comparisons with design policies adopted by governments around the world today.

Concern for design also intersected policy in a series of National Industrial Expositions, sponsored by the Ministry of the Interior as part of its efforts to 'increase production and promote industry'. Held five times between 1877 and 1903 in Tokyo, Kyoto and Osaka, a principal goal for the early expositions was to improve standards in all areas of production – including areas like agriculture and mining as well as manufacturing – through awareness and competition. The ministry also intended them as a mechanism for identifying products to showcase in Japan's sections at the international expositions. The first three expositions, held in Ueno Park in Tokyo, were organized as preparatory events for Japan's participation in the Paris expositions of 1878 and 1889 and the Chicago fair of 1893, complete with juries and prizes. Following the structure of the overseas expositions, commissioners for the first exhibition in 1877 invited submissions in six categories: metallurgy, manufactures, machinery, agriculture, gardens and fine art. The products on display covered a correspondingly wide range, from fertilizers, fruit and toothbrushes to paper, power looms and Arita

Designing Modern Japan

porcelains.[109] Workshops commonly submitted pieces intended for international expositions as a preliminary selection process, and the selection criteria for prizes explicitly referenced products' viability as exports. The expositions' use as a first selection stage for international expositions is also evident in the jury comments provided for all exhibited goods. While most jury comments described the form and style of the work, with some noting particularly pleasing aspects, some included specific statements about items' export potential. On a lacquerware tea jar exhibited in 1877, the jury wrote, 'The hammerwork and gilding both have flaws but it clearly has value. This type of jar has recently been used a lot for holding export tea so as a practical object it will be profitable.'[110] Many comments noted historical referents for the work, indicating jurors' alignment with the general shift towards historicization of styles after the 1880s.

Somewhat ironically, Ryūchikai findings may have obscured design's potential role within the Ministry of Education's plans for national education. In 1886, senior bureaucrats in the Ministry of Education decided to create a national museum system and art school. Okakura Tenshin and Ernest Fenollosa (1853–1908), an American 'foreign expert' in Tokyo, were both members of the ministry's Art Commission. Okakura and Fenollosa travelled to Europe to review possible models, including those scoped by Sano and Wagener thirteen years previously. The Tokyo School of Fine Arts (Tōkyō Bijutsu Gakkō) opened in 1889.[111] In contrast to Sano and Wagener, Fenollosa and Okakura's concern was to create a system that might preserve and promote Japan's artistic heritage against the pressures of internationalization. To this end, the art school they created focused not on product, textile and graphic design – all arguably traditional Japanese arts, but overly commercial in their eyes – but on luxury crafts that could fit European definitions of 'fine arts': painting, sculpture, lacquerware and metalworking. Exemplary artists and craftsmen like metalworker Suzuki Chōkichi and the painter Kanō Hōgai (1828–1888) who had trained in Tokugawa period ateliers were appointed as professors. In the school's early years, 'design' was not a specialism of its own but rather integral to all students' education. The two-year introductory curriculum included six hours per week of pattern design, in addition to descriptive geometry and perspective drawing; and a course called *shin'an*, literally 'new ideas', allowed students to experiment with composition and other design elements as they developed original ideas towards their final-year work.[112] An optional technical course in 'architectural decoration' (*kenchiku sōshoku*) translated artistic design skills into surface and three-dimensional decoration for rooms and buildings. Both pattern design and decorative work for buildings had been part of the Tokugawa period artist's and craftsman's commercial repertoire as well, so while on paper the new specialisms seemed to correspond to their equivalents in European art and design schools, they can also be seen as reshaping existing ideas about design as part of art and crafts practice into a 'modern' format.

Like the Tokyo School of Fine Arts, the municipal and prefectural design and craft schools discussed earlier opened in the 1880s. Comparing them allows us to articulate key aspects of the ways in which local or regional and national actors understood design. At the Tokyo School of Fine Arts, attempts to reposition early modern art and crafts practices within the internationally legible structure of the modern art school are a useful reflection of its government patrons' concern with Japan's geopolitical standing as well as the national economy. The emphasis on exporting either basic materials like raw silk and cotton thread or unique 'artistic crafts', rather than mass-produced products like textiles and tableware, meant that some bureaucrats knew of design promotion and improvement projects like the UK's South Kensington system, a system of national art education created at improving the quality of British manufactured goods from the 1850s onwards, but for the most part did not see the importance of implementing design education or even awareness campaigns on a national scale. In contrast, the municipal and prefectural schools' focus on knowledge transmission and upskilling reflect their very immediate concerns to secure the health of cities and regions dependent on crafts manufacturing during an economically volatile time. For both groups, product design had an important political and economic role to play, but the scale of that vision and communities to which they were responding differed.

Pulling back to consider design promotion in the first decades of the Meiji period more widely, we can identify some mechanisms that men in government positions and influential entrepreneurs alike employed to strengthen local and national economies through design for product exports. These included the utilization and development of systems such as education, taxation and publishing culture, as well as leadership by experts for all areas of making, from product

Designing Modern Japan

design to materials, techniques and prototypes. Implementing these mechanisms required global trade networks and communication and transportation infrastructure. They also required balancing overseas market desire for the familiar (everyday habits) with desire for the exotic, in both the vision and its implementation.

As this chapter has demonstrated, different groups of people valued these strategies in different ways, often inconsistently. Many of these initiatives – from the National Industrial Expositions to the various schools – emerged from politicians and entrepreneurs' strong, often divergent opinions about the best course forward for Japan as a nation and as an assemblage of disparate regions. The initiatives therefore waxed and waned in influence along with their advocates' power in government.

National government interventions would eventually have a direct impact on design and crafts manufacturing at all levels, but not yet. The Japonisme-fuelled export markets of the 1860s–90s also played an important role in cushioning decorative crafts industries like metalwork, ceramics and lacquerware from the disappearance of domestic demand and in ensuring the maintenance of techniques and transmission of skills to a younger generation of craftsmen. But they did not necessarily make a great impact on the design of products made for daily life at home, or even on domestic interiors, except for those of elite households who could afford Western-style homes and furnishings. Despite the importance of the European and American markets for many crafts producers, activities like the *Onchi zuroku* and the Ryūchikai's design competitions directly targeted only a small segment of manufacturers.

Indeed, local economic organization, social structures, geography and cultural attitudes continued to shape actual production organization and materials, and market demand – within Japan and overseas – the products made and techniques acquired to make them. Within this mix, design was important but had not been identified by many people as key to market success or local economic health. There were simply too many other factors at play, not least the persistent role of the powerful factors who commissioned makers' work and provided supplies in many regional industries; hierarchical social relationships within manufacturing communities and households; the relative ease or difficulty of transporting goods to market afforded by local infrastructure and geography; and the often very real financial difficulties that makers faced.[113] Ministers and civil servants enacted a series of policies around aiding makers by providing design guidance, technical expertise and exposure to new markets, although these remained minor in scale in relation to policies for developing other industries (textiles and heavy industry). As the following chapters will set out, the policy persists to this day, as does its relatively minor nature compared to other industries identified as important. Artisans, businesspeople, artists and others continue to engage with the policy, or not, for their own purposes – often but not exclusively for economic stability.

For many makers, design inspiration would continue to arise as it had in the Tokugawa period: from existing products popular with customers, from competitors and from pattern books. Regional distribution systems linking cottage industry producers in rural villages to consumers in Tokyo and Osaka through a system of dealers, wholesalers and shops continued to function as they had before 1868.[114] For industries like printed and woven patterned cotton textiles that commanded regional or even national markets, factors continued to commission specific patterns based on their popularity with existing customers, or from competitors' sample books. The material landscape of everyday life did change. Imported products – often with the cachet of the exotic – found a place in shops and homes. Makers incorporated new materials, techniques and machines into their workshops and factories. And foreign textile designs found their way into kimono fabrics, interior textiles and woodblock prints. The privileged few – members of the nobility, industrialists, government officials – who adopted European clothing and some customs from the 1880s onwards obviously saw great change in their surroundings, but internationalization had its impact on most people in some way. Changes in the market, for example a significant drop in the cost of silk compared to cotton, meant that more people could afford silk kimono. Schoolchildren became accustomed to sitting at desks thanks to compulsory elementary education. Arguably, however, these changes had more to do with the national government's large-scale designs for the nation and with local authorities' specific policy interventions than with any specific modifications in how design was understood or practised in most workshops.

As we will see in the next chapter, all of this began to change after 1900. By the 1910s, decorative crafts would decline in their strategic importance to plans for the national economy as understood by policymakers and industrialists, in relation to more mechanized industries

Designing Modern Japan

like textiles, steel and shipbuilding. Overseas, the taste for Japanese products waned, too, as the new aesthetic of Art Nouveau gained in popularity and many Japanese products came to look fussy and old-fashioned. As heavy industry gained momentum, a new class of urban consumers gained purchasing power and a new generation of bureaucrats, artists and entrepreneurs assumed responsibility for education and crafts manufacturing. The result would be renewed consciousness of the potential of design to sell products and shape the world, as well as the beginning of attempts to reshape manufacturing and consumption through design in order to fulfil that potential.

Kageyama Kōyō, *Our Newly Married 'Cultured Life' in the Jingumae Apartments*, 1934, gelatin silver print

2 '100-yen cultured living':
Design, Policy and Commerce in the Early Twentieth Century

In May 1934, photographer Kageyama Kōyō (1907–1981) decided to immortalize his breakfast. The resulting image presents Kageyama and his wife, Shizuko (b. 1904), at home surrounded by their possessions. In doing so, it captures the material world of members of the new urban middle class in early twentieth-century Japan. This world was self-consciously hybrid and modern in both provenance and style. In the Kageyamas' home, for example, Western-style furniture rests on tatami mats, rather than in a Western-style room. Husband and wife eat together on cushions at a low table, in front of an Art Deco-styled desk and matching swivel chair. Both wear kimono, hers covered with a freshly starched, ruffled white cotton apron. They have contemporary hairstyles – his a brush cut, hers gathered at the nape of the neck – and glasses perch on his nose. On the wall, calligraphy in an antique Chinese script, framed by symmetrical Art Nouveau flourishes, hangs by a printed portrait of Beethoven. Volumes in matching Western-style leather bindings line the Western-style bookshelves. Woven curtains cover a sliding glass window with wooden panes low on the wall, to be eye level when one sits on the floor, a further – and highly visible – integration of new technologies and habits with old ones.

A closer look reveals further modern touches. Breakfast was buttered toast and black tea, the former toasted on a portable electric grill, the latter brewed in a large ceramic teapot, strained and drunk from Art Deco patterned porcelain teacups with handles. A jaunty lamp sits above the desk. Someone has taken care to distinguish these particular brands of butter and tea from their competitors through logos and packaging design. Delving further into the image's history reveals further changes. The newlyweds' home was a flat in the Dōjunkai Jingū Apartments, a collective housing block completed in 1927 in the fashionable Tokyo suburb of Harajuku. Their choice to eat together at a common table rather than at individual trays was novel, too, and reflects the impact both of fashionability and of social reformers' attempts after 1900 to transform Japanese households into family-centred units, known as the *kazoku danran* (family circle) and symbolized by the family gathering around the table together.[1]

We are, of course, looking at a photograph; the cord for the pneumatic bulb release snakes from Kageyama's hand out of the frame. Kageyama Kōyō studied at one of Japan's first academic photography programmes before becoming a staff photographer at the *Asahi Shimbun*, one of Japan's largest national daily newspapers.[2] Kageyama Shizuko spent part of her childhood in Southern California and taught Western-style sewing at a modernist architecture and design college in Tokyo, the Shinkenchiku Kōgei Gakuin (School of New Architecture and Design).[3] In their work and everyday habits, the Kageyamas were participants in a self-consciously urban, planned life and its promotion to others, produced largely through design. As art historian Samuel C. Morse has noted, Kageyama Kōyō provided detailed notes on expenditures from his '100-yen cultured living' on the back of the photograph.[4] In this context, '100-yen cultured living' meant a carefully planned life, produced largely through design.

In early twentieth-century Japan, unassuming things like aprons, bookshelves, toast and photographs interested an increasingly diverse group of people. Economic and social change, including changes to the labour market, organization of work and where people worked, shaped the Kageyamas' life together, as did the disruption to household structures and daily life this entailed. As the market for mass-produced and luxury everyday items alike expanded, retailers and manufacturers recognized a business opportunity and began to devote more attention to product development, branding and advertising. Social reformers concerned with health and efficiency wanted to replace familiar elements of Japanese clothing, food, homes and social customs with other, more 'efficient' options in the name of 'rational living'. Politicians and civil servants too continued their campaign to strengthen manufacturing firms' earning power by teaching design, particularly for export markets but also for the growing domestic market. Designers, for their part, found ways to experiment and make

Designing Modern Japan

a living by embracing the roles for design created through these larger changes and initiatives.

By 1930, rising incomes, urbanization and changes in the way things were made meant that urban consumers like the Kageyamas could afford more things.[5] In the decades after 1900, design emerged as a strategy that people found useful, whether for social reform or selling products (and the line between these two was often blurred). Design improvement campaigns for the export and domestic markets pushed in different directions but were inextricably linked, not least through designers' and consumers' enthusiastic engagement with international styles.

There were a number of factors at play, including the stories and interrelations of design reform and commercial design in the context of urban consumer culture, the widening divide between urban and rural life, and Japan's continued connections with global design markets. As we saw earlier, both product improvement campaigns and a rich urban consumer culture existed in the Meiji period. By the twentieth century, the impact and scale of both campaigning and consumption shifted, and the significance of both gave design – and designers – an increasingly prominent role in guiding them. At the same time, local and national commitments to economic development through product exports continued to shape design policy, and education as part of it. This dovetailed with other efforts to improve rural conditions through design, particularly from the late 1920s. By exploring first the expansion of design education, then commercial design for the domestic market, then design for reform, the chapter offers a broadening picture. The three stories are both interconnected and run roughly in parallel chronologically. Separating education, commerce and reform activities is slightly artificial but makes it possible for us to follow the arcs of design policies, and to assess these ideas of what design could do, when played out in reality.

Promoting Design

The Kageyamas had benefited from the intensifying interest in design that swept up people in government, education and commerce in the decades preceding that photograph. Japanese design policy in this period has been little studied outside Japan itself. Rather than framed as a story of industrial structure and policy change, it is often told

as a story of aesthetic change and experimentation with new ways of expressing
Japaneseness across art, architecture and
design. Even more significant for design's
history in early twentieth-century Japan,
though, is a simpler fact: in the 1890s,
public design promotion in Japan began to
undergo substantial changes. A progression
of laws, reports, educational initiatives,
exhibitions and other acts formed a new
and increasingly cohesive effort to raise
Japanese design to the level of international
competition, led at national rather than
regional level. These occurred as part of
much larger policy decisions and initiatives.

In 1888, the Diet promulgated an Act
covering trademarks, designs and patents,
the Ishō Jōrei (Design Act). Patent Bureau
director Takahashi Korekiyo (1854–1936),
a career civil servant and politician, led its
composition after reviewing patent law in
Britain, Germany and the United States,
with particular attention to the British
Patents, Designs and Trade Marks Act of
1883.[6] The logic of Takahashi's Design Act
was simple: for export market success,
Japan had to implement a product design and manufacture system –
including design protection – similar to successful models elsewhere.
Other government entities reinforced these activities through close
observation of rivals' design and potential markets. From the 1880s,
the trade bureau in the Ministry of Agriculture and Commerce (Nōshō-
musho; MAC) commissioned reports on conditions in specific industries
in leading export nations such as Britain, France and Germany. After
1900 these intensified, and included surveys of consumer habits and
tastes in established and potential overseas markets as far as Australia
and Argentina. Competition and consumers across Qing China were
particularly interesting to the bureau, as the Japanese government,
after winning the Sino-Japanese War in 1898, began to encourage
economic as well as political expansion into the Asian continent.[7]

Designs for porcelain
dishware from Qing China
included in the Ministry of
Agriculture and Commerce
Trade Bureau's *Report on
the Survey of Craft Industry
Product Designs in Qing
China* in 1908.

Designing Modern Japan

Key for proselytization to manufacturers and the general public was a national network of product exhibition halls, surmounted by the Commercial Museum (Nōshōmushō Shōhin Chinretsukan), a state institution founded in 1887 within the MAC.[8] As led by artist turned education civil servant Matsuoka Hisashi (1862–1944), the halls' purpose was to improve Japanese products through increased exposure to good work, again similar to their inspiration, the South Kensington system of schools and museums in Britain and the commercial museums appearing in other cities around western Europe. Or, as the managers of one local hall, the Shizuoka City Product Exhibition Hall (Shizuoka-shi Bussan Chinretsukan), phrased it:

> By displaying samples and books of various products, old and new, foreign and domestic, to make them available for public inspection and to enlighten [the public with] their knowledge, supporting the advancement of agriculture, commerce, manufacturing and other industries and through this to develop the propagation and manufacturing of products.[9]

The Commercial Museum and the smaller prefectural and municipal halls exhibited domestic products for foreign buyers and brokered introductions for foreign merchants looking for Japanese products, but educating Japanese manufacturers and the public was equally if not more important.[10] The halls displayed model Japanese products and 'reference' foreign products from market leaders like Britain, France, Germany, China and India – more than 16,000 by 1900 at the Commercial Museum, and up to several thousand each at the local halls.[11] They also held seminars, lectures and study groups, attracting the general public as well as manufacturers.

The product halls were well visited. Kyoto's hall recorded over 118,000 visitors in 1909 and over 140,000 visitors in 1910.[12] Records of public lectures give a sense of who came as well as how many. In August 1911, the Kōfu Chamber of Commerce in Yamanashi, west of Tokyo, organized a week of lectures on product design, led by a lecturer from the Tokyo Higher Industrial School (Tōkyō Kōtō Kōgyō Gakkō).[13] The range of attendees was predictable. It included elementary school teachers (who were required to teach design drawing to their pupils) and employees of the local product exhibition hall, as well as students, printers and kimono shop owners, for whom a novel, visually appealing pattern or form could boost sales and income. It is not recorded what the attendees thought of the lectures from Tokyo. Records from other industrial regions show that often, local business owners found content and curricula dictated from Tokyo to be out of touch with local industrial culture, labour organization and household finances.[14] However, at the very least, events like the 1911 Kōfu Chamber

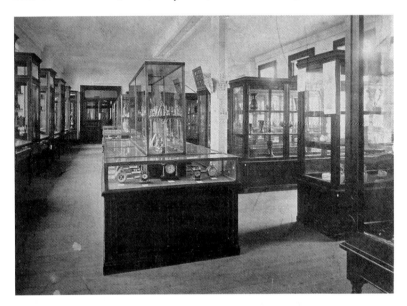

The product exhibition hall in the Ministry of Agriculture and Commerce, Tokyo, 1911, included a salon as well as rooms full of display cases.

Designing Modern Japan

of Commerce lectures show that by 1910, national and local visions of design practice and promotion were interacting.

While their establishment had been nationally mandated, the product halls were highly localized. Object selection reflected each region's local industries (including agriculture and fishing) and supported design educators' continued emphasis on improving product design for existing light manufacturing industries such as textiles and crafts. In Kyoto, the selection criteria included products that were 'fashionable', 'competitive' or which demonstrated 'inventive improvement' in materials or product design, manufacturing or use.[15] Kyoto's product exhibition hall displayed woven and dyed textiles, embroidery, thread, ceramics, lacquerware, fans, cloisonné, dolls and toys, ranging from bolts of *yūzen-* and stencil-dyed silks and antimacassars to musical instrument strings, scientific models and decorative rocks for gardens.[16] Woven and dyed textiles received twice if not more the floor space of other items, indicating the importance of textiles for Kyoto's economy.[17] At the Commercial Museum in Tokyo, woven and printed cottons and silks for Western- and Japanese-style clothing and interiors predominated in both the Japanese manufactures and foreign 'reference' sections, reflecting the importance of export textiles for Japan's economy. Other key export industries, such as ceramics, lacquerware and the like, and new industries – sundries like ribbons and gloves, metal products like water pitchers and shovels – were also well represented. Overall, the selection indicated how for many regions, the export crafts industries that had economically supported some regions in the nineteenth century – and formed the bulk of Japanese exports and domestic manufacturing alike – increasingly coexisted with new industries, both similarly scaled ones producing new goods and larger, capital-intensive ones.[18] It also underlined the continued role of indigenous export craft industries in gaining foreign income, despite arguments within government for the greater promotion of capital-intensive industry.

Trademarks, design drawings and patent applications were also on view. The Commercial Museum's guidelines mandated that halls display drawings of the products and trademarks of domestic products registered with foreign patent agencies, and local halls included a reference library with overseas trend reports and design compendia appropriate for the local industries.[19] The Shizuoka hall maintained a library of two hundred design reference books.[20] Tokugawa and Meiji period collections of design motifs applicable for lacquerware – a significant local industry – predominated. Current trend reports such as department store style magazines were also available.[21] Prefectural and local governments compiled pattern books, which they made available to businesses. Some halls, including Kyoto's, offered to analyse the attractiveness of local products' prices in comparison to those of similar foreign products, based on economic data also collected by the halls.[22]

Formal and mass media design education joined the growing network of national-level systems in place to improve product competitiveness across Japan. Design education in the late nineteenth century sat largely with local governments, who were directly responsible to local entrepreneurs and industrial communities. By the 1890s, some national politicians and civil servants felt that the existing, largely localized provision of vocational education (described in Chapter One) was insufficient for delivering the economic development they envisioned. For these politicians, Japan needed a national-level vocational education system.

The government bureaucrat and school administrator Tejima Seiichi (1850–1918) played a central role in establishing vocational education in Meiji Japan. Tejima was born into a well-connected samurai family and was sent to study in the United States in 1870, only two years after the Meiji Restoration.[23] Following his return to Japan he joined the national government, for whom he worked on the Philadelphia and Paris exhibitions before becoming head of the Tokyo Education Museum in 1881 and Tokyo Library in 1886. In 1890, he was appointed principal of the newly renamed Tokyo Industrial School (Tōkyō Kōgyō Gakkō), previously the Tokyo Industrial Workers' School (Tōkyō Shokkō Gakkō), founded in 1881 to train industrial schoolteachers and factory foremen for imported mechanized industries.[24] To this he added an appointment as the head of the Practical Education Bureau in the Ministry of Education in 1898.

Tejima and his supporters were concerned about a lack of national government attention to industrial education. Working from studies of American and European industrial education systems, Tejima and his allies convinced more senior politicians, particularly Inoue Kowashi, minister of education, that Japan's national economic and technological development required systematic worker education for children and adults alike, in both existing industries such as textiles and ceramics and new ones such as steel.[25] In their eyes, improving product quality and production capacity in new industries required a dramatic increase in shop floor level skills and expertise – in chemistry, for example, or mechanics – which could not be achieved through the existing vocational education and apprenticeship systems.[26] Tejima and others were also keen to promote the continuous integration of new techniques and technologies into existing industries.

In the 1890s, their political pressure produced results: a national system for practical vocational education from universal primary education through to elite higher institutions.[27] The Diet passed a new funding structure in 1894, allocating national funds for vocational teaching, including teacher training.[28] The reforms were not supported unanimously within the Diet, but a vocational education law subsequently passed in 1899.[29] This required prefectures to identify and offer vocational schooling, including night schools and apprentice schools, for key prefectural industries. The reforms also elevated some existing vocational schools, including the Tokyo Industrial School, to the status of higher schools or polytechnics, and created specialist teacher training schemes at national level, including the specialist vocational subjects. The Industrial Teacher Training Institute (Kōgyō Kyōin Yōseijo) opened in 1894, attached to Tejima's Tokyo Industrial School.[30] Given that individual cities and prefectures had until that point taken the initiative in providing industrial education, the laws' passage is significant. National politicians had agreed that local industries were now a matter for national scrutiny and vocational areas like weaving, fisheries and forestry appropriate to include in the national educational framework. Some 25 years after the establishment of the new national government, the balance of power was shifting, gradually, from regions to the centre.

The new laws would have major implications for design, not least because Tejima, one of the driving forces behind the national government's new policies, had identified design as a matter of national urgency. Like local leaders in centres like Kyoto and earlier bureaucrats like Sano Tsunetami, Tejima was well aware that foreign manufacturing powers like Britain and France, as well as newer exporters like the United States and Austria-Hungary, linked export and domestic product competitiveness to national design curricula and a vocational education system.[31] As Tejima wrote in the official report of the Third National Industrial Exposition in 1890, 'The textiles, ceramics and porcelains that are important to our country have no merit when they do not have design drawings. Thus, our ordinary elementary schools too should take care to teach product design.'[32] To this end, the curriculum for the Industrial Teacher Training Institute included design.

In standard schooling, the reforms prompted added emphasis on applied drawing for industry. Two-dimensional design skills had been taught as part of primary drawing education in Japan since the 1870s.[33] The 1890s reforms added handcraft (*shukō*) lessons for all children as part of universal primary education. The *shukō* curriculum included lessons in how to draw basic designs for three-dimensional objects, following Tejima's emphasis on drawing as part of practical learning.[34] The industrial school curriculum for older boys, too, taught students to read and draw two- and three-dimensional designs. Industrial education reforms were meant to prepare the future workforce for changing modes of industrial production. In many local industries, makers had previously held responsibility for determining their products' designs. Thus the emphasis on teaching design drawing as part of a standardized, systematized approach to manufacturing can be seen as part of the larger strategy, embraced by Tejima and others, to improve product competitiveness by raising awareness of design, in the sense of ideation and planning, as a stage in the making process. Tejima and colleagues looked specifically to the British government's addition of

Students at work in the classroom for Nihonga (Japanese-style painting) at the Tokyo School of Fine Arts, 1911. Drawing and painting from live birds and animals, in this case chickens, was integrated into higher-level art education, continuing practices from Tokugawa period painting training.

Designing Modern Japan

design drawing to the national curriculum as part of work to improve export income and reputation in the mid-nineteenth century, and to the larger embrace of this strategy among national governments in the following decades.[35]

Tejima's reforms led to the rapid introduction of design in a few specialist higher education courses, though these were few in number compared to courses in areas such as mechanized textiles, factory management and applied chemistry. The Tokyo School of Fine Arts already included design in the curricula for all courses. In 1896, the school added a specialist crafts design department.[36] This was followed by design departments at the Kyoto Higher School of Arts and Crafts (Kyōto Kōtō Kōgei Gakkō) and the newly elevated Tokyo Higher Industrial School, where the design curriculum began in 1897 within the Industrial Teacher Training Institute, before moving to the main school in 1899. All three schools were under direct mandate from the Ministry of Education. These elite departments functioned as platforms from which a small group of elite men could develop and disseminate design methods and aesthetics nationally.

The three new higher school design courses had different focuses, each relating closely to their specific sponsors, genesis and accordant mission. Keeping with its philosophy of promoting artistic accomplishment in indigenous media, teachers and students at the Tokyo School of Fine Arts course worked particularly in designs for bespoke, handmade crafts in materials like lacquer, ceramics and woven textiles and in interior decoration. This approach emphasized updating historical motifs for the decoration of contemporary objects. The Kyoto Higher School incorporated three departments: design, dyeing and mechanized weaving.[37] Like the selection of Nakazawa Iwata (1858–1943), a chemist who had studied in Berlin and at the Meissen potteries, as the first principal, the breadth of disciplines reflected both Kyoto's economic dependence on textile industries and civic leaders' interest in mechanizing textiles production.[38] Design department leaders Asai Chū (1856–1907) and Takeda Goichi (1872–1938) also expanded their department's remit to include pattern designs for ceramics, lacquerware and other locally important, if smaller, industries.[39] Students could also study Western-style interior decoration and architecture under Takeda, a prominent architect. This was a timely specialism, as wealthy industrialists and politicians had begun commissioning Western-style homes for entertaining in the 1890s, leading general contractors to recruit interior designers.

The house of Meiji period entrepreneur Asano Sōichirō in Tokyo's Tamachi district, 1911, was furnished with designs similar to those studied in the new design departments. Architecture and interiors are rendered in the style described as of the Nara Period, in keeping with Okakura Tenshin's vision of creating modern historicist styles for Japanese design, incorporated into design instruction at the Tokyo School of Fine Arts.

The Tokyo Higher Industrial School answered closely to national government priorities for industrial direction. Under the leadership of Hirayama Eizō, a senior figure in the Patent Bureau who had studied at the Kunstgewerbeschule in Vienna in 1874–7, its focus shifted from crafts design and interior decoration to design for 'modern' light manufacturing – preferably mechanized and mass produced.[40] The programme mirrored this mandate both in its name, the Industrial

Designing Modern Japan

Design Department, and in its education, for example by experiments into lithographic printing for decorating tableware in the ceramics course. The mandate was also visible in graduate destinations. While vocational school teaching predominated in the first years of the programme, subsequently most graduates went into design roles in private industry, with others taking design advisory roles in local product halls.[41] However, following the Russo-Japanese War of 1904–5, government emphasis shifted further towards new large-scale industries such as cotton spinning, steel and cellulose, with decreasing attention to older, smaller-scale industries.[42] The Ministry of Education pressured the school to shift its curriculum accordingly. The industrial design department stopped taking new students in 1914.

Despite differing stances and imperatives, design educators at higher schools agreed on some points. One was that two kinds of design existed: artistic crafts design for higher-end products and industrial or ordinary design for the mass production of useful, inexpensive objects.[43] A second, related principle was the importance of design in manufacturing, regardless of the product. A third was the separation, conceptually, of design for decorative, pleasurable objects and design for practical engineering purposes. Educators articulated their principles through a specific vocabulary. By 1900, two neologisms dominated: *ishō*, meaning a mental plan or design idea, and *zuan*, the design drawing that captured and conveyed the idea.[44] Komuro Shinzō (1870–1922) of the Tokyo Higher Industrial School explained their relationship and function well: 'Design [*zuan*] is the expression of a conscious particular intention or idea [*ishō*], in which form, ornament and colour are arranged in the most appropriate fashion to stimulate urbane pleasure in the viewer.'[45] *Zuan* covered both two-dimensional pattern or surface design and design for the form of three-dimensional objects, but with the implicit understanding that these would be decorative and visually pleasing, rather than predominantly practical or mechanical.[46]

Educators in Tokyo and Kyoto also tended to agree that design could be rational and scientific, and that it was ultimately teachable if standard processes were used. The design process began with the observation of nature. Elements of the sketch were then abstracted into isolated motifs from which a pattern was created and a repeat pattern generated. After settling on the object's form, the designer was then to apply this repeat pattern to the object surface.[47] This transformation from representation to pattern was known as *benka*, short

圖化便のンレハンゼウノ

彩
圖
第
二

Illustrations from Yasuda Rokuzō, *Applications for New-Style Japanese Designs* (1913). These two illustrations, read from right to left, show the initial sketch and its 'expedient conversion', the first steps in transforming a life drawing into a surface pattern design.

for *bengi-eki tenka sōshoku-hō* or 'expedient conversion decorative method'. A good design could be then evaluated – or any design improved – by judgement based on 'standard' principles of visual composition such as variety, contrast, unity, proportion, symmetry, fitness and repetition.[48]

Students commonly chose flowers as the basis for *benka* treatment, but other natural elements could form the basis of a pattern as well. A set of designs produced by Tokyo School of Fine Arts student

Designing Modern Japan

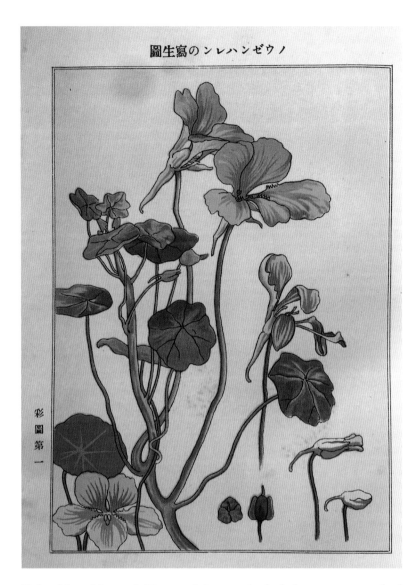

圖生寫のンレハンゼウノ

彩圖第一

Kuboshima Masao (1885–1955) in 1910 included one composed of seaweed, shellfish, rays and spiny lobsters. The process was not original: educators drew on what British design educators in the South Kensington system of the same period called 'conventional treatment' in their own textbooks.[49] But its promoters saw *benka* as a method that could produce specifically Japanese patterns. This was particularly important at the Tokyo School of Fine Arts, where educators emphasized the specifically Japanese art-historical legacy within modern formats, in line with founder Okakura Tenshin's vision of Japanese art.[50]

Benka exemplifies the way in which emergent design education and practice was shaped by the Meiji government's policy of first reviewing rules and methods used overseas, then adapting those deemed to be 'best practice' to strengthen the quality and competitiveness of Japanese industry. Underlying the claims to universality in the new language of design was a sense of the need for commensurability with definitions overseas. Educators looked to Britain, with its high-profile design school system and prominence in export products like cotton textiles – a market that Japan coveted – and closely followed books by British design educators. Under a scheme for 'practical education' launched by the MAC in 1896, a new generation of design educators also travelled to Britain, France, Germany and Austria to study design education and emerging styles in preparation for teaching or curriculum revision.[51] Nakazawa Iwata, founding principal of the Kyoto Higher School, travelled to Paris for the 1900 exposition.[52] Asai Chū, a Western-style painter and designer, had spent time in Paris before joining the Kyoto Higher School. The Ministry of Education posted Asai's colleague Takeda Goichi to Britain and France in 1901–3.[53] Design educators comprised a small fraction of the 683 students sent abroad by the Meiji government between 1876 and 1912.[54] Regardless, their emergence around 1900 alongside engineering, chemistry and medicine is significant, as an indication that Ministry of Education

Kuboshima Masao, surface pattern design with sea motifs, one of a set of designs submitted as graduate work for the Tokyo School of Fine Arts, 1910, ink on paper.

Designing Modern Japan

politicians and bureaucrats had acknowledged design's appropriateness within education.

The higher industrial schools enrolled men only. For women, formal design education could take several paths. Although enrolment rates remained low, the expansion of women's vocational high schools in the 1910s offered more girls the opportunity to continue their education, principally in domestic economy, where curricula included lessons in domestic architecture, interior design and sewing. The small number of girls fortunate enough to attend normal school received teacher training in handcrafts (*shukō*) and drawing (*zuga*), both of which incorporated aspects of design drawing: three-dimensional objects in *shukō*, and pattern design in *zuga*. Elite women educators also lobbied for the recognition of work like embroidery and artificial-flower-making as creative and economic, not only as women's hobbies.[55] In 1903, the Ministry of Education added embroidery and flower arranging (*ikebana*) to the standard girls' higher school curriculum.[56] While not included in most male educators' publishing on *zuan*, or in histories of modern Japanese design that strictly follow the categories set by men in the Meiji period and subsequently, we need to understand such subjects as offering women design skills, too.[57]

At the pinnacle of girls' education were schools like the Women's Higher Normal School (Joshi Kōtō Shihan Gakkō) in Tokyo, which offered advanced training in domestic economy and liberal arts subjects for a handful of women. Schools like the Private Girls' Art School (Shiritsu Joshi Bijutsu Gakkō), which opened in 1900 in Tokyo, offered specialist training in art and design to women from privileged backgrounds. With specialisms in domestic economy and artificial-flower-making and teacher-training streams in sewing and embroidery, higher schools offered women the opportunity to gain creative and technical design skills within spheres deemed appropriate for women's economic and domestic labour.[58] Other private vocational schools, too, provided training in sewing and embroidery. In addition to preparing women for paid work, schools offered women the skills appropriate for women's future vocations as 'good wives and wise mothers' (*ryōsai kenbō*), a role increasingly promoted by Ministry of Education bureaucrats and women's educators.[59] Significantly – both for women's agency as designers and for the future fashion industry in Japan – they also allowed women to develop Western-style clothing design for women and children, as an area that sat within the domestic sphere.[60]

Design educators adopted a combination of Western standard practices and local techniques or habits in their teaching methods and environments. For male students particularly, this included the physical experience of studying in Western-style spaces and clothing. Students sat on wooden stools at wooden desks for *zuan* teaching, in a structured classroom layout; one Kyoto design classroom featured rooflights running the length of the room in the eaves of a purpose-built two-storey wooden building, in the style of Western art studios and classrooms.[61] Students in the design programmes in Tokyo and Kyoto wore Western-style military-derived uniforms with leather shoes and caps. Students at the Girls' Art School, on the other hand, were required to wear plain black kimono. Finding them drab, students accessorized with fashionable shoes and with brightly patterned *haori*, or jackets, which they removed when approaching the school gates so as not to be seen by teachers, then replaced after lessons, when they headed to nearby cafés.[62]

Design educators' influence extended well beyond the schools. Professors like Takeda and Asai were prominent practitioners in their own right. Their paintings, buildings and designs – seen in-person and publicized in art, design and architecture magazines – helped to popularize the Arts and Crafts and Art Nouveau aesthetics, which they

Designing Modern Japan

had experienced at first hand overseas, among designers in Japan. They also functioned as 'experts', expected to shape public knowledge and opinion through speaking and publishing. They served on juries for the National Industrial Expositions and pattern design competitions sponsored by newspapers, and travelled the country lecturing to industry groups, teachers and public audiences on good design and market trends.[63] In 1904 alone, for example, Shimada Yoshinari (1870–1962), professor of design at the Tokyo School of Fine Arts, served on the juries for the Fifth National Industrial Exposition and *zuan* design competitions held by newspapers in Tokyo and Kyoto.

Higher school design professors also disseminated design principles to wider audiences through mass media forms such as lecture tours and the popular press. The Tokyo Board of Education invited Komuro to teach a course on 'design drawing for industry' aimed at teachers in general education in 1905 and 1906.[64] Komuro's lectures were published first in 1906 as a record for teachers, then as a book, *Zuan kōgihō* (Lectures on Design Methods), in 1907. His lectures at the Tokyo Higher Industrial School became the basis for a second book, *Ippan zuanhō* (General Design Principles, 1909).[65] Some books clearly targeted other markets. Tokyo Higher School graduate and lecturer Yasuda Rokuzō's (1874–1942) book *Shinshiki Nihon zuan no ōyō* (The Application of New Style Japanese Designs, 1913) named women as one target readership, connecting formal design education with a broader social education movement to develop women's aesthetic appreciation.[66] Women's educators like Ōe Sumi, too, undertook lecture tours and published manuals on domestic economy. Sections on clothing and housing included significant design aspects, but were presented and understood as domestic economy, rather than (economically productive) design.[67]

These promotional efforts gained more and more significance as European and American market taste shifted and Japanese craft exports gained a reputation as out of style and often poorly made. In 1912, Makino Nobuaki (1861–1949), Minister of Agriculture and Commerce, commissioned opinions from prominent design educators and civil servants including Nakazawa, Tejima, Matsuoka and Hirayama Eizō of the Patent Bureau on how to improve export crafts.[68] Makino, son of powerful Meiji government official and cabinet minister Ōkubo Toshimichi, was short-lived in this role but extremely well connected. The review he commissioned resulted in new initiatives, including a national Exhibition for Design and Applied Crafts, launched in 1913. The competitive exhibition, known as 'Nōten' due to its sponsorship by the MAC (Nōshōmushō), allowed design course students, graduates and teachers particularly to disseminate their ideas nationally through visitors and extensive media coverage of the exhibition. Nōten also gave emergent professional designers a national platform similar to the Ministry of Education's annual exhibition for fine artists, Bunten – also launched by Makino when he was minister of education. This was important for designers and makers who had benefited from government promotion schemes early in the Meiji period but felt short-changed by the subsequent reclassification of artistic production into fine and applied arts, along a European model. At the same time, as the exhibition progressed into the 1910s, Nōten's backers and invited jury members increasingly favoured designs for 'artistic crafts' over those for light industrial mass production. In this way, the exhibition reflected the national government's lack of investment in design for light industry in the 1910s. Simply put, design for everyday items fell between fine art and an industrial vision that increasingly valued capital-intensive industries, so received encouragement from neither camp.[69]

THINGS CHANGED IN 1914. The First World War curtailed European exporters' activities in Asia, allowing Japanese textile manufacturers particularly to increase exports and creating a boom in manufacturing. This prompted civil servants concerned with small-scale indigenous industries, too, to argue for further support for their economic development. Promoting new capital-intensive industries alone, they argued, boded dangerously for the national economy and social fabric. In 1916–17, design educator and civil servant Yasuda Rokuzō, a graduate and former lecturer in the Tokyo Higher Industrial School's industrial design department, published a strongly worded vision for a new industrial policy and the place for design within it. Yasuda's report stated that the revitalization of priority industries like dyes, celluloid, glass and cotton spinning was connected to local light industries: the metal, wood, ceramics and glass, lacquerware, printing, textile and toy industries, often composed of small- or medium-sized workshops and comprising the economic base of many urban neighbourhoods and rural regions. He accused workshops, local and national government

Designing Modern Japan

alike of preserving crafts in aspic rather than allowing them to evolve and thrive in changing markets and lifestyles, writing:

> For the most part our minds still dream of industrial crafts from the Tokugawa period of isolation. We are contented with industrial crafts that are like antiques. Thus, even today, with fierce competition between industries, we are not strategizing or connecting industrial crafts to national economic issues in order to make any large contribution to national prosperity and happiness. Instead, we seem to be forgetting the commercial and national value of industrial crafts.[70]

Yasuda argued that Japanese exports – and the economy – would not fully benefit from economic stimulation unless industrial policy addressed product improvement and the marketability of industrial crafts as well.[71] Yasuda's second target of criticism was light industry itself. He accused Japanese designs of being overly decorative and non-functional and of being too obviously Japanese, imbued with what he called the 'stench of their local region'. He saw workshops as paying insufficient attention to design, knowing too little about overseas markets, producing poor-quality goods, and not thinking to vary their products or to identify the materials, processes and forms most appropriate for them.

Yasuda's proposals echoed those of Sano and Hirayama in the 1870s, discussed in the previous chapter. They included design and industrial education based on the German system of technical schools and research institutes.[72] He also proposed reorienting the curriculum to shift attention from artistic crafts to what he termed 'designs for economy-oriented industrial crafts'.[73] He proposed aligning this with industrial rationalization within workshops and the structural reorganization of industries as a whole, including the restructuring of industry associations and a new level of cooperation between state and private enterprise. New capital investment from private backers was part of the vision, too. Industry-side change would mirror changes in state support, including better prefectural industry promotion strategies and a new industrial crafts leadership authority within the MAC. Yasuda also urged that Japan should send promising young designers overseas, sponsor visits from key overseas designers to Japan, and establish permanent design offices at the hearts of major markets and competitors – in London and Berlin for Europe, New York and San Francisco for the United States, Shanghai and Mukden (Shenyang) for China and Bombay for India – in order to identify and communicate emerging design and consumer trends.[74] The inclusion of Asian centres is significant: narratives of Japanese design often focus on transactions between Japan and the West, but design and export policy at the time also looked to the Asian mainland, particularly China, as well as to European colonies in Asia, for export markets.

Yasuda published his plan as part of a larger effort to lobby the national government for renewed support for design training for industry, which he conducted with Matsuoka Hisashi, head of the Tokyo Higher Industrial School industrial design department at the time of its closure in 1914. Their colleagues and students would ultimately implement many of Yasuda's suggestions over the following decades. So did the vocational education team in the Ministry of Education, who expanded design, printing, metalwork and woodwork departments in vocational schools nationwide after 1920. It also created a new higher school specializing in design and techniques for industrial crafts and mass-production consumer products. The Tokyo Higher School of Arts and Crafts (Tōkyō Kōtō Kōgei Gakkō) was established in 1919 and opened in 1923. The courses were taught largely by Tokyo Higher Industrial School graduates. Courses included design, woodworking, printing and precision machinery, with the products of new industries – electrical, mechanical, chemical – integrated with industrial arts.[75] Printing, for example, included photography as well as an emphasis on modernist layout and typography and current mechanized printing techniques.

A new cadre of graduates, including Kageyama Kōyō, whose breakfast we visited at the top of this chapter, emerged from these programmes. Forward-looking and interested in design reform, they entered the economy on many levels. Kageyama, of course, went on to become a photojournalist. Other graduates took teaching positions in the expanding national industrial school network and joined department store design and advertising divisions or the Industrial Arts Research Institute (Kōgei Shidōsho; IARI), a new agency created within the Ministry of Commerce and Industry.[76] As a network, these graduates would be highly influential in shaping design education and the public image of design in twentieth-century Japan; we will look closely at the activities of many of them in subsequent chapters. Before we do, it is useful to look at how graduates' skills and orientation dovetailed with the agenda set for the IARI, as another manifestation of early twentieth-century design policy.

The IARI emerged in 1928 as a way of strengthening export income through the targeted rationalization of craft and light industrial production, particularly in rural regions. The 1920s were an economically volatile period in Japan. Price collapses after the end of the First World War threatened businesses and farming households alike, leading to recession in 1920. The Great Kantō Earthquake of 1923 killed millions, destroyed infrastructure in Tokyo, Yokohama and the surrounding areas and required capital for rebuilding, all before the global economic turbulence of the late 1920s led to the Great Depression from 1929. Related to these developments, bureaucrats recognized that the industrial boom of the 1910s had fundamentally changed the balance of Japan's economy away from a reliance on agriculture, and in 1925 a new Ministry of Commerce and Industry (Shōkōshō; MCI) was created to oversee national industrial strategy and performance.[77] These two developments would create a fruitful context for design.

The IARI emerged from concern within the MCI, led by senior ministry bureaucrat Yoshino Shinji (1888–1971), that sundry goods from small- and medium-sized enterprises (SMEs) comprised over half of Japanese exports, but that the firms themselves were inefficient.[78] This, they felt, contributed to Japan's trade deficit, and required rationalization. As part of the MCI Board of Trade, the IARI's role was thus

Postcard showing export ceramic prototypes made by the Ceramics Research Institute, exhibited at the Ministry of Commerce and Industry Second Export Industrial Art Exhibition, early 1930s.

TEA CUP & SAUCER SALAD PLATE COFFE CUP & SAUCER
品作試所驗試器磁陶品出展 藝工出輸回二第者工廠

'100-yen cultured living'

to support exports of *kōgei* (the sundry goods products of industrial craft or craft-based industries, such as ceramics and lacquerware for everyday use, and including side production by agricultural households). These were distinguished from the products of *kōgyō* (new, capital-intensive industries such as cotton-spinning) and *bijutsu kōgei* (artistic crafts). Takeuchi Kakichi (1889–1948), head of the MCI Industry Agency's department of industrial policy, was tasked with organizing the institute, using funds allocated to the Board of Trade for local industrial crafts stimulus.[79] The IARI's remit could be succinctly condensed into three policy goals: to apply industrial research and rationalization methods to crafts industries, to strengthen export crafts in lucrative or strategic markets, and to popularize these products in the domestic market, with its growing purchasing power.[80]

To deliver its mandate, the IARI drew on the existing local industrial promotion system. It employed higher school graduate designers and technicians to conduct research into products, materials, machinery and techniques. IARI employees developed export product prototypes for consumer goods such as tableware, glassware, toys and lighting, made surveys of overseas market trends and studied emerging styles.[81] They shared this information with makers and with colleagues in regional industrial advisory institutes, ordinarily affiliated with the product exhibition halls discussed earlier in this chapter. Mechanisms for sharing information included seminars, lectures and exhibitions, as well as publishing technical articles and model product photographs and drawings in a monthly magazine, initially named *Kōgei shidō* (Industrial Art Direction), then *Kōgei nyūsu* (Industrial Art News). For the many design graduates who joined the IARI and their political backers, the kind of rational processes developed in design schools could supply design and technical advising for export-ready light industries, as a way to increase foreign capital. At the same time, the IARI offered these men, who were committed to a vision of design as practical, transformative and rational, the resources to further develop, proselytize and apply their ideas.

The IARI facilities in Sendai, northeast Japan, included new machinery. IARI employees often aligned their own work with that of cutting-edge international modernists, exploring aluminium chair construction along the lines of Bauhaus designers, for example. But many suggestions for local manufacturing were more pragmatic, emphasizing working with existing local strengths and materials and within existing constraints such as lack of capital. Within these, they promoted new product styles and techniques that could optimize sales in export markets. Editorials authored by IARI chief Kunii Kitarō (1883–1967) emphasized the importance of local materials, to foreground the Japaneseness of products, alongside that of rationalizing production. 'Japanese taste' could be a selling point for foreign consumers, even if incorporating it into modernist forms and materials was not always straightforward.[82] Aggressively using design to boost exports required attracting foreign buyers. In addition to the by then standard toolkit of overseas travel, imported publications and market trend reports, the IARI invited selected European modernist designers to visit Japan and develop prototypes for potential export products. German architect and designer Bruno Taut (1880–1938) was the first to arrive, in 1933. Taut would stay for three years, taking a house near Tokyo from which he wrote prolifically and advised on crafts product design, before leaving Japan for Turkey.

The IARI and related efforts are often discussed by historians as a flagship moment in Japanese design history, not least because its publications provide an unusually accessible and detailed record of activity. Also, IARI researchers participated in design organizations and activities similar to those under way in Europe and, eventually, the United States, making them more easily part of canonical design history. From a longer perspective, however, these research and dissemination activities continued the type of initiatives aimed at fuelling Japanese regions' economic development by improving the competitiveness of their products in foreign markets that previous generations had undertaken in the Meiji period and earlier. So too were the objectives of better penetration and hold in foreign markets; the decision to work with existing materials and local industries rather than to attempt to replace them; and the quest for an aesthetic that would be identifiably Japanese enough to provoke attention, but familiar enough to purchase for use at home. A few things had changed, however, not least the industrial structure and the place of indigenous craft industries within it, as well as the new language of 'scientific', 'rational' production. Bureaucrats' equation of design with export products also sat alongside an ever-growing attention to design for consumers in Japan, located largely within commerce and industry.

The Commercial Art of Design

By the time the Kageyamas sat down to breakfast in 1934, outside the window of their small apartment lay a world increasingly changed by industrially organized factories and growing commercial enterprises. Fast-moving consumer products were being made in larger numbers at falling costs and receiving increasingly nationwide distribution. Among them, confectioners and bakers produced just under 82-million-yen-worth of sweets and bread in 1925; ten years later, in 1935, this had risen to just under 138-million-yen-worth of goods.[83] Infrastructural changes – not only the railways but growing numbers of bicycles – made it easier to get materials to makers, and goods to retailers and then to consumers.[84] Major industrial and commercial cities had added new residential suburbs, further intensifying Japan's urbanization.

Increased domestic commercial activity and competition prompted an increase in corporate interest in having products stand out – in other words, in marketing, branding and advertising. The period between the 1890s and the 1930s saw both an explosion in sales of consumer goods at home and concerted interest in design – advertising, packaging, product and environment – as a technique for sales promotion. In the early twentieth century, increased access to mass-produced goods meant more customers, but also more competition. Textile, graphic and product design had been important marketing tools since the Tokugawa period, but now design would help manufacturers and retailers differentiate their products in a market with increasing circulation of products and information. Even more telling is that aggressive branding points to a competitive domestic market for products, the growth of consumer purchasing power and major social changes in the first decades of the century. As we will see, this activity was conducted largely by men, often with women as the target consumers.

Among the early adopters of an expanded design strategy were kimono merchants. In the 1880s, the industry saw increased competition and significant change. The adoption of mechanized looms increased the production capacity of the industry, while the growth of domestic post and rail infrastructure increased the scale of the market, allowing it to gain access to what had been less-connected regions. Previously, kimono merchants had purchased completed yardage from dealers who coordinated design and production. They had

Designing Modern Japan

not directed the textiles' designs themselves. This changed. In 1882, Kyoto's Takashimaya, now a major department store but at the time specializing in kimono, began to commission pattern designs directly from local painters. It established an in-house textile design department in 1885, again hiring local painters as designers.[85] Merchants in Tokyo would follow suit. The prosperous Mitsui Echigoya, now the Mitsukoshi department store, began bypassing the dealer system and taking its design requests directly to weavers and dyers in 1896.

While the concentration of people involved in the kimono industry rendered it vulnerable to economic downturns and technological disruption, Kyoto was fortunate to be a nexus of high-end design and manufacturing for national distribution, supported synergistically by the people at the heart of Kyoto's industrial ecology. These included woodblock printers and woodblock carvers, connoisseurs interested in buying the books, publishers who could run this expensive mode of publishing because of the kimono trade, merchants, weavers, dyers, painters and the makers, retailers and wholesalers of Kyoto's other industries. Within this context, merchants like Takashimaya soon began commissioning the Kyoto art publisher Unsōdō to print their own pattern books. These functioned as advertisements for both kimono and the shops themselves. Significantly, Unsōdō's work for luxury retailers also used polychrome woodblock print techniques, conceptually linking commercial clients' products with Kyoto cultural lineage. The skill of its makers demonstrated early modern luxury through the rich and colourful textures and visibly woodblock-printed images. Many of the designs employed motifs and styles recognizably drawn from Kyoto painting traditions, but in colour combinations and designs that were distinctively new.

Meiji period kimono design incorporated both existing local practices and new transnational visual languages, including those acquired through training in the new school design departments. Artist-designers took advantage of kimono merchants' increased attention to product, particularly textile, design. Many trained in early modern Kyoto painting styles before embracing a hybrid practice that encompassed decorative surface designs alongside collectable paintings, so ensuring continuity in Kyoto painting practice. Now, however, the Kyoto artist-designers could also contract directly with the kimono merchants.[86] Increased competition and industry reorganization also fostered the emergence of a new form of *hinagata-bon*. Luxurious woodblock-printed books

by Unsōdō and Unkindō, another art publisher, offered beautifully carved and printed versions of original paintings by Kyoto artist-designers like Takeuchi Seihō (1864–1942), Tsuda Seifū (1880–1978) and Kamisaka Sekka (1866–1942), rendered as potential patterns for kimono or other products.[87]

Classical references were a key part of this luxury production, as was reference to Kyoto-specific styles such as the Maruyama-Shijō, Tosa and Rinpa schools acquired through their painting education in the city. A design of irises blooming around a wooden bridge by Kamisaka Sekka, printed in a book by Unsōdō, illustrates this point. In the choice of theme and the visual rhythm, proportions and style of the irises, Sekka's print makes clear visual reference to a multi-panelled folding screen of irises by Ogata Kōrin, now in the collection of the Nezu Museum in Tokyo, which itself makes reference to a classical *waka* poem included in a revered tenth-century literary work, *The Tales of Ise* (*Ise monogatari*). While visually stunning in its own right, Sekka's design could also be applied to a kimono hem or lacquer writing box. As such it functions as a design translation from the Kōrin original. With its knowledgeable reference to multiple other artworks – the poem, the *Tales*, the painting – it participates in the culture of appreciating transmedia and transhistorical references that had been integral to connoisseurship in early modern Japan. Indeed, Sekka was not alone in referring to Kōrin's irises; they also appeared on luxury craft items for the domestic market, such as lacquered and metal boxes. Asai Chū included Rinpa-style designs in his curriculum for students at the Kyoto Higher School of Arts and Crafts. In 1905, the Mitsukoshi department store ran a competition for the best Kōrin-inspired surface pattern designs, with prizes for some 150 entries.[88] Rinpa offered more immediate visible differences from the more formal bird-and-flower compositions of historicist design. It was also broadly applicable across media from ceramics to interiors and had a passing similarity to Art Nouveau, as a native response to that style.[89]

The use of historicist styles must be understood, however, within changing industrial and design promotional paradigms. Again, Sekka provides a useful illustration. Sekka first studied under the painter Suzuki Mizuhiko (Suzuki Zuigen, 1848–1901), a proponent of the Shijō school, which had been prominent in early modern Kyoto. Sekka then joined the Kawashima textile company and studied design drawing for textiles and other decorative crafts with Shinagawa Yajirō, a

Yōshū Chikanobu, *An Array of Auspicious Customs of Eastern Japan: Rereading*, 1889, *nishiki-e* woodblock print, Tokyo. Chikanobu's print adapts the convention of the *bijinga* beautiful woman print to the moral sensibilities of Meiji elite reformers, with fashionable textiles and furnishings now presented as accoutrements for an ideal home.

Kamisaka Sekka, *Iris Pond*, from *Momoyogusa* (A World of Things), 1909, woodblock print, Unsōdō, Kyoto.

former civil servant invested in promoting design after time spent in Germany.[90] Eventually, Sekka entered the Kyoto City Painting School and studied design under Kishi Kōkei (1839–1922). Kishi was an artist-designer who owned work by Kōrin and incorporated Tosa school and Rinpa styles into his work. He was also firmly imbricated in the new model for national product improvement, having created designs for the Product Design Department for the 1876 Philadelphia exposition and the National Industrial Expositions and worked with the design educator Nōtomi Kaijirō (1844–1918) at the crafts schools in Toyama and Kagawa before arriving in Kyoto and then becoming a teacher himself in 1900.[91] As these brief biographies indicate, the schools' design teachers offered further continuity with Kyoto painting traditions within the changing industrial and design promotion structure: teachers were themselves scions of the earlier painting schools, and students incorporated their training into new work.

Unsōdō's luxurious albums were part of a larger embrace of art and design as a marketing strategy for department stores. Changes in marketing accompanied structural transformation in retail, from

Designing Modern Japan

kimono specialists to multi-category department stores along the lines of those in Paris, London and Philadelphia.[92] In 1894, Echigoya became the Mitsui Gofukuten (Dry-Goods Store); in 1904, it announced its transformation into a department store in national newspapers alongside a further renaming, to Mitsukoshi Gofukuten (Dry-Goods Store).[93] Its competitors underwent similar changes. As we saw in Chapter One, the most prominent kimono merchants employed not only fashionable clothing but culture and urban sophistication as an advertising message already in the early modern period.[94] Increased competition around 1900 saw them amplify this message, using design tools to do so. In-house publications were an important organ for disseminating this message. The Mitsui Dry-Goods Store began its campaign in 1899 with *Hanagoromo* (Flowered Robes, or Holiday Best), 350 pages of shop information, fashion illustrations and writing by well-known authors circulated to subscribers. A monthly magazine, *Jikō* (Fashion), followed in 1903. Takashimaya's *Shin ishō* (New Clothes) launched in 1902.[95] Extensively illustrated and emphasizing seasonal trends in textile design through page after page of photographic reproductions of fashionable fabrics, accompanied by fashion commentary and price lists, these magazines allowed wealthy regional customers to stay abreast of fashion through mail order and presented a luxurious aspirational lifestyle for others. Such strategies were highly successful. By 1911, *Fashion*'s successor, *Mitsukoshi taimusu* (Mitsukoshi Times), had a print run of over 50,000, and the firm employed roughly 230 people in publishing.[96]

From 1905, Mitsukoshi ran a product development group, the Ryūkōkai (literally 'fashion group'). Members included employees from the textile design group, the purchasing department and the sales floor, as well as artists, journalists and other public intellectuals. Increased awareness of design techniques for competitive branding also prompted managers to establish direct discussions with textiles producers, new pattern exhibitions and in-store advertising teams.[97] In 1909, Mitsukoshi launched a design department (*zuan-ka*) for graphic and product design. Their remit included covers and illustrations for books and magazines, designs for ceramics, lacquerware, ivory and other luxury crafts, as well as awards, trademarks, commemorative postcards, advertisements and programmes, in addition to designing all of the store's publicity.[98] Takashimaya, now also a department store, followed suit in 1913. The establishment of design sections within luxury retailers indicates how seriously they took design as a strategy for commercial differentiation and success in the changing economy. Department store design divisions became key employers and training grounds for commercial artists (graphic designers), alongside the design divisions in fast-moving consumer goods, printing, newspaper and advertising firms.

One indication of their increasing inclination to take design seriously was the way in which luxury retailers used the visual language of magazines to convey brand image. In 1908, Mitsukoshi hired Sugiura Hisui (1876–1965), a graduate in Japanese painting from the Tokyo School of Fine Arts, to direct the graphic design of *Mitsukoshi Times*.[99] Sugiura's designs transformed the magazine's image to be lighter and airier. This began with covers, which shifted from presenting textile patterns printed across the full page, in the style of the Unsōdō books, to layouts that combined hand-lettering and images with ample white space. Some covers favoured overtly European and American figural images. Often rendered in subdued, lighter colours within thick lines, these retained figural elements – birds, flowers, butterflies – but in blocky, bolder compositions. Sugiura and colleagues like Hashiguchi Goyō (1880–1921), another Tokyo School of Fine Art graduate, also attended to European Art Nouveau and the work of British illustrators like Walter Crane, often combining this style with older print techniques and visual tropes.

Their advertising amplified the desired image of the department store as a maker of respectable, sophisticated femininity through consumption. In addition to offering kimono fabrics and Western-style clothing, they offered a complete lifestyle, not only through personal adornment, and with a luxurious attention to quality. Hashiguchi's winning image for a 1911 Mitsukoshi poster competition allows us to unpick this function.[100] The woman in the poster sits on a bench, holding a large-format woodblock-printed book featuring scenes from

Cover of *Fashion*, III/6 (June 1905), Mitsukoshi Gofukuten. The cover image reproduces the fashionable patterns of kimono fabrics presented in the issue, including the Ichimatsu check, a visual reference to the Genroku period (1688–1704) in vogue in the early 1900s.

Hashiguchi Goyō, *Mitsukoshi Gofukuten* (*This Beauty*), 1911, multiple-block woodblock print, Tokyo.

Designing Modern Japan

kabuki plays on her lap. Her hair is elegantly swept up in an identifiably modern *hisashi-gami* updo. She wears a kimono with a repeat pattern of *nadeshiko* (pinks) by a stream on a deep blue ground, lined with a red stencil-dyed under-kimono. An intricate *sarasa* obi, pointing back to early modern fashion, coordinates with the bench's abstracted vegetal decoration. The wallpaper, painted or printed with elegantly branching rhododendra, provides a further contrasting pattern. In addition to its sophisticated coordination of pattern, the poster points to both past and present, Japan and Europe. In one sense, Hashiguchi's poster presented a typical Art Nouveau combination of undulating lines, simplified figural, often vegetal, motifs and a beautiful female figure with luxurious hair. The poster also clearly referenced early modern *bijinga*, woodblock prints of beautiful women, although now with a visibly married woman as the focus.[101] The positioning of the sitter in her chair, with her confident gaze, carefully figured textile repeats and luxurious goods around her, also recalls early modern European portraiture.

The juxtaposition of patterns and luxury objects thus suggests those presented in Tokugawa-period woodblock prints. But the interior furnishings arrayed in this image could themselves be acquired through Mitsukoshi – for a price. In 1904, Mitsukoshi opened a furniture and interior design department, following Takashimaya, who had launched their interiors department the previous year with a focus on soft furnishings.[102] The interiors and furniture departments designed and oversaw manufacturing of the stores' own furnishing lines, undertaking commissions for domestic and commercial properties alike as well as designing the shops' own actual interiors. The shift into furniture and interior design emerged to facilitate the stores' own interior transformations and the experience they offered visitors, as part of communicating an overall brand image particularly to female consumers. Soft furnishings continued the stores' origins in the Kyoto textile trade. But the addition of hard furnishings and interior design indicates how the stores' owners and managers had identified these design areas, too, as growing business. Early twentieth-century domestic advice manuals for women suggested that interior decoration could be an appropriate way for elite women and those emulating them to further communicate their fashionability, elegance and modernity.[103] At a time when purchasing Western-style furniture or adding a Western-style room or home extension was out of reach for nearly all Japanese, the

Designing Modern Japan

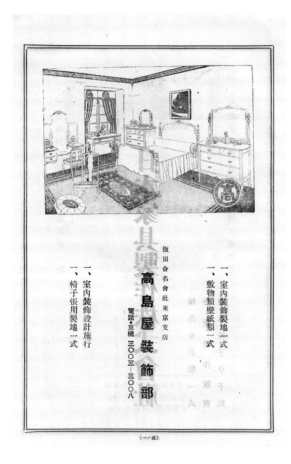

Advertisement for the Takashimaya Department Store Interior Design Department, 1919. The advertisement, which appeared in the industry journal *Woodworking and Decoration*, offers interior textiles, wallpaper, interior design and upholstery services.

opportunity to spend time in the department stores' richly furnished, spacious interiors offered temporary elegance.

In his 1911 poster, Hashiguchi offered an overt visual echo of *bijinga* while referencing this new image of elite, educated women as Mitsukoshi's model consumer. The figure in the poster looks directly at the viewer rather than casting her gaze demurely away, and her face is rendered three-dimensionally, using painting techniques Hashiguchi had practised with his teacher Hashimoto. She is educated enough to enjoy kabuki theatre, a pastime of wealthy women in the 1910s and later referenced in a famous Mitsukoshi tagline of 1913, 'Today the Imperial Theatre, tomorrow Mitsukoshi.' She also uses her family or husband's wealth to participate in Mitsukoshi's luxury lifestyle. The visual imagery of high fashion and luxury is reinforced by the print itself, famously created from 35 discrete screens, each of which was inked separately and layered with precision by technicians to create the crisp image. The time, skill, dexterity and experience required to make the image again reference the luxury industries whose clients' investment in luxury products make such production possible. Together, the poster's elements suggest access to this rarefied world, one predicated on marriage and household wealth, not the pleasure quarters, and one aimed at women specifically.

The department stores also redesigned the physical experience of shopping. Shop executives, design departments and consultant architects took establishments like Harrods in London and Wanamaker's in Philadelphia as their models. They transformed metropolitan department stores into 'retail destinations' that provided a glamorous, aspirational and consciously urban experience: the promise of acquiring a stylish, cultured life as well as new clothes.[104] Architecture provided visual advertising as well, particularly the neo-Renaissance masonry structures, sweeping entrance staircases and capacious atriums that Mitsukoshi, Takashimaya and others added after 1910. Interior design created a strikingly new experience. Early modern luxury retail happened on tatami mats, with clerks bringing goods to present to clients. Things began to change from the 1890s, with the introduction of display cases and mannequins, followed by show windows and hybrid interiors that allowed customers to sit either in chairs or on cushions on the floor, depending on their preference and attire, while consulting with clerks. The new interiors allowed customers to wander the aisles in their shoes, perusing kimono and sundries like ribbons, umbrellas and gloves, which were displayed in showcases and explained by neat, attractively attired shop girls. Department stores also added leisure and comfort facilities: cafés, children's play areas and substantial restrooms.

The shops' corporate identity campaigns worked. By 1910, department stores like Mitsukoshi, Takashimaya and their Tokyo competitor Shirokiya were tourist attractions in their own right. In the following decades, the department stores' brand communication techniques solidified their position as purveyors of total lifestyle products. They were also able to link elite customers' social status with the cachet of their own products, creating a mystique around department store clothing and furniture that lasted well into the post-war era. While different department stores became associated with clienteles of different social statuses, for example Mitsukoshi and Takashimaya at

Shoppers and clerks in the kimono section of Mitsukoshi Department Store, Tokyo, c. 1911. While the historicist treatment of ceilings and columns pointed to earlier periods in Japanese architecture, the grand atrium, glass cases and palms referred to the great department stores of London, Paris and Philadelphia.

Designing Modern Japan

the pinnacle, department store furniture as a category suggested well-made, well-designed items, often at a higher price point than one could find in the furniture shops on local shopping streets. As a result, department store interior and furniture design departments – at Mitsukoshi, Shirokiya, Takashimaya and Tokyo's Matsuzakaya, particularly – proved important employers for design graduates into the post-war period.

Architects and interior designers conformed to an earlier historicist eclecticism when designing the facades and interiors of the stores themselves, but the textiles, interiors and graphics on offer often melded Tokugawa period styles with the new design aesthetic emerging from Glasgow, Brussels, Paris and Vienna, as Hashiguchi's 1911 poster demonstrates. In this they were not alone: in the early twentieth century, the search for a new aesthetic united ambitious designers for domestic and export products alike. In a spring 1900 report on historical and current trends in craft design in Japan and overseas, Ministry of Agriculture and Commerce civil servants assessed cutting-edge taste in Europe as having changed thanks to Impressionism and Art Nouveau:

> The look of decoration today has moved away from the rich, jumbled and geometric to design that is light and airy . . . Designs based on this decorative sensibility are not bound by period styles but rather employ hybrid decoration that composes styles and forms drawn widely from across time and space. Like the pictorial style of this new movement, these artists draw not ideas and imagination but the reality of nature and colour of the light that catch the eye.[105]

Art Nouveau travelled quickly to Japan and to the artists, architects and designers responsible for advertising material. Asai Chū, for example, visited dealer Siegfried Bing's shop Art Nouveau, which had opened in Paris in 1895, as well as the Art Nouveau pavilion at the 1900 exposition, before returning to Japan. He brought with him several cases of ceramics, textiles, posters and glass slides, which he shared with students at the Kyoto Higher School of Arts and Crafts.[106] Asai and other Japanese artists in Paris associated with the Tokyo School of Fine Arts selected some fifty posters which they brought back to Japan. These went on display in public exhibitions in Tokyo, and teachers shared them with students like Hashiguchi.[107] Japanese visitors to

Paris also reported on the new style in art and literary journals, publishing photographs of the posters they had collected.

Art Nouveau architecture and its stable-mate, the luxurious but stark forms of the Vienna Secession – known as *Zesesshon* or *bunri-ha* (literally 'secession school) in Japanese – joined earlier European styles as one of a spectrum of options within the larger category of 'Western style' (*yōfu*, *yōshiki*) design. European historicism was itself a recent import to Japanese design and architectural communities. Art Nouveau therefore became the most fashionable and 'modern' of a set of possible aesthetics, rather than a self-consciously radical declaration of rejection of the others, as in Europe. The Art Nouveau aesthetic itself sometimes provoked distaste in Japanese viewers. Sekka, for instance, famously labelled it 'noodle art'.[108] In Japan, however, its stylings remained less a statement of rebellion than a strategic decision to use Western style in the first place.

Designers and management employed similarly delicate positioning to maintain Japaneseness in order to sell kimono, which were still department stores' primary merchandise, within the increasingly Westernized environment required for the overall image strategy. A gendered element shaped the negotiations of style: elite women, the shops' primary customers, incorporated fewer 'Western' elements into their lifestyle than did elite men, who might wear Western clothes and work in a Western-style office. Mitsukoshi, for example, encased its glass showcases, chairs, electrical drop lighting and potted plants under a painted patterned ceiling and ornamental mouldings modelled on Japanese palace and temple architecture. Art Nouveau and woodblock print conventions merged in Hashiguchi's poster. Rinpa textile patterns, too, could be both Japanese and modern, both historical and fresh.

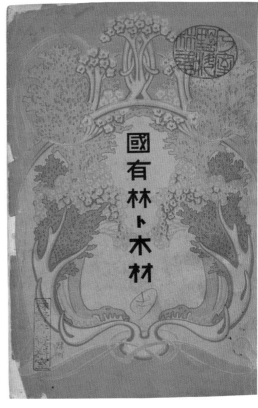

Cover, Ministry of Agriculture and Commerce Forestry Agency, *National Forests and Wood* (1907). Art nouveau designs were not only for fashionable shops and commodities.

This advertising tower advertised makers of products including fertilizer, cement, sake and mimeograph equipment.

This 1919 advertisement for the Tokyo Electrical Company presented the prize-winning design in a competition for new electrical lighting globes and fixtures.

Designing Modern Japan

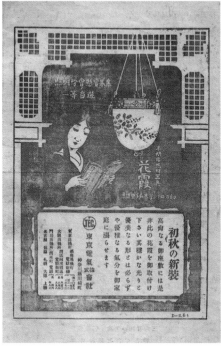

BY THE EARLY 1930S, urban Japanese consumers like the Kageyamas lived in a country awash in branded products and retailers. The Kageyamas would hardly have been able to ignore branded products like the tea and butter on their breakfast table. Furthermore, the products in the scene – kimono, curtains, desk and chair, glasses – would have been purchased in shops, very possibly a department store with a highly developed branding strategy. The Kageyamas would not have been able to read a newspaper or commercial magazine, either, without encountering advertisements. Advertisers employed multimedia advertising campaigns that took the urban landscape and domestic interior as their canvas, applying corporate logos, trademarks and slogans to advertising towers, trains, streetcars, electrical posts, billboards and sandwich men as well as to packaging and print advertisements.[109] These were accompanied by window displays, illuminations, carved and painted shop signs, promotional interiors, flagship buildings, exhibitions, showily decorated vehicles and street theatre-like processions by performers known as *chindonya*.

Newspaper circulation grew tenfold in the 1890s, reaching more than 1.5 million copies daily in 1898.[110] By 1911, the total number of periodicals (newspapers and magazines) in circulation had increased by 270 per cent from 1899.[111] This was fertile ground for new developments in advertising. Agencies specializing in placing advertisements in newspapers appeared in the 1880s; today's advertising giants, Hakuhodo (Hakuhōdō) and Dentsu (Dentsū), were founded in 1895 and 1901 respectively.[112] Initially, most newspaper and magazine advertisements were text only, either typeset or woodblock-carved texts, although printers began incorporating woodcut compositions of text with images and logomarks from the late 1870s. The popularization of other new printing technologies – lithography in the 1890s and, later in the 1920s, the HB process, which allowed images to be reproduced without hand processing and maintained resolution at any size – would allow advertisers to integrate text and image more fully. Many print advertisements were created at the printer by compositors. Manufacturers and advertising agencies commissioned paintings for chromolithographic posters from artists. Not all commentators saw the explosion of advertising as positive. In his column in the *Yomiuri Shimbun*, a large national newspaper, novelist and newspaper editor Kamitsukasa Shōken complained, 'In newspaper advertisements and all the other forms of advertising, today's advertising techniques are woefully infantile.'[113]

Prominent advertisers included Western-style confectionery makers like Morinaga and Meiji as well as manufacturers of cosmetics, soap, patent medicine, beer and sake. Fast-moving consumer goods had become highly competitive industries with national distribution and national markets, and the business models for all had changed with the advent of railways and postal subscription in particular. Brands like Kao soap and Lion toothpaste were among the first to run advertisements in newspapers nationally, promoting brand recognition to support their products' national distribution. Together, these categories of advertisers accounted for nearly half of all newspaper advertisements published by 1912.[114] Companies also produced posters, handbills and magazine advertisements.

This newspaper advertisement for Kobayashi Shōten's Lion toothpaste was reprinted in Atorie-sha, ed., *Modern Commercial Art 13: Collection of Examples from Newspapers and Magazine Advertisements* (1929).

Designing Modern Japan

In the 1910s, fast-moving consumer goods companies also established design departments, as socioeconomic change and infrastructural development increased both potential markets and competition. Urbanization accelerated after 1910 as education and cotton and steel mills attracted individuals and entire families to leave the land. Export opportunities during the First World War brought a short-lived economic boom. Consumption and advertising of national and regionally branded products increased alongside cities and incomes. Smaller textiles and sundries shops, too, increased their advertising, following the lead of the department stores. By 1919, cosmetics and medicines – the predominant advertisers in the first decade of the century – occupied only a quarter of the 1,200-page *Ōyō jizai gendai kōkoku monkū jirin* (Dictionary of Applied Universal Modern Advertising Slogans); clothing, textiles and sundries accounted for another 16 per cent.[115] Thanks in no small part to their low cost (and high calories), caramels, chocolates and other industrially made, nationally distributed Western-style confectionery were a highly competitive sector, prompting firms to invest heavily in advertising. Morinaga Seika, one of two major national confectionary firms alongside competitor Meiji Seika, opened an advertising department in 1915, with a substantial team of designers working under copywriter Kataoka Toshirō (1882–1945).[116] Morinaga's team explored the use of layouts, bold composition, photographs in print adverts, billboards and packaging, among other formats. The constant demand for new advertisements provided an opportunity for formal experimentation. As a result, the team became known as the 'Morinaga school' for the rigorous training it offered young designers.[117]

Urbanization from the 1910s changed the domestic market for design. Between 1920 and 1925, Japan's urban population grew twice as quickly as its rural population, without even counting residents of new suburbs.[118] The growth of large urban conurbations was particularly striking. The population of greater Tokyo grew 300 per cent between 1890 and 1925, to 4.5 million people.[119] The population of Osaka, Japan's industrial centre and the major metropolis in western Japan, grew nearly 40 per cent between 1910 and 1925, reaching 2.2 million people in 1926 within Osaka city limits alone.[120] The Great Kantō Earthquake of 1923 further spurred urbanization, through migration to other cities as well as reconstruction in Tokyo, the neighbouring city of Yokohama and the industrial belt between the two. A 'new middle class' of white-collar salaried workers and professionals (distinguished from the 'old middle class' of wealthy farmers and entrepreneurs) began populating the emerging commuter suburbs, which were being developed by private railways.[121] Department stores became one of a number of stylish, 'modern' urban venues for amusement and consumption, which included theatres, dance halls, cafés and cinemas, catering to urbanites of all classes.[122] Tokyo's Ginza neighbourhood was a national symbol of urban luxury for its elite shops, cafés and 'modern boys and girls' (*mobo* and *moga*), but fashionable shopping and entertainment districts emerged in cities across the country.[123] Other modern entertainment invited wider participation. Nationally, the number of cinemas – a more democratic amusement – grew from seven hundred in 1923 to more than 1,300 in 1930, attracting 140 million visits that year and supporting a substantial domestic film industry.[124] Western-style showgirl revues and jazz bands joined Japanese comic storytelling and the kabuki theatre in entertainment districts like Rokku in Tokyo and Osaka's Sennichimae. Radio, introduced in Tokyo, Osaka and Nagoya in 1925 and in regional cities by 1930, offered another medium for accessing new sounds and ideas. All of these amusements prompted publicity, spurring further employment

Postcard view of the Yamagata Prefecture Aquarium Gift Shop and Lounge, c. 1918–33. The young women visiting, wearing meisen kimono, are sitting on bentwood chairs, with bottles of Asahi beer visible on the counter.

Designing Modern Japan

Illustrator Honda Shotarō designed this cover for the February 1931 issue of children's magazine *Kodomo no kuni* (The Country of Children). Colour offset lithograph.

for graphic designers. So did children's books and magazines, an emerging genre in the 1920s as both social reformers and retailers targeted childhood, the former as an important age, the latter as a potentially lucrative market.[125]

In the 1920s, yet more manufacturers adopted comprehensive corporate identity and advertising strategies to stand out amid the visual and aural noise – only intensifying it, of course. Recession after the First World War prompted many firms to cut their advertising

Yamamura Kōka, *After Dinner*, printed in *Mitsukoshi Times,* July 1925. The caption continues, 'for cool clothing, meals and furniture, go to Mitsukoshi.' The careful depiction of fashions and furnishings recalls earlier print styles including Hashiguchi's 1911 poster (p. 108), but in the elegant pastel colour palette of the mid-1920s.

budgets and emphasize effective advertising over volume. The new constraints prompted firms and newspapers alike to pay attention to advertisements' effectiveness, leading to the rationalization (*gōrika*) of advertising.[126] While this meant smaller budgets and fewer advertisements overall, it encouraged designers to experiment with eye-catching graphical campaigns, often with a more visually simple palette, known as *tanka* (simplification).[127] Another facet in the turn to corporate identity was evident in the flagship building and café on the Ginza of the cosmetic manufacturer Shiseido, part of a campaign created by the in-house design department it had established in 1916. By defining the company's face powder, perfumes and other cosmetics – and, by extension, its consumers – as modern yet feminine, fashionable yet refined, art director Yamana Ayao's (1897–1980) distinctive graphics also defined what it meant to be chic. Shiseido's influential visual style merged languid curves, striking hand-drawn lettering and Western design elements such as arabesques in delicate, often watercolour-like shading.[128] In the 1920s, such graphics offered a visually simplified rendering of the *moderne* aesthetic – tempered simplicity in luxury materials, as shown at the 1925 Exposition Internationale des Arts Décoratifs in Paris – again emphasizing the 'modern' nature of the product for competitive ends. As the editors of *Kōkokukai* (Advertising World) opined in 1930, 'The strong point of cosmetics advertisements is their deliberate repetition of the appeal, ambition and desire for

Designing Modern Japan

beauty of modern girls, within the atmosphere of the advertisement. They don't "read" the advertisements. They "feel" the fantastic vision of their own beauty in them.'[129]

Designers applied modernist graphic language to advertise a variety of products across the visual landscape of everyday life, where it coexisted with earlier visual languages. Designers for fast-moving consumer goods firms like Kao soap and Morinaga confectionery employed stark combinations of type, white space and photolithographic images in their print advertisements.[130] Images were cropped at eye-catching angles, and the typography was obviously machine-printed. Kao's art direction team would go on to commission avant-garde advertisements, logos and packaging from photographers and graphic designers like Hara Hiromu (1903–1986) who were conversant in the new visual languages emerging from Europe: Neue Sachlichkeit (New Objectivity) photography from Germany, the stark geometrical aesthetic of De Stijl, Russian Constructivism's powerful composition and palette, the functionalist new typography of Jan Tschichold and the amalgamation of modernist aesthetics emerging from the Bauhaus. Lettering, too, came in for revision, with hand-drawn letters in particular offering expressive potential and visual appeal.[131] Many of the designers who employed the experimental European styles welcomed their philosophy of mechanical reproduction as a new mass art form. As cinema poster designer Kōno Takashi (1906–1999) wrote, 'The attraction of new advertisements is that they're regularly building the new mass life.'[132] It was not only advertisements: photographers, editors and layout men collaborated on editorial content in magazines, books and other print media. In the early 1930s, photographers, editors and designers began theorizing these possibilities in specialist journals like *Kōga* (Light Picture), dedicated to *shinkō shashin*, the Japanese name for Neue Sachlichkeit photography, and *Ai shī ōru* (I See All), edited by design educator and Bauhaus alumnus Kawakita Renshichirō (1902–1975).[133]

Left-wing and proletariat activist groups also employed the modernist visual language of their European counterparts in their publicity. The late 1920s saw not only increased consumption but increased political activity, as the 1925 General Election Law provided universal male suffrage, opening the way for new left-wing and proletarian political parties. Visually striking, simplified compositions on posters, handbills and banners often mirrored those of commercial advertisements, though with more emotively expressive forms of

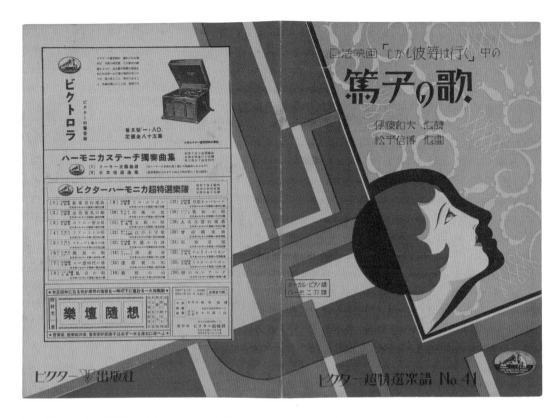

hand-lettering.[134] As with commercial advertisements in fast-moving media, political graphics needed quick, cheap and efficient printing as well as eye-catching messaging. They could be easily produced by artists and designers who had honed their skills in formal education or as advertising artists.[135]

Modernist aesthetics could also be an industrial strategy and solution to technical challenges, for example in Isesaki, a textile district north of Tokyo. As incomes rose and textile prices fell after 1890, more households were able to afford yarn-dyed, woven kimono silks in addition to the cottons worn by most Japanese previously. Both silk and cotton, however, could seem old-fashioned compared to imported wools and calicos. Regional weave patterns that had been developed in the nineteenth century sold less well to would-be sophisticates, who were absorbing cosmetic advertisements and Hollywood fashion from cinema and photographs in monthly magazines. Furthermore, many women remained unable to afford silk cloth. This combination of fashion taste and economic conditions created an opportunity for textile

'Atsuko no uta' (Atsuko's Song), cover design for the sheet music for a song from the Nikkatsu film *Shikamo karera ha yuku* (And Yet They Go On), *c.* 1931, colour offset lithograph. The design includes *tanka* elements. The inset on the back cover provides contrast with its layout reminiscent of earlier print advertising.

Designing Modern Japan

producers. It encouraged experimentation and even the emergence and popularity of a new kimono fabric, *meisen*. *Meisen* is created from lower-quality cocoons. Its production was enabled by the adoption of a new reeling technique that spun thread from the cocoons without snapping the fibres, in mechanized factory production. The process rendered the silk thread more durable – so it could woven without breaking – and able to hold brighter colours.[136] Weavers and dyers began to combine synthetic dyes with *meisen*, stencilling patterns in synthetic dyes onto *meisen* before weaving. The silk thread could be mixed with cotton or rayon – produced by Japanese mills from the late 1920s – to create a distinctive smoothness and sheen.[137] All of these reduced the prices of the raw materials required to make kimono cloth, thus making the textiles more affordable. *Meisen* commonly employed new patterns, too: boldly geometrical, abstract and floral repeats whose design echoed the motifs and composition of modernist graphics and whose generous blocks of colour showed off the textile's characteristic blur. They were sold primarily in department stores, at prices accessible to shop girls and factory workers (thus demonstrating how department stores themselves opened to a larger market). They were also available by postal order.[138] By 1930, *meisen* accounted for half of the narrow-width silk cloth that was being produced, while silks generally commanded half of the total Japanese market in textiles.[139]

Poster advertising Isesaki Meisen, 1935.

This is a good place to discuss the 'Japaneseness' of modernist style. To criticize modernist graphics and *meisen* kimono as derivative and to lament a loss of visually identifiable 'Japaneseness' would be to misread these objects. Like most nations of its size, early twentieth-century Japan did not exist in a vacuum. Designers travelled overseas, where they studied in foreign design schools, sketched in museums, visited trade fairs and expositions and sometimes worked in foreign design firms. They relayed their experiences back to colleagues through books, teaching, lectures, exhibitions and industry journals, as well as in their everyday work.[140] Overseas styles, techniques and arguments travelled to Japan too through print media and European and Hollywood films; the advertising design department at Mitsukoshi, for example, owned twenty years of back issues of the German magazine *Deutsche Kunst und Dekoration* in the 1900s.[141] Visitors to the Industrial Arts Research Institute's library in 1933 could view British, German, French and American periodicals from *The Studio* and *Mobilier et décoration* to *Popular Science* and American architectural draughtsman's magazine *Pencil Points*, and the IARI published regular excerpts and photographs from overseas publications in its monthly journal.[142] Exhibition hall and polytechnic libraries stocked foreign books and magazines purchased through specialist booksellers such as Tokyo's Maruzen. More widely, consumers experienced international trends through cinema, photography, recorded sound, sheet music and food.

As advertising demand grew, it supported the emergence of specialist designers who saw themselves as part of a transnational, cosmopolitan profession. Placed in this context, modernism was their language, too. This did not mean replacing the past; as the photograph of Kageyama Kōyō and Shizuko's flat reminds us, early twentieth-century Japan was a hybrid environment in which vernacular and imported visual languages, things and habits coincided. Modernist aesthetics did not supplant earlier typefaces, styles and motifs, nor did 'modern' products and life replace many existing habits and things (let alone reach many rural or poor urban Japanese). Within advertising, 'beautiful woman' posters further updated the woodblock print trope with highly realistic rotary photogravure images of a coquettish, lipsticked and powdered modern beauty offering anything from beer to steamship passage to Manchuria. Indeed, many shops and manufacturers retained Tokugawa or Meiji period graphics in their packaging, either consciously, as historicism came to signify tradition and quality, or – perhaps more often – for the sheer lack of any impetus to change.

The demand for compelling visual communication and accessibility of printing technologies such as photography and photocomposition typesetting offered emergent graphic designers not only a living but a creative laboratory. The new advertising forms drew on new combinations of technical skills and knowledge, not least those of photographers like Kageyama Kōyō and printing technicians like those

Designing Modern Japan

trained alongside him at the Tokyo Higher School of Arts and Crafts, alongside graphic designers, illustrators and copywriters. Writing later, in 1936, Hara Hiromu argued that design should be integrated with new production techniques and their users, within the technical capacities of the printing industry:

> What we need for the new kind of graphic work is a cooperation between good photographers, designers and good print technicians . . . In the new approach, designs were constructed on the elements of photographs, illustrations and letters.[143]

Like woodblock printing, making visual design was a collaboration between designers and technicians, constrained and enabled by the technologies available and their knowledge of them.

This environment proved fertile for theoretical and collaborative research, too. Concentration in cities – Tokyo and the Osaka–Kōbe area particularly – offered camaraderie for commercial artists intent on exploring the possibilities of their medium. In Tokyo, prompted by Sugiura Hisui, such artists formed the Shichininsha (Group of Seven) research group in 1926 as a vehicle for researching and publicizing effective poster design methods through activities such as exhibitions at Mitsukoshi and a journal, *Affiches*, published from 1927.[144] The commercial artist and theorist Hamada Masuji (1892–1936) led on a 24-volume series of commercial art reference books, the *Gendai shōgyō bijutsu zenshū* (Complete Collection of Contemporary Commercial Art).[145] Designers' activities were part of the promotion of advertising culture by newspaper and advertising more widely. Newspapers sponsored competitions for advertisements, publishers produced numerous volumes on other aspects of advertising such as slogans and catch copy, layouts, window displays and sales strategies, and specialist monthly magazines on advertising appeared, of which *Advertising World*, founded in 1926 and with a circulation of 10,000 in 1927, would become the most active.[146] In the 1920s, designers had little interaction with colleagues outside their local area. As Yamana Ayao put it, colourfully:

> At that time it was a ten-hour night train that swayed and rocked [to get from Tokyo to Osaka]. Tokyo didn't know what was going on in Osaka, Osaka didn't know what was going on

in Tokyo. Nagoya was in between but we didn't have a clue what was happening, even there. When it came to Kyushu and Hokkaidō, we had no clue what was going on where, who was doing what where. We could only see people at arm's reach.[147]

With interactions limited outside local design communities, publications allowed designers to follow developments in other regions.

Within this heady environment, increased corporate investment in advertising afforded designers the chance to experiment and to create a community and shared sense of practice. This paralleled the way in which industrial policy decisions, to stimulate industrial craft export income, were providing opportunities to product designers within the state research and advising system. And, in a way rife with gendered constraints, how the expansion of women's education enabled some women to take roles as teachers of sewing, embroidery and other creative areas conventionally associated with the domestic sphere, and with women's unpaid labour in it. Given women's lack of access to careers in commercial design, it should not be surprising that one area where they did take design leadership, in the early twentieth century, was in proposals for the rationalization and improvement of home life.

Design and Daily Life Reform

Design also appeared as a prescription for new ways of living in the guise of social reform. From the late 1910s, bureaucrats and educators increasingly saw the redesign of everyday life activities and their environment as a tool for improving national welfare. Reformers did not specifically use the language of design, preferring to talk of 'rationalization', 'reform' and 'improvement'. But their attempts to 'improve' the nation by effecting change in the things, spaces and habits that compose everyday life sat well within design practice, not only because many designers took leading roles in the project. The redesign of the material environment would redesign its users and, by redesigning their behaviour and interactions, society itself. MCI bureaucrats and IARI designers wanted to rationalize manufacturing and improve exports. Advertising agency and corporate design departments aimed at creating particular brand images for their products. At their most ambitious, daily life reformers wanted to redesign nothing less than Japanese society.[148]

Daily life reform movements emerged from earlier social reform movements which had focused particularly on improving conditions in cities undergoing industrialization. Urban reformers, inspired by studies of British working-class housing, had published reports on poor districts in Tokyo and Osaka since the 1880s. Thanks partly to their efforts, the government passed a tenement prohibition law in 1909, which signalled the appearance of state will to intervene, even if it was considered largely ineffectual in the face of restrictive land ownership and tenancy agreements.[149] Domestic economy and home economics research in the United States and Britain, respectively, further shaped daily life reform principles. Elite women's educators Ōe Sumi and Shimoda Utako, who had studied domestic economy in London, promoted a hybrid set of beliefs that combined British-style systematic domestic management with Tokugawa period social graces and Confucian morals. Ōe, Shimoda and others disseminated their vision of domestic economy through private girls' schools and publishing. By the 1910s, thanks to the popularity of work like the American researcher Christine Frederick's *The New Housekeeping* (1913), girls' school educators and domestic economy researchers were incorporating Taylorist scientific management principles for organizing workspaces and workflows into their own teachings, which included textbooks that were approved by the Ministry of Education and adopted by schools nationally. The formal government approval in 1910 of girls' vocational high schools, focusing on domestic economy, also helped to disseminate this message by providing employment for domestic economy teachers as well as educating girls. Between 1900 and 1920, the number of girls' high schools jumped by 990 per cent, and the number of girls enrolled by 1,260 per cent.[150] Girls' increased enrolment in schools ensured that the message reached more people, too.

In the 1910s, academics, reformers and a new generation of civil servants in national and local governments such as those of Tokyo and Osaka began developing more extensive policies. These aimed first at ameliorating the lives and living conditions of the poor in the cities and in rural villages, then at improving conditions for all Japanese regardless of social standing and income. Design – product, interior and dress design for improved use, and graphic and exhibition design to communicate the message – was integral to the reformers' vision for how to improve society. Following privately organized exhibitions earlier in the decade, civil servants in the Ministry of Education, working closely with girls' school educators and public health and domestic economy researchers, organized two exhibitions at the Tokyo Education Museum: in 1918 the Domestic Science Exhibition and in 1919 the Daily Life Improvement Exhibition. The latter, held over two months in winter 1919, saw roughly 110,000 visitors view panels, posters, mannequins in reform dress, housing models, table settings and rooms designed by domestic economy research groups, girls' school groups, educators and architects. Some visitors also attended lectures, demonstrations, products sales, children's music concerts and film screenings.[151]

A number of 'daily life reform' organizations followed. These included the Seikatsu Kaizen Dōmeikai (Daily Life Improvement League), which had begun in 1917 as an element of the Movement to Foster the Nation's Strength launched by the Home Ministry, before becoming an organization backed by an assortment of state and private school principals, academics and entrepreneurs, while also being supported by Buddhist and Christian women's and youth groups, female students and domestic economy research groups around Japan.[152] A 1924 publication, *Seikatsu kaizen no shiori* (Guide to Daily Life Improvement), outlined their starting point: 'from the perspective of morality, economy, hygiene and the like, daily life in our homes and society, aspects needing improvement are not few.'[153] The organization's purpose was clear: 'to educate the social public and improve and elevate the daily life of the national people'.[154] It was followed by a number of other organizations and initiatives, national and local; in discussions in rural villages, too, men's associations circulated variations of the daily life improvement message in meetings and newsletters.[155]

Print and live media provided reformers with the platform for disseminating their message. In addition to exhibitions and lectures, in 1920, the League published a 1,330-page book, *Seikatsu kaizen shosei keizai katei hyakka zensho* (Complete Dictionary of Daily Life Reform and Domestic Economy). It followed this tome with specific books outlining guidance for improved clothing, housing, food and rural customs. These were only a few of the many publications on daily life reform. While some retained the tone of moral improvement, others blended it with more commercial and aesthetic exhortations, as individual architects, furniture and interior designers, cookery experts, foodstuffs manufacturers, department stores, professional associations and women's magazines began writing and sponsoring their own books on building, furnishing and running the home.

Whether expressed in speeches, magazines or exhibitions, chief among reformers' concerns were what they saw as the unsanitary and uneconomical living conditions, poor nutrition and wasteful habits of Japanese households. Such conditions, they argued, were not only conducive to disease and endemic poverty but actually prevented the Japanese public from working efficiently, thus hampering national economic as well as social development. The solution – and the reformers' keywords – was 'rational', 'scientific' domestic management to 'improve' and 'reform' the conditions and habits of daily life. This was to be based on equally 'rational', 'scientific' research, which would make daily life more 'efficient', 'economical', 'cultured' and 'modern'. Morimoto Kōkichi (1878–1950), co-founder of another association, the Bunka Seikatsu Kenkyūkai (Culture Life Research Group), summed it up: 'It is imperative that we improve daily life and adopt a cultured life appropriate for the new age . . . Scientific research is imperative if we are to achieve actual improvement in daily life.'[156] Reformers' concrete efforts focused on promoting economy in clothing, food and housing as well as social rituals such as weddings, gift-giving and visiting, all of which they saw as overly wasteful, leading to suboptimal living and working conditions. The message was heavily gendered, positioning both urban and rural women from the middle classes to lead reform from within their own extended households by modelling frugality and thrift in social situations. Village newsletter editors exhorted rural women to save money and use simple things. Overall, reformers expected women to make change within existing social structures and class divisions: the League's 1920 doorstopper of a book included examples of reform dress for maids and model floorplans with maids' rooms.[157]

As directions for improving user efficiency and overall social outcomes through modifications to behaviour and environment, the daily life reform guidance should be seen as design, particularly the modernist sort aimed at engendering widespread social improvement in the 1920s and '30s. Some reformers' guidance called for changes in social customs to reduce expenditure. They admonished housewives to follow newly available nutrition guidelines when selecting foods for their families. They also criticized kimono and the practice of sitting on the floor as restricting movement and activity, which they saw as leading to inefficient work when compared to that conducted in Western clothing, standing or seated in chairs.

Particularly inveterate, according to reformers, was 'the double life' (*nijū seikatsu*): a household's use of both Japanese and Western clothing, interiors and other goods. While Western-style clothing, food and interiors were once the purview of Meiji elites, by the 1920s urban middle-class households enjoyed a mixture of Japanese and imported goods and habits. For reformers, combining Japanese- and Western-style living habits also required double the storage space, which only increased its wastefulness. As Morimoto opined on clothing:

> Expenditure for two kinds of clothing, however, is somewhat of a waste and can hardly be justified in an efficient standard of living. For the improvement of clothing, in the future it would be better to use one set of clothing, either European or Japanese, whichever is more practical and advantageous according to the needs of the individual.[158]

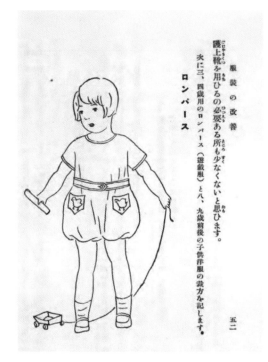

服装の改善

護上靴を用ひるの必要ある所も少なくないと思ひます。

次に三、四歳用のロンパース（遊戯服）と八、九歳前後の子供洋服の裁方を記します。

ロンパース

五二

The Daily Life Improvement League included this design for girls' rompers as reform dress in the book *Guidelines for Everyday Life Improvement in Rural Villages* (1931).

Reformers tended not to advocate kimono's complete replacement with Western-style clothing. This was largely for practical reasons: most women wore kimono outside the home. As Morimoto added in a caveat, 'It must be noted, however, that the custom of wearing European clothing is limited to certain classes of men and children. There is no possibility that the European costume will ever be commonly used by women.'[159]

Other reformers suggested new types of reform dress. The Daily Life Improvement League recommended that both men and women adopt a version of the *hakama* split trousers that had previously been worn by samurai men and been popular among girls' higher school students in the Meiji period.[160] Children, unformed by convention, were to be dressed in adapted Western-style clothing from birth.[161] Standardized garments could be used for a variety of formal occasions and, thanks to their plain design, remain in fashion, thus supporting

Designing Modern Japan

the reformers' goal of persuading households to spend less on items for different social occasions. This work was largely unsuccessful, however, not least as growing urban household incomes and the emergence of inexpensive *meisen* kimono made fashion increasingly accessible.

Housing reform activities had a greater impact, often for reasons of practicality or fashion.[162] Initially, reformers' activities and attention focused largely on alleviating housing shortages in Tokyo and Osaka. Government measures aimed to help urban middle-class families finance the construction of their own home. Collective housing blocks like the Dōjunkai Jingū Apartments, home to Kageyama Kōyō and Shizuko, appeared in Tokyo and Osaka, the former as part of local government response to the 1923 earthquake.[163] Meanwhile, real estate developers offered suburban plots. Women's magazines explained how households could not only design and build but finance their own home.[164] And furniture design educators and researchers from the Higher School system like Kogure Joichi (1881–1943) shared information about their own homes as exemplars to emulate. As with

Furniture designer and design educator Kogure Joichi included this photograph in his book *Reforming My House*, published in 1930. The girl with bobbed hair, possibly his daughter, reads in a room with tatami converted to chair-style living. The combination of books, bookshelf, clock and girl reading at a desk in Kogure's own 'reformed' house recall the Chikanobu print from 1889 (see Chapter Two).

dress reform, the primary tenet of housing reform for the middle class was for tatami to be replaced with a modified version of the Western hard floor, table and chairs.[165] Other propositions included increased provision of fresh air and sunlight, a spatial emphasis on the family over guests, and safety and hygiene taking precedence over 'empty' decoration in the construction and equipping of residences. Much attention went to construction reform, specifically the use of new materials like reinforced concrete and the adoption of international standards of measure. These propositions aligned with similar proposals advocated by reform-minded architects, planners and policymakers elsewhere.

Reformers' ideals for housing were first applied at scale in newly opened privately developed suburbs, underlining the fact that reform concerns such as housing and clothing could easily mutate into commodities. Progressive ideology advocating the rationalization of materials and design was often diluted as builders and residents introduced such 'luxurious' elements as elaborate gates and tatami-floored living areas. Despite the loud exhortations of reformers, for most households housing changed little – especially in rural areas, where some houses retained early modern features such as paper windows and earthen-floored kitchens into the 1970s.[166]

Urban reform efforts such as the promotion of reform dress or more practical interiors primarily targeted the middle classes, but some attempts reached further. The Social Bureaus of Tokyo and Osaka, for example, made recommendations for improved housing in poor districts.[167] But poorer urban residents were slower to enter the consumer class. The impoverished residents of cities did own things: in one survey conducted around 1920, some 90 per cent of households classified as 'poor' owned a table for eating, a charcoal brazier (*hibachi*) for heating, and futon bedding.[168] Over 80 per cent used electric lighting exclusively. But reformers' injunctions to own and purchase fewer things made less sense for poor urban and rural households alike. Indeed, reformers' interests in intervening in rural life through design focused more on rural making, as we will explore in the next chapter.

A KEY PARADOX THROUGHOUT this chapter has been that designers' activities sat outside the actual design and making of most products and environments in this period. Commercial artists' advertising work

Designing Modern Japan

circulated widely, but few boys, and even fewer girls, actually became commercial artists. Furniture design provides a useful illustration of this point. Through the 1930s, carpenters produced traditional wooden objects for the home in small workshops that sold either to local customers or to middlemen who commissioned products, supplied materials and managed sales to urban wholesalers or direct shops, much as they had in the Tokugawa period. Bespoke furniture-makers concentrated in specific neighbourhoods such as Tokyo's Shiba district dominated the small market for Western-style furniture. Furniture departments like those at Mitsukoshi and Takashimaya, with their teams of design graduates, were relative newcomers.

For the department stores, commissioning and selling Western-style furniture and interior decoration extended the larger commercial strategy of selling lifestyle to the burgeoning middle class. By the 1930s, the appearance of identifiably middle-class nuclear families in regional Japanese cities too expanded the stores' market even further. Their urban dwellings – often far from the multigenerational rural households in which they had grown up – required furnishing. Department stores and bespoke Western-style furniture workshops hired graduates of the Tokyo Higher School of Arts and Crafts and the local technical schools as designers. Some workshops also selected model designs out of books and magazines, as carpenters had in the early modern period. This market remained small until the 1960s but was sufficient to support a small group of manufacturers and retailers and the designers they employed.

By contrast, the self-consciously cosmopolitan researchers and educators affiliated with the Tokyo Higher School sold very little. Their key work was to disseminate ideals for both Japanese and Western-style furniture. They were able to share these ideas widely through education, expositions and publishing to the carpenters and specialist furniture-makers who designed as well as made the bulk of new furniture in this period. Their ideals and techniques travelled to women as well, through teacher training and general audience books on housing and interiors. These men who categorized themselves as 'furniture designers' were as much industry reformers who targeted both the furniture industry and the 'industry' of women who used its products at home.

If this sounds lofty, it often was. In addition to professional ties, the furniture designers were allied with the broader daily life reform movement through their goal of improving quality and lowering production costs and unit price, thus making solidly built, well-styled Western-style furniture affordable for the new middle class. More experimental designers included Tokyo Higher School lecturer and furniture designer Moriya Nobuo (1893–1927) and the Keiji Kōbō, a loose group composed of Higher School graduates and Tokyo furniture-makers whose work in steel pipe furniture, *Existenzminimum*-inspired housing and ergonomics belied both personal connections with European modernism and a focal shift from British furniture manufacturing and housing to a Bauhaus- and Le Corbusier-centred international modernism in the late 1920s.[169] The standardization of parts, processes and products would allow nothing less than the 'democratization' – in Moriya's words – of access to modern, well-made furniture.[170] Or, as Tokyo Higher School graduate Nishida Toraichi, later teacher at the Nagasaki Prefectural Normal School for Women, put it in 1935, 'Design and creation are the greatest elements of cultural progress.'[171] Efforts like these, they hoped, would bring commerce and reform together, increasing profits for industry and offering better living for all.

As educators disseminating Western-style furniture methods to new furniture-makers throughout the country through their students and shaping future trends as the much-loved teachers of department store furniture designers, men like Moriya and Nishida clearly impacted furniture design in Japan. But as the Kageyamas' hybrid breakfast

Girls learning cabinetry at the Nagasaki Prefectural Women's Normal School, c. 1935. The girls' teacher, Nishida Toraichi, included this photograph in *Compendium of the Latest Woodcraft* (1935), a woodcraft and carpentry education manual and textbook for teachers.

Designing Modern Japan

scene, with its combination of low table and Western-style desk, suggests, the researchers' concerns with standardization and universality seem somewhat blinkered. Like the Kageyamas, many Japanese lived with modern design in various forms. Carpenters were responsible for many of the things that *did* regularly furnish Japanese homes of varying incomes. This production was varied, including heavy wooden chests purchased as part of a bride's dowry, mirror stands, boxes and trays, for example. Carpenters produced such wares for general purchase and relied on several centuries of traditional carpentry based on standardized dimensions, but operated outside the emergent networks of self-consciously modern design and its production. Women and men alike, as consumers of home furnishings, were bound by budgets, convention and their position in hierarchical household structures, as well as by the actual physical construction, layout and space of their homes. For poor urban and rural households, this meant a very different experience to that of the Kageyamas, in their reinforced concrete, electrified flat.

The argument is more complex than this, but it remains worth stating: self-conscious engagement with 'design', including connections with international design trends and overseas practitioners, was only one small, if vocal, subsection of an ecosystem of designers, makers and users, in which geography, class and gender greatly determined experience. In their own way, these ecosystems were as modernist as brightly blurred *meisen* stripes or a magazine layout celebrating skiing or the mechanical rhythm of steel bridges and streetcars. Daily life, housing and furniture reformers may have had less impact on actual things, spaces and habits than they would have desired. However, their emergence alongside and sometimes within state efforts to improve export income, as well as commercial efforts to stimulate domestic retail, not only impacted design culture in early twentieth-century Japan but played an important role in shaping things to come.

ELECTRIC PERCOLATOR
電氣濾過機
350W — 100/110ᵛ—50/60
東京芝浦電氣株式會社

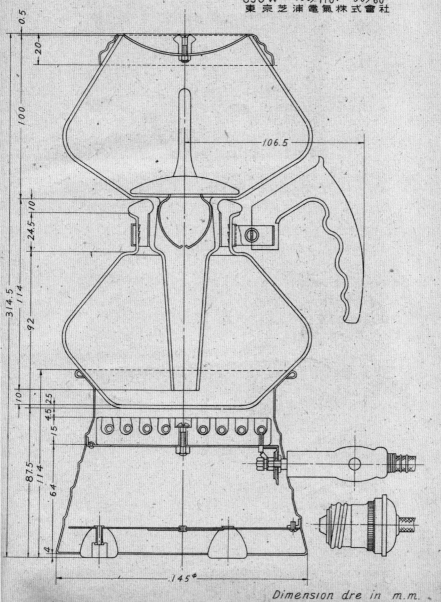

Dimension dre in m.m.

3 Coffee Sets and Militarism:
Design in Empire, War and Occupation

In August 1945, Japan capitulated to the Allied forces. This action ended the Second World War. Fifteen months later, in December 1946, the Ministry of Commerce and Industry's (MCI) Export Agency and the ministry's Industrial Arts Research Institute (IARI) published a compilation of product designs, for circulation within the IARI's network of design advisers and to manufacturers. The photographs accompanying the line drawings and technical specifications included lacquer trays, *yūzen* kimono and cloisonné vases with the decorative bird-and-flower aesthetic of Meiji export products. But the bulk of the book was taken up with glass, metal and wood homewares in the more linear, undecorated style of 1930s American products.

The product types, too – from butter bowls and cheeseboards to salad and *hors d'oeuvre* sets – clearly indicated an American market. IARI designers had worked on the project with colleagues in the MCI Export Agency, and with the encouragement of Occupation officers, in an attempt to identify light industrial objects suitable for export to the United States. IARI designers had developed the selection in the first years of the Allied Occupation, gaining direct input from Allied officials as well as from American design, home and garden literature. They hoped that the products might be popular gifts for middle-class Americans and could be sold in regional department stores, relatively inexpensive in comparison to, but visually indistinguishable from, American-made products. These goods could provide income for Japan's regional light industries to revive and, through them, to contribute to national economic reconstruction. The designs themselves are not particularly novel. Some recuperated IARI prototypes from the mid-1930s, an earlier moment in which designers had attempted

Line drawing cross-section of an electric percolator, 1946. The drawing was created as part of the technical specifications for Japanese manufacturers to produce household goods for the Allied Occupation of Japan, a project in which IARI designers played a central role.

to boost exports of industrial exports through better design. Others derived from Allied Occupation commissions to Japanese manufacturers. The motivation, to sell to export markets to gain foreign currency and through this to support Japan's economy, was familiar as well. Seen in longer perspective, this was design for regional economic development yet again, but this time embraced by civil servants and their political backers in the national government.

Today, Japan is an archipelagic nation-state lying off the coast of the Asian continent. Between 1869 and 1945, Japan was an empire, encompassing both islands and parts of the continent itself. Modern Japan's imperial expansion began in 1868, when the new national government annexed the territories to its immediate north, including the island known as Ezo or Ezochi, home to the Ainu people, renamed Hokkaidō by the Japanese government. In the 1870s, the government pursued an actively expansionist policy, employing gunboat diplomacy and unequal treaties to increase its influence in northeast Asia, countering Qing Chinese and foreign power claims to hegemony in the region. Japan formally incorporated the Ryūkyū Kingdom to the south, renamed Okinawa, in 1879, and control over Taiwan passed to Japan from Qing China after the Sino-Japanese war of 1894–5. Japan gained control over the Korean peninsula and southern Manchuria, a large area in northeastern China previously claimed by the Russians, after the Russo-Japanese War of 1904–5.[1] Over the next four decades, Japanese colonial and military governments ruled an increasingly wide swathe of East Asia. Japanese colonial expansion turned much of China into a battlefield between Chinese and Japanese forces in the 1930s, and the Japanese military occupied much of Southeast Asia as the Second World War intensified after 1940. Following Japan's capitulation to the Allied forces in 1945, Japan was itself occupied for seven years. Today, many American military bases remain in Japan. Geopolitical tensions and their histories remain integral to international relations in the region. The legacies of lived experience and its memorialization continue to shape popular sentiment, too, in East Asia and its diasporas.

While war and imperialism have played a major part in shaping modern East Asia, design and designers' role in Japan's military and colonial past is often glossed over. Japanese graphic designers were relatively open about their propaganda work in published autobiographies.[2] In the late 1970s, a generation of design historians who experienced the war as children or had not yet been born when it ended began to revisit the involvement of graphic designers and architects in propaganda production and other pro-war, state-supported activities.[3] Until very recently, however, historians have avoided discussions of design activities in colonial Korea and Taiwan and in Japanese-occupied Manchuria. Companies limit access to archival material related to their wartime support and commercial activities in colonial locations. Historical documents and oral histories related to design during war and colonial occupation have been difficult to present publicly.[4] To take one example, the export promotion activities of IARI designers in the 1930s have received some attention, but historians rarely spell out the connection between export coffee sets and militarism.[5]

There are numerous reasons for this occlusion. These include the desire to bury memories of wartime violence and post-war deprivation, as well as continued anger towards Japan in many parts of East Asia. Understandably, many historians in China, Korea and Taiwan prefer to highlight local narratives, with a preference for those that emphasize resistance to colonialism rather than the colonizers' actions or local participation in them. Within Japan, bringing to light a designer's participation in colonial and military projects can complicate an otherwise positive narrative of their careers. It also risks calling out designers for actions and stances taken by many, but ordinarily left silent in the contemporary historical record.

In the 1990s, historians began addressing these challenges, encouraged by a broader revisiting of the colonial and post-war years around 1995, the fiftieth anniversary of Japan's capitulation. In Japan, as public memory of actual war experience dies away, design historians and museum curators have been emboldened by increased archival access, changing public attitudes – which make it easier to openly discuss and exhibit colonial and wartime material culture – and by the desire of historians to counter revisionist histories that downplay or deny Japanese aggression in East Asia.[6] Across East Asia, design historians and curators in formerly occupied nations are exploring material and arguments within specific local contexts for historical memory. While regional relations remain complex and animosity has not disappeared, research into design and the role of designers in Japan's imperial expansion and war in East Asia is growing, particularly among emerging scholars. As this chapter will suggest, there is much more to be done, particularly to incorporate and reflect on more diverse experiences within Japanese design history.

The first two sections of this chapter focus on some of the roles that design played in colonial policy between 1900 and the 1930s, both overtly in colonial cultural and economic administration and at an ideological level in Japan. As part of a history of design in modern Japan, they focus on colonial policy, rather than the many ways that people in Taiwan and Korea employed design in everyday work and commerce. The intention is for the section – and, more importantly, the book – to be read alongside histories centred in Korea, Taiwan and elsewhere in East Asia, and alongside transnational regional histories.[7] The third section explores the impact of escalating war on designers, and the fourth section the design industries during the Allied Occupation of Japan (1945–52).

A recurring theme for this chapter is the sheer continuity in the work of many designers, whether creating posters and typefaces to promote an idea or product or experimenting with materials and techniques to create more functional objects. For the book introduced above, a team of designers, many of whom had been active in the 1930s, reproduced designs from that period for exports after 1945. The clients and message may have changed as war escalated and then ended. But many designers and manufacturers continued to work largely as before.[8] Design, ontologically, continued as it had: as an activity sponsored by commercial or state interests, for persuasion and profit. More often than not, products and consumer tastes also changed little in this period. Rather than looking for changes brought by empire and war, we might ask why we expect things to change in the first place.

Design in Colonial Occupation in Taiwan and Korea

The density of local manufacturers, retailers and consumers in territories across East Asia ensured a rich ecosystem of design practices and products in Okinawa and Taiwan as much as in Korea, Manchuria and indeed Japan. Regional producers of everyday products such as textiles for clothing, ceramic dishware and wooden furniture employed a variety of design sources, including existing styles, well-selling items, pattern books and instructions and orders from wholesalers, to create competitive products, largely by hand, for local and national markets. Other workshops catered for elite clients.

Designing Modern Japan

As Japanese designers, collectors and bureaucrats began to interact with newly colonized locations – whether in person or as imagined locales – they responded in various ways. Some Japanese, projecting colonial attitudes similar to those held in European nations, disparaged Taiwanese and Korean products as immature and under-developed compared to Japanese production. To give one example, in 1903, less than a decade after Taiwan's colonization, the jury for the Fifth National Industrial Exposition – generally complimentary or at least neutral in their comments for Japanese-made items – harshly criticized a display of Taiwanese woven striped cotton fabric. They asserted that it compared poorly to that of Japan and Okinawa, commenting that Taiwanese weavers would need to improve their work to be competitive in the market.[9]

Other Japanese also evaluated Taiwanese and Korean work as less 'industrial' or 'modern' than Japanese work but found in handmade objects from newly colonized locales the antidote to what they saw as the unfortunate results of Japan's own industrial modernization.

Glazed stoneware jar, 19th century, Tsutsumi (Sendai), northeastern Japan, with the aesthetic qualities valued by *mingei* proponents.

In 1914, the Tokyo collector Yanagi Muneyoshi (Sōetsu, 1889–1961) encountered Korean ceramics from the Joseon dynasty (1392–1910), the centuries-long era that preceded Japan's occupation of Korea.[10] Taken with what he saw as the simplicity, purity and honesty of Korean objects for everyday life, Yanagi began travelling to Korea to collect ceramics and other house-hold objects. He established a museum for his collection, the Korean Art Museum, in the Korean capital, Seoul, in 1924.[11] Yanagi dubbed this new category of products 'folk-craft' (*mingei*) and began to promote the connois-seurship and acquisition of similar products from around the Japanese Empire. In 1926, Yanagi along with potters Tomimoto Kenkichi (1886–1963), Kawai Kanjirō (1890–1966) and Hamada Shōji (1894–1978) published a mani-festo, the 'Prospectus for the Establishment of a Folk Craft Art Museum'. Yanagi's social position and networks ensured attention among elite collec-tors and craft patrons. Regular exhibitions in Tokyo and Kyoto, as well as the periodical *Kōgei* (Craft, published

Coffee Sets and Militarism

from 1931), further publicized this stance to a broader audience in Japan. A museum in Tokyo, the Japan Folk Crafts Museum, followed in 1936, as did workshops, retail outlets and museums in regional cities established by supporters of the 'folk-craft' ideal. Somewhat contradictorily, given the importance placed on the beauty of ordinary, anonymous objects in Yanagi's vision of folk-craft, *mingei* also emerged as a category for increasingly valuable work produced by potters like Kawai, Hamada and Bernard Leach (1887–1979) and in later years would come to overlap closely with studio pottery around the world.

Yanagi was not alone in his interests. In Korea, Taiwan, Okinawa and Hokkaidō alike, local crafts products were collected by university museums and private collectors, displayed in national and international exhibitions and classified within a value system, itself popularized in nineteenth-century Europe, that contrasted 'civilization' with 'primitive' cultures in a hierarchical racial framework. Such practices were particularly acute in Taiwan, with its indigenous communities distinct from the Han Taiwanese.[12] Within the Japanese archipelago, Leach and Tomimoto discovered their affinity with expressly 'folk' objects independently of Yanagi. So did the printmaker Yamamoto Kanae (1882–1946), who began teaching young people in Nagano prefecture to create products for sale at Mitsukoshi in 1920 and established the Japan Peasant Art Institute (Nōmin Bijutsu Kenkyūjō) for the same purpose in 1923.[13] Other socially minded entrepreneurs identified farm household crafts – the lacquer bowls, wooden toys and straw raincoats produced in the evenings and off-season – as potentially lucrative 'exports' to urban department stores, bringing welcome extra income to poor rural households.[14] Historians often describe metropolitan cultural attitudes towards rural areas in Japan, found in literature and ethnography as well as in economic development and political policy, as effectively replicating the colonial centre–periphery relationship within the archipelago itself. Projects such as *mingei* indicate how design and material culture activities, too, conveyed and amplified these political and economic agendas. For urban elites keen to align themselves with Japan's transformation, identifying crafts objects from the colonies and from poor rural communities within the archipelago as foreign, distant and suggestive of a seemingly fading artisanal and rustic past was a way to perform and solidify this position.[15]

Indeed, the emergence of folk-craft in early twentieth-century Japan corresponded with dramatic urbanization and a subsequent urban interest in rural life, including the folklore studies (*minzokugaku*) of academic Yanagita Kunio and the 'agricultural fundamentalism' (*nōhon-shugi*) of philosopher Nitobe Inazō, which provided the intellectual scaffolding for social science studies of village life.[16] Other scholars, trained in European academic disciplines, found beauty and a potentially Japanese path through modernization in the aesthetics of premodern Japanese urban life and dwellings, seen not least in the author Tanizaki Junichirō's essay *In'ei raisan* (In Praise of Shadows, 1933) and the philosopher Kuki Shūzō's *Iki no kōzō* (The Structure of Iki, 1930).[17] Yet other researchers – trained in social science and architecture – applied data collection and analysis techniques to know and measure occupied territories, including Taiwan, Korea and Manchuria.[18] Such efforts occupied a complex position. On the one hand, they overtly rejected Western modernization by embracing the local, the indigenous and the 'Oriental'. On the other, they employed Western systems of knowledge, encountered and incorporated through elite European and European-style higher education, in order to distinguish between urban modernity and rural areas, the latter being somehow closer to tradition and the past. Furthermore, and even more contentiously, the identification of Korean and Taiwanese goods with an idealized shared past, together with other similar positions, implicitly supported and normalized Japan's imperial expansion within East Asia and continued colonial occupation.

Certainly, it aligned with colonial authorities' use of design. Some Japanese authorities in colonial Korea and Taiwan saw design as an effective tool for visibly asserting their authority over the land and people, and for conveying the argument that colonialism brought an orderly, systematic and exciting modernity unattainable by local governments alone. New train stations, bridges, hospitals, shrines and administrative buildings were important visual symbols of Japanese rule built and imposed by the colonial governments.[19] With their imposing scale, masonry construction and Western historicist style, such buildings and boulevards created visual, experiential contrast with the older areas of the cities, which were home to local residents.[20] In doing so, the colonial authorities were reviving a Meiji government strategy used in the Japanese archipelago in the late nineteenth century. This simplistic dichotomy materialized one of Japan's principal arguments in favour of its right to colonize its neighbours, namely that Japanese rule brought 'progress' to otherwise 'stagnating', even

'backwards', societies.[21] On a more structural level, design education systems developed in Meiji Japan directly supported the creation and administration of colonial systems. Already by 1912, for example, graduates of the Kyoto Higher School of Arts and Crafts were employed in the printing and civil engineering agencies that formed part of the Korean and Taiwanese colonial administrations.[22]

While policies varied, colonial governments overlaid existing local practices with Japanese-style official design promotion. As in Japan, the colonial governments of Taiwan and Korea sponsored product exhibitions, aimed at manufacturers and the general public alike. In Korea, the Korean government had established a system of export promotion and exhibition bureaus in 1902. The colonial administration replaced this with a system of national and local exhibitions, similar to that established in Japan.[23] A requirement for provinces to establish product exhibition halls and chambers of commerce followed in 1914.[24] The Government-General's Commerce and Industry Promotional Hall in what is now Seoul, then known as Gyeongseong in Korean and Keijō in Japanese, offered design and trademark advising and resources, organized exhibitions, collected and displayed samples and prototypes and undertook design and technical research for Korean products, all in the service of its mission of 'product improvement and expansion of sales routes'.[25] The colonial government in Taiwan did the same, sponsoring Taiwan's first industrial fair in 1916.[26] By 1930, colonial product halls nominally existed within the same network as their 'mainland' counterparts. In 1932, for example, the Governor-General of Korea, appointed from Tokyo, sent products to Tokyo as part of an exhibition of prototypes from research institutes across Korea.[27] In 1933, the IARI lent 190 sample products to the main Taiwanese product exhibition hall.[28]

Colonial manufacturing policies in the first part of the century emphasized indigenous materials and techniques for light industry rather than the development of new heavy industry, with particular support for the redirection and development of crafts products for export markets – predominantly mainland Japan – which had been identified by the colonial governments.[29] This coincided with the period of connoisseur interest, in Japan, in studying and collecting the ancient cultural heritage both of Japan and of Asia more widely.[30] In Korea, the colonial government opened an industrial training centre in 1907 that focused on research into existing Korean crafts industries like celadon, mother-of-pearl lacquerware and papermaking.[31] In

Saeki Shunkō, *Tea and Coffee Salon (Sabō)*, 1939, ink, colour, paper and lacquer. Rustic jars line a rail along the wall in the dark-timbered café, with its modernist armchairs and waitresses in fashionable Western dress and hairstyles. The jar to the far right uses glazes, composition and form similar to those of the Tsutsumi jar on p. 141.

Taiwan, the colonial government focused infrastructural investment in agricultural output – particularly sugarcane, but also tropical fruit and rice – but also made some investment in craft industries.[32] Some of these projects piggy-backed on agricultural infrastructure, for example a training centre for woven striped cottons in 1899 opened as part of a new experimental station for agriculture.[33] By the 1920s, growing mainland Japanese taste for particular export products prompted investment in training for products made with local materials: bamboo, lacquer, ceramics, wood and so on.[34] By 1928, the colonial government in Taiwan supported a training school for lacquer, the Taichung City Craft Institute, begun originally as a private initiative.[35] These and other similar initiatives straddled a line between craft production and design for urban consumers, which has been continued in Taiwan to this day.[36]

Attitudes towards design in the archipelago also entered colonial education through industrial promotion and general education schemes. From 1902 the Taipei Normal School curriculum included drawing and handcrafts. The colonial Department of Educational Affairs in Taiwan required design drawing and manual art lessons, largely based on Japanese models, in schools from 1910 onwards.[37] A higher industrial school opened in 1918 as part of an expansion of higher education on the island, but was open only to male Japanese students until 1922, when it was opened to all male students. In Japan, as we saw in Chapter Two, the late 1910s were a heady moment for higher-level design education, leading to the establishment of new specialist programmes. In Taiwan, however, the colonial government focused the industrial school curriculum on building engineering technical capacity, primarily for settler Japanese students. Into the 1930s, enrolment in the main courses was overwhelmingly Japanese, with local students

Women working in the silkworm-rearing hall at the colonial government's sericulture training institute and in the silk-reeling works at the Chōsen Raw Thread Co., Ltd, Korea, early 1920s.

Designing Modern Japan

in the shorter, more vocational upskilling courses.[38] Given that the higher schools were directly overseen by the Department of Educational Affairs, this provides a clear indication of the persistent differentiation of Japanese and Taiwanese colonial subjects. It also suggests how the colonial government did not see design – and, more widely, products 'designed' in the modern sense of the word – as part of their vision for Taiwan's economy and culture.

The kind of industrial design education debated in 1910s Japan was not implemented in Korea, either. Again, the colonial government expected Japanese expatriates to fill skilled technical positions such as factory foremen or engineers.[39] Sons of well-situated Korean families could join their emigrant Japanese counterparts at the few state higher schools or mission schools. From the late 1920s onwards they could continue to the art department of Keijō Imperial University in Seoul. Travel to study in Japan was another elite option, building on several decades of intra-Asian experience. From the early 1900s, enterprising, well-connected and often wealthy young men from other parts of East Asia had travelled to Japan to study in the new art and design schools and polytechnics. The Kyoto Higher School of Arts and Crafts had enrolled several students from China in its first decade.[40] Some Chinese students had arrived in Japan after studying design with Japanese teachers in China, once the Qing government had started issuing invitations to Japanese design teachers in 1901. Chen Zhifo (1896–1962), for example, studied design at the Zhejiang Public Industrial Specialized School (Zhèjiāng shěnglì jiǎzhǒng gōngyè xuéxiào) under the Japanese educator Suga Masao between 1912 and 1916.[41] After his graduation, he became a lecturer at the same school before travelling to Japan and entering the Tokyo School of Fine Arts design department in 1919.[42] He graduated in 1923, then moved to Shanghai, where he became an important figure in graphic design education, publishing and practice.[43]

Following in such predecessors' footsteps, both male and female students travelled from Taiwan and Korea to study in Japan. In the 1930s, some women from elite families in Taiwan and Korea studied at the Private Women's School of Fine Arts in Tokyo, which was renamed the Women's Academy of Fine Arts (Joshi Bijutsu Senmon Gakkō) in 1929. Korean students often joined the teacher training course to gain a teaching licence, studying embroidery, before returning home to teach in girls' higher schools, which were predominantly attended by

Japanese students. Graduates formed powerful support networks for each other. As Yi Changbong, a 1939 graduate, put it, 'In Korea at the time, women who studied art in Japan were the elite, so 100 per cent of graduates secured jobs after returning home. Most of the graduates in my year taught the women in the years below us.'[44] Elite young women from the colonies could also access design education through domestic science courses at women's universities and normal schools like the Tokyo Women's Higher Normal School. Men from the colonies could also study at the IARI. In 1932, for example, the institute received a request from a young man in Chiayi, Taiwan, to spend nine months as a research student in rattan furniture and design.[45] Significantly, many of the students who travelled from Taiwan and Korea to Japan to study were ethnically Japanese. However, the few Taiwanese and Korean graduates of Japanese art and design schools would have a large impact on education in those countries after independence, with Korean graduates of the Women's Academy of Fine Arts staffing universities like Ewha Women's University and Seoul National University post-independence.

Colonial governments promoted advertising design from the 1920s onwards, possibly to further both economic development and cultural and political assimilation. After 1920, colonial governments in Korea and Taiwan abandoned military coercion in favour of an assimilationist 'cultural' regime, which sought to reposition Korea and Taiwan as extensions of Japan and Koreans and Taiwanese as colonial subjects. Under this regime, Koreans and Taiwanese could participate in what some critical historians have described as 'colonial modernity': an extension of Japanese systems and economic and cultural developments, which included urban pleasures – and economic transactions – such as shopping, cinema and cafés, but within a framework of control and discrimination that was intolerant of any overt resistance or calls for independence.[46] Colonial Taiwan and Korea therefore also saw advertising being used to promote commercial activity, as described in Chapter Two: newspapers and advertising agencies sponsored poster exhibitions, advertising competitions and publishing on commercial art. The Taipei Industrial Association launched a window display competition in 1925. Writers and artists in Seoul shared ideas from Japanese publications on commercial art.[47]

In practice, firms used advertising to attract consumers, as in mainland Japan. The many trade and export promotional events and

Postcard for Café Mon Paris, Taipei, c. 1930, published by Katsuyama Photo Studio 3-Chome, Kyomachi, Taipeh [sic], depicting the café's exterior with neon lighting, including neon advertisements for Hakutsuru sake and Kirin beer, on the top left, and waitresses and a bartender in the lavishly furnished first-floor counter in the lower right.

exhibitions organized by colonial administrations also required logos, posters, exhibition displays and other visual communication work. But discriminatory systems and culture ensured that access to prominent projects – for design and printing alike – was effectively limited to Japanese men. Indeed, colonial authorities did not enable the economic and commercial structural changes that had supported the emergence of design as a viable profession in Japan.[48] In Japan, young Japanese men could join the design departments of consumer goods manufacturers, department stores or advertising firms like Dentsu and Hakuhodo, while the expansion of design education and polytechnics after 1920 ensured demand for design teachers around the country as well. In Korea, however, the colonial administration placed structural limits on economic development, ensuring that local Korean companies did not have the consumer base or capital to form similar units and staff them with Koreans. Commercial demand for design was therefore largely monopolized by Japanese firms, either from headquarters in Japan or by Japanese employees sent to Korea. In Taiwan, too, commercial design work for the government-general and for larger Japanese firms seems to have been dominated by settler colonial Japanese.[49] This was the case into the 1930s, and in Manchuria as well.

The Visual Communication of Empire

Among the many arresting images produced for the South Manchuria Railway Company's advertising campaigns in the 1920s and '30s, the stylized illustration of an elite Manchurian woman in an elaborate beaded headdress, her richly embroidered collar with the imperial dragon motif just visible at the base of the image, stands out both for its graphical complexity and, at first, for sheer surprise. The image is the work of Itō Junzō (1890–1939), an artist and illustrator responsible for many tourist posters for the South Manchuria Railway Company (SMRC, or Mantetsu) in the 1920s and '30s.[50] Itō studied at the Tokyo School of Fine Arts, then joined the design division of Mitsukoshi in 1916. He left this position in 1923 to travel to Manchuria and worked from 1925 onwards as a contracted artist for Mantetsu.[51] In its rich decoration and depiction of a beautiful woman, the image resides within the lineage of beautiful women posters such as the Mitsukoshi posters discussed in the previous chapter, which itself continued the earlier Tokugawa period tradition of *bijinga* woodblock prints. Itō's student work at the Tokyo School of Fine Arts had included painting in the style of Hashiguchi Goyō's beautiful women.[52] In this image, Itō used the convention to create a distinctly cosmopolitan image: the woman's headdress suggests the court dress of the local Manchu dynasty, while her lightly glowing complexion, thickly lashed eyes and rosebud lips captured contemporary ideals of beauty and health.[53] The highly stylized hand-drawn lettering in English and Japanese also attests to the railway company's international ambitions, as does the abstracted style of the depiction: the woman is rendered in neat, small circles of colour. While the poster was printed in Manchuria, it was designed by a Japanese artist for a Japanese corporation, at a time when Manchuria – as well as Taiwan and Korea – lay under Japanese control.

The poster, designed to entice Japanese tourists to Manchuria, indicates design's importance for Japan's strategy of imperial expansion. From the 1900s, steamship companies employed *bijinga* posters and other eye-catching graphics as well as maps to advertise their routes between Japan and the continent, directly supporting Japanese presence and expansion in the region.[54] State agencies and powerful state-connected corporations like Mantetsu employed graphic design to recast Japan's uninvited and forcible expansion as ordinary, even inevitable, and as bringing newfound prosperity and modern infrastructure to its occupied neighbours. Style was important here. This section explores how the modernist aesthetics that designers and commissioners employed in product and transport design, in graphics, ultimately presented Japan as a world power and modern nation. As in Japan, modernist aesthetics accompanied the discourses of rationalization and industrialization, which state agencies, corporations and the military deployed to justify their actions. Conversely, commissions allowed designers to experiment with novel styles.

From the 1930s, design played a newly important role in Japanese expansion and its justification to an international as well as a domestic audience. In 1932, factional struggle in the Japanese government allowed the Kwantung Army, Japan's military force in Manchuria, to create a new 'nation' in the region and install a puppet Chinese leader as its emperor.[55] In theory, 'Manchukuo' was to be a cosmopolitan, multi-racial and independent nation; in reality it was a puppet regime that allowed Japanese interests to exploit Manchuria's rich mining and agricultural resources. Materials like coal and soybeans, processed into fuel, chemicals and agricultural fertilizer, could help increase the volume and revenue of food and exports, which was critical given the combined impact of the Great Depression and increased military expenditure. Some members of the Japanese government, concerned the archipelago would not have enough resources for Japan's growing population, also promoted Manchuria as a destination for emigrants.

Regional administration remained the purview of the South Manchuria Railway Company, a semi-public corporation established in 1911.[56] Mantetsu's engineers built railroads and bridges to facilitate sending Manchuria's natural resources to the Japanese archipelago; its bureaucrats were effectively responsible for the region's infrastructure and economy, as well as for aspects such as health and education. By 1945, Mantetsu owned and invested in over seventy companies, across transport (rails, shipping and airline), industry (steel, chemicals, oil, cement, textiles, sugar), commerce, construction, lumber, minerals (coal and gold), electric and gas power, real estate, telecommunications and the press, and hotel chains.

For social scientists, planners and architects associated with Mantetsu, Manchuria provided the mental space and physical location for a modernist experiment: to implement and test ideals for ideal cities and infrastructure which, should they prove successful, could then be introduced in Japan proper.[57] Urban plans for 48 Manchurian

SOUTH MANCHURIA RAILWAY CO.
南満洲鐵道株式會社

JUNJO ITO

Swimming pool for use by employees of the South Manchuria Railway Company and their families, Changchun, 1929.

cities continued the urban planning experiments carried out in Korea and Taiwan from the 1910s on a massive scale, materializing the argument that colonialism provided modern hygiene, efficient living and attractive spaces and providing a test bed for Mantetsu's architects, planners and social scientists.[58] The 1932–7 Five Year Plan to build a new capital, Shinkyō (Xinjing), on the existing city of Changchun consisted of grand, often tree-lined boulevards radiating from a grand plaza in front of the central train station, together with a level of physical infrastructure – electricity, running water, a sewer system, gas lines, telephone and telegraph lines, paved roads and a green belt – unseen in mainland Japan, as well as designated zones for residential, industrial and commercial uses. Through PR campaigns emphasizing that it was Japanese intervention that had created this new world, the urban plan underpinned Japanese justifications for expansion into the Asian continent, even as many of Manchuria's other residents experienced its 'modernity' primarily through systems of bureaucratic control and military force.[59]

Transport design formed part of the presentation strategy, too.[60] The Ajia-gō (Asia Express), built by Kawasaki Heavy Industries, was Mantetsu's flagship train. Launched in 1934, it swept passengers and post from Dairen to Shinkyō in eight and a half hours, at a top speed of 130 kilometres per hour.[61] The 30-metre-long steam locomotive's visual references to French and American streamlining and the rounded curves of the glassed-in panoramic viewing car embodied a message

Itō Junzō, poster for the South Manchurian Railway Company, c. 1937.

Coffee Sets and Militarism

153

大連中央大廣場

大廣場は文字通り面積一萬八百餘坪にて十餘の大道路が四方に放射し廣場內にはホテル市役所警察署等すべての樞要機關は此の一圍ドー然つて居る

（左）大連神社　（右）大連市廳

旅順要塞司令部許可　昭和十年五月二十八日　　　　　　　　　　　　　　　　　　　（4）

of everyday luxury amid speed. Styling and technology offered a double-barrelled message of progress under distinctly East Asian ownership: the locomotive's lettering was rendered by hand in antique calligraphic, spelled in Japanese *hiragana* phonetic script. Knowing that few would actually board the train, but recognizing the power of visual imagery, Mantetsu and the recently formed Japan National Tourist Board publicized the Asia Express by facilitating its appearance in model train kits, photographic postcards, tourist pamphlets, postal stamps, magazine editorial spreads, documentary films, stories in children's magazines and a primary school textbook.[62] Editors, designers, photographers and film-makers conveyed a message equating technological advancement and 'modern life' with political validity. They did so through visual iconography and avant-garde graphical styles and techniques such as photomontage, which contrasted modern Japanese-led Manchuria to 'old' China and suggested that the latter

Photographs of the central square, city hall and Shinto shrine in Dairen, c. 1935–7, published in a 1937 photo album of cities in the Japanese empire. The album employed the Meiji period convention of photographic albums of significant places, itself a development of the Tokugawa period publishing format of *meisho zue*, pictures of famous places, thus visually incorporating colonized lands into an expanded image of 'Japan'.

Designing Modern Japan

required Japan's modernizing attention.[63] The message was largely constant, whether aimed at a local, Japanese or international audience: Japanese leadership would bring modernization, speed and efficiency to the plains of northeast China. Military organization and resources would power progress with brute strength and drive. As historians have emphasized, tourism and visual modernity overlaid colonial exploitation of local labour and natural resources alike.

One rationale for military expansion into Manchuria was to boost Japan's economy by gaining access to coal, soy and other primary resources and so reduce poverty in the archipelago. But the political consequences of military aggression and the disregard of Chinese sovereignty made it more difficult to export commodities outside the empire. Exports to Taiwan, Korea and Manchuria jumped in the early 1930s, as did imports to Japan. However, Chinese and international outcry against Japan's territorial aggression in China after the Manchurian Incident of 1931 led to Japan's withdrawal from the League of Nations in 1933, triggering European and American support for

This photograph of the Ajia-gō printed in the same 1937 album emphasizes the train's speed and dynamism through the diagonal composition and cropping.

満洲旅行の栞

大連新京間快速八時間半、流線型特急「あじあ」の空氣調整裝置は旅を快適にする

南満洲鉄道株式会社

China as the war between China and Japan intensified. Despite these challenges, Japanese exporters managed to increase export income to the rest of the world impressively, rising 82 per cent in 1934 alone and doubling between 1930 and 1936, largely through increased exports of textiles.[64] But growing and maintaining export income required effort, particularly as American resistance to Japanese textile imports grew.[65] The designers and technical researchers at the IARI, with their remit to help crafts industries strengthen product exports, were among those concerned.[66] One response, mooted in the *Boeki shūhō* (Weekly Export News) and reprinted in *Kōgei nyūsu* (Industrial Art News), suggested that Japanese manufacturers and exporters promote their products as 'Manchurian':

> Since last autumn's incident, the name 'Manchuria' has swiftly become famous. Today there is not one American who has not heard of it. Thus products referring to Manchuria that are made and aimed at Americans will definitely succeed. It could be Manchurian crape, Manchurian silk or Manchurian stone; the point is to add novelty and rarity by sticking the adjective 'Manchurian' on cheap, practical Japanese products aimed at Americans.[67]

In practice, silk and cotton were two of Japan's most mechanized, large-scale industries, a far cry from the industrial crafts targeted by IARI researchers, and most manufactured product exports from Manchuria, like those from Korea and Taiwan, went to mainland Japan. Such proposals show how the rationale of regional economic development and national income through the repopularization and branding of industrial crafts exports from Japanese manufacturing regions, as explored in the first two chapters, flowed into the vision of imperial Japan as well.

The image of Manchuria was only part of a larger story: the image of the Japanese empire, archipelago and colonies alike, was an export product, with both political and economic goals. From 1934, publications like the pictorial magazine NIPPON, produced by the graphics office Nippon Kōbō (Japan Workshop), offered foreign and Japanese readers alike a select introduction to 'Japan' through images of speeding trains, exercising girls, flowering trees and austere interiors, which were by then much loved by European and American modernist

The front cover of this 1935 guidebook, *Advice for Travel in Manchuria,* overlays the Ajia-gō over a close-up of ripe wheat, again using diagonal composition and cropping to convey a message of vitality and dynamism.

Coffee Sets and Militarism

architects.[68] NIPPON was created by the German-trained photographer and editor Natori Yōnosuke (1910–1962). Natori's colleagues varied over time but included designers Yamana Ayao and Kōno Takashi, both of whose commercial work we saw in Chapter Two, and photographers Domon Ken (1909–1990), Horino Masao (1907–1998) and Kimura Ihee (Ihei, 1901–1974).[69] The magazine was first published privately, then supported by the Ministry of Foreign Affairs and Kanebō, a major textiles firm; the combination indicates how exporters and the government alike saw promoting a positive image of Japan could help increase export income. By providing a visual counter-story to anti-Japanese publicity, the backers of NIPPON and similar titles hoped that it would, as one backer phrased it banally, 'help the people of foreign countries recognize the true face of Japan'.[70] More specifically, the multilingual NIPPON invited tourism and investment by promoting an image of Japan as a technologically advanced, prosperous nation with the cultural heritage, ethnic specificity and social cohesion of a European nation. An underlying message, of course, was that Japan's modernity and cultural specificity should command international respect for its expansion in East Asia.[71] NIPPON was only one of many periodicals published in the 1930s to attract overseas interest. In 1930, Japan's Railway Board created a new agency, the Foreign Tourism Agency. Between 1930 and 1934, the agency published nearly 1 million copies of 36 different publications as part of its agenda to develop foreign tourism, particularly from the West, in Japan.[72] For graphic designers, illustrators, photographers and printers, all of these projects meant income and the opportunity to experiment with compelling graphic forms. This is important: it is very easy to interpret design created in an overtly political context through a political lens. But in addition to serving as propaganda, the emergence of magazines like NIPPON indicates how funders – in this instance government organizations and large firms invested in exports – increasingly recognized design as a valuable tool, and how graphic designers found work as a result.

As with the commercial magazines and advertisements discussed in Chapter Two, visual language was key to Nippon Kōbō's strategy for shaping the overseas reception of the magazine. NIPPON incorporated a large format, selective colour printing, European modernist techniques such as montage, regularly arrayed roman lettering, asymmetric block layout and large photographs reminiscent of German

Designing Modern Japan

Neue Sachlichkeit style, thereby offering an aesthetic that would be already familiar and legible to European and American audiences – or so the editorial team hoped.[73] Given that it required Western typography, uncommon for domestic publications, NIPPON also presented a significant design challenge, described evocatively by Yamana, the former Shiseido designer:

> What I felt strongly when I was in charge of layout on NIPPON was that the beautiful type of European lettering isn't to be found in Japan . . . I struggled with the layout, but it was the typography that regularly brought me down. For the main stories, I had to draw all the title letters from scratch. I drew them one by one for the inaugural issue; from the second issue onwards, I made a letterpress set from the alphabet that I'd drawn, then printed each letter on tracing paper and pasted it in.[74]

Hand lettering was a regular part of typographic and graphic design work through the 1930s.[75] Yamana's comment also underlines the hybrid hand–machine processes through which designers and printers created their 'machine aesthetic'.

The combination of a modernist graphic and spatial sensibility with culturally specific content also appeared in Japanese displays at 1930s international expositions. The Japanese contribution to the 1938 International Handicraft Exposition in Berlin, for example, displayed beautiful objects from 'traditional Japanese arts' such as martial arts, flower arranging and the tea ceremony against dramatically enlarged images of artisans at work. Natori's photographs for the catalogue for an exhibition of Japanese tools in Leipzig in 1938 were a triumph of *Neue Sachlichkeit* photography, with objects silhouetted silver against a black background, emphasizing geometric shapes composed on a grid.[76] Designers and photographers including Natori, Kimura and Watanabe Yoshio (1907–2000) as well as modernist typographer and educator Hara Hiromu, young designer and Tokyo Higher School of Arts and Crafts graduate Kamekura Yūsaku (1915–1997) and Bauhaus graduate and design educator Yamawaki Iwao (1898–1987), also translated magazine photomontage style into massive, immersive installations.[77] A 5.5-metre-tall photowall for the 1939–40 New York World's Fair towered over visitors.[78] The installation for the Golden Gate International

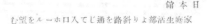
館 本 日
む望をルーホ口入てじ通を路斜りよ部生活庭家

口入のへ部傳宣化文りよ部店商 館本日

Exposition, held in San Francisco also in 1939–40, included a 51-metre-long expanse of panels 3.6 metres tall.[79]

Such work was part and parcel of the immersive, experiential displays that characterized national and corporate pavilion design in mid-twentieth-century international expositions, including the 1939 New York World's Fair. Similarly, Japan was only one of many nations to produce lushly illustrated photomagazines extolling national progress; we might think of the Soviet magazine *USSR in Construction* and the French magazine *VU* – both touchpoints for Japanese designers' work in the period – for reference here.[80] However, the Japanese pavilion interiors and publications are significant. They demonstrate not only the extent to which Japanese designers incorporated modernism's visual language and range of uses but how, in the 1930s, graphic designers and photographers in Japan moved fluidly between commercial and political work.[81] Indeed, as we will see, most of the designers named here intensified their war effort work until 1945, then enjoyed illustrious post-war careers in commercial design.

Views of the entrance hall and from the shop into the cultural publicity and propaganda section of the Japanese Pavilion at the International Exposition of Art and Technology in Modern Life in Paris, 1937. This photograph, included in the official report of the pavilion organizing committee, provides an unusually clear image of how modernist exhibition techniques – in this instance a photowall with images of modernist Japanese architecture – and industrial crafts prototypes coexisted in national promotional spaces.

Designing Modern Japan

The products presented in the IARI's 1946 book were for export, but many of them – from coffee pots to cigarette cases – would not have seemed out of place in a café, home or office across Japan. For urban Japanese, the 1930s brought yet more material pleasures, with three subway lines running in Tokyo by 1939 and 37,065 bars and cafés nation-wide in 1935.[82] While Korea remained largely rural – with 93 per cent of its population living in the countryside in 1935 – cities in colonial Korea, Taiwan and Manchuria gained department stores, cafés and cinemas, with specific neighbourhoods for locally owned and Japanese-owned businesses. Decorative shop windows, signage and advertising sprang up around cities like Taipei and Seoul. At a time when travel guides often presented modern shopping areas as tourist destinations in their own right, they were often described in Japanese-language travel guides to Taipei and Seoul in the same tone used to describe advertising in regional cities in mainland Japan. Also similar to main-land Japan, colonial governments and local business associations began promoting commercial art as a sales strategy. In 1930s Korea, commer-cial schools and newspapers promoted commercial art to male students, mirroring educational practices, styles and structures – classroom teaching, textbooks and competitions – practised in Japan, but in the context of commercial education, not design.[83] A commercial art exhi-bition shown in five cities around Taiwan in 1932 displayed all sorts of print publicity, shop windows, outdoor signs, 'electrical advertising' (neon signs) and reference materials, including statistics.[84] The aim of the exhibition was specifically to stimulate awareness of the usefulness and techniques of commercial design and advertising for advertising firms, merchants and the general public. Large trade and export pro-motional events and exhibitions required graphics – logos, adverts, communication boards – visual pictorial displays and so on. Organizers predominantly contracted Japanese designers trained in Japan for this work.[85]

Underneath the growth in commercial activity lay booming light and heavy industry production and exports in mainland Japan, as well as a new promotion of heavy industry, particularly, in Taiwan and Korea.[86] This was partly to fund the deficit and military expenditures after the Manchurian Incident in 1931. In mainland Japan, broadening consumer bases meant increased work for makers and designers across

週刊朝日

一月二十六日號

定價十三錢

特輯
聲樂の覇王シャリアピン

The Xīnshèngqiáo Tōng shopping street in Taichung, Taiwan, built in 1926 and also known as Suzuran-dōri (Lily of the Valley Street), resulted from Japanese colonial redevelopment of the existing urban fabric. It was lined with Japanese shops, restaurants, inns and other establishments catering to Japanese residents.

Cover of *Shūkan Asahi* (The Asahi Weekly), 26 January 1936. In the 1930s, popular weekly magazines disseminated an image of bright everyday modernity through cover images like this one, with its tubular steel and velvet armchair, palm plant, tiled walls and the chic attire of the actress photographed.

genres, from rattan furniture and ladies' hats to children's magazines, bicycles and lamps. The national expansion of technical school design and woodworking departments provided greater opportunities for professional training and employment.

Rural communities remained less able to enjoy the material fruits of industrialization and economic development.[87] Japanese agricultural households found themselves hit with crashing commodities prices in the Great Depression due to lowered demand for Japanese silk in the United States and lower rice prices in Japan. Several years of poor crop yields followed. By 1931, the average rural household income had fallen by two-thirds from 1925 levels, tipping many rural families into hunger.[88] One national government response was a new Rural Economic Rehabilitation Campaign (Nōson Keizai Kōsei Undō), which prompted village members to self-organize into committees in order to recommend specific rationalization plans for each village.[89] Another was to encourage mass emigration of poor rural households – and whole villages, in some cases – to Manchuria as agricultural settlers.[90]

The widely publicized suffering of rural areas returned the attention of some design researchers to the material conditions and social customs of village life. The Economic Rehabilitation Campaign offered them a vehicle through which to do so. In 1933, officials in the Ministry of Home Affairs and the Ministry of Agriculture co-founded the Research Institute for the Economy of Rural Villages in Snow Regions

(Setsugai Chōsajo) in Shinjō, a remote town in mountainous Yamagata prefecture in northern Japan. Activities included a competition for experimental improved housing, resulting in a project led by Tokyo architect Kon Wajirō (1888–1973) that incorporated suggestions for the rationalization of housework and reduction of spending that had been recommended by the Daily Life Improvement League a decade earlier.[91] In 1937, the institute's director asked *mingei* movement founder Yanagi Muneyoshi (Sōetsu) to become involved.[92] With Yanagi's advising, the institute began to commercialize the bamboo, straw and wood products that farming households made indoors as supplemental income during the winter months. Yanagi's son, the industrial designer Yanagi Sōri (1915–2011), was then serving as guide for the French designer Charlotte Perriand (1903–1999), who was in Japan by invitation of the IARI. In 1940, Perriand visited the institute in Shinjō.[93] Famously, her encounter there with a woven straw raincoat would inspire a bamboo version of her well-known chaise longue, which was exhibited in the exhibition *Sentaku dentō sōzō* (Selection, Tradition, Creation) at the Takashimaya department stores in Tokyo and Osaka in 1943.[94] Her work prompted criticism from Japanese designers at the IARI, however, some of whom found it patronizing.[95]

The IARI researchers were based in Sendai, the principal city in northeastern Japan. They researched new lacquerware, metalwork and carpentry techniques and designs for workshops in specialist light industrial areas. They also widened their experiments to include prototypes for products made for everyday use in farm households in the north, collaborating with the Shinjō institute, in yet another convergence of economic development through exports, modernist design and interest in rural 'folk' materials and methods.

Rural crisis was accompanied by political polarization and protest, as well as sharp escalations in militarism. By 1937, the Japanese military occupied China as far south as Shanghai. Military action and mass mobilization further intensified from 1938 onwards. Japanese leaders found they could use Chinese and Western resistance to Japanese expansionism to generate nationalistic public support at home, but empire cost money: even in 1937, the astonishing sum of 75 per cent of government spending went towards the military.[96] Empire appeared in the visual and material culture of everyday life: stories in pictorial magazines, the map of imperial Japan found in school classrooms and souvenirs, alongside the absence of friends and family members

Kageyama Kōyō, *One Poor Family – The Severe Bad Harvest in Tohoku*, 9 December 1934, gelatin silver print, 32.7 x 23.8 cm, Japan. Photojournalism by photographers like Kageyama, dispatched to Tohoku by the Asahi newspaper company, was a powerful medium for documenting rural conditions and communicating the crisis to the urban Japanese. The textiles worn show how poor rural households continued to wear cotton weaves, not the *meisen* silks increasingly purchased for kimono by urban working-class women. The baskets are the type of product the Shinjō institute, Perriand and others saw as potential rural crafts for the urban market.

bound for Korea, Taiwan and China as colonists, tourists and – after 1937, especially – soldiers.

Given the economic and political instability, cabinet ministers felt the need for new efforts to create and maintain popular acquiescence with an increasingly nationalist agenda. One result was a number of new policies affecting production and consumption, both directly and indirectly. A National Spiritual Mobilization Movement, launched in 1937, built on earlier campaigns to promote ideological cohesion and the reorganization of Japan's population and industry under the august will of the emperor by co-opting neighbourhood groups, industry associations and other grassroots organizations. The National General Mobilization Law of 1938 reiterated the formation of community and industry groups to align the Japanese public with the government's aims. In an unprecedented step, it also authorized the government to take all measures deemed appropriate to 'control material and human resources' in times of national emergency.[97]

The new policies affected designers, manufacturers and consumers alike. Some immediate effects were superficial. In August 1938, for example, the Industrial Arts Guidance Division of the Osaka Prefectural Industrial Promotion Hall created new guidelines for Osaka's light manufacturers, which incorporated the moral tone of the Spiritual Mobilization Campaign. These included exhortations to exercise 'thrift in the use of various materials' and 'regarding design, to remove playful elements and create products for the purpose of cultivating national spirit'.[98] The ideological campaigns were accompanied by rationing and restrictions. No surprise, then, that the Osaka guidelines also included: 'Take advantage of traditional hand-based industries,' that is, industries that would require less machinery thus avoiding restrictions on metal; and 'Research the manufacture of crafts products employing alternate materials and/or waste materials.' Colonialism had not, in fact, provided Japan with all of the raw materials necessary for producing the armaments and fuel required for a modern military, let alone light manufacturing. From autumn 1938, restrictions appeared on the use of strategic materials such as iron, tin, copper, leather and rubber. Exceptions were allowed only for military contracts or exports, necessary to gain foreign capital. Manufacturers of products as varied as ladies' hats, tea trays, neon signs, elevators and megaphones – all specifically named in the ban – had in effect four options: switch to

Designing Modern Japan

export or military products, substitute materials, obtain an exemption from local authorities or close.[99]

Some chose the military option. The Tsubame metalworking district in Niigata prefecture, known for export tableware, rejigged its metal stamping machines to produce metal parts for aircraft, small knives and helmets.[100] As dwindling metal supplies forced the military to look to alternate materials, Maruni Mokkō, a manufacturer of Western-style wooden furniture in Hiroshima prefecture, used personal connections and existing technical skills to gain contracts for wooden torpedo casings, fuel tanks and aeroplane wings.[101] The shift to military production cut across civilian and public design and manufacturing alike: experimental furniture designers at the IARI were reassigned to a Ministry of Munitions wooden aeroplane project, bringing their knowledge of plywood, which they had gained through research into modernist mass-produced furniture, to the mass production of planes.[102]

Some producers explored novel uses of other indigenous materials as a way to turn metal shortages into commercial opportunity, both for consumer and military markets. The Toyama Prefecture Paper Research Institute experimented with mulberry paper to replace the leather binding in books and photograph albums. The Shizuoka Prefecture Marine Products Division used shark and sea snake skins as a substitute material for leather bags and shoes.[103] Some Shizuoka manufacturing associations and private firms experimented with military applications for lacquer, while others reworked bamboo hats for rickshaw drivers into helmets or incorporated birch bark into the insoles for tropical infantry boots.[104]

Another strategy was to frame products as exports, thus bypassing restrictions on manufacturing for domestic consumption. Here, manufacturers had strong support from the various organizations that promoted light industry at national and local level. In September 1938, the same month as national general mobilization was announced, Kunii Kitarō, head of the IARI, articulated the institute's position:

> In the current situation it is entirely understandable that there are reasons why industrial arts could be considered leisure objects, neither urgent nor necessary. Of course, for export products, this only behoves us further to proudly display the decorative arts techniques that are the pride of

our nation, and to demonstrate their outstandingly cultured and artistic nature.[105]

In 1939, the MCI-sponsored annual salon for artistic crafts, Nōten, merged with the Export Crafts Exhibition, another MCI event launched in 1933. Product export promotion intensified into the early 1940s with a focus on potentially sympathetic markets such as Central and South America, even as stocks of materials, fuel and sympathetic overseas markets dwindled.[106] In the 1870s and '80s, the MCI's predecessor had promoted light industrial crafts exports as a way to fund the purchase of the machinery and materials necessary to establish heavy industry. From the late 1930s onwards, design and crafts industry research institutes suggested that exports of consumer products such as shoes, tableware and lamps could help purchase the raw materials and fuel for armaments – and keep their makers in business. Thus Kunii exhorted:

> Today our great and pressing need for munitions requires that we step up our promotion of exports. Japan can either dig out money from itself or take money from foreign countries. To earn money from foreign countries, it is reasonable to assume that products whose materials and production costs will earn us a good profit will be the best strategy.[107]

This strategy also extended to Taiwan and Korea. In Taiwan, Japanese craft advocates and local economic boosters alike thought folk-craft might serve this purpose.[108] In Korea, the Ministry of Commerce and Industry encouraged woodworking and lacquerware workshops to develop hairbrushes, compacts, handbags, walking sticks, napkin rings and other products deemed to be 'already appropriate for foreigners' daily life'.[109] Manufacturers of horsehair products were to explore the American market for ladies' hats.

The rebranding of consumer goods as exports also explains why bureaucrats continued to publish information about European and American design trends, despite increasingly emphatic campaigns against luxurious spending at home. It was not unusual, for example, for *Industrial Art News* in 1938 to print an article on the popularity of American 'colonial' and Swedish modern furniture at the Chicago Merchandise Mart – a prime indicator of forthcoming American

Designing Modern Japan

consumer taste – alongside an article on gold rationing for the war effort.[110] Indeed, more effective exports required better market research. As Kunii elaborated:

> Presently, the design of our nation's products is generally unpopular overseas. State design engineers must feel a great calling here. We must avoid imitation and work from an independent and original position that is Japanese, nay Oriental. I am not suggesting that we ignore research into foreign lifestyles. Rather, the more concerted the research, the more desirable fundamental knowledge will we gain.[111]

The IARI's invitations to the German designer Tilly Prill-Schloemann (b. 1902) in 1939 and Charlotte Perriand in 1940 were precisely for this purpose.[112] So was an annual meeting of local and national research institute designers in Tokyo to create books of export product designs, harking back to the Meiji period yet again.[113] Given this logic, not only did export products from urban manufacturers and rural workshops alike assume a new significance, but product designers could contribute to the war effort simply by designing attractive products. As for the graphic designers and photographers responsible for NIPPON, the onset of war reclassified designers' and makers' work as patriotic activity.

The Ministry of Commerce and Industry encouraged exports but not domestic consumption. The MCI established strict price controls for consumer as well as wholesale products, beginning in September 1940. These '9.18' controls, known by the month and date they were launched, implemented minute classification systems for all possible consumer products. The category for leather bags included 598 different products divided into sixteen subcategorics, based on an initial division between travelling bags – to be priced at 50 yen and below – and briefcases, to be priced at 20 yen or less.[114] The regulations also stipulated product 'simplification': new standardized product types, accompanied by a requirement that manufacturers conform to specifications.[115]

Rather than protest industry regulation, manufacturers' groups incorporated the guidelines into their marketing strategies. Representatives from the fashion and housewares departments of major Tokyo, Nagoya and Osaka department stores, for example, formed the New Lifestyle Research Group (Shin Seikatsu Yōshiki Kenkyūkai)

to develop commercial products appropriate for wartime life. They came up with clothing and footwear that ranged from 'reform aprons', which abstained from frills and bright decoration, to school shoes, which replaced leather uppers with cotton weave and rubber soles with indigenous oak. Ingeniously, both upheld the government regulations and created new products for purchase.[116] The group also reworked existing marketing strategies: for example, to the standard 'objects for new households' category aimed at brides and their families, it created a new category of products for newlywed apartment-dwellers, comprising 83 essential items rather than the 120 items they had identified for an ordinary new household.

Adopting the MCI's language of control and categorization allowed department stores to continue with existing retail strategies, even as the war intensified around them.[117] Advertisers even used a subsequent anti-luxury campaign, launched in July 1940 and known as the '7.7 ban', piggybacking on the call to patriotic austerity in order to publicize

Samples of synthetic or silk fabric in brightly coloured mechanically dyed patterns, some of *shibori* or mock-*shibori* (tie-dyeing), exhibited at a trade fair in April 1941, mounted on heavy card and bound into a book, *Dai gojūnikai Natsu no shinbiten shippin zuroku* (Catalogue of Submissions to the 52nd Annual Summer Shinbi Exhibition, 1941).

Designing Modern Japan

These advertisements for Tōa (Greater East Asia) Inkstands and Stout pills, published in *Asahi Aircraft* in February 1944, added the language and imagery of war to their catch copy and 'katto', or illustrations. The name of the inkstands is mirrored by a map of Southeast Asia. Catch copy for the pills suggests they are 'Nutritional supplements for victory!', accompanied by an illustration of a fighter plane.

their brand. *Meisen* silk districts, for example, began to promote their kimono cloth as 'new national clothing' with the support of the MCI, department stores and textiles merchants.[118] There were fundamental contradictions to this strategy and reception was mixed: one reviewer of 'patriotic' textile designs exhibited in Osaka in 1940 rebuked manufacturers for using the controls to offload patterns and colour schemes that were 'ten, even fifteen years out of date'. For this commentator, at least, the most important thing about fashion was not to conserve materials but to keep in style.[119] We might expect that state attempts to curb consumption would also limit the extent to which graphic designers in corporate advertising departments could overtly publicize products, too; in reality, however, many manufacturers continued to advertise, incorporating patriotic images and slogans alongside their logo.

Actions like the 9.18 controls and 7.7 ban have been understood by design historians as building on the everyday life improvement movement of the 1920s.[120] Economic and political historians of modern Japan, for their part, have emphasized how total war transformed the goals, logic and scale of such initiatives, allowing bureaucrats to realize things that had previously been an aspirational gleam in their eye. In the case of actions and rhetoric produced by designers working for and with the state, the goal of rationalization shifted from moral and economic benefits for individual households and villages to patriotism and thrift for the national war effort. The rhetoric was sometimes near-identical: the 'Rules for Wartime Living' presented at the second Exhibition of Articles for the Daily Life of the People (Kokumin seikatsu yōhinten) in 1943, sponsored by the MCI, included: 'Make the effort to organize, put things away and clean,' 'Own only a few useful pieces of furniture, and place them in the correct location' and 'Fully use space ordinarily set aside for entertainment.'[121] A sentence like 'The dining room is also the living room; it is the pleasant, warm room of the family circle' repeated the lifestyle reform tenets of the

1920s and the Rural Economic Rehabilitation Campaign rhetoric of the 1930s.

At the same time, however, things had intensified. Practical admonitions about thrift had been part of Tokugawa period morality, not least through sumptuary laws. Messages to subordinate the household to the nation had been part of Meiji period education and intensified around the Russo-Japanese War of 1904–5. Now, the first rule listed in the 1943 exhibition insisted that the Japanese public 'pray correctly to the Shintō and Buddhist home altars'. As expressed by designers, the state was asking the Japanese public to identify with what was phrased the 'spiritual' element of war: not only out of sympathy for the soldiers, but as combatants themselves on the moral home front of what propagandists increasingly termed a 'sacred' war. One editorial in *Industrial Art News* explained the extension of military discipline into the home:

> The original demand for standardization appeared most strongly in the daily life of the military, because this everyday life requires maximum functionality and effect from minimum resources and effort. Today, in terms of austerity, and given the seriousness of [conditions], the daily life of ordinary citizens is almost no different from that of soldiers. Our nation's daily life under the regime for decisive victory must go this far. Maximum function and effect from minimum resources and effort, this is the sacred responsibility the nation demands of each individual.[122]

But, like daily life rationalization two decades earlier, the rhetoric of spiritual mobilization and alignment with the war effort was often only that: rhetoric layered over daily life and production practices that in reality were shaped as much if not more by material, economic and social conditions. The 1943 Exhibition of Articles for the Daily Life of the People – launched at Mitsukoshi's flagship store in Tokyo in April 1943, then toured to cities around Japan – indicates this well. With its steamed wood lunchboxes, wooden

This illustration for 'An artistic toy shelf and box that an amateur can make', published in *Simple Furniture and Built-In Furniture That Can Be Made at Home* (1942), accompanied dreamy, poetic text listing the different kinds of toys a mother might stow away after her children played with them during the day. DIY promotion to housewives continued at the height of wartime.

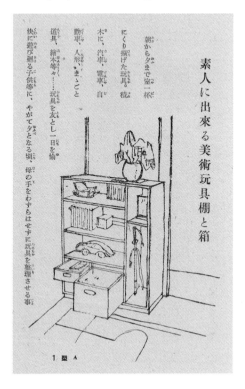

素人に出來る美術玩具棚と箱

朝から夕まで室に積む

にくり擴げた玩具。

木に、汽車・電車・自

動車、人形・まゝごと

道具、鈴木等々……玩具を友とし一日を愉

快に遊び廻る子供等に、やがて夕となる頃、母の手をわずらはせずに玩具を整理させる事

1 圖 A

Designing Modern Japan

toys, lacquer bowls, office desks and chairs and a model house filled to the brim with everyday implements, the exhibition was meant to show how standardized, well-designed products offered maximum use for minimum resources. Its plain stands and large, graphically clean explanatory panels had a modernist clarity, making the same point. But what the objects on display seemed to suggest was that patriotic life was ordinary life for most Japanese, or perhaps that exhibitors saw little functional difference between this exhibition and ordinary sales fairs.[123] In practice, though, by 1943 shortages and rationing limited what even middle-class urban households could acquire.

Attempts at standardization extended to civilian dress as well, with similar effect. Reform efforts in the 1920s had focused on simplifying women's dress to reduce expenditures and increase functionality. By contrast, the 1939 recommendations of the Great Japan Peoples' Clothing Association, an industry organization composed of representatives from textiles companies and government agencies, aimed at convincing men to adopt a civilian uniform. Known as 'national citizens' clothing' (kokuminfuku) and publicized through a national competition, the association's proposal comprised simply-cut and styled military-style suits for everyday wear, a rudimentary business suit for office workers, shoes, boots and military-derived hats, all in 'national defence colour' (kokubōshoku), meaning khaki. A competition for prosaically named women's 'standardized clothing' (hyōjunfuku) followed in 1942. The winning entries took the form of simple, V-neck, below-the-knee dresses, wrapped and tied like kimono but with a sash of the same material rather than a decorative obi. Their proportions combined kimono cutting with Western dress styling, draping over the hips and offering slightly puffed then narrowing sleeves. While some men did adopt the uniform, the women's version remained largely a prototype. The changes women did adopt were either additions to existing dress or changes required by new environments. Some women wore a patriotic white apron over their kimono. As Allied air raids made urban neighbourhoods dangerous, even uninhabitable, after 1944 and households fled to the countryside, women exchanged their kimono for monpe, baggy cotton trousers ordinarily worn by farmwomen working in the fields and disparaged by the urban women who now wore them.[124]

Government attempts to ensure popular participation in the war effort extended to domestic propaganda as well. Unlike some nations

Kids at Isohama   Sept 46

in the Second World War, the Japanese government relied on a loose network of largely voluntary graphic design and publishing groups for its domestic and external propaganda campaigns. Some of these were existing groups.[125] In the early 1930s, Japan boasted more than sixty small commercial art research groups nationwide, many of which organized poster exhibitions at department stores and galleries. With the onset of the Spiritual Mobilization Movement in 1937, these groups, like other industry organizations, shifted their overt activities. From publicizing their own design work and the discipline of 'commercial art', they started promoting a national agenda, but kept fundamental activities largely as they were.[126] The national federation of commercial artists' groups, by 1938 known as the All-Japan Industrial Art Alliance (Zen Nihon Sangyō Bijutsu Renmei), held its first exhibition after the campaign's commencement in the windows of Tokyo's Shirokiya department store, dedicating the exhibition to increasing public knowledge about air raids.[127] Other propaganda groups were new, formed by graphic designers in response to the shifting political climate and

Emery D. Middleton, *Kids at Isohama, Ibaraki, Japan*, September 1946, photograph. Among children wearing Western-style dress, one of the two girls at the centre of the photograph wears *monpe* converted from a woman's *meisen* kimono. *Monpe* wear continued after the war.

Designing Modern Japan

as increasing restrictions on the promotion of domestic consumption rendered untenable their work for department stores, confectioners, cosmetics companies and other consumer products firms.

For some designers, war work offered an income and a way to continue practising their craft. After 1940, some designers were able to continue their corporate employment. Others saw their design and publicity departments disbanded and found work at organizations more obviously aligned with national priorities. After the confectioner Morinaga dissolved its design team, graphic designer Imaizumi Takeji (1905–1995) found contract work with a bank and then, through that job, designing graphic materials for the Air Force.[128] Senior figures in the field like Sugiura Hisui, known for his work as the head of design for the Mitsukoshi department store, took on leadership positions within the groups.[129] As Imaizumi described attitudes towards war work in his milieu, while some designers disagreed with the government, many simply joined in. As he put it:

> At the time, various design groups were formed one after the other, but there was very little debate as to whether it was good or bad to participate in the war. There were a few anti-war groups active underground. [But] the war became everything, and [we] really went racing off, uncritically, in the direction of the national strategy. Without realizing it we'd become part of the flow of the war. It wasn't even as though working commercial designers got caught up in war propaganda, there were lots of designers who were determined not to miss the bus.[130]

For designers, new groups like the Society for the Study of Media Technology (Hōdō Gijutsu Kenkyūkai, founded in 1940) and the Propaganda Art Association (Hōdō Bijutsu Kyōkai), founded in 1939 as the amalgamation of several alumni groups from the Tokyo Higher School of Arts and Crafts, offered a space for debating and disseminating visual communication promotion techniques. They also gave their members a sense of participating in the war effort.[131] State interest in generating propaganda allowed the groups' research activities around effective visual techniques for sales and persuasion to continue, even to grow. Groups like the Propaganda Art Association delved deeply into propaganda techniques, including social science survey methods such as statistical visualizations, and continued to survey and introduce foreign examples of effective practice, including film as well as print, posters, packaging and point-of-purchase (POP) displays. Imaizumi wrote of his propaganda work:

> Of course we referred to overseas publicity and graphic magazines; our greatest influence was the German ones. We could get *Signal*, *Der Adler* and also magazines such as the Soviet USSR *in Construction* and France's *VU* from [Tokyo foreign bookseller] Maruzen. At that time, the montage theory of people like Eisenstein and Béla Balázs, close-up theory and cutaways were all the rage in the film world. We studied them and considered at length whether we could incorporate these film techniques into graphical compositions.[132]

Miyayama Takashi, editor of the magazine *Kōkokukai* (Advertising World) after 1935, also continued to publish articles on effective advertising techniques, from the graphic design of print advertisements to window displays and exhibitions. Like the research groups, the magazine shifted its tone. The editorial content emphasized psychological persuasion as well as effective advertising and shop design techniques, framing technical advice as useful for improving propaganda, in the service of the nation.[133] Gravures of men at work or practising *kendō* replaced those of beautiful women on the covers. Back covers featured patriotic exhortations rather than reproductions of Western fashion plates. The magazine's new direction was also evident in its English title, which changed over the course of the 1930s from *Advertising World* to *Advertising Art Monthly*, then to *Industrial Art and Propaganda*.

The designers and advertising theorists active in the groups and in *Kōkokukai* understood visual design as a technique for communicating national policy. Theorist Tsukada Isamu described this as 'publicity that controls and unites the contents of the masses' consciousness for the sake of the nation and society, directing it towards the production of high social goals and new creation'.[134] The semantic shift from *senden* (publicity), which could include commercial promotion, to *hōdō*, literally 'information direction', in both the groups' naming and the language of their projects, emphasized their focus on political or moral steering. Like the shift towards exports by manufacturers of consumer products, it also allowed commercial artists to justify their practice at a time when promoting consumption was anything but patriotic, but retailers and manufacturers still needed income.[135] As Imaizumi explained the relationship between his commercial and political work, 'through my publicity job for [confectioner] Morinaga, I was already thinking about the meaning of publicity as a kind of communication, in my own way.'[136] Seeing design as a pure practice allowed designers to relativize sales and propaganda.

A second significant point, here, is that according to some design-ers' recollections, graphic style was left up to them. In Imaizumi's telling, at least, the government officials who were commissioning the work showed a general apathy towards the visual language or content of propaganda. Designers were to make it up as they saw fit.[137] Given that many employers took a similar stance of trusting or expecting design teams to generate effective advertising, the propaganda commissioning process provided another element of continuity for designers. As with consumer products, the ideological framing had changed, but for many graphic designers practice continued as it had within a commercial context.

IN DECEMBER 1941, JAPAN bombed the American naval base at Pearl Harbor, Hawaii, and invaded Hong Kong, the Philippines, Thailand, Singapore and Malaya in Southeast Asia. This action launched war with the USA, Britain and their allies after months of rising tensions and gave Japan control over 24 million square miles in Asia and the Pacific. The impact on designers was immediate. Some designers were drafted and sent to China or Southeast Asia, as soldiers or in specialist propaganda teams. Graphic designers Kōno Takashi and Ōchi Hiroshi (1908–1974), for example, were assigned to the Propaganda Department (*Senden-bu*) of the military government in Indonesia, with the brief to create pro-Japanese posters, wall newspapers and handbills.[138] Much of their work was lost, at one point, when a ship carrying print materials to Indonesia sank.[139] Those who remained in Japan devoted increasing time to the war effort, developing designs for military materiel and creating propaganda for distribution across the empire.

Overtly military propaganda joined another form of visual com-munication that designers had begun employing in other parts of Asia, as part of Japanese imperial and military expansion. From 1940, a new conceptual framework for Japanese colonial expansion and aggression, the Greater East Asia Co-Prosperity Sphere, combined free trade with political solidarity against Western imperialism as tacit justification of Japan's expansion into Asia internationally. In addition to print media, the campaign used design as a kind of material rhetoric to make its case. Local and municipal trade organizations and museums organized exhibitions of 'Asian cultural sphere crafts products' in Japan alongside Japanese designs for sundry goods that could potentially be exported to Southeast Asia. A June 1942 exhibition at the Takashimaya department store presented Taiwanese products alongside an exhibition of Japanese crafts, and the IARI organized exhibitions of Japanese and local industrial crafts in Beijing, Taipei and other occupied cities.[140] As in the First World War, they hoped to capitalize on the withdrawal of American and European imports from the region.[141]

As part of these activities, Japanese designers travelled in occupied areas, assessing local production. In 1942, IARI designer Koike Shinji (1901–1981) spent eighty days in central and northern China. During his

'Incomparable for the coordination of the organization and the manoeuvre of diverse categories of vessels and arms', double-page spread from *Front*, 1–2 (1942), photomontage, rotogravure (images) and offset (text) printing.

Incomparable par la coordination d'organisme et de manœu-   vre des diverses catégories de bâtiments et d'armes,

Designing Modern Japan

trip he visited cities including Shanghai, Hangzhou, Suzhou, Nanjing and Beijing, meeting with representatives from regional Chinese governments and visiting workshops, as well as liaising with Japanese officials in the East Asia Development Board (Kōain, 1938–42).[142] Koike had been invited by the board as part of their programme to bring technical specialists from Japan to conduct surveys of different aspects of Chinese society – an extension of the practice of collecting data about colonized territories begun in Taiwan after 1900. Koike described his remit, to learn about craft industries in China, as falling under the rubric of 'cultural policy' rather than industry or art, suggesting the rhetoric with which the Japanese government and others sought to prettify the military presence on the continent.[143] *Mingei* and other industrial crafts proponents in mainland Japan also established schools, shops and village 'self-sufficiency' schemes in Beijing, Manchuria and other parts of northern China between 1938 and 1945, extending their vision of improving daily life and developing industrial crafts production to colonized areas.[144]

Visual communication specialists, already working in Japanese military propaganda, also expanded their activities into newly occupied areas. A group of designers and photographers led by former NIPPON editor Natori Yōnosuke, Nippon Kōbō, gained a contract for magazines in several Southeast Asian languages. Some local editions were created by Nippon Kōbō members embedded with the Japanese military in occupied territories. The magazine *Canton* was produced in Guangdong by two members, Kōno Takashi and Fujimoto Shihachi, who borrowed office space from the Japanese army. Wanting to maintain their familiar production values, with high-quality images and offset printing, Kōno and Fujimoto sent dummies off to Japan for printing, before returning to Guangdong for distribution.[145] Other periodicals were designed and published in Tokyo, with translation into local languages by students from other Asian countries who were studying in Tokyo.

Despite shortages of materials, a few designers found their work unusually well resourced. Tōhōsha (the Eastern Way Company) was a semi-covert operation whose employees included NIPPON designer Hara Hiromu as head of the art department and photographer Kimura Ihee as head of photography.[146] Their principal project was to produce *Front*, an overseas propaganda magazine printed in more than a dozen European and Asian languages.[147] One challenge for propaganda photography was the requirement to modify photographs so as not to communicate information to enemies. For the Navy issue of *Front*, for example, art department members were required to airbrush any identifying features of aircraft carriers photographed while doing exercises, in case Americans could guess their tonnage, weaponry, speed and so on from the images.[148] Production conditions could be remarkably luxurious. While the 9.18 controls and 7.7 anti-luxury laws exhorted consumers to eschew creature comforts, *Front* appeared on thick, expensive paper meant for gravure printing.[149] Tōhōsha staff were well equipped with rare imported enlargers, cameras and English watercolour paper for mock-ups, and enjoyed the luxury of time: the all-thematic issues were produced like documentary films, often beginning by contracting out the script to an external film-maker, then taking several months for production.[150] The largesse shown to *Front*'s production team was political. Tōhōsha was under the direct leadership of the Army General Staff and funded by major contributions from the Mitsubishi, Mitsui and Sumitomo combines, all of which had large military contracts. Army divisions were contracted to purchase the magazine.[151] The extent to which government and pro-military bodies valued print propaganda is also suggested by one statistic: 1943 was the most profitable year to date for the nation's largest printers.[152]

In sum, the wartime economy provided support and training for the product and graphic designers, photographers and advertising creatives who would – as we will see in Chapter Four – shape the visual and material world of Japan after the war. Designers would continue to use the comprehensive style, the use of documentary narrative and rhythmical montage of text and image of propaganda magazines postwar in corporate PR publications, and designers and technicians translated knowledge gained in munitions research to manufacturing. All of these emerged from the war effort, which provided time, materials and an environment that encouraged not only experimentation but the very basis of design activity: persuasion, styling and functional improvement. Was designers' war work straightforward 'design for war'? Or did war offer a platform for designers to continue developing their experimental practice alongside designers elsewhere, and for social and industry reformers to continue their crusades? The answer, of course, is 'both of the above', as long as their actions and communication not only sat within the parameters of officially sanctioned stances but disseminated and furthered them.

Designers' identification with the war effort must also be understood as ambiguous, and ambiguity as ordinary, even banal. Publicly dissenting voices became fainter after the launch of the National Spiritual Mobilization Campaign in 1937, and many designers joined the war effort voluntarily, even enthusiastically. We must understand their motivation as complex, however, as some were motivated by a desire for income as well as patriotism. Some younger designers especially believed that they were part of a noble cause and would eventually triumph. More cynical or pragmatic peers chose to enter the design professions or to study design rather than art, to avoid being sent to the front, as unlike art students, design students could be assigned to factory work but were exempt from conscription.[153] By 1944, however, even designers formerly enthused by or unquestioning of the war effort were finding it difficult to continue.[154] Like many Japanese across all walks of life, dire material conditions, as well as the death and destruction that followed Allied bombing raids, increasingly suggested that it was futile to continue fighting, especially when faced with the apparent strength and resources of the U.S. military. Some designers stopped going to the office and left Tokyo, distressed by the destruction around them.[155] Of course, these recollections, written and spoken after the war, also reflect the reframing of memory, unconsciously or selectively, by designers and those around them concerned to present their activities in particular ways. Regardless, the different narratives and explanations that designers provided for their wartime activities evidence the complexity and multiplicity of motivations.

Design under Occupation, 1945–50

In August 1945, Japan capitulated after the atomic bombings of Hiroshima and Nagasaki, ending fifteen years of war. The Allied Occupation, under the direction of the American general Douglas MacArthur as the Supreme Commander for the Allied Powers, set up headquarters known familiarly as SCAP in Tokyo, with military encampments and civilian administration around the Japanese archipelago. Fifteen years of war had left Japan's population exhausted, stocks of food and materials depleted, cities burned and flattened and the death toll high. The housing shortage was only exacerbated by a swelling population as an estimated 6.7 million Japanese, comprising 3.2 million military personnel and 3.2 million civilians, returned from Korea,

Taiwan, Manchuria, Russia and Southeast Asia.[156] A hunt for food overshadowed daily life: urban residents traded kimono and other household treasures for food in the countryside or on the black market.[157] Inflation was rampant. Many households emigrated temporarily to the countryside, where housing had not been destroyed and food was more abundant. Many children had been evacuated from the cities; they too often remained in the countryside instead of returning immediately to their families. An emergency housing replacement policy, established in August 1945 before the war's end, mandated the construction of 100,000 tiny wooden dwellings as a stopgap measure, but housing shortages continued into the 1950s.[158]

The hardships of daily life were mirrored in industry and Japan's larger economy. In 1947, Japan's industrial production stood at only 30 per cent of its pre-war total.[159] Shortages of materials such as steel, coal and rubber were the principal culprit, along with the loss of manufacturing equipment during air raids. Cotton milling spindles, for example, numbered 2 million, compared to a pre-war total of 13 million. In workshop-based luxury industries, materials shortages, the 7.7 luxury prohibitions and repeated mandatory orders to merge small family firms into large community-wide cooperatives hit makers hard. In Kyoto, the Nishijin weavers had switched to military fabric production, using cotton and other available fibres. Regardless, by 1944 only 40 per cent of looms were still in use, even before a bombing raid – one of the few Allied raids on Kyoto – flattened part of the

Emery D. Middleton, *Shack in Hole: Sendai, Japan – April 47*, 1947, photograph. A group of people stand with temporary housing in a large crater, in strong contrast to the new construction behind them. The painted movie signboard in the right foreground advertises an American film playing locally.

Designing Modern Japan

neighbourhood.[160] An article in the American business magazine *Fortune* described the state of manufacturing in March 1947 as follows:

> Most of the big assembly plants have closed, thereby throwing out of work a whole network of feeders, large and small. The plants that put out the machines and arms of war can do little but turn out five-and-dime-store junk – toys, scissors, notions, cheap cameras – for the open-air booths on the Ginza. Some of the aircraft factories have started turning out three-wheeled motor vehicles, a sort of combination two-passenger car and delivery wagon, but many of these plants will be hit by reparations and cease to exist. The Japanese economy is still no more than a survival economy; it is struggling to get started in an atmosphere that hardly encourages a good start.[161]

Occupation purges of large firms that had been involved in the war effort further complicated manufacturing. Given the conditions in December 1946, for the IARI and Export Agency to publish a book of designs and technical specifications for exports to the United States was wildly optimistic. Indeed, the material quality of the product design reference books was poor, testifying to the fact that makers had to work with whatever was on hand. The IARI clearly had access to ink, energy, paper and printing presses as well as ideas – likely generated from the annual design sessions held during the war – but the book combines rough, grainy Western-style paper and a hard cover with Japanese *washi* endpapers and a partially sewn binding.

It is easy to think that everything changes after a cataclysmic event. But in fact, many designers and manufacturers shifted clients and continued working as they could. Manufacturers like the Nishijin weavers who had found it difficult to adapt to the wartime economy were poorly equipped. However, many munitions and war goods factories – both plants set up for military production and existing industries like the furniture manufacturers that had shifted to military work – converted production lines and remaining resources to make ordinary objects. At Toyota, managers converted the assembly line at the company's Nakagawa plant, formerly devoted to manufacturing military aircraft, to fabricate basic metal items like pots and pans.[162] Furniture manufacturer Tendō Mokkō began as a wartime collective of carpenters producing wooden munitions boxes for companies including Tōkyō Shibaura Denki (Toshiba). Now they used stocks of wood and coal left over from their supplies, provided by the Japanese Ministry of Munitions, to produce portable dining tables for use in temporary accommodation.[163] In Okinawa, which had seen particularly fierce fighting and considerable civilian death, shrapnel and metal from downed American planes was transformed into rudimentary cookware. Around Japan, metal helmets became cookware as well.

A common immediate response among designers, not surprisingly, was to destroy all traces of wartime work. Tōhōsha, the visual communication office behind propaganda magazine *Front*, tried to burn their remaining stock, but it flew out of the furnace's air pipe, to be found in burnt-out areas all around the company.[164] Kokusai Hōdō Kōgei (previously Nippon Kōbō, the publisher of *NIPPON*), put thousands of images of front-line warfare in a wooden box, bound it with iron bands and tossed it into a river.[165] However, designers and publishers soon realized that they were not the target of purges. Roughly 1,000 new books were published between 15 August and 31 December 1945, in many cases using stocks of paper and ink left over from wartime government contracts.[166] Between 1945 and 1949, Occupation censors viewed some 13,000 different periodicals. The number of publishers jumped from three hundred in August 1945 to 2,000 in April 1946, then to 4,600 in 1948, before dropping to 1,900 in 1951.

The IARI's ability to publish a book indicates how quickly its designers turned to post-war reconstruction, in part due to direct SCAP encouragement. The IARI returned to the Ministry of Commerce and Industry, where it had been housed since 1944. Staff members who had led military projects kept a low profile initially, then returned to their posts. After burning their back issues and preparatory work for upcoming issues, *Front*'s editorial staff learned that SCAP wished to hire them to produce documents for the Occupation.[167] By November 1945, a group of former *Front* team members, newly renamed Culture Publishers (Bunka Shuppansha), were selling photographic books in the Tokyo PX, the Allied commissary. They had also found a new niche with a bilingual pictorial alphabet book for Japanese eager to improve their English; the book was a best-seller.[168] Designers at large manufacturers like Toyota and Mitsubishi, a major target for SCAP purges and corporate reorganization, were left alone; perhaps less surprisingly, so too were staff in the Tokyo and Kyoto higher school design departments. Perhaps, even though they had been involved in promoting the

Designing Modern Japan

war effort, graphic and product designers seemed less 'dangerous' than counterparts in other government and corporate positions.

There was a further pragmatism to Occupation attitudes after 1947, with the emergence of Cold War tensions between the United States and Soviet Russia. SCAP officials saw a functional economy as crucial for political stability and experts who could supply their demands as key to restarting it. For Occupation authorities, Japanese economic growth was crucial for establishing and maintaining regional political stability in East Asia: American geopolitical strategy required not only a stable democracy in Japan but the continued exclusion of the Japanese Communist Party from leadership. As the Cold War burgeoned and the United States vied for regional influence with the Soviet Union and China, the United States looked to Japan for continued support. Many in Japan wanted economic recovery, full stop.

In 1947, the Occupation implemented economic stimulus programmes and allowed private trade to resume. Japanese manufacturers were free to trade directly with U.S. importers, but all transactions had to be licensed by the new government Export Agency (Bōeki-chō) and SCAP headquarters.[169] Other controls, particularly on the combines, were rolled back in 1948. Trade, planners hoped, would allow Japan to pay the reparations demanded by Allied nations and gain the capital needed for imports, both of raw materials such as coal and steel and of staples such as food. In addition, American strategists newly concerned with the Soviet Union's potential influence on post-war Japan hoped that trade would prevent the inflation and social unrest seen in Weimar Germany 25 years earlier.

The MCI almost immediately returned to the programme of light industrial exports as a way of gaining foreign capital, now for reparations as well as reconstruction. Historians have rightly emphasized the importance of Japanese government support for heavy industry after the war, including the 1947 Priority Production programme, which allowed bureaucrats to allocate coal and fuel to steelmakers.[170] However, the Japanese government and SCAP also supported crafts industries as part of their strategy for restarting the post-war economy through manufacturing. The 1946 book embodies the ability of IARI and Export Agency officials to promote design as integral to the success of light industrial exports and testifies to the continuity of their approach.

While the IARI's designers clearly envisioned the book's products lining the shelves of American department stores, access to U.S.

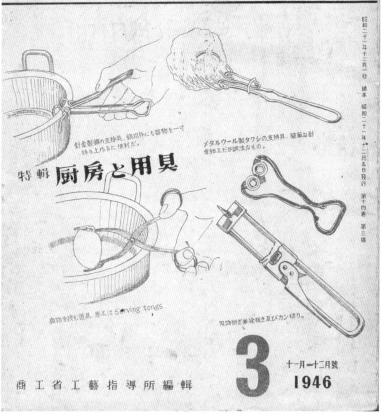

工藝ニュース

KOGEI NEWS · INDUSTRIAL ARTS RESEARCH INSTITUTE

特輯 厨房と用具

針金製鍋の支持具。鍋以外にも器物を一つ
持ち上れるに便利だ。

メタルウール製タワシの支持具。簡単な針
金細工だが調法なもの。

熱物を挟む道具。原名はServing tongs

刃物研ぎ兼徑規き及びカン切り。

商工省工藝指導所編輯

3

十一月—十二月號

1946

Line drawings of tongs made of metal wire, a scrubber of metal wire and metal wool, and other simple kitchen utensils to make, featured on the front cover of *Industrial Art News*, March 1946.

markets remained highly controlled until the San Francisco Peace Treaty of 1951. With exports to this most lucrative market limited, export strategists and manufacturers alike saw the domestic and Asian markets as a stepping-stone to eventual larger profits. In the late 1940s, Asian nations and Australia accounted for more than 60 per cent of all exports.[171] India was Japan's largest market for textiles, Thailand and Hong Kong the largest markets for electric fans.[172] Given the controls and Japan's lack of manufacturing capability, trade reopening in

1947 was partly a gesture, but it stimulated interest in export product design and manufacturing. In addition to the textile industries that once dominated exports, Occupation authorities suggested a focus on machine tools, electrical equipment, scientific instruments and other skilled manufactures that would 'complement' rather than 'compete' with those of other Asian nations. With larger industrial firms facing rebuilding and reorganization, as well as scarce materials and energy, small family-run workshops dominated immediate exports. Products from the mechanical and electrical industries were particularly successful. According to one American journalist, Japanese items that most often appeared in Korean black markets included silk, light bulbs, cosmetics, automobile and bicycle tyres, patent medicines and paper, as well as electric motors and small machine parts.[173]

The kinds of export crafts featured in the 1946 book were another

Examples of bamboo and rattan basketry export products: newspaper and magazine rack, sweets jar and a flower vase, featured in *Reference Materials for Industrial Craft Products Suitable for Export* (Ministry of Commerce Export Agency and Industrial Arts Institute, 1946).

solution identified by the IARI and Export Agency. By December 1945, the agency was again sponsoring exhibitions of crafts and light industrial export products. Some products were drawn from existing stock, while others had been hastily produced for the exhibitions, for review and selection by IARI staff and Occupation officials.[174] Six months later, from June 1946, *Industrial Art News*, the IARI journal, began disseminating model products like the electric coffee percolator in each issue. These would form the basis for the product specifications in the December 1946 book. Given their low volumes and small margins, it was unrealistic to think that cigarette cases, decanters and slippers would contribute greatly to national income. For MCI strategists, though, it was not only a first step in reconstruction but a return to standard practice, not least the IARI crafts export strategy of the 1930s. Industrial craft products had a track record of popularity and market recognition in American markets. Export craft industries were also suffering from materials shortages – lacquerware makers had become accustomed to lacquer imported from occupied China, for example. But their production processes depended less on imported coal and steel or on mechanized production, so could recommence more quickly. Industries like ceramics and basketry used local materials and had the added social and economic advantage that returning soldiers could be 'rehabilitated' as artisans. In at least one prefecture, local politicians suggested that war widows, too, could earn income by making export crafts for American homes.[175]

While a controversial marketing tactic, the 'exotic' materials and styles of many Japanese products were popular with Occupation troops, demonstrating their potential in terms of overseas market demand. In 1940, IARI designers had been uncomfortable with Charlotte Perriand's identification and use of a rural folk idiom in her furniture designs for the Takashimaya exhibition. Not a decade later, many found themselves caught between modernist design ideals and the economic reality that 'Japaneseness' could sell. Many of the photographs in the 1946 book are of traditional and elite artefacts such as *yuzen* kimono and lacquerware. While kimono and antique lacquerware, along with woodblock prints, were among the items that servicemen bought, most small firms were hardly equipped to produce new stock in the challenging conditions of the immediate post-war period. Indeed, the IARI asked an American woman who was part of the Occupation, a merchandiser at a department store recorded as 'Barr', to select the photographs for inclusion.[176]

The impact of the physical presence of foreign, mainly American soldiers, in Japan on immediate post-war design and manufacturing cannot be overstated. Occupation troops, characterized by one American commentator as a 'rather disagreeable but dependable tourist industry', were spending $160 million per year on 'souvenirs and the like' by 1951.[177] Some soldiers learned how to make Japanese crafts themselves. In autumn 1945, Occupation officers stationed in Sendai, close to the IARI, requested that the IARI offer their troops training in woodcarving, metalwork and lacquerware. Some thirty-odd soldiers participated. The IARI held an exhibition of their work at the end.[178] More conventionally, GIs purchased souvenirs directly from workshops and roadside vendors. They could also buy crafts products without leaving the Occupation compounds. Beginning in 1946, the Occupation's Central Purchasing Office (CPO) acquired craft items including

Designing Modern Japan

lacquerware, cloisonné and dolls, such as those included in the 1946 book, which it then sold in pxs.[179] Items for sale were selected by the IARI as being particularly suitable as souvenirs and purchased from IARI-organized clearinghouse companies. IARI selection responded to Occupation market demand: after the CPO declared its interest in providing textiles souvenirs for military shoppers, the MCI's Export Agency contracted with textiles manufacturers including Oritō, a wartime agglomeration of Kyōto textiles manufacturers. Where Oritō once provided uniforms to Japanese troops, the group now returned to producing kimono and other textiles. When production could not meet demand, contractors sold pre-war and wartime stock. As a result, many early CPO souvenirs were not export products per se, but rather ordinary Japanese things.

As CPO orders continued, workshops began manufacturing products designed to appeal to the Americans who shopped there, adapting vernacular materials, processes and forms to fit their customers' expectations for souvenirs. The IARI staff in Sendai, too, saw their tutelage of American soldiers as 'an opportunity to research the taste and preferences of Occupation soldiers'.[180] But souvenir purchases would not predict mass purchases for American homes and daily life in the larger export market. As during the war, Export Agency and IARI strategists saw further 'market research' as essential for cracking the American market.[181] By 1946, the IARI design department had completed a research project aimed at identifying American market tastes.[182] The research team interviewed Occupation troops as well as officials like Barr about their tastes in crafts. They invited them to product exhibitions to critique the objects on display, offer general advice on the colour, design and types of products likely to succeed in the American market and even select objects for shipment to the United States as samples.[183] IARI officials noted a difference between the Americans' taste, which they found somewhat middle-brow, with a preference for the decorative, and the modernist, 'austere' tastes of pre-war European visitors.[184] But while they acknowledged that their 'native informants' were for the most part expert in neither design nor Japan, they also recognized the value of surveying the Americans available on their doorstep at a time when travel to the United States remained restricted.

Reading libraries established in a number of Japanese cities by the Civil Information and Education Section (CIE) of the Occupation were also useful. IARI design chief Kenmochi Isamu (1912–1971) visited the CIE library in Tokyo regularly, to review American fashion and home decoration magazines like *Better Homes and Gardens* and *Vogue*. At one point, Occupation officials were sending several titles directly to Kenmochi at the IARI each month.[185] Some enterprising manufacturers simply went to magazine shops on Tokyo's Ginza shopping street, where American magazines could be picked up without waiting for Occupation contacts to share them.[186]

The continuity between this kind of export product promotion and that of earlier periods is clear. As in the Meiji period and the 1930s, IARI officials attempted to translate vernacular techniques and materials into viable products for overseas markets, by emphasizing crafts over mechanized production, working with small local manufacturers, and disseminating designs and measures of quality through print and exhibitions. As in the 1930s, vernacular crafts sat alongside contemporary export designs that competed against foreign products as ordinary objects, rather than as specifically 'Japanese' ones. The use of Occupation officials as an expert focus group continued the overseas design expert system that had earlier seen Bruno Taut, Prill-Schlemann and Perriand invited to Japan. Indeed, the IARI and Export Agency's activities can be seen as continuing pre-war and indeed wartime activity.

One major difference to earlier export strategy concerned designers and strategists' recognition that geopolitical power now sat with the United States, not Europe. In June 1946, commenting on the challenge of reconstruction, IARI designer – and chief editor of the 1946 book – Toyoguchi Katsuhei (Kappei, 1905–1991) wrote:

> All the beautifully arrayed possessions – the clothing, the munitions, the aeroplanes, the automobiles, the equipment, even the cigarettes and lighters of the Occupation forces that have overflowed the burnt-out wasteland of Japan. Our own dingy bodies. There is no way to hide this patched, cobbled-together abomination, like a woman who tries hastily to scrub up. This is the face of 'constructive Japan'.[187]

As in post-war Europe, the gap between the realities of post-war Japan and the Occupation forces' world created a seductive image of American affluence, as did the images shown in films, reading-room windows

Designing Modern Japan

and exhibitions of American daily life.[188] Within the design world, not only did the American market promise almost unfathomable demand but American design industries and their products alike were taken seriously as models to emulate. The editors of *Industrial Art News* published articles on star American designers like Charles and Ray Eames and Raymond Loewy, then expanded coverage to include reports on design promotion activities like the 'Good Design' exhibitions at New York's Museum of Modern Art (MOMA). IARI men in particular retained an interest in state design promotion systems, especially those of the UK. But the draw of American products, of the American consultant designer system and of American marketing techniques as examples of design's integration within the world's most powerful economy proved seductive, by revealing how design was integrated within business. This would lead eventually both to changes in designers' professional organization and to the incorporation of design divisions within manufacturers.[189]

The visits of American consultant designers to Japan played a role in promoting America, too. In 1951, during one such invited trip in Japan, the New York-based industrial designer Raymond Loewy (1893–1986) spoke on design's power to increase sales and corporate profit. His audience included the presidents of Toyota, Hitachi, Toshiba and major department stores, as well as the chair of the Keidanren, Japan's most powerful business association.[190] On the same trip, Loewy was paid a record-breaking 1.5 million yen, or $4,000, to redesign the packaging for Peace cigarettes. Widely reported in the business and popular press, Loewy's design fee not only raised awareness of design as a tool for growing sales but revealed that design could be a socially recognized and well-paid profession. As we will see in Chapter Four, the message would not be lost, particularly on designers keen to increase their financial compensation and social recognition.

The end of the war impacted furniture design and manufacturing as well. In January 1946, at the height of the domestic housing crisis, SCAP authorities directed the Japanese government to design, build and furnish 20,000 houses for married Occupation officers.[191] The resulting 'Dependent Houses' (DH) were designed by a team of Japanese architects under the direction of Major Heeren S. Krusé, of the Occupation Design Branch, with sizes ranging from 80 to 150 square metres. This was significantly larger than the maximum size allowed for new Japanese dwellings, restricted due to an acute shortage of construction materials.[192] A team from the IARI designed the houses' furnishings: 38 pieces of simple, American-style wooden furniture.

SCAP authorities took advantage of other wartime manufacturing conventions and organizational structures to achieve their ambitious production goals, too. With SCAP's knowledge and approval,

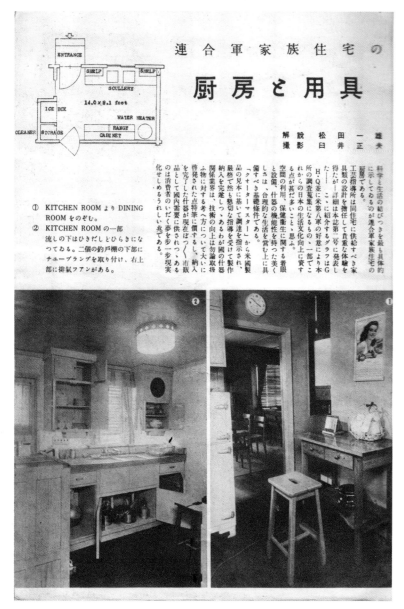

Photographs, a floorplan with dimensions and an account of the working relationships and process of producing kitchens for Allied housing, introduced to furniture designers, technical advisors and manufacturers around Japan in *Industrial Art News*, October 1947.

Senior management of furniture manufacturer Tendō Mokkō entertaining representatives from the Allied Occupation of Japan stationed in nearby Sendai, 1947. Interactions with Occupation officers enabled Tendō Mokkō to acquire machinery, materials, knowhow and support.

manufacturers located near Occupation camps formed associations to manage the bidding and assignment of contracts, in the same way as they had formed industry associations to distribute materials and fuel during the war. SCAP authorities also commissioned domestic appliances such as refrigerators, washing machines and coffee percolators from electric appliance manufacturers, including Toshiba and Mitsubishi. To disseminate these 'model pieces' to manufacturers and builders who had not worked on the project, the IARI printed technical drawings and specifications for a number of products in *Industrial Art News*. The project team also published a thick, bilingual volume of records, drawings and specifications of the buildings, furniture and appliances.

As during the war, contracts brought financial capital as well as skills, technology and connections. DH work could generate the income to rebuild a business and retain employees, as well as exemptions from wood, metal and fuel rationing and an introduction to standardized quality and mass-production methods. Noguchi Toshirō (1909–1980), an employee in Mitsukoshi's furniture department, was seconded to the DH furniture project. Noguchi later recalled,

> While the furniture was meant for temporary use by the occupying forces, its style was contemporary, its build durable and it made a great impact on the manufacturing

Coffee Sets and Militarism

industry, so it should be commemorated by our nation's furniture and manufacturing industries. That experience is one of the mothers of mass-produced furniture activities in our country. It was also the beginning of a generational shift from craftsmen to factory workers.[193]

A variant on the DH card table and chairs, for example, became a strong seller for Maruni Mokkō, the furniture manufacturer in the mountains outside Hiroshima that had made wooden parts for military aircraft during the war. It proved difficult to make DH furniture, given SCAP expectations for uniformity and quality, the poor resources of many firms and widespread inexperience with mass production of standardized products, especially American-style furnishings. Shortages of wood and fuel only compounded manufacturers' difficulties. Ultimately, however, the DH contracts would be credited with familiarizing even small manufacturers with the standardization, rationalization of production methods and simple products idealized by pre-war modernists and legislated by the wartime government. The DH commission was the large-scale project of which pre-war design reformers had dreamt: an opportunity to popularize rationally designed Western-style houses and furniture standardized for maximum durability and comfort, manufactured by small firms nationwide for use in ordinary homes.

Like the Dependent Houses, Hollywood movies and American books and magazines, which were available to schools and in the CIE-sponsored reading rooms, would become a symbol of the post-war ideal of material affluence through American-style democracy. The abstract language of democracy was met with scepticism by many Japanese, who saw it as simply replacing Japan's wartime rhetoric.[194] But housing designers, prominent architects and social activists including the architect Hamaguchi Miho (1915–1988), a rare woman in an overwhelmingly male profession, began to call for the reorganization of domestic space to reflect a more 'democratic' family structure and women's increased rights.[195]

As with the previous chapters, men led the design activity described in this chapter. Elite women with the backing of their families or husbands could study design as part of domestic economy courses or at elite modernist institutions like the Shinkenchiku Kōgei Gakuin (School of New Architecture and Design), where Kageyama Shizuko taught sewing in the 1930s. But such educational opportunities were rare and limited to women on the basis of birth and location. Like men and women in Korea and Taiwan under colonial occupation, Japanese women educated in design had limited opportunities to practise professionally. Furthermore, both men's and women's design areas were circumscribed by gender norms: architecture, interiors, graphic, textile and product design for men; and housing, clothing and embroidery for women.[196] Teaching in girls' higher schools was an approved option, but even then, women taught sewing and embroidery, with courses

Advertisements for furniture and interior decoration firms, *Industrial Art News*, October 1947. Both Takashimaya Iida and Tokyo Mokkō, the two firms advertising here, were among the manufacturers who successfully tendered to make furniture for the Dependent Houses.

in subjects like handcrafts (*shukō*) and woodworking taken by male teachers. As we saw in Chapter Two, textile work like sewing and embroidery was on the one hand an expectation for women as part of housework, but also offered women a space for design agency and creativity.[197]

The economic, social and cultural disruption of the immediate post-war period amplified these possibilities, as growing numbers of women started home-based businesses as seamstresses. Sewing kimono from lengths of cloth had been a central element of women's domestic work. In paid textile work, women composed much of the labour force for village textiles production in the Tokugawa and Meiji periods, and in large textile mills throughout the twentieth century.[198] Now, women could also earn crucial income through dressmaking, as urban and more well-off rural women began to acquire Western-style clothing for daily wear.[199] Pattern books and sewing magazines proliferated, as did sewing schools and sewing machine sales.[200] Commentators cited

'Designs in straight lines', editorial fashion spread in *Kurashi no techō* (The Notebook of Everyday Life), 1 (1948), demonstrating dresses to sew at home using techniques and forms commonly used to sew kimono and other conventional Japanese garments. *Kurashi no techō* was a popular post-war magazine whose content combined the sewing, cooking and housework content of pre-war magazines with an emphasis on women's roles in creating democratic post-war life in the home.

Designing Modern Japan

the lower cost and greater practicality of Western-style clothing as well as the glamour of American visual culture, particularly Hollywood films and women's magazines, as forces behind women's adoption of Western dress, though some dress patterns distinctly recalled the little-loved standardized dress for women suggested first by daily life reformers in the 1920s, then during wartime. Few women had the income to purchase new cloth, and both post-war dresses and their wartime predecessors used locally available textiles and derived their cut and drape from kimono, an existing piece of clothing whose pieces could be taken apart and reassembled. Women's replacement of kimono with Western-style dress provides another instance of a pre-war or wartime attempt at design reform that gained little traction when first introduced and then came to fruition in the post-war moment. But the predominance of men in this chapter also shows the persistence and depth of existing social norms and power structures. As the remark-able unity of design policy for light industrial exports from pre-war to post-war shows, too, in many ways colonialism, war and occupation offered economic support and fuel for designers' activities and the social norms that structured them, rather than changing them.

INSTRUCTIONS

NIPPON KOGAKU K. K.

Nikon S2

4 'A landscape like a picture book'
Design, Society and Economic Growth in Post-War Japan

In 1964, a pictorial feature in the popular weekly magazine *Asahi Guraffu* (Asahi Graph) described central Tokyo as 'a landscape like a picture book'. If anything, this was a sci-fi story. *Asahi Graph*'s picture-book city shone with modern infrastructure. The monorail to Tokyo's Haneda Airport curved overhead. The Tokyo Metropolitan Expressway swooped heavily as it conveyed trucks, cars and buses through a crowded city, edged by glowing billboard-sized neon signs and steel-framed buildings under construction. The material of the day was reinforced concrete, and a helicopter hovered above, completing the scene. The text, written in the *hiragana* phonetic characters also used in Japanese children's books and employing a similar language and tone, speaks in awe of aeroplanes, expressway, helicopter and monorail.

The image acknowledges that not everything was shiny and new. The expressway overshadowed a cluster of wooden houses, as though residents were simply in the way. Other dirt lots, below, were strewn with rubbish. But overall, the story in this picture book is one of work and prosperity, of investment and industry designed to move people and products efficiently from place to place. It is also, less overtly, a story of design: of design's role in corporate and state strategy, of engineering and, increasingly, the design industries themselves. The monorail, cars, trucks and buses, the expressway's signage, the neon signs and the magazine spread itself – its typography, its layout – were designed by professionals. These designers had been trained and worked as designers in an economic, social and industrial system whose other members increasingly acknowledged their role, particularly if they were men.

Economic recovery is inseparable from the story of design in post-war Japan. In Japan, as elsewhere, the period began in rubble and

Kamekura Yūsaku, cover design for the instruction manual for the Nikon s2 camera, Nikon Kōgaku Kabushiki Gaisha, early 1950s.

poverty, with dramatic political, economic and social restructuring to encourage democratization and economic growth. It closed with sometimes violent discontent with the mechanisms and fruits of the new peace and prosperity, in a society riven by inequal access to design's improvements. In the 1950s and '60s, centralized industrial policy, focused on exports, and rising domestic consumption indicated a place for design within the manufacturing and distribution process. Between 1950 and 1973, exports and rising domestic consumption propelled Japan's economy to grow roughly 10 per cent annually, with particularly accelerated growth in the five years after 1955.[1]

As we will see in this chapter, self-identified professional designers were keen to position their industries within the emerging economic systems and quick to take up this opportunity. They were also relatively effective: the categories and definitions of design established in Japan in the 1950s set standards for education, publishing and the design professions for the half-century to come. Self-consciously modern *dezain* did not infiltrate all areas of production, whether in craft or in heavy industry. But by the mid-1960s it was clearly part of the picture-book landscape. However, this vision of the future was not universally supported. The chapter also explores how dissent to design's alignment with commerce and the state shaped dialogue and decisions alike, throughout the period.

Looking back now, both the visual styles of the period and the questions that concerned designers in the 1950s and '60s may seem familiar. A small and influential group of graphic, furniture and industrial designers active in the period have documented their own work and that of colleagues in publications and design industry association gallery exhibitions.[2] Printing firms, electrical goods manufacturers, advertising firms and other enterprises that continue to work closely with designers have also invested in exhibitions, research and other documentation and publicity of designers' social and economic contributions in post-war Japan.[3] Museums in Japan and abroad have contextualized their work, along with iconic products from the era, through period and individual retrospectives and publications.[4] Universities, too, have carefully documented and publicized their own contributions and those of influential design educators and graduates.[5] An aim of this chapter is to add the rich social texture of designers' working lives and experiences to the more well-known designs and to embed these stories within the economic trajectory

Designing Modern Japan

of the period. Whether monorails or picture books, there is much more to tell.

Economic Incentives, Export Policy and Product Design

In December 1949, the design critic, educator and former Industrial Art Research Institute employee Koike Shinji gave several presentations on 'industrial design' to designers, manufacturers, students, bureaucrats and citizens' groups. Recalling the presentations a few years later, colleague and friend Akashi Kazuo (1911–2006) explained how Koike's equation of industrial design, exports and prosperity had fuelled his own passion for his work:

> With conditions like cramped land, overabundant population and poor natural resources, Japan is bound to its fate: dependency on manufacturing for the export market. So, for us, industrial design seemed like the obvious method for promoting and supporting manufacturing exports. Ever since then, I have thought I would give my all for the promotion of industrial design.[6]

Akashi had indeed done so, first as a designer at the state IARI in the late 1940s and early 1950s, then as a consultant designer and design educator. Along with Koike and other colleagues in education, the public sector and the corporate world, Akashi worked hard to stay abreast of international trends in design practice, industrial technology and consumer taste, and to share these insights with Japanese manufacturers, students and the public. A defining aspect of post-war Japanese manufacturing was an emphasis on exports for reconstruction and economic growth, based on the perception that, as many put it, Japan's position was to 'export or die'.[7] This created an opening for Akashi, Koike and their colleagues to promote industrial design as a specialist and necessary part of manufacturing and consumer society – more simply put, its professionalization.

In 1949 Japan's economy remained well below pre-war standards. Foreign trade was less than half that of 1937.[8] A common concern among policymakers in the Japanese government and the Allied Occupation authorities, mirrored neatly in Koike's comment, was that Japan's limited natural resources and increased population presented an economic and demographic ticking time bomb. Without the resources to feed and clothe Japan's population at home, policy-makers saw a solution in foreign currency accumulation through the export of manufactured goods. Foreign currency – particularly U.S. dollars – could then be used to purchase the things needed from overseas. Strict measures to help increase exports and balance the budget followed. By 1950, Japan's gross national product was the highest in Asia. Japan's foreign currency deposits increased by 450 per cent between 1949 and 1951.[9] Stimulus arrived partly via the Cold War: American foreign aid, support from the World Bank and the Korean War of 1950–53, for which the American military placed contracts with suppliers ranging in size from conglomerates to corner workshops. In 1951, Japan's trade deficit with the United States was offset by what one American commentator described as 'a favorable invisible balance' of $763 million, which included $327 million in 'special procurement' goods and services and $297 million for the expenses of U.S. forces in Japan.[10] By 1953, special procurements for the U.S. military accounted for 64 per cent of Japan's total exports, and Americans spent more than $1 billion in Japan during the Korean War.

More conventional exports mattered, too. The San Francisco Peace Treaty reopened trade and diplomatic relations between Japan and its former enemies in 1952, significantly simplifying the export process. The Japanese government immediately applied to join the General Agreement on Tariffs and Trade (GATT), created in 1947 as a mechanism to facilitate free trade and economic development internationally after the Second World War. Japan was granted accession to GATT in 1955.[11] Policymakers in the Ministry of International Trade and Industry (MITI) and bureaucrats in its trade agency, the Japan External Trade Relations Organization (JETRO), sought to support economic reconstruction through exports of textiles, ceramics and the products of other established industries, allowing manufacturers in mechanized new industries like audio equipment the time to develop competitive products. This was a similar strategy to the 1930s, but the imperative was reconstruction rather than imperial growth. The scope of policy also widened, from light industrial products made from local materials – wood, lacquer, ceramics and so on – to include those from new, mechanical and electrical industries. Cotton and rayon textiles and clothing were the most important manufacturing export, and optical equipment was growing in importance, but small items like stainless steel cutlery, ceramic dishes and toys, mostly from SMEs – and known

Designing Modern Japan

collectively as *zakka*, or 'sundry goods' – were also major exports, as well as the industrial and economic basis for many communities.

By the early 1950s, policymakers and entrepreneurs alike focused their efforts on the U.S. market. Some 46 per cent of Japanese clothing and tableware exports went to the United States, for example.[12] The desire to export to the United States may seem unnoteworthy, even obvious: Japan had only just emerged from an eight-year occupation led by an American military and civil administration. But as in European countries like France and Italy, this was an economic as well as a geopolitical decision. In the early 1950s, Southeast Asia, Latin and South America and Africa remained Japan's most significant actual export markets. But the U.S. market offered greater potential profit. Exports to Communist China and the USSR were politically difficult, given Japan's commitment to the U.S.-aligned trading bloc. Furthermore, American dollars were convertible currency, unlike currencies like the UK's pound sterling. With trade liberalization, the total value of exports from Japan grew between 23 and 30 per cent annually from 1954.[13] Total national income nearly doubled between 1950 and 1955, from 3,361 billion yen to 6,574 billion yen.

As exports grew, so too did Japanese products' presence in the United States. Exports of ceramic dishes and stainless-steel cutlery to the United States more than doubled in value annually in the mid-1950s.[14] Japanese-made items proved popular with American department store buyers and their customers. But American and other foreign manufacturers aiming for the lucrative U.S. market campaigned actively to the U.S. government to limit imports from precisely the industries that Koike, Akashi and their colleagues sought to support. From the 1950s to the 1980s, other GATT members often blocked Japan from trading under GATT terms, due to pressure from domestic industries concerned that Japanese imports would threaten their profits, particularly in textiles, stainless steel tableware and ceramic dishes. American gingham and velveteen manufacturers lobbied national politicians. So did the owners of woollen sweater mills in Scotland and American makers of pillowcases and women's blouses. The issue was cost. Japan's lower wages meant that exporters could sell pillowcases, blouses and table settings at lower cost than was possible for manufacturers based in the United States and western Europe. Given this situation, Akashi Kazuo's argument that industrial design could promote and support manufacturing exports made even more sense: design could provide novelty or aesthetic pleasure to counterbalance the image of Japanese products

Bamboo-wares

Paper lanterns

Magazine rack

Bamboo baskets

Sundry goods for export, c. 1957: paper lanterns, bamboo and rattan baskets, and a bamboo magazine rack, likely a prototype from the Industrial Arts Institute.

as cheap and undercutting local or European labour. So too is where Akashi published his comment: in his preface to a guide to designing light electrical equipment for export markets, published in 1956.

Both Akashi and Koike began the post-war period at the Industrial Arts Research Institute. The IARI played an important role in positioning design as integral to effective exporting, in both practice and

Designing Modern Japan

in government guidance. The institute's name and affiliation changed several times between 1949 and 1952, eventually becoming the Sangyō Kōgei Shikenjo ('Sankōshi', the Industrial Arts Institute or IAI) within MITI's Agency for Industrial Science and Technology (AIST).[15] As we saw previously, Institute designers responded to the war's end in 1945 by immediately offering design, technical and logistic advice to makers working with local materials. By 1950, they were advising large firms as well, and exploring the application of new manufacturing technologies. For example, following the critical praise and visibility of Charles and Ray Eames's DCM-1 plywood chair within the United States in the late 1940s, the IAI's technical and design sections turned their attention to electrical heat-moulding for plywood furniture. In widely publicized experiments from 1948 onwards, Institute researchers hoped to demystify and popularize the heat-moulding process among manufacturers, then to support them in adopting it for mass production and export. Other projects looked at toys and at homewares in local materials and modernist forms, and at using new materials like plastics and fibreglass. Plywood presses remained expensive, but IAI experiments did impact local manufacturers' work, particularly through one-on-one advising at the IAI and the wider network of locally based technical institutes.

In practice, much design and technical advising for small manufacturers fell to prefectural and municipal research institutes. IAI

Table settings, tablewares and table linens made for export, c. 1957.

'A landscape like a picture book'

researchers acted as national leads for the network of local industrial research institutes, disseminating information through workshops, lectures and meetings. While the IAI experimented with adopting international design and technical advances for Japanese industry, local organizations directly supported local industries in implementing them, continuing relationships and networks begun decades earlier but with new product types in mind. Design advising was highly localized. In Aomori, in northern Japan, the prefectural industrial research institute experimented with plywood skis, appropriate for the region's deep snows and plentiful timber.[16] In Shizuoka, home to industries including lacquerware, furniture and wooden sandals (*geta*), researchers continued to advise on traditional products. But they also promoted new materials like particleboard for cabinetry and supported an industry pivot from wooden footwear to 'chemical sandals' made of vinyl – in other words, a shift from woodworking to resin injection moulding – in order to retain the domestic footwear market and capture export markets.[17]

For the IAI and local organizations alike, acquiring and sharing information about overseas competitors and market trends was an important part of their work. The most common mechanism for scouting foreign market tastes and emerging design trends in the 1950s remained American design and home magazines, including magazines like *House and Garden* that largely targeted a female consumer readership. Another, more cost-intensive, way of doing this was to invite foreign – most often American – designers to visit Japan. Visiting designers and critics included Bernard Rudofsky and Charlotte Perriand in 1953, Walter Gropius in 1954 and George Nelson in 1957.[18]

Invitations had a geopolitical edge, showing how designers, too, incorporated Japan's post-war 'pivot' to the USA. Designers and curators worked closely with American government agencies and with foundations like the Ford Foundation and Rockefeller Foundation, all of which were interested in promoting American culture to Japan.[19] In July 1955, a number of Japanese graphic and industrial designers, architects and photographers were invited to Tokyo for seminars on 'American Design'. There they joined young American practitioners who were in Japan on prestigious one-year Fulbright fellowships, including architect William Alexander, ceramicist Maurice Grossman and his wife Marilyn, and Richard Haag, a landscape architect.[20] The seminars had been proposed by staff at the U.S. Embassy; they were

The December 1948 issue of *Industrial Art News* presented the IAI's research into radio heat conduction plywood technology. Cover artist Amano Takeo, a graduate of the Tokyo Higher School of Arts and Crafts design department and an IARI employee, would go on to design export tablewares and metal cutlery for the Institute.

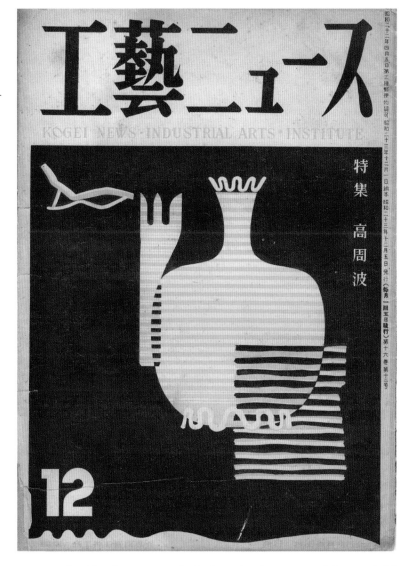

co-organized by the U.S. Board of Education in Japan and the IAI. Cold War U.S. policy to strengthen Japan economically – and keep Japanese business from turning to China or the USSR – supported design as well. The strategy was mutually beneficial. In the 1950s, America offered an unparalleled target for Japanese goods. American designers could advise on their home markets, while influential Japanese designers like Kenmochi Isamu, head of the IAI Design Section, could identify U.S. designers like the Eameses and institutions like MOMA as the forefront

George Jergensen from the Automotive Design Department at the Art Center College of Design in Pasadena, California, correcting sketches made using the highlight technique at a seminar at the Industrial Arts Institute in Tokyo, 1956.

of modern taste, and as a style to adopt, for successful repositioning of Japanese exports – and their own practice – in the American market.

Once again, on-the-ground observation was important for acquiring information. The San Francisco Peace Treaty cleared the way for Japanese nationals to travel overseas again; initially much travel was to the USA. In 1952, MITI posted Kenmochi to the United States for six months.[21] Kenmochi travelled from San Francisco to Los Angeles, then crossed the country via Chicago and Grand Rapids before spending time in New York, with trips to Philadelphia and Boston. As in the Meiji period, acquiring useful knowledge to grow export profits was the goal.[22] After the end of the Occupation – and of Occupation facilitation of travel to the United States – MITI formalized a travel scheme for individual corporate and research institute designers to study in the United States and Europe. MITI also sponsored group educational trips, mirroring the Meiji period scheme for foreign education. Study areas tended towards the pragmatic, with an emphasis on styling both design and engineering for manufacturing efficiency and maximum sales. Travel to the USA was expensive, given the fixed exchange rate of 360 yen to the dollar, and the Japanese government restricted overseas travel for Japanese citizens until 1964. That MITI would sponsor designers' trips, then, indicates that designers were successful at presenting their profession as an integral, crucial aspect of export promotion.

Designing Modern Japan

Kenmochi's 1952 trip to the United States illustrates this point. During his six-month stay, he visited well-known designers, design firms, design-led manufacturers and university design departments. In New York alone, he visited the offices of well-known industrial and interior designers including Raymond Loewy, Walter Dorwin Teague and George Nelson, and spent considerable time with senior staff at MOMA. Across the country, designers including Nelson, Charles and Ray Eames and Crombie Taylor, architect and acting principal of the IIT Institute of Design in Chicago, invited him to stay in their homes and hosted parties for him.

Visits allowed Kenmochi to learn at first hand how successful consultant designers in the United States worked. He also gained an understanding of their perceptions of Japan. Networking also allowed him to present Japanese exports as 'design', with the added value and sense of quality this presented, and to build relationships with key U.S. and international tastemakers. But his remit went beyond acquiring information about consumer taste and product design. For the IAI and MITI more widely, design was only one part of the vision for increasing American sales, along with packaging, materials and marketing and advertising. Kenmochi travelled with slides, flyers and other publicity material from the IAI showing types of Japanese export products, and took notes on how his U.S. interlocutors reacted to them. He met with high-end craft homeware retailers, particularly those focusing on Scandinavian imports, to identify Japanese products that would sell in their local markets and to initiate potential retail agreements. He also visited packaging and materials specialists like Container Corporation, the Forest Products Laboratory of the U.S. Department of Agriculture, and Shell Oil, makers of Formica, noting in letters to IAI colleagues his inability to comprehend the technical details.

Thanks to the internationally networked nature of elite design in Japan and design's privileged position in the IAI, institute designers were well placed to reconnect local Japanese makers and their products to international markets and communities. The emphasis on economic recovery through exports allowed design to gain attention and resources. Unlike cognate fields like engineering and materials science – also crucial for product quality and appeal – design may also have seemed less threatening, more 'cultural', to overseas audiences in the United States and elsewhere. In the 1950s, American and Japanese philanthropists actively worked to change American perceptions of

Japan, in part by promoting Japanese art and performance in the USA.[23] Design in the sense of 'art and design' could be part of post-war cultural diplomacy overseas, while sitting within industrial and economic strategy at home.

But international encounters also raised questions about what 'Japanese design' was and should be, for the designers fortunate enough to take on these roles. The question was particularly acute for Kenmochi, whose role as the head of the IAI Design Section meant regular interactions with foreigners, during which the topic could arise. More concretely, he had to decide how best to represent Japanese design at key trade fairs, where he played a lead role in overseeing Japan's national booth.

After hosting trade fairs for international buyers in Japan during the Occupation, the Japanese government sent model rooms to fairs in Toronto and Seattle, then invested more heavily in an exhibit for the International Exhibition of Architecture and Industrial Design in Hälsingborg (now Helsingborg), Sweden, in 1955.[24] The IAI designers took trade fairs seriously. As with international expositions in the Meiji period, not only were they one of the most important mechanisms and sites at which foreign buyers entered into contracts with Japanese exporters, they also offered an opportunity for designers, particularly, to shape wider perception through the overall aesthetic of the national showroom.

In the IAI model room in Hälsingborg, Kenmochi chose a combination of household items that he felt displayed 'the main thread [*suji*] of good design', across traditional, *mingei* and modern design aesthetics.[25] Most furnishings and products were IAI prototypes, with other objects such as an easy chair by institute-alumnus-turned-consultant-designer Watanabe Riki (1912–2013) and *yukata* fabric designed by modernist artists Inokuma Genichirō (1902–1993) and Okamoto Tarō (1911–1996). The objects displayed in the room represented MITI's strategy of selling the products of both existing and new industries. Electrical appliances included a Matsushita Denki radio designed by the firm's design lead, Mano Zenichi (1916–2003). Consultant designer Yanagi Sōri contributed a white porcelain coffee set for the ceramics company Hakusan Tōki. The model room also featured more conventional light industry exports – toys, lighting, lacquer and bamboo objects, teawares – as well as a decorative 'objet' by artist Teshigahara Sōfū (1900–1979). Kenmochi brought these two categories together

Designing Modern Japan

through a unifying aesthetic he called 'Japanese Modern' and 'Modern Japanese Style': Japanese materials, techniques and functions that embodied the post-war tenets of international good design, such as simplicity, solid colours and an emphasis on enhancing the existing properties of the materials used.[26] He saw this as a response to 'Japonica', the intentionally exoticizing decoration of souvenirs and domestic furniture that he had observed in American homes and magazines during his travels. For Kenmochi, Japonica was both economically damaging to Japan's export prospects and embarrassing, as the antithesis of good design tenets.

Kenmochi and his colleagues thus felt that Japanese design had to be 'good design', aligned with the modernist ideals of simplicity and functionality. These had emerged from Europe in the 1920s and '30s before finding a new champion in New York's Museum of Modern Art, particularly MOMA curator Edgar Kaufmann, Jr. At MOMA, Kaufmann promoted the take-up of modernist design principles in U.S. homes through the project *Good Design, A Joint Program to Stimulate the Best Modern Design of Home Furnishings*, organizing exhibitions in collaboration with retailers at the Merchandise Mart in Chicago, 1950–55. IAI designers assiduously researched and published information on the furniture, lighting, products, packaging and interiors that curators at MOMA and similar institutions presented as having these qualities. In graphic design, too, designers working on export advertisements and packaging, like Kamekura Yūsaku, incorporated the block colours, highly graphical typography and pared-down but visually powerful aesthetic of the movement then becoming known in the United States

Matsushita DX-350 radio, plastic, fibreboard and electronic parts, designed 1952. Matsushita lead designer Mano Zenichi's design won the grand prize in the second annual Mainichi Industrial Design Competition in 1953. The radio was unusual for its phenol resin plastic cabinet at a time when many radios used wood, a less expensive material with better local manufacturing infrastructure across Japan.

'A landscape like a picture book'

as Swiss typography or the Swiss style. Adopting the visual language of post-war international modernism allowed graphic designers – and the marketing managers who approved their work – to position Japanese products less obviously as 'Japanese', to foreign consumers. At the same time, the modernist visual presentation of products from Japan countered the earlier aesthetic of cherry blossoms, Mount Fuji and geisha disseminated by 1930s and '40s propaganda – often from the same designers.[27]

'Good design' would also support small firms to rationalize production and perform effectively in lucrative markets. As such, it needed embracing as an integral and powerful element of export strategy. An editorial in a 1954 special issue of *Industrial Art News* explained:

> Today's good design movement is a new design eye-opener
> for our nation's wide variety of industrial crafts objects
> and daily life goods. Even more importantly, it can sound
> a warning about the lack of individuality – if not the imitations,
> then the sycophantic, simplistic geisha girl SIMPLICITY – that
> has been the greatest reason for our nation's sluggish exports.
> It tells us that the situation demands an internationalist
> outlook, a new ethnic creativity that will capture the
> attention, and efforts at ingenuity.[28]

Yet again, designers working within government identified and advocated design as a solution for the problem presented by Japan's exports. Yet again, product and packaging design was a way to add a sense of 'Japaneseness' to exports that otherwise fitted the expected parameters for certain object types. Given the very real trade frictions prompted by American textile, cutlery and ceramics manufacturers' appeals to the U.S. Congress, emphasizing 'Japaneseness' might suggest that Japanese imports sought not to compete with American products but to complement them.

The mid-1950s saw a barrage of activities from like-minded designers, curators and critics aimed at educating a wide audience, particularly urban women, about the principles of 'good design'. Design critic and educator Katsumie Masaru (1909–1983) founded a magazine, *Ribingu dezain* (Living Design), in 1955. The Japan Design Committee (Nihon Dezain Komitī), a group of architects, designers and critics including Kenmochi and Katsumie, selected objects for a permanent sales and

Japan Design Committee, product selection meeting for the Good Design Corner at Ginza Matsuya, Tokyo, 1956.

didactic display at the Matsuya Ginza department store, named the Good Design Selection (Guddo Dezain Sentei).[29] Curators at the Tokyo National Museum of Modern Art persuaded their counterparts at MOMA in New York to lend 'good design' objects from the MOMA collection for an exhibition in 1957. As Takada Tadashi, head of the Patent Office Design Section, explained, 'design promotion must involve efforts to create education to train designers, to improve recognition among manufacturers and to educate mass consumers who purchase the products.'[30] Once again, 'good design' promotion activities were intended not only to sell products but to change daily life habits.

Japanese designers' embrace of 'good design' formed part of a longer history of synchronizing their work with international trends, for domestic as well as export markets. 'Good design' allowed privileged designers like Kenmochi and his IAI colleagues to participate in an international community linked by shared beliefs, and to educate a next generation of designers – and consumers – within this internationalist model. It was also a strategy to position Japanese goods overseas. As such, it sat within the IAI's larger remits to strengthen and rationalize local industry and boost manufacturing export income. It continued the IAI's pre-war and wartime connections and contributions to the everyday life and industrial rationalization movements, which were themselves part of an effort to participate in international trends. 'Good design' mirrored teachings on ethics and aesthetics from the Meiji period and earlier that connected beauty with morality. Significantly, however, its promoters wrote and spoke of *guddo dezain* rather than translating the concept. Many of the men who promoted *guddo dezain* had been involved in pre-war and wartime rationalization campaigns. Using the English transliteration allowed them to align their work with post-war America rather than the pre-war and wartime campaigns for design and daily life rationalization.

Guddo dezain also helped promote the originality of Japanese exports against claims of copying, legal and illegal. Licensing technologies from American and western European firms was an important part of machinery manufacturers' restart after the war, but in the 1950s Japanese electrical goods manufacturers shifted from licensing foreign technology to designing their own.[31] Tokyo Tsūshin Kōgyō (now Sony), for example, licensed technology for transistor radios from the Western Electric Company, a U.S. firm, in 1953 before developing their own transistors the following year.[32] Other manufacturers licensed the full product from American firms like RCA and Philips or manufactured components for them. Profit margins were however higher for original products. For the MITI-affiliated men at the IAI, charged with increasing export profits through design, associating Japanese products with *guddo dezain* emphasized originality and quality.

Guddo dezain thus became part of formalized initiatives to counter charges of imitation and poor quality. In 1954, following complaints from British textile manufacturers, British and Japanese manufacturers' representatives agreed joint steps including a voluntary system by which manufacturers would submit their export products for checks by industry associations.[33] American ceramic tableware and textiles manufacturers, too, raised concerns with the U.S. government.[34] Claims continued to mount, eventually resulting in Japanese lawmakers becoming directly implicated, sometimes publicly with no warning. In 1957, the British designer Robin Day confronted Japanese Foreign Minister

Designing Modern Japan

Fujiyama Aiichirō on live British television regarding Japanese copies of British ball-bearing packaging.[35] The year ended with a delegation of U.S. congressmen flying to Tokyo specifically to discuss American manufacturers' allegations of poor practices among Japanese exporters. As part of its efforts to mitigate external pressure, MITI established a design advisory committee (Ishō Shōrei Shingikai) comprised of internationally respected designers and architects, many of them also members of the Japan Design Committee responsible for Matsuya's Good Design Selection. The Good Design Selection System, a mechanism by which manufacturers could have their products formally tagged as 'Good Design' and labelled with a 'G-Mark', followed.[36]

By 1958, the Japan External Trade Relations Organization (JETRO) had a Design Section. For its part, the Patent Office launched a publicity campaign aimed at manufacturers and industrial designers. This included an exhibition co-sponsored by MITI, 'An exhibition to protect design', at the Shirokiya department store in Tokyo. The exhibition compared seventy sets of original and copy products to illustrate design copying infringement and impress on viewers their moral responsibility to use only original designs for the good of Japan.[37] Alongside such carrots, more formal sticks included the 1959 Export Commodities Design Protection Law (Yūshutsuhin Dezain-hō), which required manufacturers of particularly contentious products to register their designs and have them certified by a named organization. The Japan Textile Color and Design Center was responsible for textiles, the Sundry Goods Design Center for exports of everything from fountain pens to vinyl chloride toys, and the Mechanical Design Center for tape recorders, projectors and cameras.[38] As a result of these and other efforts, patent applications rose from 175,022 in 1961 to an estimated 265,000 in 1963, although nearly 70 per cent of applications came from large manufacturers, in other words those most likely to receive and be impacted by scrutiny.[39] Of course, neither *guddo dezain* nor patent legislation immediately resolved the association of Japanese manufacturers with intellectual property theft in the U.S. or UK markets. In 1961, the *Wall Street Journal* reported:

> At an exhibition of steel making equipment in Cleveland not long ago, a sales executive was fuming because he was unable to prevent some Japanese visitors from snapping pictures of a model of an oxygen steel making plant. 'You tell them no

pictures are allowed and when you turn your back you hear their shutters clicking', he said.[40]

For American consumers in the late 1950s and early 1960s, however, this mattered less than price and quality. Thanks to low labour costs, resultingly low prices and increasingly consistent product quality, Japan's electrical appliance manufacturers hit their stride in the U.S. market. Exports of mechanical goods boomed in the 1950s, growing 990 per cent over the decade.[41] Japanese firms began exporting transistor radios in 1955, and by 1959 they were the country's second most profitable manufactured item. Exports increased 240 per cent in 1958–9 alone, described by the authors of MITI's annual report on exports as 'a wondrous increase', and accounted for $104 million dollars' worth of trade that year.[42] Electrical equipment, too, increased 80 per cent in 1958–9, and a further 38 per cent in 1959–60.[43]

Despite these export successes, officials in MITI remained concerned about the product quality and viability of the small-scale enterprises that produced more than half of Japan's exports into the mid-1960s, including 56 per cent of sewing machines, 90 per cent of small electric lightbulbs and fully 100 per cent of metal toys and tableware in the mid-1950s.[44] Intricate networks of small suppliers characterized both traditional craft industries like lacquerware and

A worker at the NGK Insulators Ltd plant in Mizuho, Aichi Prefecture, 1963. NGK's mechanized mass-production facilities, in a historic ceramics production region, illustrate the transition to capital-intensive, rationalized manufacturing encouraged by MITI.

Designing Modern Japan

Artisan weaving silk in a workshop in Nishijin, Kyoto, c. 1957.

furniture and the mechanical and electrical industries. Small workshops were important for the economy and relevant for the vision of transforming manufacturing to emphasize higher-value-added mechanical products. But MITI officials and others often saw them as underproductive and inefficient.

Given the combined concerns of export originality and SME viability, public design advising took on a new role of supporting small-scale manufacturers in producing products that would clear the originality hurdles. By doing so, they might also give firms more negotiating power and agency to thrive outside wholesaler networks and subcontracting relationships with large firms. To support small-scale manufacturers and local industrial research institutes alike, the IAI lobbied for and received a new funding stream specifically to support SMES' designs.[45]

Civil servants also began promoting 'design' to SMES specifically as a business strategy. Designers like Kenmochi and civil servants like Takada published popular business paperbacks. The National Small and Medium-sized Enterprise Association Central Committee commissioned a contribution for its 'onsite techniques' series, which presented guidance on management and production techniques ranging from injection moulding to accounting. Co-authored by a team of consultant industrial designers and IAI researchers, the design volumes presented good product and graphic design as fundamental elements in product creation – rather than as superficial styling at the final stage – and a potential saviour for small companies in times of economic duress and fluctuations in demand.[46] Of course, the volumes also advocated for original design over imitation, noting that this would pre-empt charges of copying. For their part, *zakka* manufacturers had mixed responses to the offers of design support. Some manufacturers took advantage of the opportunities for advice. Others found the schemes to be well-intentioned but missing the point: product and advertising design alone could not improve relationships with suppliers or wholesalers, or reduce taxation and transport costs.

Curating and display design for trade fairs and expositions was an area that state designers could control more easily. As cameras, radios and other electro-mechanical products became increasingly important exports in the late 1950s, exhibition commissioners and designers had to combine these new objects with the existing Japanese modern aesthetic and the *zakka* products it had promoted. Curatorial decisions to combine textures, materials, patterns and forms visibly reminiscent of craft-based industries with electrical machinery and modernist furniture reflected actual MITI priorities. They also satisfied the political requirement to balance different constituencies of manufacturing industries – and politicians concerned with maintaining economic growth in their own regions – and reflected the actual mix of Japan's manufacturing.

The combination of objects could also function as a potentially beneficial narrative framing. The theme of the Japanese pavilion at Expo 58 in Brussels was 'The Japanese Hand', or, as the British journal *Industrial Design*'s reviewer paraphrased it, 'the skill of her people, their intelligence and love of beauty, their mechanical and artistic talent'.[47] When displayed next to *mingei* pots, electric machinery could be recharacterized as partly attributable to Japanese affinity for craft; as a report in the *New York Times* put it, 'Japanese hand-skill is said to be particularly fitted for this kind of precise work.'[48] A message of cultural specificity, artistic and craft heritage supported the message

The Japanese national exhibit for the twelfth Triennale di Milano in 1960, previewed at the Takashimaya department store in Tokyo. The exhibit, designed by architect Sakakura Junzō's office, combined lacquer trays and cushions on the floor with scooters, 8 mm film projectors and modernist plywood furniture.

Designing Modern Japan

of technical excellence in objects and appliances for modern life worldwide. Skill in craft could also counteract the image of Japanese manufactured goods as cheap, shoddy or pirated.

The choice to emphasize a legibly 'Japanese' craft aesthetic drew heavily on Scandinavian countries' design promotion and export strategies. Kenmochi met repeatedly with retailers of Scandinavian housewares during his 1952 American trip. Japan's Foreign Ministry brought the travelling exhibition 'Design in Scandinavia', first shown in the United States in 1954, to Tokyo in 1955. Kenmochi explained:

> Today, in the competitive ring we know as the Good Design show, Japan is no more than the source for exhibitions of native craft. Most products exhibited by Sweden, Denmark and Italy are designs made by designers, but almost all of the Japanese things are well-made products by anonymous makers. That's not a bad thing. But I don't want people to go on thinking that Japan is a country that only has native craft (the kind of things that Mexicans or Indians make) and doesn't have contemporary Japanese [products] like the Scandinavians make.[49]

The perception that Scandinavian goods embodied a unique sensibility within their universally usable product types suggested a way to offer novelty and distinction, potentially increasing export sales and securing higher price points.[50] It also offered a model for nationally branded design that used styling and materials to suggest a connection to storied craft tradition, anti-commercial 'good design' *and* specific national culture as used by European and North American countries. In the Meiji period, export craft strategists in the national government had sought to position Japan as an equal, conceptually, to Western imperial powers through objects, while seeking export income to support infrastructural development. In the 1950s, again, positioning Japanese exports as equal to European ones, outside the conceptual framework of 'Asia' or 'the non-West', carried political as well as financial weight.[51]

'Japanese Modern' was not without its critics. For some, its products could seem derivative: during a later visit to Tokyo, George Nelson remarked that the IAI's export chairs for its New York Trade Center were 'too Scandinavian'.[52] At a time when many Nordic and West German crafts industry exporters looked to minimalist Japanese forms for inspiration, this was a bit rich.[53] Regardless, for others, 'Japaneseness' tipped into self-exoticization: Kenmochi's own experiments with 'Modern Japanese Style' led to criticism among some colleagues in the design and architecture communities in Japan. But like Swiss style for camera packaging, the strategy stuck. Young designers in the early 1960s particularly were often sent to Denmark and Sweden. The vast majority of prototypes collected by designers and JETRO employees posted overseas were Nordic craft design.

By 1960, craft manufacturing was becoming marginalized domestically as household incomes grew. Japanese consumers switched from wooden *geta* to plastic chemical sandals, and from metal and wood rice-cooking pots to electrical rice cookers.[54] Some *zakka* manufacturers' products continued to find markets overseas and at home. Other, often highly skilled, makers of luxury crafts products increasingly categorized their work specifically as craft (*kōgei* or *kurafuto*), aligning themselves with initiatives to preserve Japan's cultural heritage or with avant-garde practice.[55] As we will see later in this chapter, Japan's consumer landscape was changing rapidly, with real impact on makers; the point here is that yet again, as in the Meiji period, changes in industrial policy impacted the categories of design and craft, product and work.

Kenmochi's comments on craft also highlight a new relationship to Japan's design history. Rather than learning from Nishijin weavers, Kyoto *yūzen* painters or Arita potters, Kenmochi and his cohort imposed 'international standard' methods and frameworks for design and technical R&D as a way to help *zakka* manufacturers access new markets. This may have been partly a function of time passing. By the 1950s, research institute designers, design educators and consultant designers alike were all several generations away from pre-Meiji design education. They had emerged from and worked to propagate and develop a system that separated 'educated' designers – in higher schools and corporate design departments – from designers who learned on the job as part of their making practice. The landscape for designers themselves had changed.

Design in Industry and Education in Post-War Japan

Like confectioners and cosmetics firms, manufacturers of electrical appliances had adopted commercial art advertising practices – publicity, point of sales, marketing, advertising – before the war. In the 1950s, they began to invest in industrial design. Tōkyō Shibaura Denki (Toshiba) provides a useful case in point. Designer Yoshiharu Iwata and colleagues at the company had begun experimenting with styling design in 1947, replacing the plain black casing it had used for its electric fans since the 1930s with colourful resins.[56] The firm was already Japan's market leader in electrical fans, both domestically and in the then important Southeast Asian export market. The potential for expansion into the American market prompted its sales division leadership to explore styling design. So too did managers' awareness that the Japanese domestic market would become more competitive as the economy improved, increasing domestic consumption.

In 1950, the IAI proposed a series of styling design experiments to Toshiba and its competitors, using consumer reactions in the domestic market as the test. For the IAI–Toshiba project, researchers changed the colour and casing form of electrical fans – both aspects that would not impact fans' technical performance – and observed consumer reaction. Based on test results, the partners deemed the project a success. The firm adopted the strategy of releasing new models that updated the product's styling without radically changing the motor or other mechanical features – in other words, styling design. The new fans featured new colours, forms and additional features such as a mirror or function that sprayed fragrance into the air. Toshiba's marketing department began experiments with product naming as well, and shifted from the numbers and letters of pre-war products to flower names: the Himawari-R (Sunflower-R) in 1951, the Nadeshiko (Pink) in 1953 and the Cosmos in 1954.[57] In addition to showing how the firm adopted the doctrine of styling design, the feminine, floral names indicated the firm's rising recognition of the home as a market for electrical goods, with women as its primary managers.

In the early 1950s, some prominent manufacturers began establishing in-house design divisions. Matsushita Kōnosuke (1894–1989), founder and president of the eponymous Osaka-based company responsible for the National and Panasonic brands, instituted a design division at Matsushita Denki in 1951, hiring industrial design educator Mano Zenichi to lead the new initiative.[58] Following the fan experiments, Toshiba created a design section in the marketing department in 1953, then moved it to the production department in 1954.[59] Other manufacturers reorganized existing design staff into named product design sections. Mitsubishi had hired designer Itō Hiroyoshi in 1936 to handle product and catalogue design following his graduation from the Tokyo Higher School of Arts and Crafts. A second academically trained designer, Niboshi Jun, followed in 1942. In 1949, Mitsubishi created a cross-department design committee composed of designers, engineers and managers who met to draw up design standards for products including fans, radios, fluorescent lights, refrigerators, irons, toasters and washing machines. The Standardization Section was renamed the Development Division in 1954 and given responsibility for 'industrial design', with particular attention to colour. It became the Design Division in 1957, with six staff under the division head and two apprentices.[60] Some manufacturers preferred to use outside talent. Tōkyō Tsūshin Kōgyō worked with consultant designers like Akashi Kazuo and Yanagi Sōri until 1961, when it opened an in-house design section.

Integrating design into the production process took time. Designers' responsibilities and location in the corporate structure at conglomerates reflected unease about industrial design's relationship to marketing and engineering. The product design section at Matsushita Denki was composed of section chief Mano, two designers working on radio cabinets and one student intern.[61] According to Mano, the new design employees had little knowledge of materials or manufacturing processes and functioned primarily as 'artistic advisers'.[62] The design section was responsible solely for styling radio cabinets; Matsushita Denki's other products were designed by engineers based on images from American catalogues, with colour and labelling by the public relations department.[63] In other words, the product design section and the idea of creating original designs for new products were experiments. Colleagues in management had to be convinced that design was a specialist activity and a useful one. They often saw design as an element of persuading consumers to buy products, rather than part of the production process.

Managers' understanding of the role that industrial design could play deepened as firms' profits increased, through the growth in sales. In 1954, Matsushita Denki exported 200,000 portable radios to the United States and opened a new central research centre.[64] Design became a separate division within the technology department, thus moving from marketing to engineering. Managers hired three newly graduated industrial designers and gave the Design Division full responsibility for all product styling. The firm began sending its designers overseas for market research and training, and hosted talks by visiting foreign designers invited to Japan through the IAI. With

The workshop at Matsuda Kenkyūjo, 1960, one of two model-making facilities used by the Design Division at Toshiba to fabricate models in wood, metal and plastic after initial prototyping in-house.

corporate reorganization in 1958, design was integrated into each of the company's six product divisions, and the number of designers employed increased to thirty. An in-house publication, *Nashonaru dezain nyūsu* (National Design News), followed in 1960.[65] By 1960, the Design Department at Toshiba, too, employed 44 people.[66]

Automobile design was another growth area for designers in post-war Japan. In 1952, automotive manufacturing was the second-largest industry by production value after machinery.[67] Japan had 88,000 passenger vehicles registered, but these were primarily police cars, taxicabs, cars for government use and ambulances, and overwhelmingly American imports.[68] Some Japanese manufacturers focused on trucks, including lightweight three-wheeled models that could navigate post-war Japan's potholed, bumpy roads and narrow lanes. Three-wheeled trucks were subject to fewer manufacturing restrictions and used fewer materials than larger vehicles. Similarly, 50cc two-stroke engine scooters like Yamaha's Rabbit and Honda's Cub were popular for their naviga-bility and durability. Other firms specialized in buses and train cars.[69] Regardless, Toyota and Nissan, two major auto manufacturers, identi-fied passenger vehicle production as key. Theirs was a long game. The first goal was to increase and claim the domestic market from foreign, largely American, imports. The second was exports.

Automotive design nicely illustrates how some firms understood the relationship between design and technical development for the domestic and export markets. For Toyota and Nissan, the strategy was to concentrate on small cars. There was an immediate reason for this: smaller cars were more appropriate for Japanese roads and the purchasing budgets of Japanese consumers. Small cars would also mean less obvious competition with American auto manufacturers, who concentrated on larger ones – hence reducing possible friction should Japanese manufacturers begin exporting their products to the American market. Given the large numbers of Americans in Japan, growing domestic auto use could also serve as advertising for exports. As one Toyota manager put it, colourfully, 'We should make the kind of cars that will make foreigners who've come for sight-seeing say, "Japan has cars like this" and take them home as presents [*omiyage*].'[70] Toyota's flagship passenger car, the Toyota Crown RS, launched in January 1955 after a three-year development period that included market surveys of taxi drivers and a year of road testing covering 100,000 kilometres.[71] Toyota previewed it in the firm's central Tokyo showroom to a crowd of 18,000 people gathered in the streets outside.[72]

Some officials in MITI, too, identified automobiles as a strategic export area. This was highly optimistic in the early 1950s but fell within MITI's larger strategy to shift exports from existing local industries to new mechanical and chemical ones. In 1950–51, officials in MITI's Automotive Section interviewed manufacturers to gauge the seriousness of their commitment to making passenger vehicles.[73] The Automotive Section wanted to limit production to two companies

アメリカでも実証された実用性

ダットサン 1000 乗用車

ご用命はもよりの特約販売店にお申付け願います

気軽に使える経済車 ダットサンはアメリカ本 国でも大好評で、ぞく ぞく輸出されています

NISSAN 日産自動車株式会社

'Practicality also verified in the United States', magazine advertisement for the Datsun 1000, Nissan Jidōsha Co., Ltd. Like the Toyopet, the Datsun 1000 was celebrated as one of the first domestically made cars in Japan.

Designing Modern Japan

– Toyota and Nissan – and to use competition between them to develop a domestic passenger car that would be competitive with foreign imports.[74] In 1952, the Automotive Section published a book, *To Understand Domestic Passenger Vehicles*, for distribution to members of the Diet to lobby for government support.[75] The book clearly placed the automotive industry within MITI's wider plan:

> From now on, our country, given its poor resources and massive population, will develop each type of manufacturing and processing industry using our plentiful workforce and highly skilled technology, plan the promotion of exports and conduct processed products exports to maintain the economy and stabilize the daily life of the nation.[76]

The echoes of Koike's 1949 statement should be clearly legible: again, this was industrial promotion for reconstruction. Given the complexity of automobiles as products, however, exports required a longer plan. Testing in the domestic market could be part of this. To this end, members of the Automotive Section began to plan products for take-up specifically within Japan, analysing consumer demographics and sales pricing in several countries overseas and using this data to formulate provisional guidelines for the speed, size, price and passenger numbers for domestically produced cars.[77] While firms like Honda Giken achieved success with motorcycle exports in the 1960s, it would be in the 1970s that Toyota, Nissan and their domestic competitors achieved traction. Behind this success, however, lay over two decades of R&D and testing, using the domestic market.

Many industrial designers participated in this work, designing internal parts such as motor casings as well as car bodies and interiors. The conceptual shift in the late 1950s from seeing automobiles as mechanical apparatuses to understanding them as planned, designed products and commodities created an opening for designers.[78] At Toyota, a design desk within the general drafting division began handling the styling of all non-mechanical parts, such as the body, interiors and faces of dashboard instruments, except the chassis.[79] Toyota's designers were subordinate to the company's chief engineer, who moved between design, production, marketing and sales and ultimately controlled the design of each model. Other firms hired consultant industrial designers like Kosugi Jirō (1915–1981), a pre-war graduate of the Tokyo School of Fine Arts design programme who gained familiarity with automotive engineering through working as a mechanic in Manchuria during the war.[80] Design teams adopted practices learned from the United States, not least clay modelling. For the Toyota Crown RS, the firm's chief designer, Iwata Hiroshi, studied foreign cars, both American and European, drawing their components, and assigned details to the head of the Tokyo branch office art section, Morimoto Masao (b. 1918).[81] Understanding the dimensions of foreign cars could be a challenge. Without actual cars to use as models, the team worked from photographs, calculating the scale of each car based on the size of willow trees reflected in the shiny car body.[82] For the Toyota Crown RS, the design team made full-size metal models of five body ideas, ranging from tailfins, Cadillac style, to a more rounded, 'European' model and a boxy model with flush sides.[83] The final style was boxier, with more 'American styling' than originally planned. After feedback from cab drivers, the team included doors that opened outwards from a central hinge, unlike American models.[84] Iwata's grille, inspired by the grille of the de Havilland Comet jetliner, was derided by other members of the design team as an 'upside-down brassiere'.[85]

Whether in-house or outsourced, the purpose of design in car production was relatively consistent. Like fans and space heaters, cars required engineers. And sales could be improved, in theory at least, by hiring designers for styling. Parts like motor casings could become more durable and less expensive to manufacture, too, through attention from designers. But automotive designers could find their roles challenged by colleagues unfamiliar with design. Here is how Nissan chief designer Satō Shōzō (d. 1981) described the design process of the Nissan Junior truck in 1957:

> the company has no trust in us designers, and we are treated as though we do little more than draw posters. The more novel our design, the more unrecognizable and poorly made the prototype will be, and we lack the time and preparation to support its implementation. Without an art director, even this is hard to do – our suggestions are seen simply as the designer's whim.[86]

Thanks to their active research into their American counterparts and dissemination of that information, designers were familiar with the roles of people like Harley Earl at General Motors and with

Clay modelling in the design division at the Nissan Jidōsha Co., Ltd, mid-1950s.

developments in design management such as the art director system. But they could feel that this knowledge was not always shared or appreciated by their colleagues.

Constant changes to the brief during the design process presented further difficulties. Comparing the challenges of working in a corporate setting to the relative ease of posting off a design entry to a competition, Satō wrote:

> It's like close combat when the sun's setting and you can see 40 square metres in each direction, you've just lost touch with your comrades and can't even fight with your fists. You spend one, two, three weeks growing thin from the effort. This kind of thing isn't confined to vehicle design, it's surely ordinary in any company. But it's not like drawing a picture to enter a popular magazine competition.[87]

Satō closed by commenting that the solution would be to include both styling and engineering design upstream in product development. He also noted that the corporate structure at most large organizations would render this impossible.

Large manufacturers' quandaries over how to incorporate product designers into corporate structure indicate the extent of fundamental questions about design's nature and purpose. Was design about superficial styling or integral structure; for optimizing a product's function or for marketing? Which department's employees should lead on design? How should engineers and designers divide duties, and who should have the final say? Matsushita and its competitors stand out for having embraced design as a sales strategy. But at many manufacturers, designers remained subordinate to both marketing and engineering.

The relationship was clearer for graphic design. As we have seen in previous chapters, department stores, fast-moving consumer goods manufacturers, film studios and other makers and retailers created positions for designers as part of their advertising work for the domestic market in the early twentieth century. After the war's end, this work resumed. Graphic design also mattered because of the sheer volume of publishing in post-war Japan and the importance advertisers placed on advertising within them. In 1960, Japan boasted 1,000 different monthly and weekly periodicals.[88] The most popular magazine remained the farming journal *Ie no hikari* (Light of the Home), with a monthly circulation of 1.7 million. Between them, the top ten titles could boast a total circulation of 8 million.[89] Intense publishing activity meant editorial and advertising work for illustrators, designers, photographers and printing technicians, with particularly high demand for eye-catching advertisements. Manufacturers in major export categories like textiles, cameras and electrical machinery also contracted consultant designers for posters and packaging.

While work was to be had, here again tension between designers and the marketing division was not unknown. There was systemic change, too. Many designers who had cut their teeth working in corporate design divisions in the 1930s and the war effort until 1945 launched independent consultancies in the 1950s, often combining this work with teaching in the new design universities. New graphic design graduates continued to join department stores and corporate design divisions in other established industries, but they could also join the consultancies, where lead designers like Sugiura Hisui and Hara Hiromu harnessed their interwar and wartime connections for contracts. By the mid-1950s, large manufacturers' adoption of styling design as a sales strategy meant sufficient work and recognition that some graduates – again with good connections – could found their own consultancies. GK Design began in 1954 as the brainchild of educator Koike Iwatarō (1913–1992), and seven students, male and female, in Koike's design programme at Tokyo University of the Arts (Tokyo Geijutsu Daigaku, known as Geidai), previously the Tokyo School of

Fine Arts. The group won a Special Prize at the Mainichi Industrial Design Competition in 1954 while still students, and incorporated GK Design upon their graduation in 1957.[90] Early products included a piano and hi-fi portable stereo and tuner for Yamaha, a motorcycle, also for Yamaha, and a bicycle for Maruichi.[91] According to founding member Ekuan Kenji (1929–2015), members were inspired by the heady ideals of the age, particularly the idea that they might contribute to the public good through industrial design.[92] GK Design would become a major consultancy with international impact, thanks not least to Ekuan's inspirational writing and personality.

A second change involved restructuring within firms themselves. After the mid-1950s, advertising agencies like Dentsu and Hakuhodo moved from an atelier-style chief designer supported by a junior team to an 'American-style' art director (AD) system, in which the AD had creative control over the project and delegated production to a photographer, graphic designer, typographer and illustrator. Dentsu's Arai Seiichirō (1907–1990) had observed the AD system during a stay in New York and publicized it to the advertising and graphic design communities following his return to Tokyo.93 He established an American-style copywriter division at Dentsu and co-founded the Tokyo Art Directors Club (ADC) in 1952, drawing on his observations of the Art Directors Club in New York.[94] Dentsu and its competitors also shifted from selling advertising space to creating advertisements themselves, and became major employers for graphic designers. These developments were part of a larger process of observation and adoption of American-style advertising and marketing practices in Japan in the 1950s, including market research and a restructuring of advertising management.[95] Explanations of current developments in commercial design techniques appeared regularly in both advertising industry journals *Senden kaigi* – literally 'advertising meeting', although its official English title was *Marketing and Creativity* – and in business paperbacks about effective sales techniques.[96] While lauded at the time, however, some designers who had worked in the more 'all hands on deck' mode before and during the war found the AD system limiting in unexpected ways. Design's increased recognition brought resources, structure and employment. But formalized structures that compartmentalized work into specific sub-tasks, as part of creating an advertisement, a poster or a package, could constrain designers from implementing their creative vision.

In response to working conditions within industry, designers created support structures. Unsurprisingly, interwar and wartime connections remained alive, as professional groups created for the war effort transformed into post-war industry associations and friends and colleagues created formal groups. Organizations provided strength in numbers, camaraderie and shared inspiration. Some groups also offered an economic alliance married with aesthetic agreement. To give one example, the Shinseisaku Art Association began in Tokyo as an artists' group in 1936, then expanded to include architecture in 1949.[97] While its focus was modern art and architecture, it presented furniture designed by architect members like Tange Kenzō (1913–2005) at annual exhibitions. From the early 1950s, the group showed furniture by designers like Kenmochi. Eventually, it included several designers as members. Groups like Shinseisaku were underpinned by personal friendships, common background and professional affinities: between artists seeking social relevance for their work, architects exploring work on smaller scale, craftspeople experimenting with new applications and markets for traditional materials like clay, and designers eager to contemplate abstract concepts in form-making. But at a time when the contemporary aesthetic of modernist art, design and architecture exhibitions belied the very real economic and material challenges that exhibitors faced, interdisciplinary networking and socializing were also important for designers' incomes. As architects like Tange gained commissions for rebuilding civic buildings and erecting new corporate headquarters from the early 1950s onwards, they brought designers like Kenmochi and Watanabe Riki – both Shinseisaku affiliates – and manufacturers like Tendo Mokkō onto the projects, too.

Professional organizations were another important way for designers to strengthen their position within industry. There was a certain continuity for graphic designers, who as we have seen converted existing commercial art networks into research groups for propaganda in the late 1930s.[98] Graphic designers Kamekura Yūsaku, Itoh Kenji, Ōhashi Tadashi (1916–1998) and other colleagues had collaborated on propaganda work during the war.[99] In 1951, they established a professional organization in Tokyo, the Japan Advertising Artists' Club (JAAC, known as Nissenbi), one of several graphic design organizations active in Tokyo that decade.[100] For industrial designers, the prompt was the rising amount of work without professional recognition. In 1952, a group of forty product and industrial designers formed the Japan Industrial Design Association (JIDA).[101] While many of its founders were based in Tokyo, JIDA's membership were located nationwide.

These were explicitly professional organizations. JIDA, for example, required prospective members to have at least five years' professional experience and to have designed at least three products for manufacture, whose design principles and technical accomplishment were scrutinized closely by the membership committee upon application.[102]

They were also overwhelmingly male. Women were not explicitly barred from applying to join the new professional organizations, but the relative youth of female design graduates and expectations that women would leave the profession once they were married, ending their careers, meant that in practice, few women were qualified to apply.

Some designers saw artistic groups and professional organizations as extremely different: one being for lofty aesthetic pursuits, the other for commercial gain. But both functioned to raise awareness of design as a body of specialist professionals. And both could offer lucrative connections, allow designers to raise their fees, and advance careers. Organizations also offered a collective front for lobbying clients to respect designers' intellectual property and to address other issues around poor treatment, at a time when many designers complained about low, uneven design fees and idea theft. Here again, travel allowed designers to gain potentially useful information for strengthening their bargaining power and position. Kenmochi Isamu, for example, used his 1952 U.S. trip to answer key questions about the status and working conditions of designers in industry, including standards for remuneration, pensions, intellectual property and other contractual arrangements, commenting dryly, 'a little different to the in-house designers at Japan's Mitsukoshi and Takashimaya, constrained by their monthly salaries'.[103]

Visitors view posters at the annual exhibition of the Japan Advertising Artists' Club (Nissenbi) at Ginza Matsuya, 1953.

Designing Modern Japan

Organizers of the third annual exhibition of the Japan Advertising Artists' Club (Nissenbi), 1954.

Raising the public profile of professional design practice was part of the lobbying, too. Annual exhibitions and competitions advertised the idea of the designer generally and offered a platform for individual designers to promote their work. Placing work in Nissenbi's annual competition with member and open strands, similar to the pre-war poster competitions exhibited at department stores in Tokyo and regionally, became an important career step for early career designers. The recognition helped them to secure jobs and to build their networks, not least by gaining backing from more established JAAC members. Regular meetings allowed the organizations to function as a social hub and create a sense of community.

Education was part of creating structures for professional design practice, too. Post-war educational reforms reclassified subjects like design as university subjects and incorporated the national higher schools in Tokyo and Kyoto, polytechnic vocational programmes and prefectural industrial and normal schools into four-year universities, often through institutional mergers.[104] The Tokyo Higher School of Arts and Crafts, for example, became the Department of Industrial Design within the Faculty of Engineering at Chiba University, with Koike Shinji, the inspirational speaker and former IAI employee, as its head. Private art schools and sewing schools became private universities, some co-educational, some for women only. The technical high schools established from the Meiji period onwards, too, continued to offer design education. High schools also often had prominent designers as lecturers.

The growing design industries and educators' drive for public aesthetic education supported an expansion in design publishing.

IDEA, the influential graphic design monthly, appeared in 1953, from the previous editor and publisher of the pre-war journal *Kōkokukai* (Advertising World).[105] Graphic designers like Itoh Kenji, Kamekura Yūsaku and Imatake Shichirō (1905–2000) enthusiastically contributed articles about designers' work and new trends in Europe and the United States, as well as offering their own work, making the journal an important reference for designers in Japan and promoting Japanese graphic design overseas. Significantly, *IDEA* read from left to right like a European or American magazine, rather than following Japanese convention and opening from right to left. In Osaka, *Puresu āto* (Press Art) publicized work by graphic designers like Tanaka Ikkō (1930–2002) and functioned as an important mechanism to connect younger designers to more established ones.[106] Designers and critics also wrote prolifically for art, architecture and business magazines and published paperbacks outlining their interpretations of modernist design theory for general audiences.

Post-war reforms increased access to higher education across class and gender lines. Higher education was expensive through the 1960s. Accordingly, many universities offered four- and two-year routes as well as night school pathways and degrees by correspondence. In 1920, less than 2 per cent of the Japanese population had attended university. In 1950, this had risen to more than 10 per cent, and in 1963 to nearly 16 per cent.[107] Women's participation in higher education overall rose from almost 10 per cent of first-year university students in 1950 to nearly 16 per cent of first-year university students in 1963, and from over 41 per cent of first-year junior college students in 1950 to over 72 per cent in 1963.[108] Women also comprised significant proportions of design programme students. Some women joined the newly co-educational design programmes at universities like Geidai. Others continued to study fashion, textiles, interior design and architecture within the home economics departments of women's universities and junior colleges.

A 1956 roundtable between the architect and researcher Kon Wajirō and five young female designers, all based in Tokyo, offers unusual insight into women's experiences in design education and work in post-war Japan.[109] Of the five women interviewed, three had studied at women-only universities and colleges, and two in newly co-educational universities. When asked about their experiences, responses were mixed. The women were passionate about their work

Designing Modern Japan

as designers but less enthused about their education, particularly the theory courses and general education requirements. Contract interior furniture designer Matsuzawa Hatsue noted that she was happier once she had graduated and could follow her own interests. Working provided her with challenges, autonomy and professional identity. All five of the women worked for prominent post-war firms – two in apparel, two in architecture practices and one with a well-known stage designer.

From their responses, the women seem to have been respected and taken seriously by clients, colleagues and bosses, but both Kon as moderator and the women in their comments modulated between their roles as designers and as women, with particular societal expectations for homemaking, marriage and aesthetic education. Nakahara Nobuko (1929–2008), an architect, commented that design as a practice offered women a previously rare opportunity for self-expression and as such was good for women regardless of their aspirations to professional practice. Aoki Ikuko, a fashion designer employed at the textile conglomerate Sanyō Shōkai, agreed that studying design could 'enrich one's home life with a designer's sensibility' and explained that she herself felt torn between her attachment to her work and her previous expectations that she would quit soon into her career to become a homemaker.[110] As for Kon, the moderator, his final question addressed the women not as designers but as consumers buying teacups and 'pretty' stationery.

The five women's experiences in moving from education to work were not unique. At both co-educational and women's universities, strong alumni networks and the close connection between professors on prestigious programmes and employers were important. Like their pre-war predecessors, male and female graduates alike found employment at cosmetics and confectionery manufacturers, advertising agencies, department stores and regional universities, colleges and research institutes. White goods manufacturers like Matsushita Denki and apparel firms like Renown, Aoki's employer, became important employers as they added design departments. Here again, hierarchy and connections ruled. Thanks to their networks, graduates from universities like Chiba University and Geidai staffed the design divisions of manufacturers such as Mitsubishi and Hitachi, as well as the design advisory teams at the IAI and many regional research institutes. More widely, the fact that many senior graphic and industrial designers had taken professorships and leadership positions in university design programmes meant that they could serve as matchmakers for students and firms, using their professional connections. Among well-networked programmes, fashion designer Kuwasawa Yōko's (1910–1977) Kuwasawa Design School (Kuwasawa Dezain Kenkyūjo, KDS), an entirely new post-war school in Tokyo with significant profile, drew on her personal and professional connections. KDS offered night courses in industrial design, dressmaking and fashion design and other disciplines, taught by Kuwasawa and other key industry figures, including Akashi Kazuo.[111] KDS was unusual for offering fashion design alongside product and graphic design; most fashion programmes in higher education operated as part of clothing-specific schools like the storied Bunka Fashion College (Bunka Fukusō Gakuin), or in the home economics faculties of women's universities and junior colleges.

Whether products, magazine covers or posters in train stations, designers showed their work to public audiences all the time. But this work was not necessarily noticed as the products of design. To raise awareness of design as an industry, promoters had to point out that *someone* had designed these things. From 1952, the *Mainichi Shimbun*, a major national newspaper, sponsored a competition, the New Japan Industrial Design Competition (Shin Nihon Kōgyō Dezain Shō, renamed the Mainichi Industrial Design Concours in 1955), with prizes in commercial design and industrial design. The competition offered winners prominent publicity in the newspaper and a touring exhibition, as well as prizes up to 300,000 yen, a substantial amount when working households had an average annual income of 315,999 yen in 1952–3.[112] Significantly, the jury looked both at overall aesthetic appeal and the designers' rationalization of production and use – the 'industrial' aspect of industrial design, underlining the centrality of design to economic development to paper readers and exhibition visitors. The Minister of International Trade and Industry and the head of the Agency for Industrial Science and Technology also sponsored prizes, further indicating the link between economic development, industrial rationalization and design for mass production. Yanagi Sōri won the 1953 competition for his record player design for Tōkyō Tsūshin Kōgyō (Sony). Fellow consultant designer Kosugi Jirō triumphed in 1954 with a sewing machine for Janome, a major competitor to Singer in Japan and overseas.[113] The exhibitions, substantial prize money and promotion in a national newspaper raised design's profile and aligned the

Kuwasawa Yōko teaching Western-style lingerie construction at the Kuwasawa Design School, 1955.

image of design with new industries, not traditional ones. So did Graphic 55, an exhibition of work by a loosely affiliated group of illustrators and graphic designers including Kamekura, Kōno Takashi and Hayakawa Yoshio (1917–2009), along with the work of American designer Paul Rand. The object of the show, held at the Takashimaya department store in Tokyo in 1955, was to display posters by each designer as a creative work to be admired and appreciated in and of itself. As such the exhibition presented an alternative assessment of design's value as creative art, beyond or alongside its commercial impact.

It is telling that the list of Mainichi award winners in commercial and industrial categories contains many designers well known today, outside as well as within Japan. Also telling is that by 1955, women were placing in the awards but few of these women appear further, prominently, in the historical record. As if to underline why this was, commentary on the achievements of female award-winners foregrounded their gender, while those of the male award-winners did not. One commentary on the 1956 competition connected the number of women winning prizes with the clear success of industrial design's popularization among the general public, and described an entry by two female designers, a camera, as possessing a 'feminine sense'.[114] At the same time, publicly circulated rosters of industrial designers available for contracts included no women.[115] Societal expectations that women would marry and stop working after marriage to have children and manage the household ended most careers before women achieved senior positions, let alone their own offices, and shaped women's experiences of professional design.

For male designers as well, experience was not equal. Class and family wealth often determined whether young men could access university design courses or join corporate design teams. Young men from poor backgrounds apprenticed or studied design at vocational high schools before going into work locally. Graphic designer Kimura Tsunehisa (1928–2008), for example, worked as a sign painter in a black market in Osaka for three years, between the ages of eighteen and 21, before apprenticing to an established designer.[116] Networks and geography shaped university-educated designers' experience and opportunities, with work clustering around the cities home to large manufacturers, department stores and ad agencies: Tokyo, Osaka and, to a lesser degree, Aichi prefecture, with its automotive and ceramics sectors. Where designers chose to work was driven partly by family and familiarity. In 1956, Geidai reported that its graduates received 'many passionate requests' from firms in Osaka and Aichi who wished to recruit them but noted that almost no graduates accepted these offers.[117] The report's analysis of graduates' geographical destinations commented that graduates preferred to remain in Tokyo as the centre of design activity. Tellingly, however, it also noted that continuing food and housing shortages and household financial precarity meant that most Geidai applicants were already Tokyo residents and wanted to stay there. Whether as students or as professionals, many designers starting out had to stay where they were, whether that was Tokyo, Osaka or a regional city.

Local industry continued to shape design education in each place, as design areas seeded and developed in response to industry and consumer demands. In graphic design, Osaka and Tokyo continued to house two largely separate design communities, each responding to different local needs. Designers often suggested that the two cities' different client bases – commerce and industry in Osaka, government and trade in Tokyo – had created strikingly different visual styles. Osaka-born designer Kōno Takashi commented in 1952:

> Tokyo has a lot of government commissions while Osaka commissions are largely from individual shops that give the designer the freedom to do as he likes. So a lot of the Tokyo work feels extremely orthodox, and Osaka produces a lot of

Designing Modern Japan

daringly original work . . . I wish that Tokyo graphics would smile a little more, and Osaka graphics remove their loud Hawaiian shirts.[118]

Locality could be an advantage. Emerging designers could develop ties with more established designers in study groups as well as through work, and designers could develop mutually beneficial relationships with local businesses. The Osaka designer and illustrator Hayakawa Yoshio, like other several other prominent graphic designers from Kansai area, honed his skills working for the Kintetsu Department Store and gained professional networks during his time there. But by the late 1950s, the importance of advertising, an industry increasingly centred in Tokyo, made Tokyo the most attractive location for ambitious designers. So too did the emergence of industrial and graphic design consultancies, from small firms launched by former IAI designers like Kenmochi to the Nippon Design Center, established in 1959 as the creative consultancy for eight major corporations including Nippon Steel and Toyota. As Kimura Tsunehisa memorably described his decision to leave his home town of Osaka for Tokyo:

At that time, Osaka was troubled physically and economically by subsidence. The munitions factories had pumped up all the groundwater during the war. Buildings in the industrial area along the bay had subsided so much that you needed to enter and exit through the third-floor window. The water damage was unbearable. Osaka, previously the centre of Japanese commerce and industry, sank to the level of a regional city after the war. The centre became overconcentrated in Tokyo. It was nearly impossible to work as a designer in Osaka, so in 1960, I moved to Tokyo, too, to join Nippon Design Center.[119]

Tokyo-based designers dictated much of the post-war history, not least because colocation in Tokyo allowed designers to work more directly with the most prominent design organizations and publications, themselves Tokyo-based. Working in consultancies, rather than in-house design divisions, also allowed designers to speak up. And public prominence could be part of a consultancy's marketing strategy.

Expansion and change in the graphic and industrial design communities required new language, as did responses to international trends.

Universities, professional societies, publications, exhibitions and consultancy work offered a stage on which designers and critics could define their industry through the language they chose to describe it. Graphic designers replaced the pre-war term 'commercial art' (*shōgyō bijutsu*) and the words *zuan* and *ishō* with 'graphic design' (*gurafikku dezain*) and a transliteration of 'design', *dezain*. Product designers sought accurate, precise language for translating 'industrial design' into Japanese. Some promoted the translations *sangyō ishō* (manufacturing design) and *kōgyō ishō* (industrial design). Other young designers were attracted to *indasutoriaru dezain* itself, with its internationalism and reference to industry rather than to heavy industry (*kōgyō*) or manufacturing (*sangyō*), but found that others had not kept up with them. GK Design's Ekuan explained:

> Every time we met someone, we had to start by explaining the meaning of '*indasutoriaru dezain*' . . . We told people about the goals, value and methods of industrial design and the dreams of industrial designers and began with activities that introduced the 'way of making things' they proposed.[120]

By 1971, GK Design had published nearly three hundred books and articles, including translations from American industrial designers and several books on their approach to the field.

Not everyone agreed. IAI chief and metalwork specialist Matsuzaki Fukusaburō thought that *kōgei*, used in the pre-war period to include design and craft alike and often translated as 'industrial art', remained most appropriate. For Matsuzaki, design was the technique that allowed makers to produce the best results for an everyday product, applied in any form of manufacturing, hand or machine, workshop or factory, and *kōgei* described it well:

> *Kōgei* grows with the times . . . *Kōgei* is definitely not a set of decorative techniques, nor is it a smug, self-righteous form of fine art. It is the technical ability to generate the results most appropriate to a product to make that product easily usable by the people who will use it.[121]

While Matsuzaki's employer, the IAI, expressly supported industrial crafts through the 1960s, this was to be a losing battle. Increasingly in

Hayakawa Yoshio, the eleventh autumn Shūsaikai, poster for a kimono fair at the Kintetsu Department Store in Abeno, Osaka, 1973, advertising 'The chicness of the kimono fashion of autumn '53' and the beauty of 'French colour schemes' through Hayakawa's elegant illustration as well as the catch copy. Kimono sales to the women in prosperous families remained an important aspect of fashion and department store business, and department stores remained an important employer for graphic designers, as earlier in the century.

the 1950s, *kōgei* became identified with craft design, itself an evolving category as some designers and small workshops aligned themselves more and more with the creative, original and handmade, rather than with production for everyday sales. Koike, Ekuan and others' embrace of 'industrial design' and rejection of *kōgei* aligned with the MITI shift towards valuing and promoting machinery, electrical goods and other higher-added-value, higher-productivity industries over existing local industries. It demonstrated how design could continue to take part in the export industrial vision, even as its applications changed.

'Electrified Life': Design and Domestic Consumption

The domestic market mattered for manufacturers and designers, too. Another compelling image, this time a colour photograph, helps us pick up the story here. In the photograph, a young woman neatly clad in a jumper, skirt and apron, shopping basket over one arm, offers an apple to a small, pinafored girl holding a vacuum cleaner hose. This image from the early 1960s suggests that while mother went shopping, her small daughter played housewife. The family seem secure and comfortable, perhaps because they have been fortunate enough to win a new flat in a public housing block, trading a tin-roofed wooden rowhouse or worse for a bright, airy interior that, as we can see, is also easy to clean. Cleaning no longer means wiping the floor on hands and knees: now, an electric vacuum cleaner does the hard work. The bright colours and contrast of the image, too, suggest prosperity: this is a country with the technological capacity to print colour photographs in high resolution as book covers. Altogether, the image is anodyne yet telling, potentially illustrating many stories yet remarkably apt for the one it does. The photograph, by photographer Ōhashi Haruzō (b. 1927), appeared as the front cover to *Denka seikatsu annai: Hyūzu kara kūrā made* (A Guide to Electrified Life: From Fuses to Air Conditioners), a manual for domestic electrical appliances published in Tokyo in 1962.[122]

In the breakfast vignette that opened Chapter Two, we saw how households adopted electrical appliances beginning in the 1920s. After the war's end, policymakers, researchers and old and new electrical machinery firms alike put effort into developing export products like electric fans. As incomes rose in the 1950s, domestic consumers became an important market for such products as well.[123] Growth in domestic and export sales increased production volumes, allowing manufacturers

Ōhashi Haruzō (photographer), illustration in Zenji Katagata, *A Guide to Electrified Life* (1962).

to lower their prices and spurring further purchases at home. By 1961, 62.5 per cent of urban households and 28.5 per cent of rural households owned a television set, respectively a 40 per cent and 150 per cent jump in ownership in one year alone.[124] Ownership of electric refrigerators, fans and vacuum cleaners had increased noticeably as well. Within Japan, consumption provided further fertile ground for designers and formed an important part of the 'landscape like a picture book'.

The period of high economic growth, also known as Japan's economic miracle, did not benefit everyone equally. Poor urban housing and household poverty remained endemic issues. Hard working conditions continued for many, from agricultural households to coal miners. But the combination of rising national income and public intervention into living conditions affected everyone: it was a matter of degree rather than absolutes. Growing household incomes and expectations that people would own more things, including fuses and air conditioners, created yet more work for designers.

One area for direct public intervention was everyday life spaces and practices in rural communities. One national effort was spearheaded by the Everyday Life Improvement Department (Seikatsu Kaizen-ka) in the Ministry of Agriculture and Forests (Nōrinshō), led from 1948 by Yamamoto Matsuyo, a domestic economy specialist who had studied in the United States in the 1930s.[125] Yamamoto oversaw a national network of 'daily life improvement proselytizers', women with two years of university education who advised villages. As a system, this network of women paralleled the network of male technical advisers charged with rationalizing regional industry through their work in industrial research and advisory institutes, but for a literally domestic economy – non-waged work within the home – rather than production for market profit.

Yamamoto's remit added an emphasis on 'democratizing' village society to existing pre-war concerns with rationality, efficiency and the replacement of 'outdated' customs with more rational ones. In one project, department team members tried to improve rural women's working conditions and decrease the amount of time they had to spend on laundry by reforming rural dress, published in the farming household magazine *Ie no hikari*. Another proposal, in the late 1950s, was for rural women to adopt a revised form of *monpe*, the loose-fitting trousers women wore in the fields, made with a synthetic fabric (*biniron*) that dried more quickly than natural fibres. *Biniron* was eventually

Designing Modern Japan

produced as a fabric for agricultural workwear by Kurashiki Rayon, a major textile manufacturer, and distributed by the national agricultural association.[126] The agricultural cooperatives of Japan's rural areas may seem far from the fashionable environs of Tokyo's design communities, but both fashion designer and educator Kuwasawa Yōko and researcher Kon Wajirō participated in this project. Koike Shinji's point about designers 'giving their all' extended to domestic development as well.

In cities, public intervention into housing had a knock-on effect for furniture manufacturers. Urban housing was part of government investment in physical infrastructure as well. In 1956, just over a decade after the war, the government's Economic Planning Agency commented that while Japanese daily life had recovered in terms of food and clothing, housing remained insufficient in quality or quantity.[127] Bureaucrats in the Ministry of Construction estimated that the country still lacked 2.7 million residences, affecting 16 per cent of Japan's population, with average living space still smaller than before the war. Much urban housing remained wooden rowhouses with thin walls, a communal alleyway courtyard and toilets, and a public bath nearby. Space was at a premium: through the early 1960s, it was not unusual for an urban couple or family to occupy one 4.5-tatami-mat room with a shared toilet and no bath, with bedding closets used as makeshift bunk beds.[128]

In response to the urban housing shortage and concerns over the quality of available housing, architects, officials and construction firms began developing large communal housing schemes known as *danchi*. Among them, those of the Housing Corporation (Jūtaku Eidan), formed in 1923, were most prominent. The Housing Corporation succeeded the Dōjunkai, the association formed in Tokyo in 1923 to provide housing after the Great Kantō Earthquake (and responsible for the Dōjunkai Jingū Apartments discussed in Chapter Two). In 1955, the corporation became the Japan Housing Corporation (Nihon Jūtaku Kōdan, JHC), known familiarly as Kōdan.[129] The corporation's standardized interiors, particularly the 51-c unit launched in 1951, would have an immense impact on post-war housing.[130] The 51-c unit provided an expandable formula for flats known as 'nDK', comprising n number of rooms with a separate combined dining-kitchen (DK) area and toilet. 51-c dining-kitchens had hard flooring for sanitation, requiring a dining table and chairs for comfort. Tatami mats covered the floors in the rooms for living, allowing residents to use whatever furnishings they already owned. The 51-c unit was based on a design by the architect Nishiyama

Uzō (1911–1994), who saw its floorplan as reorganizing social relations, for example by requiring the head of the household to enter the feminized workspace of the kitchen to eat.[131] It also reflected the ideals of the 1920s housing reform movement. The nDK model became the national standard for new housing, such as that photographed in the *Guide to Electrified Life* illustration, not least through the JHC's unique role in providing housing at scale: estimates suggest it provided 27 per cent of the total housing units built in Japan between 1945 and 1973.[132] It also inspired the design of other public organizations' housing estates, as well as estates by private developers. By 1957, Tokyo alone had 68,000 public housing flats, including those operated by the metropolitan government as well as the JHC.[133]

Reformers saw dining-kitchens as improving hygiene and familial social roles and interactions. But some residents were less pleased when the materials and layout of the space began to change their living habits. One university-educated housewife, Sasaki Kyōko, recorded that she and her husband spent part of his annual bonus on a dining set, after finding sitting at a low table uncomfortable in the space. As she expressed her bemusement:

> With the dining set, the room finally looked right, and
> mealtimes became a lot more convenient. It took some
> of my pleasure away, though, to look at our home as a
> whole and see how crammed it had become with furniture.[134]

Getting rid of things would eventually become a challenge as well, particularly in the twenty-first century, as Japan's baby-boomers downsize and younger generations show little interest in the dish sets, decorations and kimono chests they accumulated.[135]

In the post-war period, however, furnishing homes took precedence. Families with the means to do so purchased three-piece sets for living rooms and bedrooms, including a kimono chest, as a dowry for daughters getting married; this was important for the many couples moving to larger cities and forming nuclear households there. All of this meant work – and income – for furniture manufacturers and retailers. In the early 1950s, furniture manufacturers around the country channelled profits and designs from the Occupation-era Dependent House project into goods for the domestic market, despite materials shortages and high taxation on furniture as luxury items. Department

Designing Modern Japan

stores resumed furniture displays. Given furniture's associations with wealth – the wealthier the household, the larger the home and the more furniture they could acquire – having an active furniture and interiors department allowed department stores to position themselves as more upmarket than competitors. An editorial in *Living Design* in 1955 opined, 'The furniture department is the barometer of a department store's prosperity, and it is said that the greater effort a store makes in its furniture department, the higher its class.'[136] Department stores' in-house furniture designers – often graduates of the key design universities – created many of their products; department stores also sold furniture from high-end Western- and Japanese-style manufacturers.

With furniture from Mitsukoshi and Takashimaya out of reach for most households, specialist furniture shops in local shopping areas furnished most homes. Local retailers remained in sway to powerful regional wholesalers and distributors, as in the Tokugawa period, as did most furniture manufacturers.[137] Most furniture continued to be made in specialized industrial districts, with district industry organizations handling negotiations with wholesalers and distributors and organizing trade fairs. Individual districts specialized in particular kinds of furniture, ordinarily either legged (*ashimono*) or boxy (*hakomono*). The furniture districts in Shizuoka and Tokushima, for example, specialized in mirror stands, while those in Ōkawa made chests. Both were boxy, in contrast to the furniture makers of Asahikawa, in Hokkaidō, who provided chairs and tables with legs.

Industrial organization and the preponderance of family micro-businesses precluded most home furniture producers from having in-house designers. Instead, businesses looked at competitors' products, discussed market trends through their local industry associations and consulted with the design sections at local industrial research institutes. Institutes served an important role in creating prototypes of new designs, using competition entries to test them in national markets and supporting local makers in adopting new designs for manufacture within the limitations of local workshops. Prototypes often addressed changing lifestyles and purchasing habits. In Shizuoka, institute designers developed mirror stands that could rest on table-tops.[138] Mirror-stand makers also branched into radio cabinets and sewing machine tables, latching on to those booming industries.

While graphic and product design were growth areas for designers in the 1950s and '60s, furniture design remained unreliable as a professional specialization. Employment in department stores, the few design consultancies, elite architecture firms and industrial advisory institutes allowed some designers to work in furniture design, often for contract interiors. By the 1960s, Tendō Mokkō and other contract furniture firms with integrated production created specific in-house design teams, although they too continued to work with consultant designers like Watanabe Riki and Yanagi Sōri rather than bringing design fully in-house. But the small-scale, distributed nature of the industry meant that few furniture manufacturers could offer design positions. Perhaps as a result, few young designers chose furniture as their métier. One anecdote illustrates this well. In 1961, Tendō Mokkō launched an annual furniture design competition, judged by a jury of elite designers and architects.[139] The competition lasted five years, with judges noting the lacklustre nature of entries by the 1963 competition.[140] Furniture design was simply less viable as a specialization. In overseas museum collections, consultant designers like Kenmochi, Yanagi and Watanabe are known for their furniture. But they all worked across packaging, interiors, industrial and craft design as well as furniture for their income.

In contrast, apparel design was a growth area. The woman and child on the cover of *A Guide to Electrified Life* wear Western-style clothing. Among the reasons for women's adoption of Western dress as standard daywear was the low cost of Western-style clothing relative to that of kimono, making it easier for women to look smart on a low budget.[141] The greater ease of wearing, washing and maintaining Western-style clothing similarly made it less expensive and more convenient. The bulk and expense of kimono storage chests particularly in post-war urban housing may also have played a role in kimono's decline as everyday wear. Post-war fashion magazines included both Western-style and kimono patterns and editorial spreads, but kimono became a choice rather than the default option.

The growth of women's Western-style clothing as an industry followed, at two very different scales.[142] At one end were home sewing and made-to-measure dress shops. In 1947, Japan had four hundred sewing schools with 45,000 students; in 1951, there were 2,400 schools and 360,000 students, a 600 per cent increase in the number of schools and an 800 per cent increase in the number of students in only four years.[143] The rise in schools related directly to the growth in popularity of Western-style clothing and the belief that machine- rather than

Designing Modern Japan

Architect Tange Kenzō reviewing fabrication of the т-7304 chair, known familiarly as the *dakko isu* (hug chair), at the Tendō Mokkō factory in Yamagata Prefecture, Japan.

hand-sewing was the most appropriate way of making it.[144] Following the convention of sewing kimono at home, many women learned Western-sewing techniques so that they could continue to make clothes for themselves and their households, using sewing machines and following magazine patterns. For other sewing school students, seamstress work was the goal. The number of Western-style dress shops in Japan increased from 1,300 in 1943 to 15,000 in 1955.[145] For the most part these were small, made-to-measure neighbourhood shops; 90 per cent of dressmakers were women sewing at home or in workshops contracted to small retailers.[146] Sewing machines were a key design brief for industrial designers throughout the 1950s, not only for export but for domestic sales.

Women's adoption of Western-style clothing also impacted existing textile manufacturers, not least by providing a market. Textile production relaunched in 1949, enabling the exports that so troubled American and European manufacturers in the 1950s.[147] By the 1960s, however, textile exports were declining. Both large textile firms like the Osaka spinning mills and small family firms in industrial districts that had specialized in export textiles wanted new income sources. So did the large firms that specialized in artificial textiles such as rayon, acetate and nylon: Tokyo Rayon (now Toray), Mitsubishi Rayon, Asahi Kasei and others. Large manufacturers and wholesalers established ready-to-wear apparel divisions, using vertical integration to manage clothing production and distribution, and selling largely through department stores.[148] While Japan had not historically had a significant ready-to-wear industry – kimono being sewn at home, from bolts of cloth – women's adoption of Western-style dress presented an opportunity. At the same time, the rapid decline in women wearing kimono as everyday dress removed a major market from the domestic garment industry, affecting kimono cloth and obi weavers and dyers as well as accessory manufacturers, wholesalers and retailers.[149] Some firms switched from producing and providing kimono cloth and accessories to manufacturing and distribution of Western-style clothing in Japan, including subcontracting for larger firms.[150]

All of these developments created new fashion careers, including fashion illustration, design and pattern-making for Western-style clothing. The most prominent schools for women interested in a career in Western-style fashion and dressmaking, including Bunka Fashion

'Your own seamstress', advertisement for Pine Sewing Machines Co., Ltd, 1954.

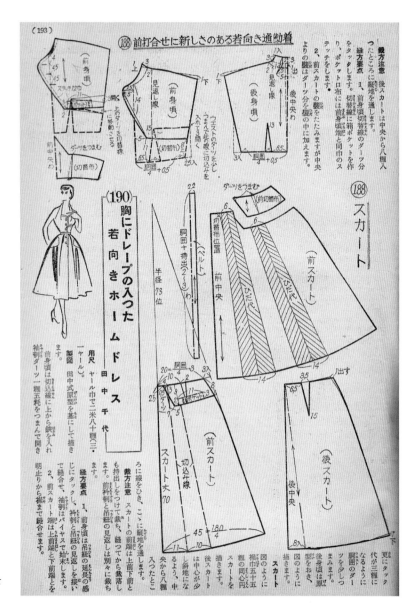

Dress designs including 'a youthful home dress with a drape in the bust' by leading Western-style sewing and fashion educator Tanaka Chiyo, in *Summer Clothing for Home and for Going Out* (1954).

College and Doresumēkā Jogakuin, known as 'Doremē', were located in Tokyo. In addition to training women, schools like Bunka and Doremē publicized Western-style fashion as an industry and consumer item, by hosting visits from prominent Paris designers like Christian Dior and Pierre Cardin, launching design competitions and publishing fashion magazines. *Sōen*, published by Bunka, had a circulation of

350,000 in 1960; its competitor *Dressmaking*, published by Doremē, had a circulation of 250,000.[151] Graduates of the specialist fashion and sewing schools and from the home economics departments at prestigious women's universities could go into employment in the design sections at department stores, firms like Renown and Sanyō Shōkai, the employer of Aoki Ikuko, interviewed by Kon Wajirō in 1956. Women's fashion careers in industry remained largely separate from kimono and obi textile design, which continued to be a largely masculine practice, centred in Kyoto.

As household income increased and expenditures stabilized, homes became increasingly electrified. Household electrical usage nearly doubled between 1960 and 1965.[152] It grew 500 per cent by the end of the 1960s. In 1965, 90 per cent of households owned a television. By 1970, 90 per cent of households owned a refrigerator and a washing machine as well. Smaller electric appliances populated homes, too: more than 80 per cent of households owned at least one electric footwarmer in 1965, and period films depicted urban and rural housewives alike pining after electric knitting machines. Along with magazines and radio programmes, books like *Guide for Electrified Life* encouraged women not only to purchase electrical appliances but to become expert users, both to lighten the burden of household chores and, with sewing and knitting machines, to earn an income by undertaking piecework from home.

Increased domestic purchases – powered partly by domestic piecework – fuelled design industry growth, not least as competition prompted manufacturers to invest in marketing and styling design to differentiate vacuum cleaners and washing powder on the shelves and at home. Catchphrases such as the 'three sacred regalia', playing on sacred objects enshrined in the imperial family shrine at Ise, allowed marketers to promote purchases of

'Like wearing a cool breeze: "Cool and airy style" summer wear', advertisement for Asahi Cashmeron summer knits by Uematsu Kuniomi (designer) and Fukishida Takeshi (photographer), Asahi Kasei, 1963.

涼風を着る〈空冷式〉サマーウエア

旭化成
カシミロン

サマー
ニット

Designing Modern Japan

'This happiness tells everything about a car', Nippon Design Center (art director Kaji Yūsuke, designer Shibanaga Fumio, copywriter Tanaka Tōru, photographer Takanashi Yutaka), print advertisement for Toyota Motor Co., Ltd, 1965.

white goods such as refrigerators, washing machines and black-and-white televisions in sets of three.[153] The new comprehensive visual communication consultancy Nippon Design Center, launched in 1959 with investment from corporations including Toshiba, Toyota and beverage maker Asahi, must be understood in this context.[154] Run by well-connected graphic designers, photographers and illustrators including Kamekura Yūsaku, Tanaka Ikkō and Hara Hiromu, the NDC provided advertising campaigns for their backers across media channels including radio, television and environmental graphics, including neon signs. Advertisers like Matsushita also invested in PR work, from newspaper advertisements to glossy corporate magazines, to publicize the company rather than to sell a particular product. Magazines themselves were growing in number, from a total of 290 million magazines published annually in 1950 to 774 million magazines in 1957.[155] All of this meant more work for advertisers and, as a result, for designers.

The visual look of advertising changed dramatically in the early 1960s with the wide adoption of new technologies. Among them, the introduction of colour film and four-colour halftone printing allowed printers to replace the previous standard – three-colour-filtered monochrome images, layered on posters and magazine covers to create colourful, blocky images – with multi-colour compositions in which colour photographs, rather than illustrations, featured prominently.[156] Design teams began experimenting with new materials as printers developed inks and techniques for printing on plastics, metals, vinyl and cellophane. The widespread adoption of television – and the presence of commercial channels – in the early 1960s also created demand for film-makers and animators to create television advertisements, as advertising firms sold television sponsorships as well as ad time. Environmental graphics such as neon signs and wayfinding systems presented yet another growth area.[157]

Working in multidisciplinary teams, with film-makers and animators as well as printing technicians, allowed graphic designers and illustrators to work across new media and to build networks for commissions. In 1964, graphic designer, illustrator and artist Yokoo Tadanori (b. 1936) left the Nippon Design Center to start his own studio. Yokoo had gained media and critical attention for his bright Pop art paintings. In a series of television advertisements for Vonnel Casuals, a knitwear line from Mitsubishi Rayon, flashes of Yokoo's highly distinctive imagery punctuate filmed footage of four young women striding over bridges, through stadium seating and by a group of apprentice geisha at a shrine. The women's hair is cropped and their eyeliner heavy, like Twiggy or Jean Shrimpton, to match the style of their knitwear separates and minidresses. Jump cuts and the insouciant, irreverent animations emphasized the youthful, modern and urban image Mitsubishi Rayon had chosen for the Vonnel line. The fast jazz soundtrack and audio overlay of the women's quick footsteps suggested progress towards a more modern – as well as stylish and empowered – future through ready-to-wear fashion. While not as overt, the advertisement also indicates how two decades after the war's end, the combination of export-driven industries and the growing domestic economy, together with designers' and their allies' concerted and persistent lobbying for design's role in these systems, had created design jobs and embedded designers' work in commerce.

But some members of the design community, particularly those with international connections, thought that design was overly in service to commerce. Debate was particularly fierce in graphic design, where some designers felt that advertising's commercial imperative, quantitative techniques and technological advances in printing subsumed creativity. A decade after graphic designers presented posters in the manner of a group painting show at the Graphic 1955 exhibition, the exhibition Persona 65, held like its precedessor at the Matsuya department store in Tokyo's Ginza, presented posters by prominent illustrators and graphic designers including Tanaka Ikkō, Nagai Kazumasa (b. 1929) and Yokoo, whose eponymous poster advertised nothing but the artist himself.[158]

This understanding of the designer as auteur emerged from both sides of the art and design, or crafts and design, divide. Japanese *mingei* historian Mizuo Hiroshi's (b. 1930) 1962 book *Dezainā no tanjō* (The Birth of the Designer) looked back to early modern and premodern

Yokoo Tadanori, *Untitled (Having Reached a Climax at the Age of 29, I Was Dead)*, 1965, silkscreen poster, ink on paper, displayed at the Persona graphic design exhibition at Ginza Matsuya in 1965.

Designing Modern Japan

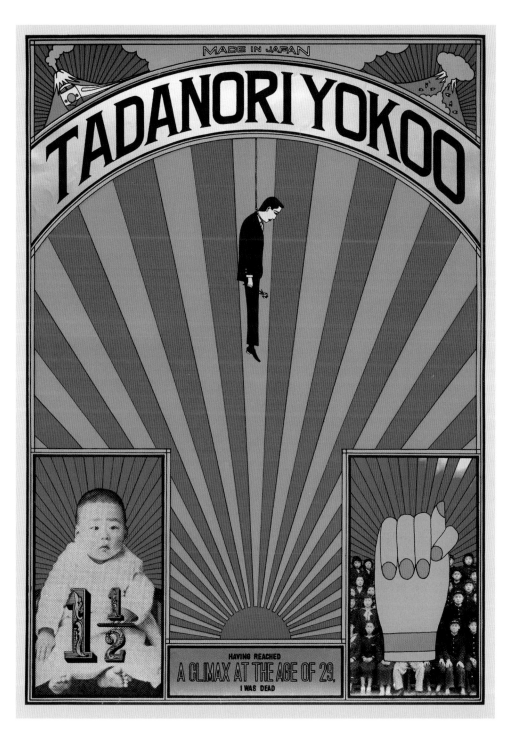

Japanese art history to find parallels with contemporary occupational archetypes.[159] Hokusai and Hiroshige were 'photographers'; Rinpa painter Tawayara Sōtatsu was a 'layout man'. Honami Kōetsu, the prolific Rinpa designer, was an 'art director'. The obverse of this was, as Mizuo phrased it in his conclusion, 'today's designers are artists.' As he continued, 'They know what beauty is, and they are always searching for ways to create beauty. They flex their spirits to find the best way express their own individuality and artistic sensibility in [their work].'[160] In the Meiji period, designers like Kamisaka Sekka had sought to bring Rinpa style into their designs for modern life. In the post-war period, designers including Kenmochi and Yokoo pursued a distinctly Japanese visual and object language. By suggesting that art and crafts production in premodern Japan corresponded to modern design, Mizuo sought to position the design industries in Japan as themselves part of a longer continuum – to claim not only modern design aesthetics but the design process, with its combination of art and commerce, as already Japanese.

By 1960, many prominent and commercially well-connected designers had begun to reconsider design's social role. This came partly from their active participation in international organizations like the International Council of Societies of Industrial Design (ICSID, now the World Design Organization), of which JIDA was a founding member in 1957.[161] In 1960, some four hundred Japanese and foreign designers, architects and critics explored design's purpose at the World Design Conference (WoDeCo), a three-day conference in Tokyo.[162] Prominent American and European designers like Saul Bass, Walter Landau and Max Huber, invited through Japanese designers' and architects' active networking in the United States and Europe, joined Japanese design figures like Akashi, Kenmochi and Kamekura and architectural luminaries like Tange and Sakakura Junzō (1901–1969) for discussions around designers' responsibilities towards humanity, rather than the practicalities of working as a designer, although designer Herbert Bayer's address urged participants to bridge the gap between design idealism and commercial work.[163]

By the early 1960s, however, a younger generation of male designers like Yokoo, Kimura, Awazu Kiyoshi (1929–2009) and Uno Akira (aka Aquirax Uno, b. 1934) were becoming involved with countercultural and critical art, film and theatre groups and projects, incorporating their often radical visual language into both avant-garde work – much of it linked to social and political protest – and corporate and government campaigns like the 1964 Summer Olympics.[164] As we will see in the next chapter, graphic design practice became more politicized over the course of the 1960s. Even in the early 1960s, however, events like the 1960 renegotiation of the U.S.–Japan Security Treaty, known as Anpo, and trade union activism around the closure of coal mines nationally, had created public dissent in which designers, too, participated.[165]

For designers, the 1964 Summer Olympics brought many of these questions – about art and commerce, and designers' sovereignty versus

Kamekura Yūsaku (design), Murakoshi Jō (director of photography), Hayasaki Osamu (photographer), *The Start of the Sprinters' Dash*, poster, Tokyo, 1962, colour photogravure.

their roles as contributing to something greater – together. The Olympics were the first to be held in Asia, after the 1940 Summer Olympics in Tokyo were cancelled, and the first major international event to be held in Japan. As such, they offered a message regarding Japanese economic recovery and internationally recognizable cultural values, mediated through design and sport. Preparation for the Olympics was a major factor in creating the 'landscape like a picture book' with which this chapter opened: the national government's infrastructural investment included Japan's first motorway as well as the New Tōkaidō Trunk Line, better known as the bullet train or Shinkansen, between Tokyo and Osaka.[166]

Mirroring the embrace of design within MITI export policy and export manufacturers' sale strategies alike, the Olympic organizing committee invited prominent and well-connected designers to form a Design Headquarters and to create an overall branding strategy.[167] Design critic and editor Katsumie Masaru was appointed as overall lead, and the Nippon Design Center commissioned to provide graphics. The NDC's Tanaka Ikkō and Sugiura Hisui directed the official design style guide.[168] For the games, designers sought to develop a clear and unified visual language that could then be applied to everything from invitations, programmes and the telephone directory for the Olympic Village to signage, promotional cigarette packaging and third-party souvenirs – and in doing so to incorporate the new theories of practice around visual communication (*shikaku dentatsu*) that they had discussed with overseas colleagues at the WoDeCo. The Olympics' visual campaign was made possible by designers' participation in international circuits and conversations, but also by their experiences both in wartime propaganda and in competitive marketing environments.

The style they chose combined a restrained high modernist typography – highly symmetrical and reliant on the visual appeal of the letterforms – with visually identifiable Japanese symbols whose aesthetic allowed them to appear seamlessly within the modernist visual idiom. The message was obvious: the Japanese nation, and Japanese designers, as comfortably part of an exclusive club of technologically adept, democratic post-war nations. Kamekura's official emblem for the games, a solid red circle on a white background, interlocked gold rings and 'Tokyo 1964' underneath, articulated the style strategy directly with its clear, simple visuals and an obviously Japanese symbol. Kamekura explained:

Designing Modern Japan

I don't want to show ingratiating Japaneseness to foreigners.
It will just get in the way, to be looked at with fascination like
they're looking at some kind of primitive art. We need to fight
at an international level of culture and show that Japaneseness
is what oozes from the Japanese people.[169]

More subtly, the style guide mandated Neue Haas Grotesk (Helvetica)
for roman letters and Tokutai Gothic, a particularly fat Gothic typeface,
to draw the eye to the Japanese lettering. The design team also speci-
fied *washi*, Japanese paper, for tickets, and Nishijin silk for the medal
ribbons. The design team emphasized identifiably Japanese materials and visual icons in their designs but found other aspects of the
Olympic work nationalistic in a different way. The Olympic committee
asked the design team to work for free, a stance the design team felt
recalled the working practices of wartime propaganda and suggested
that some organizers had not moved past the wartime understanding
of citizens' obligations to the state. In one recollection of the Olympics
work, graphic designer Nagai Kazumasa used the word *sōdōin* (total
mobilization), a phrase from the war.[170] This vision felt even further
from the ideal of the designer as creative individual.

For some, the sense of mobilization hit a nerve, as had design's
increased positioning as a commercial technique. In the 1960s, a decade
of political protest and the emergence of radical design practices worldwide, Japan too saw a growing critique of commercial, profit-driven
design as colluding with grand political schemes. The concern was
that capital and established political classes were co-opting creativity,
absorbing and thus neutralizing counterculture. The real flashpoint
would come later in the 1960s. But as work like Yokoo's Vonnel advertisements suggests, critical and commercial work were hardly mutually
exclusive – rather, critique was part of intensifying consumption in
the designed, commercial world of late 1960s Japan.[171] Whether accep-
tance or antagonism, countercultural design work too was part of
'electrified life'.

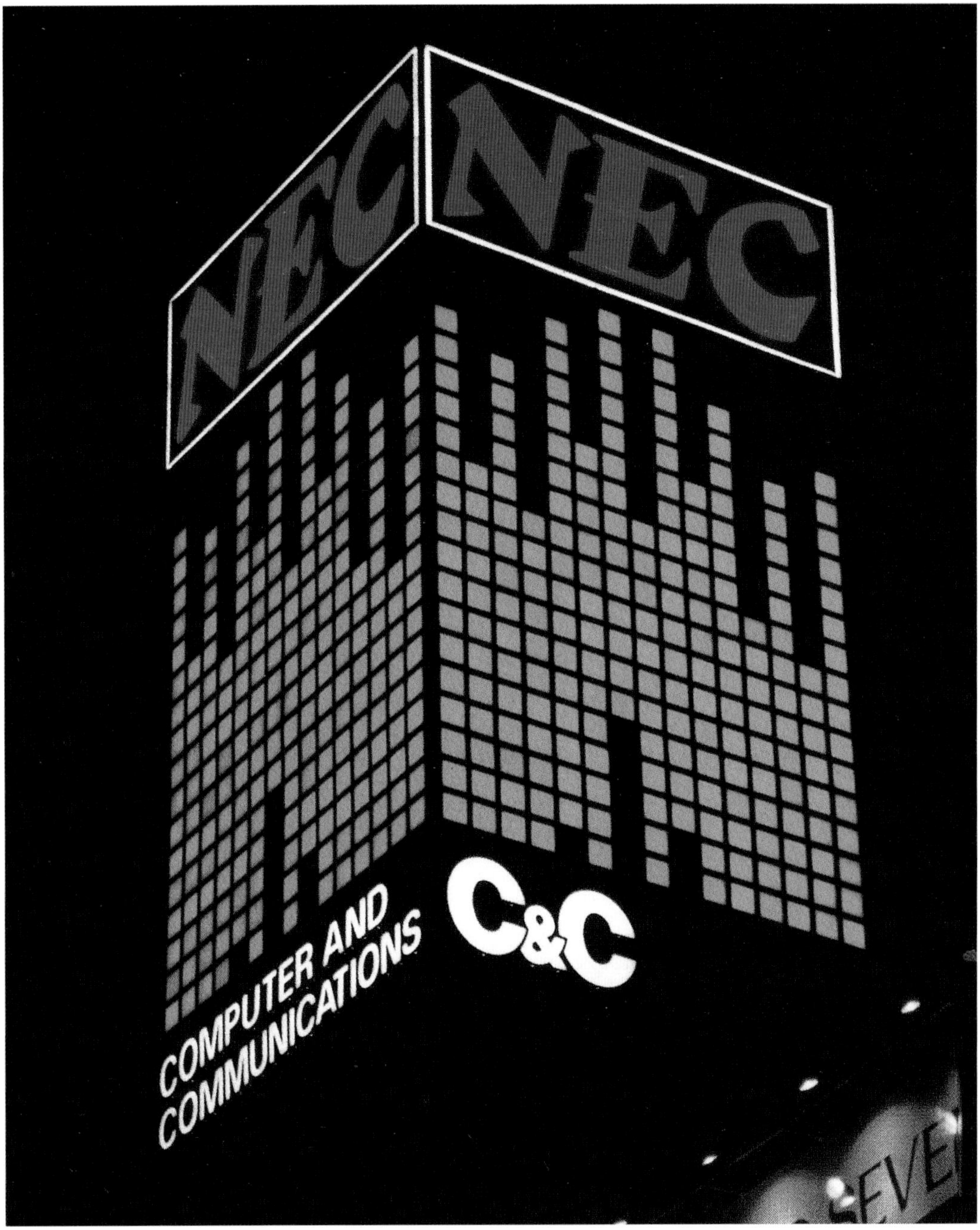
NEC
NEC
COMPUTER AND
COMMUNICATIONS
C&C

5 'Generosity and tolerance'
Design and the Information Industries in Late Twentieth-Century Japan

In September 1981, Hamano Yasuhiro (b. 1941), founding editor of design magazine *AXIS*, explained that the conditions for designing in Japan had changed:

> Design has become an extremely important factor in mature industrial societies.
>
> I think we can say that we have left the era of technological competition and competition over production volume and entered a new era which is based on these things but is clearly the era of design.
>
> In this world, which cannot be summed up in the binary of 'Culture' and 'Civilization', we are at a point now where the word 'Art' has come to look musty and mouldy. In these conditions, the generosity and tolerance offered by the concept of 'Design' has received much attention.[1]

Hamano's statement was boosterish but not hubris. The new magazine presented product and furniture design within a highly corporate, mass-produced context: it admitted that 'design' included mass-manufactured products, but insisted that design and designers had played an integral role in the success these products enjoyed on the market. Some of the products examined in the first issue included the City Honda, a smaller version of the Honda Civic, the Sony Walkman and Shape Pants by Wacoal, a modified sports girdle redesigned for everyday wear. By 1981, designers played a significant role both in the creation and promotion of consumer goods and services in Japan and in the critique of Japanese society as one of mass consumption fuelled

Itoh Kenji, neon sign for NEC, 1964. The sign's message, 'Computer and communications', signals the new direction that large electrical and electronic machinery firms like NEC had begun to take by the mid-1960s.

261

by industrial capitalism. If designers were in the spotlight, it was not down to their stellar performance alone. Rather, designers were part of a larger system predicated on continuous economic growth: one of many supporting roles without which the production would have limped on, but without the same finesse.

The magazine's presentation indicated the increased integration of design within business. The editors and journalists at *AXIS* presented design in the visual and written language of business, advertising and marketing research. Layouts layered colour blocks in a cut-and-paste collage effect over the modernist grid of post-war design magazines. Rounded sans serif type for both titles and text, bright colours and glossy paper gave its articles a feel similar to a popular business magazine or general weekly. Some articles drew on approaches from sociology and media studies to describe contemporary social phenomena, with an 'in the know' excitement that might convince corporate leaders and managers that design was on fire. The visual language of *AXIS* communicated design as a populist business practice aimed at gathering attention.

The emergence of *AXIS* in 1981 testifies to considerable change in the environment for design in the preceding decade. In the late 1960s, leaders at Japan's large industrial manufacturing firms and policymakers in the Ministry of International Trade and Industry (MITI) alike shifted their focus from supporting heavy industry and lower-end electrical goods towards the creation of a high-skilled, information economy. A second planned shift entailed moving from a vision of economic growth based in production to one of a more mature economy in which consumption played a larger part – and the environmental and social costs of growth were acknowledged.[2] In their vision, both large-scale manufacturing and government support for industries were to focus on electronics, information technology, automobiles, fashion and other high-added-value sectors, most if not all of them reliant on Japan adapting and creating advanced technologies. In 1969, the Japanese economy overtook that of West Germany with the second-largest GNP in the world, following the United States.

The strengthening domestic economy and growing trade income made everyday life in Japan increasingly comfortable. As people in cities and rural areas acquired basic life items, manufacturers and service providers, supported by advertising firms and commercial media, encouraged people to spend money on lifestyle goods and

Designing Modern Japan

leisure activities. Changing lifestyles meant that existing products took on new values and sometimes different functions, but often lost their markets. Manufacturers in both new and old product categories – cameras and cars, kimono and ceramics – adapted to changing markets and policies by changing products as well as manufacturing lines. For designers, all of this meant more work. It also stabilized the professional systems and relationships that designers and some entrepreneurs had worked to establish, in some industries, since the 1900s.

The aesthetic of designers' work shifted as products, manufacturing processes and consumer tastes themselves changed. Sony Handycams, Comme des Garçons jumpers and Nissin ramen adverts etched themselves into many minds – domestically and overseas – as offering a fresh and stylish way of living. But this chapter contends that for design practice itself, the 1970s and '80s must be seen as a moment of acceleration and consolidation, rather than dramatic change.[3]

Osaka Expo 70 and Changes in Design Practice and Theory, 1965–80

In many ways, the organization and design of Osaka Expo 70, a celebration of national economic power, technical ability and design ingenuity, embodied these shifts in policy vision: from heavy industry to information, and from production to consumption. Designers' involvement in the fair also illustrates how as a profession, designers were both complicit in that shift and ambivalent about their role in enabling it. The Osaka World Exposition 1970 drew 64 million visitors, including over half of Japan's population.[4] Economically and culturally, the expo's organisers aimed to capitalize on rising domestic income and growing domestic travel, as well as interest in Japan from a new generation of overseas visitors.[5] To this end, planned investment was five times the national investment in the 1964 Tokyo Olympics.[6]

Expo design drew on a roster of well-known designers, all networked through their commercial work, wartime activities and involvement in professional organizations in earlier decades. At the core organizing committee level, a thirteen-member Design Small Committee comprised of luminaries of post-war graphic and industrial design including Kamekura Yūsaku, Kenmochi Isamu and Mano Zenichi, lead designer at Matsushita, oversaw the visual identity and design guidelines for the event. The influential design critic, editor and writer Katsumie Masaru

served as design advisor, like Kamekura and others reprising his role from the 1964 Summer Olympics. Ekuan Kenji of GK Design organized the design of street furniture and wayfinding on the Expo site. GK Design handled telephone booths, post boxes, outdoor clocks and the physical signage, building on their own research into street furniture and small, modular buildings.[7] Kenmochi Design Associates, the consultancy led by Kenmochi Isamu, the former Industrial Arts Institute (IAI) Design Section chief, designed the benches and other outdoor seating, and the firm Total Design Associates the lighting. Graphic designer Fukuda Shigeo (1932–2009) created wayfaring pictograms for the signage.

The Japanese designers involved had benefited from the rise in leisure consumption in 1960s Japan. Both the Design Small Committee and the Japan Pavilion design team included designers known for their work in corporate leisure and entertainment environments.[8] By the mid-1960s, Kenmochi was known as much for his interiors, which included the first-class cabins for Japan Airlines' first Boeing 747 planes, as for his design promotion work at the IAI. Nakamura Hideya, on the Japan Pavilion team, provided interior design for the rapidly expanding Tōkyū Hotel chain, among other clients. Growing incomes and the rise

Visitors to Osaka Expo 70 had their day at the fair facilitated by the lights, loudspeakers, wayfinding signage and bins placed along the pedestrian thoroughfares. Compared to the spectacular pavilions, the public toilets, long, low modular buildings with grey and yellow side panels, were less noticeable but crucial, GK Design's Ekuan Kenji argued, for successful delivery of the experience.

Designing Modern Japan

of the domestic leisure economy – corporations and consumers with money to spend on hotel stays, theatre spectacles and dining out – had allowed designers to develop skills and specialisms in interior design and scenography, including more avant-garde film and performance.[9] Japanese artists and designers like the film-maker Matsumoto Toshio and graphic designer and illustrator Yokoo Tadanori joined international peers like the German composer Karl Heinz Stockhausen and the American group Experiments in Art and Technology (E.A.T.) in fusing avant-garde artistic expertise and vision with cutting-edge technology, using national and corporate funding to push new boundaries of immersive media performance.[10]

From steel and chemicals to the automotive and textile industries, corporate pavilions represented prominent industrial sectors and companies. But planners saw Expo 70 as an opportunity to show the world Japan's emergent industrial leadership in systems, environments and information. This reflected a larger shift in both industrial policy and commercial interest towards sectors increasingly seen as adding

Takara Beautylion (1970)/ TAKARA BELMONT CO., LTD. Architecture: Kisho Kurokawa Architect & Associates. Capsule unit: GK Industrial Design Associates, Osaka Expo 70. The capsules' deep plush carpet, brass features and liberal use of moulded plastics and vinyl upholstery were commonly used for luxury interior design in Japan around 1970. The shapes recall those of space capsules reported in Japan, as around the world, in the late 1960s.

higher value. In 1957, following several years of corporate activity and MITI support for Japan's electrical machinery industries, the Diet had passed a law to support the development of a homegrown computing industry. Firms like Hitachi and Tōshiba Shibaura Denki, soon to be Toshiba, were beginning to prosper in the United States and domestic markets, making everything from transistor radios to industrial electronics. Now, they would take on computers as well. MITI introduced a suite of financial initiatives designed to support Japanese firms in making the necessary capital investment in equipment and to enable firms to acquire Japanese-made computers.[11] Protectionist legal measures limited the access that foreign firms – particularly the American firm IBM, then the world market leader – had to the Japanese market. MITI and industry leaders agreed to apportion product categories among manufacturers. Together, these measures ensured that Japanese firms were not knocked out of the domestic market by more sophisticated foreign competitors, while retaining some competition to strengthen their offers. State–corporate partnerships for research and development in computing followed, too, in the 1960s, as did moves by consortia of Japanese firms, supported by MITI, to license IBM and other American companies' hardware. By 1968, Japanese companies and research organizations owned roughly 3,000 computers, a similar number to West Germany and behind only the United States in total computer ownership.

Hitachi's first digital computer, the HIPAC MK-1, was developed for power-transmission-line design calculations, at the time of development, c. 1957.

Investment in IT production capacity was part of a larger attempt by bureaucrats and the leaders of large mechanical electrical manufacturing firms to reshape Japan's industrial landscape to 'knowledge-intensive' areas such as computers and robotics.[12] Japan's post-war economic reconstruction had been supported substantially first by the export of 'sundry goods' or *zakka* – ceramics, textiles, thermos flasks and so on, then by both export and domestic market purchases of electrical and mechanical goods: electric fans, cameras, radios and the like. Shipbuilding, steel and coal also continued to be major employers. The new direction displaced both *zakka* and heavy industry for new forms of value-added manufacturing, including information technology.

Designing Modern Japan

Expo 70 amplified national ambitions around IT in some spectacular ways.[13] The Festival Plaza, an immense roofed space designed by Isozaki Arata (b. 1931) with engineering by a consortium of Japanese construction firms, sat at the heart of the expo both spatially and conceptually. As the Festival Plaza's key attraction, 'a giant traveling crane with electronic brains [*dennō*] will be installed as a gargantuan robot', as the Ministry of Foreign Affairs put it in a press release, using the literal translation of the new Japanese word for computer.[14] Each robot – there were actually two – incorporated control rooms for operators on their head, although the control systems were non-functional. Robots appeared in multiple pavilions as well. The Fujipan Robot Pavilion, for example, entertained children and adults with 41 robots undertaking common human tasks.

Less spectacularly, engineers and designers at Osaka 70 embedded control systems into the site and pavilion infrastructure alike.[15] Exhibition planners envisioned an environment composed of an artificial climate to mitigate Osaka's humid summer weather, with automated walkways delivering visitors around the site and communications equipment allowing workers to manage their experience in real time. A central information system would facilitate this and in doing so showcase Japanese advances in IT. As the fair's official report phrased it, 'Utilizing the highest level of Japanese technology, inclusive of computers and telecommunication equipment, studies were made of a fully automatic central information control system based on a large computer connected to branch computers.'[16] In the auto industry association pavilion, children could ride a 'computer car' designed by GK Design along a route controlled by an automated traffic control system, powered by a Japanese computer.[17] More sensationally, Mitsubishi's pavilion used an automatic feedback loop to make its lighting and sound respond to visitors' presence. The emphasis on IT was noticed: the fair's key themes as reported in *Bijutsu techō* (Art Notebook), a prominent contemporary art monthly, included 'information and matter, humanity – orientations towards space, information and media, robots, control systems, inflatable construction, light, fire, water, design as thing [*mono*], the arts as thing [*mono*]'.[18] The robots were for sensation; the control systems were more important.

Expo 70 was also shaped by prominent Japanese designers' embrace of systems thinking in the 1960s. The master plan, set largely by architect and urbanist Tange Kenzō and his lab at the University of Tokyo,

お祭り広場のロボット・デメ

The Auto Pavilion at Osaka Expo 70 allowed visitors to ride in 'computer cars' designed by GK Design, in an electronically controlled automated traffic system.

Women in kimono, haori and scarves and men in Western-style suits walk by Deme, one of two Demonstration Robots designed by Isozaki Arata for use in performances in the Festival Plaza, Osaka Expo 70. The robots' bodies could rise 7.3 m in the air to create a stage on the base for performances.

presented architecture as the support structure for plug-ins of light, sound, water, multimedia and electronic media and live performance.[19] GK Design's street furniture underlined the systems approach and the concept of built environment as support through modular construction, smooth surfaces, gently angular forms and monotone colours, and through the use of computer simulations of expected user numbers to refine the designs.[20] The plan for street furniture was that it would unify the different spaces of the site for visitors, creating a more seamless experience of the Expo for visitors, while also simplifying the logistics of moving thousands of people a day through the spaces smoothly and safely. The idea was that removing decision-making, irritations and distractions – where to find a shady place to sit to eat lunch, or the sight of sweet wrappers on the ground, for example – would lead visitors to focus their attention on the exhibits, not the unplanned spectacle created by other visitors.[21] Roughly speaking, advocates of systems thinking sought to rationalize the design process by applying logic models and heuristics from mechanical and systems engineering, operations research, psychology and the nascent field of cybernetics. Ekuan Kenji of GK Design participated in the Metabolism group, whose members, inspired partly by Tange's work, were known for their explorations of visionary systems futures for buildings and cities.[22]

For many industrial designers in Japan, however, American human factors engineering (now better known as ergonomics) and the field of man–machine relations (now human-computer interaction or HCI) were equally if not more intriguing. By the mid-1960s, designers in Japan were experimenting with techniques from these approaches to improve the functionality of the form of electrical machinery such as optical and medical equipment. Through participation in the International Council of Societies of Industrial Design (ICSID), study abroad in the United States and West Germany, and American and European design books and magazines, some industrial designers in Japan also kept abreast of the research into systematic design methods being undertaken among designers and engineers like Christopher Alexander, L. Bruce Archer and J. Christopher Jones. In 1969, the Industrial Arts Institute hosted Jones and his colleague R. Charles Grey for a seminar on design methods.[23] A seminar with Archer followed several months later.[24]

For designers interested in the nascent field of design methods, the new language of systems offered a way of designing – and of communicating design's value and process – more closely aligned with shifts in industrial production and planning. By the late 1960s, electrical machinery firms like Fujitsū and Hitachi who had joined the state–private consortium, along with universities and the national telecommunications corporation NTT, had established labs to explore computers' applications for engineering design, in areas ranging from circuitry and electrical power grids to aviation and naval engineering. Some researchers, inspired by American and British research, were experimenting with computer-aided decision-making to optimize transport plans and building footprints for efficiency. Researchers on one project at the University of Tokyo in 1966 made isometric drawings to model optimal housing clustering, using digital plotters, microfilm plotters and cathode-ray tubes (CRT) with light pens, run in the computer programmes FORTRAN IV and HISAP on a HITAC 5020 computer from Hitachi.[25]

Researchers explored using graphical plotting and decision-making tools in industrial design and manufacturing as well. Most early computer-aided design (CAD) research was conducted in engineering

Designing Modern Japan

and computer science, rather than in design, not least because of the technical skills and hardware required. However, in the post-war university reforms, some universities, including Chiba University, had put design departments into the engineering faculty. This meant unusual proximity to CAD experiments, expertise and facilities for the designers in these universities. In one experiment at Chiba University, engineering researcher Minato Yukie used a graphical plotter to optimize the direction of the wood grain used in boards cut to fabricate shoe lasts, the idea being that this might maximize wood use and product strength.[26] Computer-aided decision-making and design allowed designers to generate quantitative evidence that design was more than styling, and to demonstrate how designers could improve efficiency and user experience, not only increase sales. Some designers, including the team at Chiba, were also at pains to stress that computers – known also as 'artificial brains', or *jinkō dennō* – would complement human capacities, not replace them.

Designers further from the designated tech hubs could still access information about computer-aided design, machine-aided cognition

Minato Yukie, Faculty of Engineering, Chiba University, design methods decision-making diagram for optimizing the form of the Coca-Cola bottle, using computer logic and similar in form to circuitry, 1968.

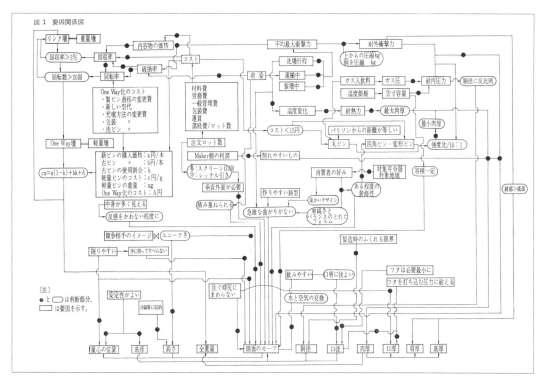

and graphical systems for human–machine communication, including the Sketchpad system developed at MIT and the 'Cybernetic Serendipity' exhibition at the Institute of Contemporary Art in London in 1968, through study abroad, foreign publications and Japanese researchers' own publications in Japanese.[27] Sympathetic firms offered access to the technology in Japan. In 1967–8, the Computer Art Group, a group of recent art and design university graduates, won a competition sponsored by IBM's Tokyo office and received access to IBM's computing facilities. Their work was included in the groundbreaking 'Cybernetic Serendipity' exhibition at the Institute of Contemporary Arts in London. Three years later, in November 1971, a group of illustrators, computer programmers, urban systems designers, paper company representatives, photographers, editors and art printers met to discuss art, computers and creativity, and human–machine relations. Some members of the group experimented with an XY plotter to generate patterns. Others, including designers at NHK, the national broadcaster, began using graphic displays and video to make animated films. Soon, the research group had morphed into a more established entity, the Computer Art Center. Members took on commercial work, applying their image-making skills to commissions for book covers and illustrations for publications in medical systems, geography, cluster analysis and image processing, as well as science textbooks.[28]

Despite these inroads, many designers would not work with computers for at least another decade. Computers presented new technical possibilities, but the production systems and economics for the hotel interiors, knitwear lines, school desks, product packaging, corporate logos and other commissions that occupied most designers' time did not require them. More immediately, the sheer cost of computers meant that few if any consultancies had the capital to procure computer hardware. For most designers, the greatest impact of computers within their working practices – as opposed to the world around them – would remain conceptual until the 1980s, if not the 1990s.

In this context, some consultancies began to incorporate computer logic into their processes, exploring the conceptual implications of digital logic as a compositional tool. The idea was that without using computers physically in the design process, designers could experiment with thinking like computers. For the cover of the 1968 *Kōgei nyūsu* (Industrial Art News) special issue on computers and design, graphic designer Sugiura Kōhei (b. 1932), recently returned from two years' teaching at the Hochschule für Gestaltung Ulm (HfG Ulm) in West Germany, used photomechanical printing techniques to represent a complex grid of pixels, the result of an experiment to generate pattern through the programmatic application of noise across x and y axes. Sugiura's image and the technical process used to generate it prompted questions about logic, randomness and human creativity, and about the extent to which effective design was generated by human creativity and skill or by machines. Designer Mukai Shutarō (b. 1932) was also recently returned from the HfG Ulm, where he encountered the nascent field of design methods. For Mukai, the Ulm vision of design as rational, theorizable practice corresponded neatly to the potentials of information technology industries. He proposed 'designerly thinking' to 'respond to the era of the electronic calculator', focusing on the application of logical methods and the concepts of control systems and feedback loops to theorize more effective protocols for designing anything.[29] Or as researchers at the IAI put it in 1968:

> considering the introduction of computers into the design process requires us to rethink the very action of designing befor we even consider the great potential of computers as as 'tool' or learn the limitations of this work. It presents an opportunity to contrast [computer logic] with design, which we might call the most human of the activities of the natural sciences, with their unwavering logic, and to reconsider design thinking and prices from the perspective of logic.[30]

Whether as hardware and software or as a conceptual logic system, computing could offer new design protocols.

By disrupting the human-run, human-centred processes and relationships that comprised manufacturing, there was also a chance, or a danger, that the binary decision-making imposed by early digital systems – 0s and 1s, yesses and nos – could disrupt designers' roles and employment. The consensus – if there was one – that manufacturing required specialist designers was a few decades old, if that. These questions troubled some industries more than others. Designers working with traditional local industries like ceramics and wood furniture had their own issues to contend with, not least changes in consumer taste and government support that in many cases were beginning to

工芸ニュース

5

industrial
art
news
1968
vol.36
no.5

発行一九番株式会社 編集一工業技術院産業工芸試験所

特集「コンピューターとデザイン」

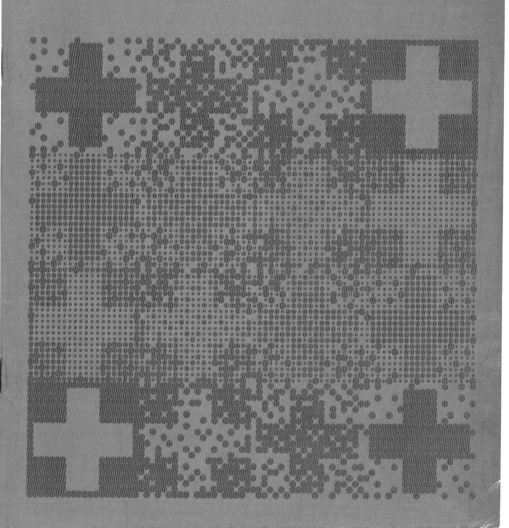

challenge industry survival. But small firms were far from being able to access computers. Large electrical equipment and electronics manufacturers, on the other hand, had the capital and connections to integrate computers into their design and production systems. By the late 1960s, many also had dedicated design divisions.

For manufacturers and systems engineers, much of the excitement centred around computers' potential applications for automating manufacturing. Computers could make supply chains more efficient by automating the communication and ordering of parts and products. Automated decision-making could monitor outgoing product quality, ensuring greater standardization and closer correlation to product specifications. Inputting component combinations to computers also allowed managers to respond quickly to new orders and assemble several different products on a single production line, making it possible to use production facilities more efficiently.

Some designers in industry were concerned that managers would identify elements of their roles as similarly open to streamlining, or that an increasingly computerized system would preclude designers' ways of working. By the mid-1960s, numerically controlled (NC) design and modelling allowed American auto manufacturers like General Motors to automate drafting and die-making, offering new tools for designers and draughtsmen but also potentially displacing them. In Japan, some auto designers felt that advances in Japanese-made computers and infrastructure, too, would soon enable Japanese auto manufacturers to adopt NC systems. In Japan, Yaegashi Mamoru and Iwata Dai were veteran automotive designers with Toyota. Yaegashi and Iwata felt that it was only a matter of time before advances in Japanese-made computers and infrastructure, too, allowed Japanese auto manufacturers to adopt NC systems. In a commentary for colleagues across design disciplines delivered in 1968, the same year Toyota introduced its first CAD system, they emphasized the importance of learning to work within a highly binary decision-making environment, in which discussions around form would need to be answered with a direct yes or no. As they put it, designers must 'understand the essence of the "systems" that accompany the rapid development of "computers"'.[31] They wrote, 'We need to consider how to understand and apply [these systems], so that we don't lose our way. Exchanges and integration with specialist technicians are desirable.' Yaegashi and Iwata also suggested more interaction and a greater degree of integration

Sugiura Kōhei, cover art for *Industrial Art News*, January 1969, a special issue on computers and design.

between designers and technicians as a way for designers to 'future proof' their jobs.

Both Yaegashi and Iwata were veteran designers at Toyota, accustomed to asserting design's role to engineers and management. Their comments could be seen as a warning to colleagues across industries. Failure to integrate into new production systems, and to forge a compelling role for designers' as creatives within it, could result in their displacement – especially possible given that Japanese automotive firms had added design divisions and begun working with consultant designers only a decade previously. Given the Japanese government's industrial policy shift to embracing IT, the questions were relevant for designers across disciplines, from craft and graphics to apparel. Strategizing and publicizing a new vision of design for manufacturing that continued to require specialist designers would become an important theme for designers in a number of industries, from that point onwards.

Some designers were also thinking differently about the political and social role and responsibility of design. Public critique and anger had grown over the course of the 1960s, beginning with wide-scale citizen anger at the renewal of Japan's defence treaty with the United States in 1960. Environmental activism was on the rise, following the discovery in 1956 that residents of Minamata in southern Japan were being poisoned by mercury effluent from a large agricultural fertilizer plant.[32] Action against industrial pollution increasingly occupied media attention and contributed to further rises in citizen activism about environmental pollution across the country. After four major court cases over industrial pollution in the late 1960s, the Diet passed strict environmental and industrial pollution legislation, but campaigning against the industrial destruction of rural environments and livelihoods remained volatile throughout the 1970s. Japan's facilitation through military bases of the U.S. involvement in the Vietnam War, and the United States' continued occupation of Okinawa, prompted anger and activism as well, including student protests in 1968.[33]

Among designers, Osaka Expo 70 particularly became a lightning rod for both self-reflection and a critique of design's complicity in postwar nationalism and capitalism.[34] Critic Haryū Ichirō (1925–2010), a frequent contributor to the journal *Dezain hihyō* (Design Review) noted that 'design in the age of social improvement has single-mindedly created design pollution, connected with industrial pollution. How

Designing Modern Japan

to overcome this will be the post-Expo departure point.'[35] Haryū outlined the issue well. If the significant contribution that design and designers had made to national economic growth also resulted in environmental pollution and measurable human suffering, then not only the post-war Japanese social, economic and political compact but designers, operating within it and for it, needed to reconsider and redefine their value system.

Haryū's critiques mirrored a larger concern among some designers about the impact of design's complicity within a growth-minded, consumption-fuelled economic framework. This included misgivings about the ease with which this framework could commodify or absorb critique and countercultural practice within it.[36] The 1960s had seen a number of popular design manifestos published, including the graphic designer Awazu Kiyoshi's *Dezain no hakken* (Discovery of Design, 1966), which presented design as a humanist approach for making a social contribution, rather than primarily as a tool for generating corporate profit. The journal *Design Review*, created and powered by a group of politically, socially active designers and critics like Awazu and Haryū, was part of this movement too.[37] This was not critique from outside: many highly critical voices had made their names as commercial design-ers, not least Awazu, who had worked at the Nippon Design Center. Ekuan Kenji of GK Design was another prominent voice, in his writings particularly, for design as nothing less than socially transformative.[38] Thanks to newspaper and television reporting, publishing and their own personal and professional networks within Japan and overseas, Japanese designers and critics like Ekuan, Awazu and Haryū were famil-iar with the political, economic and environmental protests taking place across the globe in the late 1960s, including among design communities. Like protest movements in late 1960s and early 1970s Japan more widely, their positions and actions must be understood both in transnational context and as having stemmed from conditions specific to post-war Japan.[39]

Design students catalysed some of the most decisive self-reflection and critique. In August 1969, a group of students invaded a meeting of the jury for the Japan Advertising Artists' Club (JAAC) annual com-petition and demanded the end of the organization. The activists' critique – which many JAAC members subsequently went on the record to say they recognized – had been the club and its members' lack of engagement with the pressing issues of the time. On 30 June 1970, the JAAC disbanded after ten months of reflection and conflict. Designer Kanda Akio's (b. 1935) comment usefully describes how the mood had changed:

[Around 1960,] when I had just started my career, Nissenbi's symposiums and seminars provided something fresh that I had not gained from my design education to that point, and I learned a lot. But it might be worth flagging that the contents emphasized the importance of technique. As technical accomplishments made around 1960 were absorbed into the advertising industry along with the subsequent economic advances, humans and design, or society and design, the issues that formed the intellectual bedrock started working primarily for commercialism. At the same time, basic issues for making a living like how to understand design as a profession, what to do about the relationship between designer and client and what to do about designers' working conditions were neglected. And we might need to reflect critically on the fact that as an organization, we weren't sufficiently able to explain the multiple conditions of graphic design today, in relation to the aggression between students and society.[40]

Yomiuri News Photography Unit, helmeted students enter the JAAC general meeting and protest, 5 August 1969.

Designing Modern Japan

Majima Seiichi, *The Age in Which Everything in the World Is Advertising, Overflowing Advertisements Are Contemporary Culture,* young woman walking in front of a wall of painted demands from left-wing university activists, 1971. At a time when advertisements seemed inescapable in urban environments, political protest, too, could be subsumed into commercialism.

By 1970, these concerns were well at the heart of the hastily constructed post-war design establishment, too. Designers Kenmochi Isamu, Watanabe Riki and Kamekura Yūsaku, all of whom had worked on government projects, including wartime work, the 1964 Summer Olympics and Expo 70, stepped down from Expo 70 committees following the student protests.[41] At the May 1970 opening of his solo show at Matsuya Ginza, a prominent venue for design, Yokoo Tadanori, who like Awazu worked across countercultural and corporate clients alike and had profited from the Expo, announced a two-year moratorium on work.[42] These designers and their colleagues had worked to raise the social status of graphic design and contribute to the modernist state project of national economic and social betterment through design. This meant contributing to corporate sales and national GNP, subsuming one's well-being and private life to achieve corporate and public aims, and seeking recognition for creativity and individuality within these frameworks. By 1970, Japan's economic strength and the subsumption of design practice into advertising to further fuel consumption framed design's contribution differently. Now, auteurist practice could seem narcissistic and solipsistic, rather than contributing to society.

The critiques of the design industry went beyond complicity with the state. Some designers pointed out that the concentration of powerful national clients in Tokyo created an unequal playing field for designers elsewhere. They saw the lack of parity as an issue of representation and voice: designers in Tokyo were able to represent the national picture without actually experiencing or recognizing it. Others were concerned about income inequality as a result. For yet others, however, inequality was a necessary evil, given the concentration of large clients – and therefore profit-making potential – in Tokyo. Using the metaphor of broadcasting, graphic designer Nishijima Isao (1923– 2001) commented:

> Tokyo is the only flagship station in contemporary communication. There is only tiny appetite in the regions for presentations of new designs. It is unavoidable that our work, which is graphically reproduced, cannot grow as it does in Tokyo. No matter what we do we cannot create a nationwide trend, and we can't become stars. Given all of this, there is little point for young people to become involved in regional design activity. That said, I'd like for the thirty or so people at the centre who have name value and are financially fortunate to create a group and continue to mount exhibitions as they have until now, with the stance that 'we're the ones who represent Japan', to be a foil for the regions and their juniors.[43]

Of course, all of this commentary was by male designers. Simply being female remained a still larger disadvantage for women going into design. Female designers continued to work against the wider social expectation that women would leave industry for marriage and motherhood, and that this path was incompatible with the requirements of professional paid work. Going into the 1970s, Japan gained prominent female designers, of whom art director Ishioka Eiko (1938–2012) and illustrator Yamaguchi Harumi (b. 1941) were particularly prominent.[44] Young women design graduates continued to join consultancies and in-house design firms. Many women worked – as they do now – as personal assistants to prominent designers and in other facilitation, management, editorial and translation roles behind the scenes. But the profile of designers published, debated and critiqued, at least within professional organizations and publications for graphic, industrial and interior design, remained almost solely male. In the early 1970s, feminist activists in Japan formed groups and began public campaigns to promote gender equality in law, including in family matters and in the workplace.[45] Public attitudes towards women's equal abilities and work began to shift as well. But critical discourse within mainstream design communities continued to ignore inequalities of gender within the design profession. Debates about 'designers' were tacitly about men.

Some male designers were tired, after decades of contributing to their particular visions of the national or professional project. Kimura Tsunehisa, the successful Tokyo-based graphic designer, offered an anecdote about a well-known colleague to describe how JAAC designers had prioritized industry promotion and work over personal life:

> Ōhashi Tadashi once grumbled, 'For more than twenty years, I've not gone with my kids to the sea', and I was shocked. Every summer, in the midst of the hot, humid summer when everyone else was resting, we were immersed in exhibition preparation, whether it was useful for us or not. In that moment of irritation and exhaustion, it's like we lost the ability to judge things.[46]

For these male designers, burnout and disillusionment were closely related to the sense of having worked for the national project. There was an implied critical self-questioning about designers' social roles and how designers might atone for their unintended but evident role in promoting environmental destruction and capitalism. Indeed, to fully understand design in 1970s Japan, we need to look to commerce and consumption as well. As a set of design briefs, Osaka Expo 70 revealed elite, cutting-edge concerns about technology, designers' social responsibilities and the downsides of development among the men contracted to design it, in many ways mirroring the new economic and industrial vision behind the fair. But like the persistence of local industries whose small firms were far from incorporating control systems into manufacturing, most designers in Japan in 1970 were engaged in less self-conscious, more commercial practice. The picture that emerges from looking at design in 1970s Japan more widely suggests that in addition to thinking like a computer, as Mukai Shūtarō and others had suggested, successful design still required thinking like a stylist.

'A brand that could propose a total lifestyle': Commerce and Design in the 1970s and Early 1980s

In 1974, D'Urban, a spinoff company from the large apparel firm Renown, decided to launch a new brand: íxí:z. Ten years later, the brand's design team was profiled as a marketing and design success story in a special issue of *Bijutsu techō* devoted to design consultancies and corporate design departments:

> Ten years ago, D'Urban had gained a position as an adult apparel brand. But would it be able to keep on capturing consumers' hearts if it continued with the same ideas from the Western-style clothing industry? Rather than the vertical thinking of considering itself as operating within the Western-style clothing industry alone, [the firm decided to] target a particular generation's consumers, responding in the same way to their desires to buy not just Western-style clothes but also other things like domestic appliances and motorbikes. If they didn't think up a brand that could propose a total lifestyle, ultimately they'd never be able to shrug off being a Western-style clothing shop.[47]

íxí:z sold men's casual fashions, aligned closely with European and American fashion trends, in vertically integrated boutiques in key department stores and shopping zones. íxí:z ran as a separate office within D'Urban with sole control of product development, including design, marketing and distribution. The design team included European designers based in European capitals. íxí:z boutiques also sold furniture, bicycles, stationery and shoes, all product categories that young men with disposable income might buy. Rather than make capital investments in equipment for producing these goods, Renown liaised with established manufacturers for branded production.

D'Urban launched íxí:z in response to the expansion and diversification of consumption identified in the Economic Planning Agency Economic White Papers around 1970. In the 1970s, design in Japan became research-driven and largely identified with large modern

Designing Modern Japan

industries predicated on mechanized mass production, rather than with the small and medium-sized enterprises to whom design bureaucrats promoted design in the 1960s. Designers' target markets changed, too, from the immediate post-war emphasis on exports to domestic consumers. There were economic factors behind these shifts. By the late 1960s, the Japanese domestic economy strengthened to the extent that exports accounted for only 9 per cent of GDP.[48] The 1970s, however, were turbulent. The end in 1971 of the Bretton Woods system of fixed exchange rates – a series of events known as the Nixon shock – decoupled the yen from the rate of 360 yen to the U.S. dollar, set during the Allied occupation of 1945–52 to encourage economic reconstruction in Japan. The yen soared in value, rendering Japanese exports immediately more expensive for overseas consumers, and weakening sales. Labour costs in Japan were rising as well. For manufacturers, these conditions meant that the strategy of gaining and retaining market share through low-price goods would no longer work. Further disruption came in 1973 with the oil crisis. Oil prices

The íxí:z stationery range for 1983, fully branded with the íxí:z logo.

quadrupled, lowering GNP and prompting consumer price inflation. With manufacturing costs higher and household incomes rising at a slower rate, the manufacturers and retailers on whom most designers depended for work had to change their business models.

Changes in lifestyles and living environments had an impact on both designers' prospects and what would sell. By the early 1970s, Western-style clothing predominated. Most women wore kimono only for special occasions such as weddings. Few men wore kimono at all. Textile designers, weavers and dyers in Kyoto continued to create high-end kimono, particularly for older women and for wealthy families who continued to provide them to daughters at marriage. But the market was shrinking and would continue to fall.[49] Changing relationships to kimono also impacted the design of kimono and accessories, as young people born after the war into a world based on Western dress were less likely to know how to dress themselves in kimono or to understand distinctions in pattern, colour, weave, decoration or accessories in order to select and combine them appropriately.[50] Department stores had already expanded from kimono into Western-style clothing, furniture, homewares, cosmetics and other areas; now, diversification became even more important.

The growing market for ready-to-wear Western-style clothing, manufactured by large apparel makers and sold in branded boutiques in department stores, supported more women especially to enter fashion design. Living at home until marriage provided young women and men – the target clientele for íxí:z – with disposable income, even as the economic fluctuations of the 1970s impacted salaries and prices. In contrast to the vertically integrated brands operated by apparel manufacturers, DC brands ('designers and characters' brands) emerged in the early 1970s from independent designers like Yamamoto Yōhji (b. 1943) of Y's and Kawakubo Rei (b. 1942) of Comme des Garçons. DC brands sat at a higher price point and emphasized the individual creativity and character of the designer, the brand and – by extension – its wearers. These designers were known as 'manshon makers' for the popular impression that they worked from their flats, manshon being the word for new multistorey reinforced concrete housing blocks.[51] The international success of Japanese designer Takada Kenzō (1939–2020), who launched his brand Jungle Jap in Paris in 1970, was one inspiration. Some DC brands had their own boutiques in areas like Jingu-mae and Aoyama in Tokyo. Others hired space in new 'tenant buildings'

Kansai Yamamoto was the first Japanese fashion designer to show in London, 1974. His designs for his first London fashion show included a mask T-shirt which bleeped when the eyes and the nose were pushed. Designer seen here with model Marie Helvin.

full of fashion boutiques, like Parco, launched in 1969 by Tsutsumi Seiji (1927–2013), president of the Seibu department store.[52] DC brand designers including Matsuda Mitsuhiro (1934–2008) and Kaneko Isao (b. 1939) banded together in 1974 to create the organization Top Designer 6 (TD6), to jointly produce fashion shows and publicize their brands to retailers. The emergence of new youth-oriented fashion and lifestyle magazines, most prominently *an an* in 1970 from publisher Heibonsha and *Non-no*, its competitor from Shūeisha, launched in 1971, gave DC brands a national platform for young people through fashion editorials and advertisements. While post-war fashion magazines like *Sōen* and *Ryūkō tsūshin* targeted the librarians, teachers and students at Western-style sewing schools, and the owners of Western-style fashion boutiques, *an an* and *Non-no* were for young female consumers. The first issue of *an an* sold 60,000 copies.[53] Media attention to the DC brands also promoted fashion schools like Bunka Fashion College (Bunka Fukusō Gakuin), alma mater of Takada, Matsuda, Kaneko and many other DC brand designers.

With their narrative of independence, creativity and self-expression and distinctive house styles ranging from the feminine sophistication of Matsuda's brand Nicole to the folkloric patterns and voluminous silhouette of Kaneko's brand Pink House, DC brands became popular among unmarried young adults. Collaborations with avant-garde interior designers like Kuramata Shirō (1934–1991), who designed boutiques for Miyake Issey (b. 1938), and Sugimoto Takashi (b. 1945) of Super Potato, contracted with Seibu to deliver Parco boutique interiors, enhanced the DC brands' aura of cutting-edge fashionability.[54] So too did the striking interiors, with their raw concrete floors and walls, exposed lighting and ductwork on the ceilings, spotlights and wire-frame fixtures supporting a few carefully placed garments. By the late 1970s, as the baby boomers became parents, DC brands also included monotone, colour-blocked children's wear from brands like Comme ça du Mode, with their own highly styled boutiques.

Furniture and home furnishings had to respond to changing demand as well. By the early 1970s, most Japanese lived in cities and their suburbs, rather than in agricultural or fishing villages. While multigenerational households persisted, particularly in the countryside, the number of nuclear households increased. High population density and the high price of land in major cities like Tokyo and Osaka meant small living spaces. But growing household incomes allowed more families to leave rented flats or rowhouses and purchase flats in *manshon* or two-storey family homes in new commuter suburbs.

Changing housing forms and family structures had an impact on the furnishings that households needed and that would literally fit in homes. The use of flooring – wooden or vinyl – rather than tatami mats in *manshon* and the new suburban homes required chairs, tables and beds. Unlike apartments (*apāto*) in wooden buildings, which often had a Japanese-style toilet and no bath, requiring residents to use local public baths, *manshon* flats ordinarily included a Western-style toilet and a bath and shower. For sanitaryware manufacturers, new housing types meant new product opportunities. Ina Seitō, a large firm based

Yoshikawa Hideko, a young couple in unique original T-shirts strolling in Jingūmae, a fashionable area of Harajuku, 1972.

Designing Modern Japan

Sugimoto Takashi
(Super Potato), shop
interiors for the boutique
Pashu, 1983, Sapporo.

near Nagoya, a hub of large-scale ceramics production, had begun selling fibre-reinforced plastic (FRP) bathtubs in 1958.[55] In 1967, Ina Seitō followed with both Japan's first integrated plastic shower-toilet unit, the Sanitary Ina 61, and the country's first shower-toilet. Ina Seitō began as a kiln producing ceramic dishware in 1766. The firm began firing tiles for Western-style buildings in 1910, then moved into sanitaryware in 1945. For ceramics manufacturers like Ina Seitō and its rival Tokyo Tōki, the popularity of standalone homes and higher-end *manshon*, with their separate bathroom and toilet, presented yet another opportunity to develop and market new product types for rapidly expanding markets. This meant new design work for designers as well.

New residential styles and rising incomes substantially affected the demand for new furniture. As members of the post-war baby boom married and started new households, they did not have kimono to store or want dowry sets of kimono chests and mirror stands, previously a strong seller for furniture manufacturers and department stores. New flats were not scaled to fit them. Competition from foreign furniture firms presented a further challenge. Rising corporate

Designing Modern Japan

and domestic incomes attracted American and European furniture manufacturers like Arflex and Artemide to open shops in Tokyo and other cities.[56] Japanese manufacturers also licensed designs from American and European firms like Herman Miller. Japanese consumers, attracted to the novelty, cachet and often lighter look of European designs, began to purchase imported and licensed furniture in increasingly high volumes, particularly to furnish flats in new *manshon*.[57] The value of furniture imported from western Europe, for example, rose by 400 per cent between 1971 and 1975.[58] The trend would eventually support the emergence of Tokyo, particularly, as a centre for contemporary furniture design in its own right. Entrepreneur Kurosaki Teruo (b. 1949) began importing European furniture from London in 1975, before expanding in the early 1980s to produce and sell furniture specifically for his Idée brand, with designers including Philippe Starck and Kuramata Shirō.

Faced with declining popularity after a decade of strong sales, some furniture designers and manufacturers changed tactics. Product planners and designers at the high-end furniture manufacturer Maruni Mokkō presented both cheery painted furniture and heavier, more formal European styles constructed with Southeast Asian hardwoods, sold through established department stores such as Mitsukoshi and Takashimaya. Sazaby, begun in 1970 as a European furniture importer for department stores, branched into bags and printed textile design and manufacturing before opening a restaurant in Tokyo's fashionable

This 1970 catalogue photograph for the Edinburgh eight-piece set from furniture manufacturer Maruni Mokkō suggested that the seating, with its leather upholstery and solid forms, would suit a household able to afford a modern standalone home with a garden.

'Generosity and tolerance'

Jingu-mae district in 1975. Shop interiors were part of the sell. Sazaby and its competitors' aesthetic was light and airy or rendered in bright primary colours, high-gloss paint and tubular steel rather than dark wood furniture. Pitched at baby boomers in their thirties, their appeal to individuality and fashionability aligned with the approach taken by the DC brands in fashion. So did the wastebins, mirrors, dishes and other accoutrements sold at the new homewares shops that opened in fashionable residential suburbs. Unlike the homeware shops in local shopping streets, these new shops offered particular aesthetics in interiors that could be mistaken for a fashion boutique.[59] Interiors magazines like *Modan ribingu* (Modern Living) promoted the shops as a way to consume 'design', specifically. Both the magazines and the idea of consuming 'design' interiors were popular. The publisher Heibonsha launched the men's lifestyle magazine BRUTUS in 1980. By 1983, reader demographics allowed BRUTUS to run a three-hundred-page special issue on housing and interiors.[60] Design boutiques, interiors magazines and a diversification of aesthetics, ranging from high-tech minimalism to country style, appeared in many parts of Europe and North America as well in the late 1970s and early 1980s. In Japan, purchasing these items went far beyond changing taste. More significantly, for younger,

Photographs for these Maruni Mokkō furnishings, from the same 1970 catalogue, suggest that residents in standardized apartment blocks or *manshon* would prefer white gloss-painted furnishings with thinner lines for a fresh, airy feel. The white-painted furniture represented a major shift for high-end modern furniture manufacturers, whose products had previously been finished with clear varnishes to reveal the wood grain of the veneers underneath.

Designing Modern Japan

more affluent people, particularly in cities, they represented a change in bodily comportment, social relations and other fundamental ways of living.

But many manufacturers and retailers, including many of the small family firms that comprised Japan's historical furniture manufacturing districts, struggled to adapt their products to changing fashions and living spaces. In Shizuoka, known for its lacquered chests and mirrored stands, the number of manufacturers began to decline in the 1970s, then fell precipitously, by over 80 per cent, in the thirty years after 1980.[61] Others – including family firms in districts like Shizuoka – capitalized on the popularity of the *mai hōmu* (my home) dream of home ownership to sell homewares and furniture that promised a particular lifestyle.

New living habits, the high yen and the new MITI emphasis on electronics and other high value-added products also affected industries like metalwork and lacquerware and the designers working with them, now often known as 'craft designers' to differentiate them from designers working for mechanized mass-production industries. MITI no longer promoted these exports, and the high yen made Japanese sundry goods – the toys and jewellery boxes that helped to support post-war reconstruction – uncompetitive against products from Taiwan and other countries with lower labour costs. Baby boom consumers and their parents alike preferred the convenience of electric hot water pots to iron kettles heated on gas hobs, and metal and injection-moulded lunchboxes to lunchboxes made of steamed wood. Lacquerware makers were increasingly using plastic cores rather than turned wooden ones.

Implicitly, these changes in lifestyle contributed to the association of design with mechanized mass-manufacturing. With changes in consumer tastes driving the demise of entire industrial sectors, local and national governments, industry associations and department stores reframed industries as traditional craft. A 1974 law offered financial support for industries that met particular conditions such as employing local materials, using hand techniques and making products for everyday use.[62] The reclassification of many local industries as 'craft' affected designers at local industry research and guidance institutes. The policy shift to supporting high-tech industries weakened the position of these publicly employed designers and in many cases their funding was reallocated to sectors like precision machinery and electronics. The reclassification of traditional industries as craft allowed these design advisers to reposition their own practice. Now, many encouraged SMEs to create products that emphasized their craft nature and local origins within the aesthetic of contemporary domestic interiors. For a century, design advisers had helped manufacturers strike a balance between exoticism and familiarity for export markets. Now, they supported local firms in similar exercises for urban Japanese markets.[63] For traditional industries, 'craft' could be a useful category for enticing consumers to buy things out of taste and desire, not necessity. Regardless, and despite these efforts, community industries making everything from ceramics and lacquerware to obi and Buddhist altars shrank dramatically in the 1970s. Their disappearance further strengthened the association of design with mechanized mass-manufacturing and materials like plastic and metal.

There was another reason why design in 1970s Japan became increasingly associated with mechanized, mass-produced products. By the time household incomes slowed their stratospheric growth, most households, including rural ones, had already acquired luxury as well as everyday household goods. With 95 per cent of households owning a colour television by 1974, for example, manufacturers had to create yet new product categories or to persuade households to trade up. Fast-moving consumer goods like beer and confectionery were often purchased at local shops, where familiarity, habit and relationships with shopkeepers tended to determine the brands and products shoppers chose.[64] But these were highly competitive markets. Branding and advertising, along with new product launches (*shinhatsubai*), were a way for larger manufacturers to sway consumer decisions in other lucrative situations like after-work drinks. In this context, design to provoke desire through differentiation in styling, functionality or the image around a product became ever more important.

'Large variety, small volume production' – *tahinshu shōryō seisan*, often abbreviated as *tahinshu-ka* – was a key strategy. Japanese manufacturers, retailers and advertisers developed this approach to respond to market saturation and fierce competition from other firms.[65] By diversifying production from large lots of a few products to smaller lots of many different products, often differing only in styling and the combination of functions offered, manufacturers and retailers could create and target multiple micro-audiences based on market research, and generate demand for additional purchases and model upgrades alike. The IT strategy of the early 1970s, implemented on large-scale factory production lines and to manage supply chains between manufacturers,

Designing Modern Japan

Sanshū ibushi tiles, 1976, showing a tile artisan at work in Aichi Prefecture. Images such as these aestheticized Japan's remaining industries that manufactured everyday items largely by hand, using local materials.

subcontractors and suppliers, contributed to making this possible. So did efficiency and productivity drives within companies, prompted by falling profit margins in the mid-1970s due to the high yen and oil crisis.[66] By 1980, thanks to MITI promotion, corporate investment and the situation within domestic manufacturing, Japan led the world in the number of industrial robots in use in assembly lines.

The ability to create a larger number of products within the same constraints increased product styling work for corporate design teams and consultancies. Designs both had to stand out and to be producible within constraints of time, labour and tooling. *Tahinshu-ka* also placed additional demands on capital-intensive machinery, production lines, tooling and supply chains. Given the considerable capital investment required to produce new tooling, products needed to be interchangeable on production lines, resulting in multiple products with the same basic form and materials, distinguished by details such as controls.[67]

It was easiest to house a VCR, for example, in a sheet-metal box. Creating a distinctive product, then, became a matter of individuating products through details. At Victor, the design team for the HR-D120 VCR created a visual language of rectangles, triangles, circles and squares in bright primary colours, which they used for the controls. Differentiation emerged from the VCR's specific functions, its distinctive visual language and the substantive ad campaign prepared for its launch. The emergence of branded cross-industry 'character goods', unified by particular illustrated characters and their back stories – Sanrio's Hello Kitty most prominently – must be understood within this context as well, as a way to differentiate a pencil case in the shop from one already on the desk at home, and in doing so to create a sales opportunity.

With production lines at large manufacturers, at least, increasingly able to shift between products, manufacturers and marketing consultants like D'Urban began to use research techniques from social science to identify new and lucrative target users and their tastes, to launch brands like íxí:z. Japanese advertising agencies like Dentsu and Hakuhodo and manufacturers like Matsushita already used American consumer research techniques to describe trends in Japanese consumers' tastes and living habits, which they disseminated through annual reports. Researchers at the IAI undertook contract research for electrical

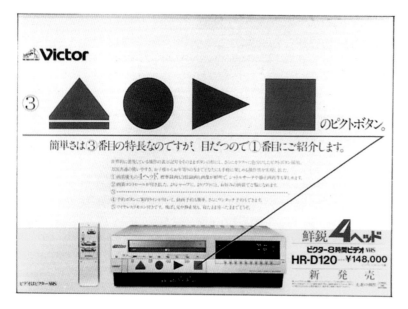

Advertising poster for the Victor HR-D120 video cassette recorder, designed for use in commuter trains, c. 1983. Four colour pictograms chosen by the design team represent the function buttons on the VCR's boxy exterior. While the VCR also boasted four playback heads and the ability to play Victor's eight-hour VHS tapes, the buttons' dominant presence in the main catch copy helped to differentiate the HR-D120 from competitor products.

Designing Modern Japan

Packaging design for multiple different occasions, Suntory Nama beer, 1983, Suntory Holdings.

appliance manufacturers into the ergonomics of household chores, from the early 1960s. In the increasingly saturated market of the 1970s onwards, manufacturers and retailers drew even more heavily on market research to define lucrative markets and write product development, design and marketing briefs to target them.[68] Department stores and manufacturers in highly competitive arenas like apparel, electronics and home electrical appliances began to focus on users' everyday life (*seikatsu*, with users known as *seikatsusha*). Like D'Urban, electrical appliance makers like Sanyo and Toshiba established integrated life-style research centres that handled product development from user (no longer market) research to design and launch, creating designs for segmented user groups and designing based on assessment of their needs and lifestyle.[69] Whether in 'everyday life' and 'product science' (*shōhin kagaku*) research centres within companies or by contracting research to advertising agencies, manufacturers sought to understand not only the aesthetic preferences and visual prompts that would attract *seikatsusha* to product images but consumers' everyday life habits, in the belief that understanding use would allow them to design features that would appeal to these sub-markets.

Market research focused as much on who had purchasing power as on what they purchased and how they used their new possessions. Housewives in their thirties were a key market, as they managed the household budget. So were unmarried wage earners of both genders. Young adults working or studying were most likely to live at home until marriage. From the late 1960s, no or low housing costs meant higher expendable income on lifestyle goods. Sales of stereo equipment, skis and mountaineering boots, to give only three examples, boomed.[70] D'Urban's plan for íxí:z provides a clear example of demographic targeting. Based on their analysis of age-specific purchasing power data, D'Urban's researchers identified university-age men, or men between 20 and 24, as having the greatest purchasing power. The target demographic was chosen with scale and brand longevity in mind as well: young men were one of Japan's fastest-growing demographics and twenty- to forty-year-olds were expected to comprise 75 per cent of the population by 1990. In the late 1970s, men between the ages of 25 and 34 spent 88 per cent of their income, and women in the same age bracket 96 per cent.[71] Women's purchasing power, in particular, had increased prodigiously from earlier decades. Men, however, both earned more and spent more on consumables, with 48 per cent of their income going towards clothing, accessories, snacks, eating out, education and

Young women licking ice cream cones on Omotesandō, in Harajuku, 1976. Omotesandō's place as a fashion hub was established in the early 1970s. Young, unmarried women's conspicuous consumption included simply being in fashionable neighbourhoods. In this instance, newspaper *Mainichi Shimbun* used this image to illustrate the potential moral hazards of youth lifestyles.

entertainment, compared to 40 per cent of income for women the same age. In the 1960s, D'Urban's parent company, Renown, had created Western-style ready-to-wear brands for young women as the post-war generation came of age. íxí:z was a chance to capitalize on young men's incomes as well. Marketing researchers would continue to direct product development towards young women into the 1980s, labelling unmarried, working women in their twenties as 'single nobility' for their purchasing power and predilection to put their earnings towards fashion, cosmetics and experiences.[72] As the creative director for one Nagoya-based advertising agency put it in 1983, 'Go after "singles"!'[73]

The Sony Walkman, perhaps the most iconic design from 1970s Japan, was another product of the focus on the youth market.[74] The Sony PP Center, a recently founded design division led by designer Kuroki Yasuo (1932–2007), created design and marketing strategy for all product development and the firm's overall image in an

Designing Modern Japan

WM-2 Walkman® stereo cassette player, Sony Corporation, 1981.

integrated unit.[75] The Sony PP Center provided a number of teenagers and young people with a prototype to see how they responded to it, then targeted product development to meet the functionality and price point appropriate for the target market.[76] By January 1982, two years after the product launch, Sony had sold 4 million Walkmans and prompted numerous competitors, including a growing variety of models from Sony itself. For this reason, the Walkman also illustrates conditions for designers' corporate work in late 1970s Japan. In a highly competitive domestic market with many companies making similar products, manufacturers put resources towards product development, design and marketing, including for product design and design for advertisements and packaging. This heightened competition, thus creating yet more incentive to put resources into design and marketing.

D'Urban's creation of íxí:z as a standalone lifestyle brand with its own design and management team also points to designers' integration into corporate strategizing. Corporate adoption of *tahinshuka* and market segmentation as fundamental business strategies changed the nature and the timing of designers' contributions to product development and marketing. Many companies continued to ask design teams and consultancies to create styling design and advertising campaigns once brand identities and products had been developed.

'Generosity and tolerance'

But the highly competitive domestic market and ability to vary product image, whether by changing production lines or – as D'Urban did for íxí:z, subcontracting production to small specialist firms – prompted some managers to adopt design differently. As a form of art direction and a corporate strategy in its own right, design moved upstream in brand and product development. It also contributed to corporate image creation across the entire company.

One well-known example of companies adopting art direction as a facet of business strategy is the Seibu Group, under the leadership of president Tsutsumi Seiji. Seibu's companies included the Seiyū chain of supermarkets as well as the mid-range Seibu department store in the commuter hub of Ikebukuro, on Tokyo's northern edge. Seibu began diversifying its range of shops to attract younger consumers in the late 1960s by opening the Parco tenant building for fashion boutiques. Graphic designers and art directors like Awazu Kiyoshi, Ishioka Eiko and Yamaguchi Harumi, contracted by Parco managing director Matsuda Tsuji (1926–2007) to produce Parco's advertisements, combined eye-catching colour photography – saturated colours, unusual narrative moments, striking landscapes, foreign models – or equally saturated illustration with emotionally charged messages and the Parco logo, to brand Parco as a point of origin for cutting-edge youth culture through fashion.[77]

Seibu also created a design advisory committee, with members including Tanaka Ikkō as art director and the copywriter Koike Kazuko (b. 1936), to advise on corporate image (CI) and brand and product development across Seibu's companies. In the late 1970s, Tanaka led on the development of a new 'branded non-brand' for Seiyū supermarkets, initially developed by Seiyū's product science research institute, founded in 1975. After consulting with the design advisory board to determine the new brand's concept of trustworthiness and reliably good quality, avoiding wastefulness – initial products included processed salmon made from offcuts – Seiyū priced its products slightly higher than competitor supermarkets' own-brand products.[78] Mujirushi Ryōhin ('No logo, good quality'), better known overseas as MUJI, launched in Seiyū stores in 1980 with a small line-up of foods and household goods, assembled like the íxí:z range by subcontracting manufacturers across Japan. By 1983, Seibu repositioned Mujirushi as a standalone brand, not least by opening a flagship shop on Tokyo's fashionable – and expensive – Aoyama-dōri.[79]

Ishioka Eiko (creative director and art director), Nagasawa Takeo (copy), Miyake Issey (styling), poster, *Fashion Isn't Right If It's Just Imitation*, Parco campaign for Miyake Issey, 1975.

Designing Modern Japan

ファッションだって真似だけじゃダメなんだ。

PARCO

Mujirushi's aesthetic, carried into retail design as well as products, packaging and advertising, would contribute greatly to the image of Japanese design overseas as minimalist, authentic and natural.[80] It needs to be understood, however, as sophisticated branding, originally created to stand out in a saturated domestic market in which appealing to 'authenticity' over fashion, natural materials over processed ones, and neutral colours over bright ones offered visual and emotional difference to competitors' products. Mujirushi's brand identity of authenticity and 'anti-fashion as fashion' was a far cry from Parco's bright, fast-moving image, but both demonstrated how bringing design and designers – in the form of art direction for brand and corporate identity – could offer competitive advantage by selling image in a crowded market. In doing so, Mujirushi's aesthetic perpetuated the image of Japanese design as authentic and natural promoted by European and American architects, designers and curators from the late nineteenth century as an antidote to what they saw as overly commercial styling design. In the 1980s, Japan itself became a brand.

Tanaka Ikkō (art direction) and Koike Kazuko (copy), *There's a Reason It's Cheap*, advertisement for the Mujirushi Ryōhin line, Seiyu Stores, 1980. Tanaka's art direction for Mujirushi Ryōhin packaging and promotions emphasized the brand message through functional copy, the use of recycled and unbleached paper for the packaging, matte red ink recalling the red ink used for signature seals, and packaging and advertisements that used illustrations rather than photography.

As the editorial in AXIS that opened this chapter indicated, the adoption of design as business strategy had a major impact on designers, both qualitatively and quantitatively. Seibu's adoption of corporate and brand identity signalled a step change in design's role in business in modern Japan. Branding and corporate identity through advertising and packaging design were not new, as we have already seen with kimono merchants in the Tokugawa period, confectioners like Morinaga from the 1910s and cosmetics firms like Shiseido from the 1920s. In the 1950s, electrical and mechanical goods manufacturers like Matsushita and Toyota added designers for product styling along with advertising teams to create compelling campaigns, with a strong emphasis on outreach to potential consumers through tied retailers and direct contact with potential consumers.[81] In embracing branding

Designing Modern Japan

and CI design as part of business strategy, Seibu Group and others who adopted a similar strategy from the 1970s accelerated a trend already under way. This approach also helped to sell products. While production figures must be understood in light of greater economic, political and technological factors such as exchange rates, wages, overseas anti-dumping campaigns and production line automation, the production of durable consumer goods more than doubled in Japan between 1975 and 1980.[82] Advertising spending nearly tripled between 1970 and 1980. By 1984, continued growth meant that ad spending was more than 1,600 per cent of what it had been in 1960.[83] Again, this meant more work for designers.

Tahinshuka did not remove designers from the design process, despite the fears around the potential for automation that so concerned vehicle designers in the 1960s. While CAD changed the modelling process – one of the vehicle designers' main fears – and the increased use of market and user research channelled designers' creativity, the immediate impact of the 'large variety, small volume production' model was to increase the involvement of graphic and industrial designers in product development and corporate communication more widely. Whether for a discrete brand or an entire company, identity campaigns required generating a conceptual identity and the visual language with which to communicate it, then applying this identity across all forms of brand or corporate communication, including advertising design, product design, interior design, architecture and corporate communications. This increased work for designers in multiple disciplines, as demands for design work grew within companies that already employed or hired designers, and as other companies began engaging them. According to the national census, the number of people giving their occupation as 'designer' grew more than 25 per cent between 1970 and 1975, from 70,630 to 88,725 people.[84] Most firms or design teams were small. The exceptions were at large manufacturers like Toyota, who employed 430 people in the design department in the early 1980s, and Sharp, who operated a two-hundred-person-strong corporate design centre.[85]

Increased work for designers across disciplines in the 1970s did not necessarily improve working conditions. Among graphic and product consultant designers, concerns remained about low fees, clients stealing or not fully acknowledging designers' intellectual property and inequal relationships with clients that meant designers had little if any negotiating power. In graphic design, these concerns prompted a new wave of labour organization. In 1978, 705 designers, mostly owners or employees at small independent design offices, became founding members of the Japan Graphic Designers Association (JAGDA).[86] Its founders intended JAGDA to serve as a union, with a collective voice that could lobby for better treatment from clients. An inaugural survey to determine members' needs also identified the public promotion of members' work through publishing and exhibitions as a key desired function. Significantly, members also wanted highly practical support: information sharing about materials and jobs, joint purchasing of materials and printing to bring down costs for small firms, and insurance, mutual aid and legal consulting for freelancers especially.[87] Into the 1980s, designers complained of low design fees, clients not complying with contracts and in other ways not respecting designers in business interactions.

Increased adoption of design as a business strategy diversified the work that designers did within and for companies. Both smaller retailers and manufacturers and some larger firms also retained designers as consultants, sometimes to advise on CI and brand identity, sometimes to deliver all the materials for related campaigns. Conglomerates like Sony and Seibu divided design work between centrally positioned design teams like the Sony PP Center who worked laterally to create CI and the parameters for new product lines, and large design divisions with graphic, product, packaging and retail designers who delivered the myriad materials, from packaging and advertisements to promotional products, commissioned to express brand and corporate identity. In 1989, Matsushita's comprehensive design centre employed fifty industrial designers, with another 350 industrial designers distributed across product teams in the firm and its subsidiaries.[88] Other large firms drew members from the design, marketing and product development teams into new central committees to set CI, brand and product parameters, before handing them over to design departments.[89] Yet others began approaching advertising agencies not just for ad campaigns but for product development, in other words much further upstream.

All of this meant more design work at two levels: determining corporate and brand identity and new product lines, and the actual design work required to realize their physical components. In 1985, packaging designer Hirohashi Keiko (b. 1931) explained the relationships of integrated product development and design for its individual elements in the product segmentation model:

Originally, it was good enough for packaging design to emphasize and express the unique points about a product. But segmentation to create various unique features for products and to establish them as separate items has advanced in response to consumers' demands. As a result, to sell more of just one product means we need to create differential advantage between that product and others, through packaging design that emphasizes the segmentation concept. One maker makes many different brands. Each brand needs to have its image decided, then everything from naming to brand colour, logo, models and characters, packaging design and advertising is developed together.[90]

Hirobashi was referring to packaging design, but her explanation articulates how the new corporate design practice not only brought design further upstream in the product development process but increased the amount of work expected of designers.

A further aspect of *tahinshuka* that increased designers' work was the insight that one product could be repackaged for use in multiple different occasions, effectively creating multiple products from one product, and multiple and often overlapping markets for it. A good example here is beer. Beverages, particularly beer, were known as a highly competitive industry in the 1970s and '80s, with a few major players dominating the national market. While the beers themselves varied little, manufacturers like Kirin, Asahi, Suntory and Sapporo regularly released new products with distinctive marketing to create new revenue streams. Advertising tried and trusted products in new packaging could be an effective strategy as well. In 1986, Asahi repackaged one of its existing beers in a distinctive silver can with strong black lettering and advertising that drew attention to the fact that a familiar product was inside. Asahi Super Dry became the second-highest selling beer in Japan soon afterwards.[91] Existing beers could also be repackaged for celebratory occasions and the changing seasons. Beers and other everyday use products like cooking oil and soy sauce could also be repackaged for the twice-annual gift-giving seasons and for seasonal events. Packaging design allowed companies to capitalize on brand loyalty across product categories. Marketing one product across different categories of use – everyday own use, gifts, corporate use and so on – also required considerably less outlay and time than to develop new product lines altogether. In one sense, diversifying packaging while retaining a constant product inside realized the rationalization of production that mid-twentieth-century campaigners wanted. On the other hand, the efflorescence of product choices did anything but rationalize packaging design and retail. It encouraged consumers to spend money on special events. It also increased packaging waste.[92]

The embrace of brand identity and CI extended to retail space design. Shop interiors could communicate identity through the physical experience of shopping and, as much if not more powerfully, through their reproduction in magazines. The emergence of tenant buildings like Parco and boutiques for DC brands offered opportunities for designers like Sugimoto Takashi of the consultancy Super Potato, now a member of the Seibu Group's design advisory committee, and Kuramata Shirō, who designed interiors for the Issey Miyake boutiques in addition to highly conceptual furniture. One British designer, visiting the flagship boutique for shoe brand Himiko, designed by Takayama Fujio (b. 1956) of Plastic Stock, explained his impression of this approach: 'Stock, as is usual in Japan, is subordinate to the interior design: the idea is to create an atmosphere for the shop rather than to pile the merchandise up high.'[93] Luxurious interiors that presented a visual contrast to existing retail spaces, photographed and distributed nationally in newspapers and in tourist guidebooks, had been a major tool for the new department stores like Mitsukoshi and Takashimaya in the early 1900s. Commercial designers and fast-moving goods manufacturers like Shiseido and Morinaga explored visual merchandising and point-of-purchase (POP) design beginning in the 1920s. From the 1970s, the proliferation of fashion brands, fashion buildings, fashion magazines and fashion consumers created a new rationale for companies to invest in design for retail spaces for a much wider demographic. íxí:z, for example, was a mid-range brand with carefully styled interiors for its concessions in tenant buildings. The circulation of photographs and reports on Japanese retail interiors in overseas magazines like *Blueprint* and *Vogue*, together with the establishment of boutiques for avant-garde brands Issey Miyake and Comme des Garçons in Paris and New York, also extended their fame or notoriety to foreign audiences interested in design as well, conflating their minimalist, materials-heavy aesthetic with 'Japanese design' in general.

The concentration of 'designerly' boutiques in specific neighbourhoods and tenant buildings amplified the effect that each could have.

By the late 1970s, it also created neighbourhoods known for fashion and design. Some could be found on newly branded streets like Shibuya's Faiya-dōri (Fire Street), others in existing fashion centres like Osaka's Shinsaibashi-suji, home to the art deco Daimaru and Sogō department stores. Whether laterally adjacent or vertically stacked in tenant buildings, the new shopping destinations retained the function and organization of the department store: entertainment as well as shopping, with fashion boutiques alongside cultural amenities like bookshops, galleries and cafés. Some neighbourhoods, most notably Aoyama in Tokyo, became associated with design practice thanks to the colocation of prominent graphic, product, interior and furniture design consultancies and DC brand boutiques within them – and publicity around these neighbourhoods in interior and furniture design magazines.

Fashion neighbourhoods were also the result of land development, as conglomerates with interests in railways, retail and real estate like Seibu and its rival Tōkyū established multiple tenant buildings on land in targeted locations. Seibu's first Parco opened in the Ikebukuro area of northern Tokyo, near the conglomerate's main department store and railway terminus. By 1975, Seibu had opened two further Parcos in Shibuya, closer to Aoyama and other fashionable neighbourhoods. Tōkyū and others followed with their own tenant buildings in Shibuya, Aoyama and other nearby areas and in other cities around Japan, creating concentrations of shopping and lifestyle venues, which could be advertised as design lifestyle destinations as well as the points of origin for national fashion trends. Further publicity came from editorial profiles of these neighbourhoods – or, even more compellingly, the young women and men who shopped and played there – in women's fashion magazines like *an an* and similar magazines for young men, which were launched in the late 1970s, and from national television programmes. For designers, again, this both increased demand for design work and increased the public profile of design as a profession. It also associated design, as a profession, with fashionability and with Tokyo, in particular.

Design in the Era of 'Corporaturgy'

Underlying all of this was corporate investment in design as business strategy. In the 1980s, domestic market competition propelled design and designers in Japan to even greater prominence and recognition, at home and overseas. This section focuses on domestic activity to explore how members of the design community, along with advertising agencies, increased their promotion of 'design' as business strategy, in order to point out how Japanese firms with strong brand and corporate identity campaigns succeeded in the domestic market. Some prominent members of the design community responded to increased abundance, lifestyle and commercialism – and to the opportunities it brought designers – with critiques based in a concern for the social values they represented. With companies funding cultural facilities and activities as part of their branding, these critiques, too, could be subsumed within a design-conscious experience economy, for consumption as part of the experience. Trenchant critiques actually enhanced brand image. Books like design critic and historian Kashiwagi Hiroshi's (b. 1946) *Seiji no dōgu to media* (The Politics of Tools and Media), a Frankfurt School-inspired critique, presented Shibuya Parco as the epitome of capital's co-option of culture, particularly design. Come 1989, it could be purchased in the Shibuya Parco's in-house bookshop. All of this activity created the conditions for the products, interiors and fashions that captured overseas attention. Perhaps the most important international driver, however, was the exchange rate.

Yet again, trade with the United States and negotiations over currency exchange rates shaped domestic economic conditions, creating particular parameters for designers' work. In 1985, Japan and the Federal Republic of Germany agreed to inflate the value of their currencies against the u.s. dollar as a way to help American manufacturers compete in their home market, the world's largest, by artificially raising the price of Japanese and West German goods. The high yen allowed overseas purchases by Japanese companies and consumers to go further, whether in the form of raw materials for manufacturing or travel and shopping overseas. At the same time, American consumers continued to buy Japanese exports, despite highly publicized protests against Japanese cars, increasing exporters' profits.

Striking exhibitions of Japanese design overseas played a role in persuading consumers to abandon prejudices towards 'made in Japan' and embrace the concept of 'Japanese design'. Beginning with 'Tsutsumu: The Art of the Japanese Package' in New York in 1975, a number of exhibitions and publications in the United States and Europe presented an image of Japanese objects and architecture – and through them, Japan – as thoughtfully designed, exquisitely crafted, miniaturized, playful, close to nature and deeply ingrained in Japanese

Designing Modern Japan

religious beliefs and cultural traditions which, they suggested, continued to shape a unique national aesthetic and sensibility.[94] The Japan Foundation, the Japanese government organization founded in 1972 to promote international cultural exchange with Japan, provided backing, as did cultural charities affiliated with prominent companies. In contrast to the mass-produced cars, VCRs and cosmetics that prompted protectionist responses from U.S. and other foreign manufacturers and workers in the 1970s and '80s, such exhibitions and publications presented Japanese design as admirable, cultural and deeply non-capitalist. By the mid-1980s, curators, designers and promoters had identified a further trope: Japan as the physical manifestation of postmodernity or the technological sublime. For fashion audiences, the inventive forms and unconventional use of tailoring and materials offered by avant-garde fashion designers like Miyake Issey and Kawakubo Rei challenged then prevalent visions of feminine beauty when presented in catwalk shows or boutiques in Paris and New York. In the U.S. market, the promotion and novelty of such goods helped distance exports on the shelves from trade frictions and the lingering association of Japanese goods with poor quality. For designers and consumers outside the United States, too, they offered 'visions of Japan', to cite the name of a memorable exhibition in London in 1991, in which a celebration of design pleasure was integrated into everyday life.[95]

Domestic and export sales and the savings afforded by the high yen meant profit. Japan's national government used the increased tax revenue to support rural regions, far from the large exporters' bases in metropolitan areas like Tokyo, Osaka and Aichi. Exporters invested in assets, particularly land. Urban and suburban land prices soared, especially in Tokyo, where the average price of land grew 87 per cent in 1987 alone.[96] The capital gain in land assets equalled 367 per cent of Japan's gross domestic product between 1986 and 1990.[97] Share prices rose as well. The Nikkei Stock Average, which reflected conditions on the Tokyo Stock Exchange, hit 10,000 yen per share in 1984. By 1989, it had nearly quadrupled in value, to 38,915 yen per share.[98]

Growing affluence further accelerated corporate use of the *tahinshu* strategy. In 1991, towards the end of the economic bubble, some 348 types of refrigerator were on the market in Japan.[99] At Sanyo, the electrical goods manufacturer, the design team styled multiple product lines for different user groups: the Retro modern collection for sophisticated older couples, Floor Gang for 'young individualists', Mymy

for young women, Urbanesque for young adults living alone and Robo toys for children.[100] Product development teams at firms like Sanyo launched incrementally different products on the market several times a year, enabling constant new model availability and constant new advertising campaigns. Increased functionality, not only in personal cassette players, mini CD players and video cameras but in rice cookers, bathtubs and toilets, was one way to do this. Miniaturization was another common technique, often used to target younger consumers. In the publicity for its Handycam 55 video recorder, released in 1989, Sony emphasized that the camera was no larger than a Japanese passport, with a delicately styled interface. Sony shipped 71,000 cameras in the Handycam 55's first month of sales, 40 per cent of the industry total.[101] Eventually, a prominent economist would describe the *tahinshuka* model as the 'overdiversification of products, frequent model changes and useless versatility'.[102] It also meant big design teams. Sanyo assigned 45 people, predominantly designers, to its 'life creative room', responsible for creating product concepts.[103] Sanyo's design department, responsible for creating the actual catalogues, flyers, POP items, promotional goods and other materials for each campaign, numbered over three hundred employees.[104]

Another strategy for appealing to consumers in the saturated market of late 1980s Japan was to commodify information about commodities itself. Information (*jōhō*) became a key branding concept adopted by firms such as Seibu Group, whose core businesses consisted of retail, land developments and railways but described itself as a 'Broadcasting centre for information' – that is, fashion.[105] Along with retailers and powerful advertising firms like Dentsu and Hakuhodo, media outlets suggested that consuming information about the latest fashions was a way to fully participate in an affluent, abundant society. Tokyo publisher World Photo Press launched *Mono magajin* (Things, commonly known as *Mono*) in 1982, with the strapline 'SUPER GOODS MAGAZINE for discovering the things you want'. *Mono* made its remit explicit: the delivery of 'new product information', specifically for young men. *Mono* and its competitors enumerated the qualities, prices and retailers for watches, shoes, lighters, bicycles, cars, wallets and other commercially available items in editorial features composed of finely detailed text and images. Meanwhile, advertisements presented corporate image more often than products. Editorials and special issues like 'The Three Sacred Regalia for Men' – watch, wallet and lighter – with

Tamago-tsuto (Egg Tube), (*Yamagata Prefecture*), colour photograph by Sakai Michikazu, in Oka Hideyuki, *Tsutsumu*, Mainichi Shinbunsha, 1972. With their modernist, minimalist composition and reverent visual treatment of rural Japanese objects like the egg carrier fashioned out of straw, Sakai's photographs, included in Oka's book *How to Wrap Five Eggs* and exhibitions it prompted in the USA and Europe, supported a particular perception of Japanese design.

the subtitle 'Discover the Exquisite Articles for You Alone', emphasized readers' ability to achieve personalization through shopping, but within mass-produced commodities available widely on the national market, and within product categories closely associated with readers' gender and age.[106] Economic growth in the 1960s rendered standard commodities accessible to most households regardless of income and geography. The bubble economy of the 1980s presented highly subdivided but still standardized commodities as personalized, promising to create and express individuality. In some ways, the Tokugawa period concept of the *tsū*, or connoisseur, had now returned for a mass market rather than for men of privileged status alone.

But *tahinshuka* was losing its power in some markets. By 1989, Dentsu described Japanese consumers as demanding something new:

> With increased diversification and personalization of lifestyles, people are trying to select, out of the vast array of products and services, items that best match their individual needs and represent their unique identities. Seeking quality in this world rich with things, consumers are starting to pursue affluence of the mind, time and environment. The day has come when people are beginning to savor 'a sense of personal betterment,' and individuality.[107]

Social researchers first identified *monobanare* – 'leaving things behind', or a loss of interest in acquiring things – as an emergent phenomenon in the late 1960s. The phrase came to the fore in the early 1980s to describe a new trend: some consumers' reluctance to buy things at all.[108] As assessed by Dentsu, the issue was partly one of information overload: too many products to choose from, and too much information available about each of them. Faced with so much information, and already possessing the goods they needed, some people purchased none. Social researchers also suggested that consumers of all ages and genders were widening their sense of self, rendering demographically targeted product design and marketing less effective.

Both *monobanare* and unpredictable shopping habits posed potential challenges to manufacturers, retailers and the ad agencies that handled promotional campaigns for many large firms. In response, Dentsu, Hakuhodo and the art directors working as consultants for brands or within corporate central design units shifted to create

Designing Modern Japan

indirect, imagistic advertising campaigns and product packaging intended to capture attention and communicate a general corporate identity, rather than to inform potential consumers about the performance and identity of specific products or a product line.[109] Packaging designer Hirohashi Keiko, summing up successful packaging in 1985, explained that rather than selling the product, packaging should express playfulness, humour and a sense of expansiveness and freedom.[110] Like posters for Parco from the late 1960s onwards, this was advertising to evoke an emotional response, rather than to communicate product demographic, functionality or performance.[111]

Manufacturers' and retailers' turn to corporate identity required designers to retune their designs, whether for advertising graphics, packaging, products or retail interiors. Most of the examples in this book demonstrate how designers conveyed product and brand image through the styling of product forms, by creating a recognizable visual language in packaging and advertisements, and by associating products and brands with particular external things. As influential manufacturers and retailers embraced CI around 1980, the subject of designers' work shifted increasingly from products like the Sony Walkman or brands like íxí:z to the firms behind them. This did not change how designers worked, particularly, but it integrated design even further into business and marketing strategy and changed firms' expectations of what designers – at the strategic level, at least – would deliver. It also produced the kind of advertisements for which Japanese art direction from the 1980s onwards has become known internationally: imagistic, technically accomplished compositions that juxtapose visually stunning photography or film footage with short, obtuse captions or voiceovers and a discrete corporate name and logo, which refers to neither an actual product nor the company's main business.

Seibu was an early adopter of the CI strategy. Seibu transformed its design advisory team into an affiliated design firm, Japan Creative, for overall creative direction as well as the design of Seibu homewares and other projects. Tanaka Ikkō remained as art director, with Koizumi Keiko as lead copywriter and Sugimoto Takashi of Super Potato as lead interior designer for Seibu's retail spaces. Together, they oversaw a CI campaign that ranged across advertisements and interiors through to tenant building location, as well as boutique and designer selection. The campaign also included Seibu LOFT, a multistorey destination for lifestyle goods, stationery and homewares, and considerable investment in cultural facilities such as the Saison Museum in Ikebukuro and an arts and culture publishing imprint, Libroport. Through carefully imagistic advertisements for both these initiatives and the group itself, along with the association of selected Seibu subsidiaries with high-end design, art and culture, Seibu – the Saison Group, as it became in 1985 – positioned itself as responsive, fashionable and cutting-edge.[112] As one measure of success, Seibu's sales more than doubled between 1983 and 1988, from over 400 million yen to 1 billion yen.[113] While sales at Parco actually declined from their peak in 1979, Seibu's CI campaign and the fashionability of its branches, particularly Parco and Mujirushi, began to impact public and industry perceptions of design as well. In 1987, Tanaka Ikkō came first in a survey of most admired designers.[114] More broadly, in one survey of four hundred major corporations published in 1987, 56 per cent of the managers who responded on behalf of their firms wanted designers who could be ahead of the times and convey new trends, and 55 per cent wanted designers who could improve corporate image. Only 42 per cent wanted designers who could improve the sales of products.[115]

'Culture' (*bunka*) became a keyword for companies and branding teams eager to communicate a less overtly commercial face to corporate activity. Its adoption echoed the 'culture' boom of the 1920s, though without acknowledging the connection, at least in marketing material. Suntory president Saji Keizō (1919–1999), for example, presented Suntory as 'selling everyday life culture', not beverages.[116] Suntory opened the Suntory Museum of Art in Tokyo in 1961, showcasing premodern Japanese artistic treasures. A range of new artistic corporate sponsorship initiatives in the 1980s included Suntory Hall, a concert hall for Western classical music opened in 1986. The transport, retail and real estate conglomerate Tōkyū, a direct competitor to Seibu, decided to foreground the cultural concept, opening the Bunkamura ('culture village') complex in 1989 as part of an eight-year urban redevelopment plan for an area of Shibuya.[117] Bunkamura's combination of art gallery, bookshops, cafés, cinema and performing arts spaces for theatre and Western classical music included an official extension of Les Deux Magots, the café on the Rive Gauche in Paris known for its association with bohemian artists and intellectuals.

Some firms already associated with architecture and design began supporting cultural production in these areas. The sanitaryware firm Ina Seitō, newly renamed INAX, sponsored a new journal of architectural theory and criticism, *10+1*. Exhibitions at the INAX Showroom near the Ginza and a publication series, INAX Booklets, recorded and celebrated twentieth-century Japanese design and architecture. Competitor TOTO, formerly Tōyō Tōki, opened Gallery MA in 1985 as an exhibition space for work by contemporary architects, with an advisory board of architect Andō Tadao (b. 1941), furniture designer Kawakami Motomi (b. 1940), industrial designer Kurokawa Masayuki (b. 1937), interior designer Sugimoto Takashi and graphic designer Tanaka Ikkō, the latter two also advisors of course to Seibu. Gallery MA would become synonymous worldwide with avant-garde Japanese architecture.[118] For its part, lingerie manufacturer Wacoal, maker of the Shape Pants introduced earlier in this chapter, opened Spiral, a multipurpose cultural complex and office designed by architect Maki Fumihiko (b. 1928) with interiors by Kuramato Shirō, in 1985, at the junction of designerly Aoyama and emergent youth culture epicentre Jingū-mae. Less obviously, the AXIS building in Tokyo's Minato ward, home to AXIS magazine as well as numerous design showrooms, craft boutiques, cafés and the Tokyo Design Space Gallery, was sponsored by Bridgestone tyres, whose other cultural initiatives included the Bridgestone Museum of Art, a leading private museum for European art.[119] Carefully sited facilities like the AXIS building, Spiral and Bunkamura only intensified the association of specific Tokyo neighbourhoods with design and fashionability within Japan, and raised the profile of Tokyo itself as a design capital worldwide.

For eagle-eyed cultural critics, who were well versed in post-war French philosophers' theories of signs, consumption and spectacle, as well as the Frankfurt School philosophers' critique of capitalism as commodifying culture, the physical manifestations of CI and cultural strategy – the cafés, the tenant buildings, the creation of design and fashion epicentres and their reproduction in national media – were symbolic of the way in which Japanese late industrial capitalism was transforming urban living space itself into a sign and a commodity, ready for consumption at distance. Kashiwagi Hiroshi's essays, published in both popular general readership weeklies and prominent philosophy and literary journals, described Parco's cafés as more important as information than as a destination. As Kashiwagi explained, the café could be redeveloped and a new café installed instantaneously: what mattered was not visiting the café but knowing of it.[120] For the developer, Seibu, design as fashion information helped to maintain high land and share prices. CI and the cultural strategy, in this sense, did sell the company.[121] No surprise, perhaps, that the sociologist Yoshimi Shunya (b. 1957) landed on dramaturgy as a useful concept for explaining how Parco's management created a form of urban space as artificial experience.[122]

There were also critiques within the CI business itself. Already by 1985, corporate identity consultant Nakanishi Motoo (b. 1938), founder of leading CI consultancy PAOS, criticized the cultural infrastructure strategy as superficial, given that so many corporations were undertaking it. For Nakanishi, sponsoring concert halls, galleries or art books – and publicizing these activities by associating them with beautiful, cutting-edge design – was insufficient. Companies had to grow and publicize their own internal cultures, or, as Nakanishi explained, to shift from a culture strategy to a one of 'culturization'. In Nakanishi's diagnosis, presented in the graphic design and typography industry journal *Tategumi Yokogumi* (Vertical Typesetting, Horizontal Typesetting), designers' role was to communicate internal culture through materials like annual reports, rather than to decorate streetscapes and homes with corporate image.[123] For Nakanishi, too, this was best facilitated through the conceptual practices of the stage: in his words, 'From CI to cultural strategy, and now to the era of corporaturgy'.[124]

In corporate design practice itself, the proposition was hardly novel, whether in Japan or overseas. For its part, from the transmedia designs of Honami Kōetsu in the early Tokugawa period, subsequently the basis for Rinpa, to the early twentieth-century campaigns of firms like Mitsukoshi and Shiseido, Japanese business history was replete with managers, art directors and designers who had created strong CIS for their firms, then integrated these across advertising, packaging, retail interiors and media messaging. Now, the hope was that if market segmentation and product differentiation no longer sold products, corporate image, aligned to flatter consumers' self-image, might.

Design business magazines were promoting mass-manufacturing and large retail design divisions and critics focusing on urban dreamscapes like Shibuya, but in reality products, retailers, advertising and consumers existed in a much more complex retail and urban ecosystem. In the Shinsaibashi area of Osaka, for example, the postmodern Kirin Plaza building by architect Takamatsu Shin (b. 1948) prominently represented the beverage maker's CI and cultural strategy. Osaka Parco, opened in 1972, was a few minutes' walk away. But both were embedded in one of Japan's most storied shopping streets, Shinsaibashi-suji, home to confectioners, stationers, and shops selling tea and dried seaweed since the Edo period as well as to smart post-war cafés, book-shops, fashion retailers, two major department stores – Daimaru and Sogō – and competitors' own tenant buildings. A short walk away was Amerika-mura, home to American second-hand clothing shops and record shops, and Yoroppa-mura (Europe village), a neighbourhood intended for more sophisticated fashion boutiques for women. Shinsaibashi-suji abutted the Senba wholesale textile district, once Japan's largest, to the north. To the south were the massive Takashimaya department store and specialist wholesale neighbourhoods for electronics, kitchenware, furniture and other items. Shops and cafés needed interior designers. Apparel manufacturers required textile and fashion designers. Sales on Shinsaibashi-suji and the surrounding wholesale streets also supported shoe designers, packaging designers, product designers, furniture designers, and graphic designers creating everything from signage and advertising posters to clothing tags and café menus. The neighbourhoods' business associations hired designers for street furniture, including lighting and signage.

In sum, the new attention to design for CI, including design as cultural strategy, existed within a much larger and longer-lived design ecosystem, in which many people made a living for design work, including many still not named as designers. In many ways, this was not so far from urban manufacturing and retail in the Tokugawa period. At the same time, design had become big business. More people from across social classes could access these urban pleasures, particularly more women.[125] Design's prominence was also underpinned as much by land prices, companies' stock prices and foreign exchange rates as by what shoppers bought at Parco or the seaweed shop.

Corporate attention to design increased both the amount of design work and the number of design roles. The number of people identifying their profession as design in the national census rose only slightly between 1975 and 1980, then jumped nearly 30 per cent between 1980 and 1985, from 92,636 to 120,500 people, before growing by 33 per cent again in the five years to 1990, to 160,800 people.[126] The number of companies identifying themselves as design firms also grew in the early 1980s, from 5,718 in 1981 to 7,801 in 1986, an increase of over 36 per cent.[127] Underneath the numbers, many seemingly independent firms were spinoff companies or otherwise affiliated with large printing firms, ad agencies, design firms or powerful clients. The engagement of designers by businesses and the prominent role of design in creating fashion neighbourhoods raised the profile of design as a career path to creatively minded young people across the country. Publisher Bijutsu Shuppansha launched *Dezain no genba* (Designers' Workshop), a journal profiling different design professions for interested students and others considering entering the design industries. The project had begun as a series of special issues in the contemporary art journal *Bijutsu techō*; in 1984, readership was strong enough for the publisher to turn the concept into a standalone journal with its own editorial staff. For new design graduates, it was a sellers' market; small consultancies complained of not being able to hire even two-year design college graduates, let alone design graduates with four-year university degrees.[128] Whether for *tahinshuka* or for CI and cultural strategy, increased corporate engagement with designers also supported the emergence of a peripheral design infrastructure, including editorial firms such as Arushīvu (Archives)-sha in Tokyo, which produced publications by designers. In the background – on purpose – the design media infrastructure of writers, translators, editors and photographers enabled the high volume of public outputs by designers on design, further contributing to the design professions' association with cutting-edge urban fashionability.

While work was abundant, designers' feelings about their working conditions remained mixed. Time and workload were an issue. A 1987 survey of 254 designers across disciplines indicated an average workday of ten hours. Twenty per cent of respondents, including 30 per cent of designers working in corporate teams, said their workload was impossible.[129] Average pay across the sector was relatively low, and corporate design team members earned only 60 per cent of the average pay for all designers, possibly because they were younger and had not yet left to go freelance after building their portfolio.[130]

By the early 1980s, corporate design teams and consultancies alike were staffed by both men and women. Within large firms, most team leaders were men, as were most corporate managers, with women working both in the teams assigned to generate product, brand and corporate concepts and in the practical roles to execute them.[131] Women's prospects to lead on design projects and gain recognition as a result were limited by entrenched gender bias. Hiring practices channelled many women into the non-career path (*ippanshoku*), and

The product development team at Panasonic, c. 1983, selecting the colour panels for a new washing machine from a number of options. The clear distinction between younger office ladies (OLS) in company uniforms and mostly older career-track male employees in shirts and ties indicates how gender could structure lived experience in corporate product development in 1980s Japan.

the expected long working hours were incompatible with family life for employees on the corporate advancement career path (*sōgōshoku*). Long working hours, unpredictable ending times and the need to be on call or responsive to clients and managers made it difficult for women to stay on after marriage and motherhood. There were also gender politics to play in work transactions. Osaka graphic designer Ōnishi Chizuko, who counted a large beverage maker among her clients, explained how gender biases increased the amount of work she needed to put into managing her relationships with them. In her experience, Ōnishi reported, 'There is no comparison between the amount of labour I need to put into flattering men, behind-the-scenes work and pointless meetings, and the effort I can put into the actual design work.'[132] In a 1989 roundtable initiated by industry magazine *Nikkei dezain* (Nikkei Design), product and corporate strategist Kubota Yūko explained how clients continued to see female designers and consumers as supplemental to core business and the core team.

> A certain manufacturer came to talk with me about a project they wanted to run as an addition to core business, to be developed by women. As they explained the talk, [it became clear that] they were going to give part of the project to women to do, but the rest would be done by men. The project was neatly divided up that way. I told the company that if they were actually going to commission the project, it would be good not to make

'Generosity and tolerance'

some kind of strange division like 'she's a woman so she can't do more than that' and 'he's a man so he can do more than that.'[133]

As successful consultants with strong track records, Ōnishi and Kubota were able to comment publicly on gender discrimination they faced at work. This was less the case for women in corporate design divisions. Women's outsized purchasing power did not guarantee social status within the workplace, creating a complex environment for female designers to negotiate. The conversations also show how product development for segmented markets continued apace, underneath the buzz around CI and cultural strategy.

The popularity of CI also prompted the major advertising agencies, Dentsu and Hakuhodo, to take a larger interest in design, as clients increasingly approached them about comprehensive CI and product development work, as well as downstream advertising and publicity. Hakuhodo opened a CI department in 1983. At Dentsu, employees across a number of departments organized an unofficial research group on the concept of 'Designing' as business strategy in 1984, after the marketing department began getting requests from firms to handle comprehensive product planning work, from conceptualization through to total design, including product and retail space design.[134] Dentsu's senior management turned the group into a summer seminar for employees, inviting star designers, critics and academics to brief Dentsu's teams on design practice and relevant cultural and social theories such as semiotics and postmodernism. As part of its own brand repositioning, Dentsu then published the seminar transcripts as a book, *Dezainingu* (Designing), within its line-up of marketing and advertising titles for general business readers.[135] The 'ing' in the title was expressly intended to situate design as a business strategy, alongside marketing, advertising and branding.[136]

Advertising was not alone in appropriating and promoting design as a business strategy. Following the launch of AXIS in 1981, business and financial media firm Nikkei established *Nikkei Design* in 1987. Like *Designers' Workshop*, editorial content in both magazines focused on designers, design management and hit products. But whereas *Designers' Workshop* profiled craft designers, illustrators and Kyoto textile firms as well as Honda's motorbike design team, as part of its remit to present design as professional practice, AXIS and *Nikkei Design* very clearly emphasized design for mass-manufacturing and large-scale retail.[137]

Profiles of 'design-oriented' (DO) companies like Matsushita and Sanyo presented the 'how-to' of establishing and running a design team that increased sales and market share, as well as creating a corporate structure and management system to maximize the design team's impact.[138] Statements by company presidents explaining how design was integral to their business strategy, together with surveys of Nikkei 500 firms identifiable as DO companies, further associated successful corporate leadership and business strategy with an embrace of design.[139] The magazines fleshed out their accounts of design teams' process from initial product concept to market success with flowcharts and sketches, prototypes, sample parts and design team office spaces and meetings. In doing so, they publicly labelled popular products as 'designed', highlighting designers' roles in creating business success as well as the commodities that populated everyday environments.

Design industry associations like the Japan Industrial Design Association (JIDA), along with the state Japan Industrial Promotion Organization (JIDPO), began promoting design management as well, in JIDA's case linking with similar efforts among design academics, organizations and publications in Britain and elsewhere. Some regional officials saw design for business as a potentially useful strategy for place-branding and business promotion. In 1985, the governments of Nagoya and surrounding Aichi prefecture, along with representatives from leading local companies, bid to host the 1989 conference of the International Congress of Societies of Industrial Design (ICSID). By 1989, events included Nagoya's self-designation as a 'Design City' and – more substantially – a world's fair, the Design Expo. The International Design Center Nagoya (IdcN), an exhibition and event space aimed at promoting design's take-up by local Nagoya businesses and showcasing existing design accomplishments, followed in 1992.[140] Events like the Design Expo targeted an international audience, but regional politics and positioning were significant drivers as well. Design promotion had come full circle, from designer-civil servants' efforts earlier in the twentieth century to raise local manufacturers' awareness of design as corporate strategy, to manufacturers and politicians identifying design as a lever for economic growth and political capital. This was design for cultural strategy and city branding, as well as an extended, well-resourced effort to wrest some of the investment in design – and its cultural cachet, not to mention international attention – from Tokyo to Nagoya and Aichi, with their great manufacturing base.[141]

The geography of design in 1980s Japan did skew towards Tokyo. Design consultancies and advertising firms were located across the country. Design consultancies and teams in regional cities contracted with local clients, from large, regionally based manufacturers to small firms. Osaka was important for consumer electronics and electrical goods design, with major firms like Matsushita, Sharp and Sanyo headquartered there. But Tokyo was the clear centre for both design offices and design's consumption as a cultural commodity. Tokyo housed an estimated 40 per cent of all design firms in Japan and 50 per cent of designers, with Osaka home to another 20 per cent.[142] By 1986, the Tokyo telephone directories listed 3,634 commercial design offices, handling advertising, packaging and the like; 953 offices offered product, industrial and furniture design services, and 850 offices specialized in interior design.[143] This only grew over the course of the bubble period: in 1989, another survey found 5,912 firms listed in the Tokyo telephone directories.[144]

Within Tokyo, design industries had a particular geography. While consultancies were scattered across the city, they were most densely concentrated in the neighbourhoods home to advertising firm and television station headquarters, convenient for regular liaising, and in fashion epicentres.[145] Tokyo's Minato ward was the undisputed hub, with Shibuya ward and Chūo ward, home to the Ginza, close behind. Building on the existing format of fashion neighbourhood profiles, the new design industry journals publicized designers who had located their offices in these areas in insider accounts about designers as celebrities, as exciting, stylish, breathlessly of the now.[146]

Such celebrations of corporate design and star designers' offices obscured the fact that design firms also operated in regional cities, providing logos, packaging design and the like to small local firms, be they a tinned fish manufacturer or an optician. One consultant graphic designer who worked in a regional city between Tokyo and Nagoya explained his feelings:

Most of the marketing information and design information in specialist design journals until now has concerned large firms or presentations to large firms. We local designers buy the magazines to have something to talk about, but in reality they're next to useless for us.

I can understand that there are particular circumstances necessary for editorial planning and high sales numbers, but I'd like for you to put more of a spotlight on small firms around the country.

Specifically, I'd like you to plan things like a special issue on unique advertisements for small firms. Regional advertisements for small firms can't be like the concepts and forms of expression pursued by large firms. I hope you will increase this direction going forward.[147]

A graphic designer based in Kyushu put it more succinctly: 'Places like Tokyo and Osaka aren't the only audiences for design.'[148] They weren't, but for design's audiences outside the design industry, the association of design with metropolitan culture was important. While *tahinshuka* and market segmentation fundamentally changed manufacturing for national distribution, the products of the national design media, for the most part, remained one-size-fits-all. Local logo and packaging design fit less comfortably with the image of design as cultural strategy, lifestyle brand or youth fashion that rendered design attractive to audiences as diverse as students and Nikkei 500 companies.

Thus far, this chapter has focused on design within Japan in the 1970s and '80s, as a way to emphasize the economic and social conditions that shaped design practice and products and the lived experience of designers within it. Of course, design was a major Japanese export throughout the period as well. Designed commodities were major exports. To give only a few indications, in 1983, Shiseido had the third highest revenue for a cosmetics firm in the world, following Avon and L'Oréal.[149] Some analyses of its success noted the presence of Shiseido counters at the Galeries Lafayette in Paris, but Shiseido's global sales came primarily from other countries in Asia, where Shiseido was a luxury brand. At the peak of exports in 1985, before the artificial inflation of the yen, 60 per cent of Japanese electrical items were exported.[150] Even after the yen's increase in value, in 1987, Japanese electric machinery manufacturers had 24 per cent of the global market, or 30–35 per cent if products from overseas plants and joint companies were included.[151]

For many foreign designers, Japan's design industries appealed. One draw was the combination of large corporate budgets for design and the sheer availability of work. Others were the allure of Japanese fashion, products, interior and graphic design, and the image of Tokyo in particular as a phantasmagoria of designed goods and environments. China was emerging into a new era of trade and diplomatic relations after Mao Zedong's death in 1977. For educators in the PRC's few university design departments and designers at product development institutes in places like the new economic zone in Shenzhen, on the border with Hong Kong, Japanese design expertise could be useful.[152] Japanese graphic designers like Sugiura Kōhei established relationships with counterparts in China, offering seminars and sharing knowledge. Chinese designers travelled to Japan to spend time in university design departments and design consultancies.

For European and other Western designers, Japan could offer work. For some, this meant one-off commissions, for others ongoing relationships and even employment. Japanese companies and design organizations continued to consult prominent foreign designers, but Japan's economic strength and the resources available to designers drew emergent practitioners as well. íxí:z employed the British textile designer Penny Jarvis at the brand's design office in Paris.[153] In 1988, 26-year-old Australian designer Marc Newson had a solo show in the gallery at AXIS and was on a retainer with Idée.[154] For ambitious young designers from overseas, Japanese firms offered adventure and corporate backing and resources for aesthetic and technical experimentation, as well as the opportunity to experience Japan's design culture from the inside. For entrepreneurs in Japan, eye-catching café interiors and corporate headquarters by international architects like Starck and the UK's Nigel Coates fulfilled the brief as well. Photogenic interiors were not the corporaturgy that CI consultant Nakanishi Motoo had urged for, but they demonstrated corporate capital at home and abroad. Far from designers' concerns about the state co-option of design's power at Osaka Expo 70, this was design as both beneficiary and driver of corporate and national success.

'This has led to considerable difficulties in halting the inclination toward expanding the industry': Restructuring Design after 1991

From *tahinshuka* and market segmentation to CI and cultural strategies, Japanese corporate engagement with design in the 1970s and '80s offered designers work, income and resources. It also exposed designers to market fluctuations, specifically downturns. In 1991, the

Designing Modern Japan

economic bubble collapsed.[155] The Nikkei Index fell to 14,309 yen by the end of the year, 63 per cent lower than its high in 1989.[156] From its high of 367 per cent the value of nominal GDP in 1987, land prices sank to roughly half of nominal GDP in 1992.[157] In a more tangible measure, in spring 1991, the national media announced that for the first time in a generation, the hiring market for university graduates favoured employers, not graduates.

For manufacturers and retailers alike, the crash in stock and land prices lowered corporate value immediately. Consumer hesitation, followed by income losses as companies began to restructure their labour forces or accelerated manufacturing offshoring to China, slowed purchasing. The yen, however, remained strong, making Japanese goods more expensive against competitors in markets overseas. The economist Takeuchi Kei, writing in 1994, set out the issues in distinctively Japanese understatement, with reference to electrical goods:

> Now with the prolonged recession and the high value of the yen, each company in the home electric appliance industry has been forced to proceed with restructuring. Up to now the home electric appliance industry had carried out continual expansion, while passing through product cycles of major goods. This has led to considerable difficulties in halting the inclination toward expanding the industry. Viewed from a midterm perspective, any more expansion of the domestic market cannot be anticipated. In addition, because of the rapid growth of industries in Chinese and the NIES countries and the anchoring of the high yen in the international marketplace, not only is the expansion of exports unlikely, but an increase of exports from abroad can be expected as well.
>
> Under such circumstances home electric appliance corporations have proceeded with policies that expand overseas production and partially scale down domestic production. Furthermore they are now revising their rules of rivalry in order to alter their excessive competitiveness and promote strategic cooperation, including partnerships with foreign corporations.[158]

The course of export-driven manufacturing as the dominant industrial policy from the 1870s onwards – and, arguably, of domains' exports to other domains as a growing economic mainstay in the Tokugawa period – had stopped. Economic growth slowed to an average of 1.3 per cent in the 1990s. A major restructuring of banking resulted in negative interest rates from 1998. While some new product types like digital cameras and household computers captured consumer attention, for the most part households already owned their big-ticket items and were less likely to replace them. In 1993, MITI and the major manufacturers announced a new policy promoting 'long-life' product development.

Neither exports nor domestic consumption disappeared, of course. The fashion epicentres in Tokyo, Osaka and regional cities remained, as did fashion and design media. Product development and advertising campaigns continued, meaning work for both in-house design teams and consultancies, but budgets fell and the production cycle slowed. Consultant graphic designers who provided advertising campaigns for retailers found that budgets disappeared.[159] One graphic design insider, Ōseko Nobumitsu (b. 1953) of JAGDA, described budgets for print media as dropping by 30 per cent a year in the 1990s.[160] Ad agency Hakuhodo closed its CI department in 1993. Overall, shrinking advertising and product budgets meant less work for designers, illustrators and photographers, lower rates, and pressure on designers to reduce fees or submit low tenders for new work. Among younger designers who had benefited less from the bubble period's expense accounts and high fees and had less responsibility for overall company welfare, creativity and exploration continued unabated, with a renewed interest in 'indie' brands like Hysteric Glamour, 'select shops' like Beams, and independent book, magazine and record labels over those owned by established firms. Older male designers who led teams or owned consultancies felt the changes more acutely. The decline in work was also determined by geography. Tokyo's economy remained stronger than that of the rest of the country, whereas Osaka and the surrounding region were hard hit by local events like the Kōbe earthquake of 1995 and the offshoring of textile production, including kimono, to China. The concept of the designer as 'creator' re-emerged, with a neologism, kuriētā, replacing 'designer' in many profiles. Design students travelled overseas to study in London, Paris and New York, drawn by the renewed vibrance of design scenes in these cities.

Computers began to appear in design offices, although their adoption varied widely from firm to firm. For every type foundry creating digital type or manufacturer investing in CAD there was an art director who preferred the mat and X-Acto knife.[161] The marriage of digital technology and children's and youth culture was creating a new visual language and set of specialisms in digital and game design, drawing on and contributing to the accomplishments of firms like Nintendo, Sega and animation leader Studio Ghibli.[162] Technical advances – the introduction of Japanese typefaces, graphical user interface (GUI) and OS software that functioned in the Japanese language, along with faster processors, cheaper memory and advances in software like Adobe Photoshop and Illustrator – allowed amateurs to take on graphic design projects using desktop publishing software, and to enter the web design industry.[163] As in design communities elsewhere, professional designers in Japan often greeted digital design's increased accessibility with mixed feelings. In 2000, designer Ogawa Shunji noted:

> Homepages are set up so that anyone can become involved in GUI design, amateur-level GUI is emerging in great volumes at the moment. Today it continues to appear. I think this in itself is good, but within these conditions the existence of developers and managers who aren't able to tell the difference between the work of designers and that of amateurs has become even more clear.[164]

Ogawa's concern was that the GUI of popular web design software like Dreamweaver prompted professional users to design using predetermined 'wizards', rather than programming code directly. Unlike the Toyota designers in 1968, Ogawa was not concerned that design software would replace his profession. Rather, it was the lack of texture and expressive breadth afforded by digital shortcuts – something he compared to thick make-up on the skin of a beautiful woman – that concerned him. Other designers, however, celebrated digital aesthetics, particularly in highly simplified colour-block graphics like those of Groovisions and Satō Kashiwa (b. 1965). The Toyota designers' predictions were also partly correct. Speaking in 2007, Oseko Nobumitsu of JAGDA reflected that designers' adoption of computers – particularly the Apple Macintosh – had often resulted in clients and managers expecting designers to do more work, faster, and to take on additional work such as copy-editing for the same fee.[165]

By the mid-1990s, design remained important for many firms' business strategy, providing work for designers. But the era of 'corporaturgy'

was over, with the end of economic growth. This rendered design work more precarious while also freeing designers to explore new clients and practices. The digital tools explored by some designers in the 1970s had disrupted some hard-won professional practices, but also offered a new visual language and new work opportunities. Working hours remained long, intellectual property (IP) issues a concern and pay uneven, but the era of working for the national good had long passed, not least as the next generation of designers had themselves grown up with *tahinshuka* and extreme individuation. Many of the changes predicted by designers around 1970 were not that far off the mark.

This chapter began with comments by *AXIS* editor Hamano Yasuhiro to the effect that design offered a particular 'generosity and tolerance' well suited to advanced industrial societies like that of Japan in 1981. The Economic White Papers of the early 1970s had outlined two related shifts in direction, from a production-oriented economy to one in which consumption played a larger role and the cost of growth was acknowledged, and from heavy and lower-end manufacturing industries to a high-skilled information economy. Early on, some designers worried that the adoption of information and control systems would weaken their roles. Others felt that design was overly complicit in a national project to achieve economic growth and political stability, regardless of the environmental and social fallout. But as the shift took hold, designers benefited. Employing designers and adopting ideas of 'designing' allowed larger firms, especially, to drive sales through the

Designing Modern Japan

fine differentiation of product lines, the intensification of shopping as an immersive leisure experience and the rebranding of companies themselves. In the domestic market, engaging designers became a way for existing firms to retain customers, as everyday life habits and consumer taste changed. Increased corporate engagement with design resulted in more opportunities for designers. So did increased public awareness of design as a viable profession and practice. But this primary association with commerce and consumption – an association actively promoted, in different ways, since the Meiji period – also locked design into a form predicated on economic growth. When the market collapsed and growth slowed, designers, like other industries, were left exposed. While individual designers and firms reconfigured their business models to adapt to scaled-down budgets and fewer clients, a broader challenge would be to reinvent design as something whose generosity and tolerance offered advantages to causes beyond economic growth.

Epilogue

This story began with an encounter with a magazine rack in an Osaka bookshop, in the autumn of 1991. It ended a few years later, with designers facing frozen budgets, lost clients, new technologies influencing client expectations and the style of work, and a recession that, once it began, sometimes seemed as if it would never end.

In the three decades since that moment, yet further changes, some of them occurring outside Japan, have further impacted how designers in Japan work, what they make, and with and for whom they make things. Japan's 'lost decade', as the 1990s are popularly known, represented a moment of gradual change as designers, clients and consumers alike adapted to lower economic growth, lower interest rates, the offshoring of manufacturing and a string of disasters, not least the Great Hanshin Earthquake of 1995 and a sarin gas attack on the Tokyo subway in 1996.[1] These events shook national confidence. The earthquake left western Japan's economy fragile. Changes in employment structures removed the certainty of secure work for men and women alike, particularly for younger people, and wages, like prices, stagnated.[2] But people continued to buy things and designers to create them, if not at the rate they had before.[3]

Towards the turn of the millennium, new consumer digital technologies, most prominently mobile phones but also laptops and digital cameras, became the focus of much design activity among product designers and art directors alike.[4] In 2000, Docomo, the mobile phone branch of telecommunications giant NTT, launched a new generation of mobile phones equipped with iMode, an interface for mobile web use. Sales of web-equipped mobile phones and computers supported the expansion of digital design with products ranging from software to animation to interfaces. Character design – the creation of mascots for uses ranging from regional branding to the beloved email software PostPet, created by Hachiya Kazuhiko (b. 1966), in which an energetic pink bear handled incoming and outgoing emails in between baths, sleeping, meals and playtime – became a growth area, with universities establishing specialist courses, as they had for digital and information design.[5]

The digital turn presented opportunities for differentiation through design, continuing the commercial design strategies embraced by manufacturers and retailers in the 1970s and '80s. Sony Network Communications Inc. incorporated the entertaining, appealing Post-Pet interface into its Internet service. Docomo and some competitors invested in upgrading the user interface and capacities for mobile web browsing. Other mobile phone providers, most prominently KDDI, the telecommunications firm behind the Au network and handset brand, contracted prominent product designers like Fukasawa Naoto (b. 1956), a consultant designer who had previously led the Tokyo office of the Californian design firm IDEO, to create handsets whose tactility, feel in the hand and colour scheme – in other words, old-fashioned styling design – provided their appeal. Fukasawa's Infobar, a brightly coloured plastic handset available in a number of colour schemes, won a top prize in the 2003 Good Design Awards. Designs like the Sony VAIO, a light, slender laptop with a distinctive lavender-grey colour and subtly curved corners, and the Canon IXY digital camera, advertised as a necklace by AC Perugia footballer and Japanese national side star Nakata Hidetoshi to emphasize its elegant proportions and features, sold well and continued the new return to product styling. So did Fukasawa's designs for Mujirushi Ryōhin and the work of new creative director Hara Kenya (b. 1958), which overlaid the brand's reputation for simplicity and quality with the concept of 'emptiness': interpretive flexibility allowing consumers to see in MUJI products what they wanted to see.

As the generation of male designers most closely associated with post-war graphics and products reached their seventies and eighties, a younger generation including Fukasawa, graphic designers like Hara, Satō Kashiwa (b. 1965) and Satoh Taku (b. 1955) and the designer Miyake Issey assumed new public roles as design curators and thinkers, publishing popular books on their design philosophies and taking on roles as cultural producers for design. The private design institute

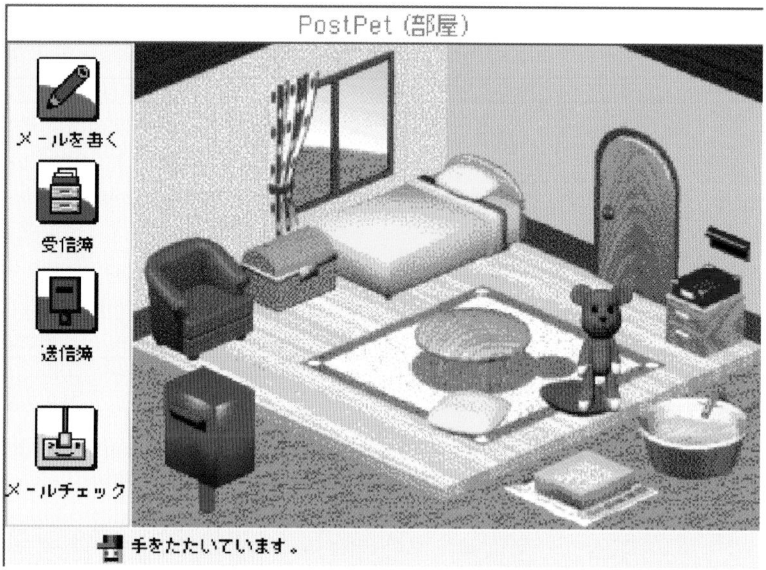

PostPet (部屋)

メールを書く

受信簿

送信簿

メールチェック

手をたたいています。

Hachiya Kazuhiko, PostPet™ © Sony Network Communications Inc., 1997.

21_21 DESIGN SIGHT opened in 2007 on the grounds of Tokyo Midtown, a new real estate development on the site of former Ministry of Defence grounds in central Tokyo. Developer Mitsui Fudōsan incorporated spaces for design organizations and universities as well as shops, creating an accessible but high-end hub for graphic, product, fashion and craft design. Miyake, Fukasawa, Satoh and design journalist and curator Kawakami Noriko wanted to secure a venue for promoting a wide range of design through exhibitions as a form of creative problem-solving and cultural practice. Kawakami and Moriyama Akiko (b. 1953), who like Kawakami edited a design magazine in Tokyo in the 1980s (Kawakami was editor of *AXIS*, and Moriyama of *Nikkei Design*), became prominent design advisers. With the exception of fashion and textiles designers like Kawakubo Rei and Sudo Reiko (b. 1953) of experimental textile studio NUNO, most women active in design retained lower profiles than their male counterparts, working in facilitating and cultural production roles as curators, editors, journalists and business managers, or as members of design teams. Within large manufacturers and advertising agencies, female designers progressed internally to leadership roles, but corporate protocols of crediting the firm rather than the lead designer, among other factors, often kept corporate design leads from gaining the publicity accorded to their consultant counterparts.

Designing Modern Japan

Demographic shifts drove many changes in design practice and the factors shaping it. Increased internationalization through media and study abroad and the presence of foreign designers practising in Japan helped build the momentum for design promotion events like Tokyo Design Week and Tokyo Designers Block, which took events like the Salone del Mobile in Milan as a model for promoting designers and shops to trade and public audiences. While the youth, housewife and corporate markets remained important for manufacturers and retailers, Japan's ageing society created an impetus for designing and providing products and spaces more obviously accessible to older people. Kōdan, the public housing corporation, refurbished post-war public housing units with no-step thresholds to minimize the risk of falls. Matsushita's home appliance design team embraced universal design principles and in 2003, based on consumer research, developed a washing machine with a drum opening placed at an angle on the front facade, the VR2200, for users of different heights and mobilities. Matsushita popularized the new washing machine through advertising that specifically showed its functionality for differently-abled and -shaped people. The VR2200 incorporated a 32 MB processor to automatically calibrate washing functions and water use for laundry weight through 'fuzzy logic'. Its application of user research and IT extended and further developed the research-intensive design practices developed at the IAI and the large manufacturers in the 1960s.

Canon, IXY 310 digital camera, 1997. With their fractional technical advances, emphasis on styling design and extensive advertising image campaigns, digital cameras indicate how the product design strategy of the 1980s continued in some areas.

The ageing population and the continued migration of young people from rural villages to cities accelerated the depopulation of rural areas, creating another new area of practice for designers.[6] Until the mid-1990s, national tax revenue redistribution to towns and regions dependent on slowing primary industries – agriculture, fisheries, forestry and mining – had provided funding for rural areas and regional cities to attract tourism through cultural initiatives. This stopped, and in the early 2000s the national government consolidated many towns and villages into larger political entities.[7] Many local industries, too, were failing en masse. Clothing and household goods manufactured overseas undercut prices of Japanese ones. Many of the remaining workshops were unable to recalibrate their products to reach contemporary tastes at prices competitive with offshore mass-manufactured goods.[8] Faced with falling tax revenues from depopulation and deindustrialization, many rural councils cut services and looked for routes to revitalization.[9] Contemporary art initiatives like Benesse Art Site Naoshima, on a group of islands in the Seto Inland Sea, and the Echigo-Tsumari Art Triennale, in mountainous Niigata Prefecture, provided site-specific events and installations to encourage tourism and investment into areas facing depopulation and a disappearance of economic activity.[10] In the 2000s, Nagaoka Kenmei, a Tokyo-based designer, began championing 'long lasting design'. Projects in D&DEPARTMENT, Nagaoka's umbrella initiative and lifestyle brand, have included the 60VISION and NIPPON VISION schemes, which reframed post-war Japanese home furnishings and industrial craft as Japan's own modern design heritage. The d47 project, launched in 2009, produces design-led tourist guidebooks, exhibitions and shops, designed to entice urban residents to travel regionally in Japan for design-led experiences.[11]

For their part, some locally based designers across Japan and some art and design universities responded to decreased services and funding in regional cities and rural communities with design consulting schemes. Some of these supported remaining local industries by offering product development for urban Japanese markets. In other schemes, designers applied their skills in brand and corporate identity to rebrand villages, cities and regions to attract tourism and investment.[12] Other design-led revitalization projects sought to connect young designers with older manufacturing communities.[13] From the late 2000s, *komyuniti dezain* (community design), popularized by the Osaka designer Yamaguchi Ryō, emerged as another design strategy for empowering local communities.[14] Yamaguchi's approach uses design ideation, communication and prototyping methods to encourage and support communities to rethink local services and to engage with local and prefectural government to determine their delivery. *Komyuniti dezain* would become particularly relevant after the nuclear power plant failure and tsunami of March 2011, known in Japan as '3.11' or the Great Tōhoku Disaster, devastated hundreds of towns and villages across northeastern Japan.[15] Many designers responded to 3.11 with pro bono initiatives, from working with local community members to design products for urban consumers and producing exhibitions showcasing Tohoku products to volunteering in disaster shelters and clearing rubble.[16]

Design promotion for economic revitalization at the national level re-emerged. The Good Design Award system, now operated by the Japan Institute of Design Promotion, continued as an important recognition and publicity system for manufacturers.[17] Its organizers expanded the submission categories to include environmental and systems design. The Cool Japan initiative, adopted by the Ministry of Economy, Trade and Industry in 2012 to promote exports from small and medium-sized firms in Japan's creative industries, was most closely linked with support for the global popularization of Japanese pop culture forms such as anime, manga and J-pop music, but also supported small-scale industrial and crafts manufacturing.[18] Local authorities, industry associations and firms could apply for Cool Japan funding for overseas trade fair participation, for example at the annual Salone del Mobile or London Design Week, or for a new round of regional product branding initiatives.

Design associations became involved as well, concerned to retain the contemporary saliency of their activities and to contribute designers' particular skills to help resolve national challenges, as well as to advocate for members' working conditions. Together, the Japan Industrial Design Association and the Tsubamesanjō Regional Industries Promotion Center (Tsubame Sanjō Jiba Sangyō Fukkō Sentā), a metal tableware manufacturing community in Niigata, in northern Japan, launched an initiative to pair industrial designers with Tsubame firms. Collaborations between districts and individual firms producing eyewear, ceramics, lighting and other historical industrial products and designers – sometimes prominent overseas figures or Japanese celebrities – followed. These ranged from ongoing design work by Fukasawa

Naoto and the prominent UK designer Jasper Morrison for Hiroshima-based furniture manufacturer Maruni from 2008 onwards, to a collaboration in 2013 between football star Nakata Hidetoshi, designer Sato Oki (b. 1977) of design firm nendo, and sake brewery Takagi Shuzō. Industry and academic design associations also began to collaborate more closely on conferences and information-sharing with East Asian counterparts, most prominently in South Korea and Taiwan. Consultant designers expanded their practice to China, as China entered a new stage in its own period of rapid economic growth, shifting from heavy industry to a focus on domestic consumption, and fuelling demand for luxury interiors and high-end Japanese industrial crafts.

Within this activity, some members of the design community felt it was time to archive the rich history of design practice and culture in modern Japan. Curators and academics at university and public museums like the Musashino Art University Museum and Library and the Utsunomiya Museum of Art, already owners of significant design collections, further expanded both their collections and their research, exhibitions and publishing activities.[19] Concerned that many design firms and manufacturers, particularly smaller ones, did not have the means to preserve their archives, and that Japan was in danger of losing the material evidence of its modern design heritage, both curators and the professional design associations began promotional work to build public momentum and lobbying power to establish a national design museum.[20] A fundamental aim of this book is to contribute to that momentum, towards the long-term support needed to collect, preserve and share the objects – but also the experiences – of design in modern Japan.

Hara Kenya (art direction) and Fujii Tamotsu (photography), poster for the Mujirushi (MUJI) Ryōhin 'Horizon' campaign, Uyuni Salt Flats, Bolivia, 2003.

Poster for 'TEMA HIMA The Art of Living in Tohoku', 21_21 DESIGN SIGHT, Tokyo, 2012. The TEMA HIMA exhibition, oneof many design communityinitiatives in response to the 3.11 disaster, aimed to raisevisitor awareness of thecraft expertise and artistry of manufacturers in the Tohoku region.

Designing Modern Japan

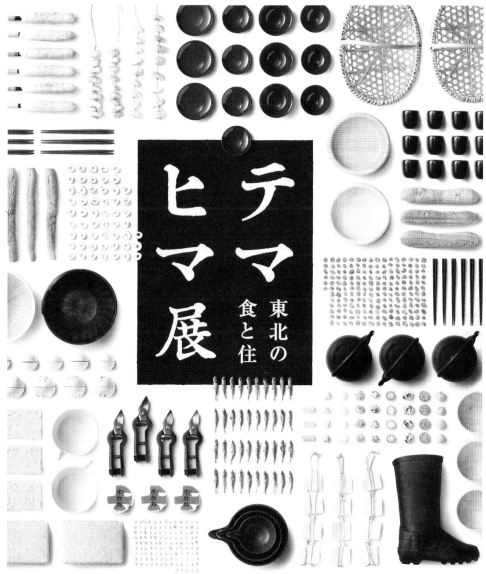

テマ
ヒマ展
東北の
食と住

21_21 DESIGN SIGHT 企画展
テマヒマ展〈東北の食と住〉
会場：21_21 DESIGN SIGHT（東京ミッドタウン・ガーデン内）

2012年4月27日（金）−8月26日（日）

休館日：火曜日（但し5月1日は開館）　開館時間：11:00-20:00（入場は19:30まで）／主催：21_21 DESIGN SIGHT、公益財団法人 三宅一生デザイン文化財団　後援：文化庁、経済産業省、青森県、秋田県、岩手県、山形県、宮城県、福島県、東京都、港区　特別協賛：三井不動産株式会社　特別協力：株式会社 虎屋　協力：キヤノンマーケティングジャパン株式会社、マックスレイ株式会社／展覧会ディレクター：佐藤 卓、深澤直人　企画協力：奥村文絵、川上典李子　映像制作：トム・ヴィンセント、山中 有　写真：西部裕介　学術協力：東北芸術工科大学　東北文化研究センター／21_21 DESIGN SIGHTディレクター：三宅一生、佐藤 卓、深澤直人　アソシエイトディレクター：川上典李子

Exhibition "TEMA HIMA : the Art of Living in Tohoku"　Date：Fri Apr 27 - Sun Aug 26, 2012
Closed on Tuesdays（Except May 1）Time：11:00-20:00（Entrance until 19:30）　www.2121designsight.jp

21_21

THERE ARE MANY OTHER stories to tell. Perhaps more than most, for this book. *Designing Modern Japan* has tried to show how the concepts of design, the social structures within its industries and the external factors shaping them all have much longer histories than that of the word 'dezain' in Japan. More than anything, the book is an attempt to recount the historical conditions and events, particularly those within Japanese economy and society, that shaped both the practices of designing and the results of those practices. It also seeks to anchor the discussion of these within the way in which they were motivated and understood within Japan, rather than in perspectives on Japanese design from overseas. While the book incorporates overseas events and attitudes towards Japanese design as relevant for the domestic story, the narrative focuses on design as practised, experienced and perceived by people working and living in Japan. People overseas admired, disparaged, collected and competed with products designed in Japan throughout the time span discussed in this book. What has been less evident, at least in the English-language record, is how designers worked, whom they worked with and for, and how they fit into Japan's industrial, social and economic systems. By providing this narrative, the book aims to add new depth to existing awareness of designs from Japan, and to identify design's role within the larger social and economic history of modern Japan.

Key changes with design practice and its industries over the period described here include, of course, the categories of products that were included in design and the scope and remit of designers within their production process. Design expanded its remit from surface and formal design for the products of local industries and their advertising to include corporate identity campaigns and, by the 2000s, ways of empowering members of local communities to have a say in immediate decisions affecting their daily life. Despite this, the products designed throughout the book were largely physical, tangible items. It was not until 2020 that Japan's Patent Office revised its definition of design (*ishō*) to include intangible work like a user interface. Even so, to be registered as a design, work such as this must be obviously connected with a tangible artefact such as a mobile phone or screen.[21]

The people associated with design also changed. From design as an activity conducted predominantly by the people making things, sometimes following directions from commissioning agents or pattern books, design became one conducted by people whose job title

A sample of D&DEPARTMENT activities, promoting engagement with recycling, reuse and regional craft communities.

'365 Charming Everyday Things', a project led by itochu fashion system co., Ltd., launched during Maison et Objet, Paris, 2012, selling local products as part of the Cool Japan initiative.

Designing Modern Japan

includes 'designer', if not 'art director', 'creative director' or simply 'creator'. The loci of design promotion shifted as well, from domain officials responsible for *shokusan kōgyō* policies in the Tokugawa period to former domain officials working in the Meiji bureaucracy and their spiritual descendants in the IARI, who used design techniques from Europe, Japan and eventually the United States to promote foreign currency revenue through sales of export products. In the late 1960s, however, the growth of the domestic market and change in industrial policy direction agreed between MITI and large manufacturers shifted the locus of design promotion to manufacturing and retail conglomerates, advertising agencies and design consultancies. This swung back again, in the 1990s, to encompass design as a tool or mechanism for economic and social sustainability as Japan faced demographic and other challenges. Looking at the social compositions of designers, family backgrounds for designers are now more diverse, generations away from the status system of the Tokugawa period. In contrast to these changes, gender bias and related expectations for men's and women's behaviour and life courses mean that while many women study and then work in design, prominent designers – particularly outside fashion, textiles and areas of craft design like accessory design associated with female consumers – remain predominantly male.

The focus on product, industrial, graphic and to a lesser extent furniture and interior design in the book, and the relatively light treatment of fashion and textile design, means that women's practice is overshadowed, given the predominantly male composition and leadership of the fields explored during the period covered in the book. What the book has tried to do is to indicate some of the intersections between domestic economy, social reform and fashion design (as an area gendered more female) and product, graphic and interior design – all areas in which business, discourse and histories alike are dominated by men. There are excellent histories of women's unpaid design and making labour, of fashion, and of the kimono and Western apparel industries, cited throughout the text. But there is more to be done to connect those communities and industries to the industries and communities written about here.

This book has been shaped to a great extent by the stories commonly told about design in Japan and the materials preserved in archives. This means that it leaves substantial room for further scholarship. The overemphasis on Tokyo, and to a lesser extent Osaka, in

Designing Modern Japan

the national design media means that the stories of designers in other regions are greatly underrepresented, despite the fact that design for industry, like design promotion, design education and indeed design critique, occurred across Japan. Also overrepresented are the voices and stories of people working specifically as designers, rather than people who designed as part of their work. In the first half of this book, particularly, there are very few voices of makers, due partly to persistence of the Tokugawa social hierarchy, with makers – artisans and rural households engaging in cottage industries – low in the hierarchy and often poor. As a result, while they may have made the objects discussed in the book, they were not the ones compiling or archiving the records on which the book also relies. After the Second World War, factors including the expansion of design education and recognition of design as a specialist practice by managers in influential large industries created a context in which designers could record their own voices. It would be another project to amplify the voices of the many creative practitioners in post-war Japan who undertook design regularly as part of their work making iron kettles, kimono chests or indeed kimono themselves.

Were the people discussed in this book 'designers'? Would they have called themselves 'designers'? Arguably, what they did is more important. Whether the bureaucrats in the Product Design Department in the 1880s or the painters contributing advertisements, book covers and textile patterns at the turn of the last century saw themselves as designers or not, their work sat firmly within parameters of design as an activity at the time, and certainly within how design has been understood subsequently. By the 1920s, for some people in Japan it mattered very much whether one was a designer – or a commercial artist – or not. Professional organizations' work contributed greatly to regularizing the idea of design as specialist practice in the post-war years. But again, recognizing work as 'design' based on whether someone was categorized as a 'designer' at the time or not shapes both in-time interactions and the historical record, leading to very different accounts.

In most histories, including this one, a woman drawing on her specialist education and working from published principles in order to reorganize her living room or to create a lunchbox for her child has a very different status to a man with 'designer' in his job title. Historians have documented some women's participation in the spheres of practice understood in the design history world as 'design'.[22] Other feminist historians across architecture, craft and design have written both empirical and theoretical histories of women's making and their design agency within it.[23] This book has tried to do some of this work, for example by discussing design education for women in the 1920s and '30s. But there is much more to say about the creative practice of women, both those whose work was understood at the time as falling within the remit of design but was not recorded as significant, and those who designed things, spaces and experiences but whose efforts occurred in feminized spheres such as domestic economy and so were not classified as 'design' at the time (because 'design' was a masculine space). The later chapters, especially, point to the impact of social attitudes around class and gender on participation in design. That this occurs increasingly in the later chapters indicates the increased documentation both of women's design practice and of their comfort with – or tacit activism in – publicizing their frustrations with gender bias within the industry.

A further reason for women's lack of recognition within this story is that both the recognized story of design in Japan and the one this book has told focus on economic activity: activity by people who were paid for their work, outside the home.[24] While it necessarily muffles the work of people, especially women, whose design work occurred outside the waged economy, following the red thread of economics does something particular and important for design history. Historians often discuss design activities, political motivations and implications and economic policy and activities, but largely without connecting design activity to economics. In contrast, this book has argued that design's history is predicated on political economy – on policy and on markets. In the 1870s and '80s, and again in the 1970s and '80s, designers helped makers adjust to changing markets by suggesting new products and by influencing policies favourable to domestic light manufacturing and craft industries. For much of the twentieth century, designers hung their hats on state policies, attempting to shape them to support their vision of local or national systems made better through design, and to secure a stable economic role and income for people talented at design. At the same time, designers aligned with leftist causes and other positions critical of the state used their expressive powers to critique, counteract and provoke dissent with the state vision of a people aligned behind national development. In the 1960s

Designing Modern Japan

particularly, designers began expressing their discomfort with the state project and shifted to countercultural and commercial work. Critique of this work continued, too, often subsumed into the system it critiqued by the status of design, by the 1980s, as a desirable cultural commodity in its own right.

The book has focused on what designers wanted and how they presented themselves, within a larger social history of design practice. As a result, there is more to say about how consumers and users experienced designed products, to connect consumption history perspectives with those from the social history of design. This book should be read alongside those that explore everyday life in modern Japan, in rural areas as in cities, and that present, through those narratives of lived experience, how social structures shaped experiences in modern Japan and how these structures changed over time. For example, in her history of consumption in modern Japan, the economic historian Penelope Francks points out that much of the material culture of the 1970s – ready-to-wear clothing, for example – cut bonds between family members by not requiring women to defer to mothers and mothers-in-law to learn how to do these things, an instance in which behaviours afforded by new material goods had an impact on social relations.[25]

Sputniko!, *Tranceflora*, 2015. For this project, commissioned by Gucci and exhibited in their Tokyo flagship store, artist Sputniko! worked with partners including the National Institute of Agribiological Sciences and Hosoo Textiles, a silk-weaving firm in Kyoto's Nishijin district founded in 1688, to create and display an outfit from transgenic glowing silk.

This book was unable to foreground how people reacted to or used designs, what they thought of designs and designers, or whether they thought of them at all. It was also unable to represent fully the contingent and collaborative nature of design production. From technicians, manufacturers and clients to retailers, there is further research to be done to document the interactions and contributions of the diverse networks of practitioners who actually made designs.

There is also more to be said about the interplay between images of 'Japanese design' outside Japan and design practices within Japan.[26] In many countries, 'Japanese design' could mean MUJI's brand vision of simplicity and practicality, delivered through a carefully neutral aesthetic of emptiness. It could mean Uniqlo's ubiquitous low-cost, high-quality puffer jackets and cashmere jumpers, available in a rainbow of colours and made possible through standardization, high-volume sales, IT-managed supply chains and offshore manufacturing.[27] It could mean a particular kind of creative, experimental high fashion, or minimalist interiors constructed of concrete or wood and glass which bring the outside in and prioritize visual pleasure over furnishings.[28] Beyond the high end, it could mean video games, animation and pop music: the plethora of arts, industries and hobbies categorized as 'Japanese popular culture', which are enjoyed by millions overseas as in Japan and promoted by the Japanese government as cultural soft power.[29] In professional design circles, it could also mean the kind of technologically informed, carefully considered design engineering of groups like Takram (Tagawa Kinya, b. 1976), or work by designer-artists like Sputniko! (Hiromi Ozaki, b. 1985), whose video, photography and installation work combines pop culture and technological innovation into critical, speculative practice designed to entertain, engage and trouble audiences at the same time. In some cities in East Asia, Japanese design means these things, but it can also mean a particular kind of lifestyle goods and aesthetic: workshop craft items that are well-made, true to their materials and imply social, cultural and economic capital through connoisseurship, not bling.[30] These experiential understandings of design from Japan impact design production in Japan not only through market demand and the image they perpetuate but through the personal interactions of designers, colleagues and fans.

There are still yet other stories to be told, and many aspects of design in modern and contemporary Japan left untouched or underdeveloped. Histories that incorporate environmental factors and impact, for

Designing Modern Japan

example calculating the energy impact of design's activities and relating this to national energy policies and resources, would be valuable, as would work that connects the strong scholarship on labour history in modern Japan to design's role in manufacturing and society. There is more research to be done on design in Japan within the larger regional context of northeast and, more widely, east Asia, on the relationship of local design practices and values to colonial ones in Japanese-occupied East Asia, and of design among the Japanese diaspora worldwide. As much as anything else, *Designing Modern Japan* is intended to serve as a prompt for further explorations.

As for design in Japan, the story continues. Young people continue to study design, then to find work in graphic design, product design, interiors, fashion and particularly digital and user experience design, creating immersive environments that blend physical and digital sensations, place-making and pleasure. Practices like community design, when taken seriously, allow designers to use their skill and experience to democratize planning: helping people to make decisions about their future and to have a say in how resources are allocated to achieve those futures. Here design blurs into community activism, local politics and participatory place-making (*machi-zukuri*), all lively areas in post-1990s Japan.[31] Sharing design's capacities within communities challenges the professional roles designers worked hard to create, but also continues the alignment of design practice with government policy: design taking different forms but continuing to promote reform and transformation. Policymakers and business groups continue to set policies to steer the nation and its regions, seeing economic sustainability if not development as the key to national well-being. Entrepreneurs and corporate managers continue to view design as providing differential advantage. Between these two poles and emergent areas such as social and community design, designers continue to find ways to have their work supported and to make their practice meaningful and viable. This includes travelling across borders: when we speak of design in Japan, now, this includes the thousands of students and practitioners from Korea, China and further afield in Asia and the world who study and work in Japan. Across these examples lies a commitment to design as both a personal professional identity and practice, and a practice that can contribute something to one's community as the surrounding society and resources change. That commitment lies at the heart of design – in modern Japan and beyond.

References

Introduction

1 A study of design, consumerism and everyday life in 1980s Japan through magazines is Hui-Ying Kerr, 'Envisioning the Bubble: Creating and Consuming Lifestyles through Magazines in the Culture of the Japanese Bubble Economy (1986–1991)', unpublished PhD dissertation, Victoria and Albert Museum and Royal College of Art, London, 2017. On women's economic and social agency in accessing design through lifestyle magazines in 1980s and early 1990s Japan see Lise Skov and Brian Moeran, eds, *Women, Media and Consumption in Japan* (Richmond, Surrey, 1995). My own encounter with magazines resulted in Sarah Teasley, '(Anti-)Hysteric Glamour: Masquerade, Cross-Dressing and the Construction of Identity in Japanese Fashion Magazines', *Critical Matrix*, IX/1 (1995), pp. 45–66.

2 The *bakumatsu* period refers to the final years of the Tokugawa regime, roughly between 1853, when the American Commodore Perry visited Japan, and the Meiji Restoration in 1868. The Heisei period began in 1989. In its periodization this book follows the conventions agreed by an international group of scholars for the forthcoming *Cambridge History of Japan*, vol. III: *Modern Japan*.

3 On the historical impact of consumption in modern East Asia, see Sheldon Garon and Patricia Maclachlan, eds, *The Ambivalent Consumer* (Ithaca, NY, 2006).

4 There is extensive literature on user agency in the history of technology, science and technology studies (STS) and design history. See for example Nelly Oudshoorn and Trevor Pinch, eds, *How Users Matter: The Co-Construction of Users and Technologies* (Cambridge, MA, 2003). The journal *CoDesign* provides rich information on co-design as a practice, process and stance.

5 There is a rich discourse on designing in Japan among professional designers, within the research community and in media aimed at wider audiences. *Dezaingaku kenkyū* (Journal of the Science of Design), the journal of the Japanese Society for the Science of Design, provides a rich introduction to current debates and theories around design in Japan.

6 Here, the book aligns with work like Penelope Francks and Janet Hunter's excellent *The Historical Consumer: Consumption and Everyday Life in Japan,*

344

1850–2000 (Oxford, 2012), which has similar interdisciplinary aims to broaden economic history's scope and readership.

7 For an overview of the history of modern and contemporary Japan, see Andrew Gordon, *A Modern History of Japan*, 4th edn (Oxford, 2020).

8 On seeing comparisons, similarities and connections as a method, see Glenn Adamson, Giorgio Riello and Sarah Teasley, 'Introduction', in *Global Design History*, ed. Adamson, Riello and Teasley (London, 2011), pp. 1–30.

9 Similar national design histories that focus on local and national stories within an acknowledged global context in the modern period include Jeremy Aynsley, *Designing Modern Germany* (London, 2009); Paul Betts, *The Authority of Everyday Objects: A Cultural History of West German Industrial Design* (Berkeley, CA, and London, 2007); Cheryl Buckley, *Designing Modern Britain* (London, 2007); Kjetil Fallan, *Designing Modern Norway: A History of Design Discourse* (London, 2018); and Grace Lees-Maffei and Kjetil Fallan, eds, *Made in Italy* (London, 2013). Pat Kirkham and Susan Weber, eds, *History of Design: Decorative Arts and Material Culture, 1400–2000* (New Haven, CT, and London, 2013) and Haruhiko Fujita and Christine Guth, eds, *Encyclopedia of Asian Design* (London, 2020) present multiple national design histories side by side. On the significance of national design history as a mode of history-writing see Javier Gimeno Martínez, *Design and National Identity* (London, 2016) and Kjetil Fallan and Grace Lees-Maffei, 'Introduction: National Design Histories in an Age of Globalization', in *Designing Worlds: National Design Histories in an Age of Globalization*, ed. Fallan and Lees-Maffei (New York and Oxford, 2016), pp. 1–21.

10 On this argument see also Ignacio Adriasola, Sarah Teasley and Jilly Traganou, 'Design and Society in Modern Japan: An Introduction', in *Review of Japanese Culture and Society*, 28 (2016), pp. 1–3.

11 See Morgan Pitelka, ed., *Japanese Tea Culture: Art, History and Practice* (London, 2003) and Kristin Surak, *Making Tea, Making Japan: Cultural Nationalism in Practice* (Stanford, CA, 2012).

12 An exception to this rule is Patricia Jane Graham, *Japanese Design: Art, Aesthetics and Culture* (Tokyo, 2014), which offers historical context for aesthetic qualities often associated with things designed in Japan from the premodern period to today.

13 Comparable discussions of globally networked professional and creative communities in modern Japan include Jordan Sand, *House and Home in Modern Japan: Architecture, Domestic Space and Bourgeois Culture 1880–1930* (Cambridge, MA, 2003); Laura Elizabeth Hein, *Reasonable Men, Powerful Words: Political Culture and Expertise in Twentieth-Century Japan* (Washington, DC, and Berkeley, CA, 2004); Lisbeth Kim Brandt, *Kingdom of Beauty Mingei and the Politics of Folk Art in Imperial Japan* (Durham, NC, 2007); Ken Tadashi Ōshima, *International Architecture in Interwar Japan: Constructing 'Kokusai Kenchiku'* (Seattle, WA, 2010); and Alicia Volk, *In Pursuit of Universalism: Yorozu Tetsugorô and Japanese Modern Art* (Berkeley, CA, 2010).

14 Key English-language accounts of modern Japanese industrial policy are Chalmers A. Johnson, *MITI and the Japanese Miracle: The Growth of Industrial Policy, 1925–1975* (Stanford, CA, 1982) and Mikio Sumiya, *History of Japanese Trade and Industrial Policy* (Oxford, 2000).

15 On material history methods and Japanese history, see Christine Guth, *Craft Culture in Early Modern Japan: Materials, Makers, and Mastery* (Berkeley, CA, and London, 2021) and Carolina Hirasawa and Benedetta Lomi, eds, *Japanese Journal of Religious Studies*, XLV/2 (2018): *Modest Materialities: The Social Lives and Afterlives of Sacred Things in Japan*. More widely, see Karen Harvey, ed., *History and Material Culture: A Student's Guide to Approaching Alternative Sources*, 2nd edn (Abingdon, 2018); Giorgio Riello, 'Things that Shape History: Material Culture and Historical Narratives', in *History and Material Culture*, ed. Harvey, pp. 24–47; and Anne Gerritsen and Giorgio Riello, eds, *Writing Material Culture History*, 2nd edn (London, 2021).

16 I have argued for this elsewhere. See Sarah Teasley, 'Contemporary Design History', in *The Blackwell Companion to Contemporary Design since 1945*, ed. Anne Massey (London, 2019), pp. 9–31 and Sarah Teasley, '"Methods of Reasoning and Imagination": History's Failures and Capacities in Anglophone Design Research', in *Theories of History: History Read Across the Humanities*, ed. Michael Kelly and Arthur Rose (London, 2018), pp. 183–206. On environmental history and design history see Kjetil Fallan and Finn Arne Jørgensen, 'Environmental Histories of Design: Towards a New Research Agenda', *Journal of Design History*, XXX/2 (2017), pp. 103–21.

17 Felice Fischer and Katherine B. Hiesinger, *Japanese Design: A Survey since 1950* (New York, 1995). See also Penny Sparke, *Japanese Design* (London, 1988).

18 See Fujita and Guth, eds, *Encyclopedia of Asian Design*, and the work of Yuko Kikuchi, Yunah Lee and Wendy Siuyi Wong to translate and publish East Asia-based researchers' work in English, as described in Yuko Kikuchi and Yunah Lee, 'Transnational Modern Design Histories in East Asia: An Introduction', *Journal of Design History*, XXVII/4 (2014), pp. 323–34.

19 For such an approach see also Daniel Huppatz, *Modern Asian Design* (London, 2018).

20 See Sand, *House and Home in Modern Japan*; Brandt, *Kingdom of Beauty*; and Penelope Francks, *The Japanese Consumer: An Alternative Economic History of Modern Japan* (Cambridge, 2009).

1 'As a practical object it will be profitable': Design, Industry and Internationalization from the Tokugawa to the Meiji Periods

1 On the history of Arita, see Oliver Impey, *The Early Porcelain Kilns of Japan: Arita in the First Half of the Seventeenth Century* (Oxford, 1996); Tai Wei Lim, *Japanese Trade Ceramics in the Premodern Global Trading Space* (Lanham, MD, 2014); and Nicole Coolidge Rousmaniere, *Vessels of Influence: China and the Birth of Porcelain in Medieval and Early Modern Japan* (London, 2013).

2 On Japan's display in Philadelphia, see Sakamoto Hisako, Kawakami Hideto and Matsuoka Takahiro, 'Firaderufia bankoku hakurankai ni okeru Nihon no shuppinbutsu no kaijō kōsei', *Kenkyū kiyō*, 27 (1997), pp. 89–116. On Japanese exhibition practices in international expositions in this period, see Tōkyō Kokuritsu Hakubutsukan, *Seiki no saiten bankoku hakurankai no bijutsu: Pari Uīn Shikago banpaku ni miru tōzai no meihin* (Tokyo, 2004).

3 To understand Japan's visual impact and strategy in context, see Paul Greenhalgh, *Ephemeral Vistas: The Expositions Universelles, Great Exhibitions and World's Fairs, 1851–1939* (Manchester, 1990), and David Raizman and Ethan Robey, eds, *Expanding Nationalisms at World's Fairs: Identity, Diversity, and Exchange, 1851–1915* (London and New York, 2017).

4 On Tokugawa period history see John Whitney Hall, ed., *The Cambridge History of Japan*, vol. IV: *Early Modern Japan* (Cambridge, 1991). Andrew Gordon, *A Modern History of Japan: From Tokugawa Times to the Present*, 4th edn (Oxford, 2020), provides a succinct and useful history of the period.

5 Tessa Morris-Suzuki, *The Technological Transformation of Japan: From the Seventeenth to the Twenty-First Century* (Cambridge, 1994), pp. 27–32.

6 On the culture engendered by this system, known as *sankin kōtai*, see Constantine Vaporis, *Tour of Duty: Samurai, Military Service in Edo, and the Culture of Early Modern Japan* (Honolulu, HI, 2016).

7 Eiko Ikegami, *Bonds of Civility: Aesthetic Networks and the Political Origins of Japanese Culture* (Cambridge, 2005), p. 259.

8 Donald H. Shively, 'Sumptuary Regulation and Status in Early Tokugawa Japan', *Harvard Journal of Asiatic Studies*, XXV (1964), p. 126.

9 Ibid., p. 127. Key arguments that market economics challenged the political status system include David L. Howell, *Capitalism from Within: Economy, Society, and the State from a Japanese Fishery* (Berkeley, CA, 1995), and Kären Wigen, *The Making of a Japanese Periphery, 1750–1920* (Berkeley, CA, 1995).

10 On lived experience in early modern Japan, including ways in which people negotiated social status, see Takeshi Moriyama, *Crossing Boundaries in Tokugawa Society: Suzuki Bokushi, a Rural Elite Commoner* (Leiden, 2013); Amy Stanley, *Selling Women: Prostitution, Markets, and the Household in Early Modern Japan* (Berkeley, CA, 2012); Amy Stanley, *Stranger in the Shogun's City: A Japanese Woman and Her World* (New York, 2020); and Anne Walthall, *The Weak Body of a Useless Woman: Matsuo Taseko and the Meiji Restoration* (Chicago, IL, 1998).

11 On proto-industry within village social organization, see Edward E. Pratt, *Japan's Protoindustrial Elite: The Economic Foundations of the Gōnō* (Cambridge, MA, 1999).

12 On the putting-out system, see Masayuki Tanimoto, ed., *The Role of Tradition in Japan's Industrialization* (Oxford, 2006).

13 See Thomas C. Smith, 'Farm Family By-Employments in Preindustrial Japan', *Journal of Economic History*, XXIX/4 (December 1969), pp. 687–715. Accounts of farm women's lives are helpful for understanding this shift. See Kathleen S. Uno, 'Women and Changes in the Household Division of Labor', in *Recreating Japanese Women, 1600–1945*, ed. Gail Bernstein (Berkeley, CA, 1991), pp. 17–41, and Anne Walthall, 'Life Cycle of Farm Women in Tokugawa Japan', in *Recreating Japanese Women*, pp. 42–70.

14 On the history of Kiryū weaving, see Kiryū Orimono Hensankai, *Kiryū Orimono-shi* (Kiryū, 1935). On the diffusion of urban production technology to rural regions, see Pratt, *Japan's Protoindustrial Elite*, pp. 53–61.

15 Christopher Dresser, *Japan: Its Architecture, Art, and Art Manufactures* [1882] (Cambridge, 2015), pp. 159–62.

16 On consumption in Tokugawa-period Japan, see Penelope Francks, *The Japanese Consumer: An Alternative Economic History of Modern Japan*

(Cambridge, 2009), pp. 11–73, and E. Taylor Atkins, *A History of Popular Culture in Japan: From the Seventeenth Century to the Present* (London, 2017), pp. 33–78.

17 On Edo, see James L McClain, John M. Merriman and Kaoru Ugawa, eds, *Edo and Paris: Urban Life and the State in the Early Modern Era* (Ithaca, NY, 1994).

18 A thorough social history of premodern textile production is Nagahara Keiji, *Choma, kinu, momen no shakaishi* (Tokyo, 2004).

19 On tea ceramics production and culture in early modern Kyoto, see Morgan Pitelka, *Handmade Culture: Raku Potters, Patrons, and Tea Practitioners in Japan* (Honolulu, HI, 2014), and Richard L. Wilson, *The Art of Ogata Kenzan: Persona and Production in Japanese Ceramics* (New York, 1991).

20 On shopping for luxury ceramics in Kyoto, albeit in an earlier period, see Louise Cort, 'Shopping for Pots in Momoyama Japan', in *Japanese Tea Culture: Art, History and Practice,* ed. Morgan Pitelka (London, 2003), pp. 61–85.

21 On the history of Nishijin, see Sasaki Shinzaburō, *Nishijin-shi* (Kyoto, 1932). On Nishijin in English, see Tamara Hareven, *The Silk Weavers of Kyoto: Family and Work in a Changing Traditional Industry* (Berkeley, CA, 2003).

22 On learning in painting workshops, another major Kyoto industry, see Brenda G. Jordan and Victoria Weston, eds, *Copying the Master and Stealing His Secrets: Talent and Training in Japanese Painting* (Honolulu, HI, 2003).

23 On Nabeshima porcelain, see Nabeshima Hōkōkai, ed., *Nabeshima denrai tōjiki meihinten*, exh. cat., Chōkokan, Saga (Saga, 2013).

24 On fashionability and prints, see Julie N. Davis, *Partners in Print: Artistic Collaboration and the Ukiyo-e Market* (Honolulu, HI, 2015), pp. 61–107, and Ikegami, *Bonds of Civility*, pp. 245–60 and 271–85.

25 There is a large literature on Rinpa. In English, see Tomoko Emura, 'Rinpa Artists and the Samurai Class', *Bulletin of the Detroit Institute of Arts*, LXXXVIII/1 (2014), pp. 70–85. See also Yūzō Yamane, Masato Naitō and Timothy Clark, *Rimpa Art from the Idemitsu Collection, Tokyo*, exh. cat., Idemitsu Bijutsukan, Tokyo, and British Museum, London (London, 1998).

26 On *hinagata-bon* and kimono fashion, see Iwao Nagasaki, 'Designs for a Thousand Ages: Printed Pattern Books and Kosode', in *When Art Became Fashion: Kosode in Edo-Period Japan*, ed. Carolyn Gluckman and Sharon Sadako Takeda, exh. cat., Los Angeles County Museum of Art, Los Angeles (Los Angeles, CA, 1992), pp. 95–113, and Terry Satsuki Milhaupt, *Kimono: A Modern History* (London, 2014), pp. 46–52.

27 On the circulation of print materials, see Mary Elizabeth Berry, *Japan in Print: Information and Nation in the Early Modern Period* (Berkeley, CA, 2007), and Ikegami, *Bonds of Civility*, pp. 286–323.

28 On kimono retail and shopping, see Anna Jackson and Iwao Nagasaki, 'Creation and Commerce', in *Kimono to Catwalk*, ed. Anna Jackson, exh. cat., Victoria and Albert Museum, London (London, 2020), pp. 81–90.

29 On *kosode* see *Edo Mōdo zukan: Kosode moyō ni miru bi no keitō*, exh. cat., Japanese National Museum of History, Sakura (Sakura, 1999); Gluckman and Takeda, eds, *When Art Became Fashion*; Amanda Mayer Stinchecum,

Kosode, 16th–19th Century Textiles from the Nomura Collection, exh. cat., Japan House Gallery, New York, and Japanese National Museum of History, Sakura (New York, 1984); and *Miyako no yūga: Kosode to byōbu*, exh. cat., Museum of Kyoto (Kyoto, 2005).

30 On commoners' clothing see Amy Stanley, 'Fashioning the Family: A Temple, a Daughter, and a Wardrobe', in *What Is a Family? Answers from Early Modern Japan*, ed. Mary Elizabeth Berry and Marcia Yonemoto (Berkeley, CA, 2019), pp. 174–94. On samurai clothing see Vaporis, *Tour of Duty*, pp. 28–37.

31 Jackson, ed., *Kimono: Kyoto to Catwalk*, provides an excellent overview of changing fashion in early modern Japan, as does Milhaupt, *Kimono*, pp. 31–55.

32 Stanley, *Stranger in the Shogun's City*, describes the difficulties that poor households faced acquiring and maintaining clothes.

33 On stencils in Japanese textiles, see Susanna Campbell Kuo, *Carved Paper: The Art of the Japanese Stencil*, exh. cat., Santa Barbara Museum of Art (New York and Tokyo, 1998).

34 On *sarasa* see Kayoko Fujita, 'Japan Indianized: The Material Culture of Imported Textiles in Japan, 1550–1850', in *The Spinning World: A Global History of Cotton Textiles, 1200–1850*, ed. Giorgio Riello and Prasannan Parthasarathi (Oxford, 2011), pp. 181–204. On stripes, see Hoshimi Uchida, 'Narrow Cotton Stripes and their Substitutes: Fashion, Technical Progress and Manufacturing Organisation in Japanese Popular Clothing', *Textile History*, XIX/2 (1988), pp. 159–70.

35 Ibid., p. 186.

36 On this transition, see Louis Cullen, 'The Nagasaki Trade of the Tokugawa Era: Archives, Statistics, and Management', *Japan Review*, 31 (2017), pp. 69–104, and Robert I. Hellyer, *Defining Engagement: Japan and Global Contexts, 1640–1868* (Cambridge, MA, 2010), pp. 73–115.

37 On learning from European objects see Martha Chaiklin, *Cultural Commerce and Dutch Commercial Culture: The Influence of European Material Culture on Japan, 1700–1850* (Leiden, 2003). On *rangaku* see Terrence Jackson, *Network of Knowledge: Western Science and the Tokugawa Information Revolution* (Honolulu, HI, 2016). An excellent case study of the translation of European science and technology is Yulia Frumer, 'Translating Time: Habits of Western-Style Timekeeping in Late Edo Japan', *Technology and Culture*, LV/4 (2014), pp. 785–820.

38 On lacquerware in the Tokugawa period see Arawaka Hirokazu, ed., *Nihon no shitsugei* (Tokyo, 2003), vols III and IV.

39 On appreciation as an element of tea culture, see Patricia J. Graham, *Tea of the Sages: The Art of Sencha* (Honolulu, HI, 1999).

40 Dresser, *Japan, Its Architecture, Art and Art Manufactures*, p. 159.

41 On connoisseurship, including its transformation in the Meiji period, see Christine Guth, *Art, Tea, and Industry: Masuda Takashi and the Mitsui Circle* (Princeton, NJ, 1993). On an earlier history of connoisseurship and sociality, see Morgan Pitelka, *Spectacular Accumulation: Material Culture, Tokugawa Ieyasu, and Samurai Sociability* (Honolulu, HI, 2018).

42 An illustrative example of connoisseurship and connoisseur knowledge in print is Christine Guth, 'The Aesthetics of Rayskin in Edo-Period Japan: Materials, Making and Meaning', *Impressions*, 37 (2016), pp. 98–100.

43 On this multi-decade process see David L. Howell, 'Foreign Encounters and Informal Diplomacy in Early Modern Japan', *Journal of Japanese Studies*, XL/2 (Summer 2014), pp. 295–327.

44 On fluctuating finances and government policy responses, see Steven J. Ericson, *Financial Stabilization in Meiji Japan: The Impact of the Matsukata Reform* (Ithaca, NY, 2019).

45 Ibid.

46 On the economic fluctuations of the cotton and silk industries, see Tanimoto Masayuki, *Nihon ni okeru zairaiteki keizai hatten to orimonogyō: Shijō keisei to kazoku keizai* (Nagoya, 1998).

47 On this transition, known as the Meiji Restoration, see Robert Hellyer and Harald Fuess, eds, *The Meiji Restoration: Japan as a Global Nation* (Cambridge, 2020). On the impact of political change on social structures and experience across Japan, see David L. Howell, *Geographies of Identity in Nineteenth-Century Japan* (Berkeley, CA, 2005).

48 On the transition within lacquer production see Malcolm Fairley, Oliver Impey and Joe Earle, eds, *Treasures of Imperial Japan*, vol. IV, parts 1 and 2: *Lacquer* (London, 1995). On lacquer production during the Meiji period, see Nihon Kōgakukai, *Meiji kōgyō-shi: Kagaku kōgyō-hen* (Tokyo, 1930), pp. 603–29.

49 On Shibata Zeshin, see Joe Earle, *Treasures of Imperial Japan: Masterpieces by Shibata Zeshin* (London, 1996).

50 For the economic history of the ceramics industry in the Meiji period, see Takehisa Yamada, 'The Export-Oriented Industrialization of Japanese Pottery: The Adoption and Adaptation of Overseas Technology and Market Information', in *The Role of Tradition*, ed. Tanimoto, pp. 217–40. Detail on kilns and ceramics districts nationwide is in Dai-Nihon Tōgyō Kyōkai, ed., *Nihon kinsei tōgyō-shi* (Tokyo, 1922), vol. III, pp. 1440–49.

51 Clare Pollard, 'Gorgeous with Glitter and Gold', in *Challenging Past and Present: The Metamorphosis of Nineteenth-Century Japanese Art*, ed. Ellen P. Conant (Honolulu, HI, 2006), p. 134.

52 Clare Pollard, *Master Potter of Meiji Japan: Makuzu Kôzan (1842–1916) and His Workshop* (Oxford, 2002), p. 48 n. 7.

53 Economic historian Naramoto Tatsuya calculated that the value of national ceramics production dropped 42 per cent in 1881–3. Ibid., p. 48 n. 5.

54 Yamada, 'The Export-Oriented Industrialization of Japanese Pottery', p. 228.

55 Suzuda Yukio, 'Arita seiki no Edo to Meiji', in *Kindai Nihon dezain shi*, ed. Nagata Kenichi, Hida Toyorō and Mori Hitoshi (Tokyo, 2006), p. 45.

56 See the argument ibid., particularly pp. 42–6.

57 See Victoria and Albert Museum, London, inv. no. 367-1877, http://collections.vam.ac.uk, accessed 25 October 2020.

58 On production changes in ceramics, see Pollard, 'Gorgeous with Glitter and Gold', and *Seramikkusu Japan: Tōjiki de tadoru Nihon no modan*, exh. cat., Museum of Modern Ceramic Art, Gifu, Tajimi City; Ishikawa Prefectural Museum of History, Kanazawa; Museum of Ceramic Art, Hyōgo, Tamba-Sasayama; and Shōtō Museum of Art, Tokyo (Tajimi, 2016).

59 Yamada, 'The Export-Oriented Industrialization of Japanese Pottery', p. 223. They were not the first to use blanks for mass production. Already

Designing Modern Japan

in the Tokugawa period, kilns had supplied blanks for Ogata Kenzan's studio, for him to decorate in his celebrated style. See Richard L. Wilson and Saeko Ogasawara, *The Potter's Brush: The Kenzan Style in Japanese Ceramics*, exh. cat., Freer Gallery of Art, Arthur M. Sackler Gallery, Smithsonian Institution, Washington, DC (Washington, DC, 2001), p. 139.

60 Tōkyō Kokuritsu Hakubutsukan, *Seiki no saiten bankoku hakurankai no bijutsu*, p. 71.

61 Koto Shōkoshi and Kawamura Terumasa, 'Kinsei kinu orimono no tenkai', in *Koza: Nihon gijutsu no shakaishi*, vol. III: *Bōshoku*, ed. Nagahara Keiji and Yamaguchi Keiji (Tokyo, 1983), p. 142.

62 Hiroko T. McDermott, 'Meiji Kyoto Textile Art and Takashimaya', *Monumenta Nipponica*, LXV/1 (2010), pp. 43–4.

63 Ibid., p. 42.

64 On the Kyoto Prefectural Painting School see Yoshio Sakakibara, 'The Kyoto-Prefecture Painting School and the Kyoto Municipal Special School of Painting', in *Nihonga: Transcending the Past*, exh. cat., St Louis Art Museum (St Louis, MI, 1995), pp. 84–5. See also Julia Sapin, 'Naturalism Fusing Past and Present: The Reconfiguration of the Kyoto School of Painting and the Revival of the Textile Industry', in *Kyoto Visual Culture in the Early Edo and Meiji Periods: The Arts of Reinvention*, ed. Morgan Pitelka and Alice Y. Tseng (London, 2016), pp. 138–60, and Sato, *Modern Japanese Art and the Meiji State*, pp. 54–5.

65 Haruhiko Fujita, 'Notomi Kaijiro: An Industrial Art Pioneer and the First Design Educator of Modern Japan', *Design Issues*, XVII/2 (2001), p. 24.

66 The Kanazawa Industrial School's first principal, Nōtomi Kaijirō, was the son of an elite samurai family from the Hizen domain who had participated in the preparation and delivery of Japan's displays in Vienna and Philadelphia before becoming an independent technical researcher and adviser. For Nōtomi and design education, see Fujita, 'Notomi Kaijiro'; Yamazaki Takafumi, 'Nōtomi Kaijirō no sangyō kyōiku: Sono rinen keisei to zuan shidō o megutte', in *Kindai Nihon dezain-shi*, ed. Nagata, Hida and Mori, pp. 85–99.

67 Yokoi Tokifuyu, *Nihon kōgyōshi* (Tokyo, 1898), p. 204.

68 Ibid., pp. 3–5.

69 Penelope Francks, *Japanese Economic Development: Theory and Practice*, 3rd edn (London, 2015), p. 53. This figure includes both textiles from 'modern' industries such as silk filatures and those from 'traditional' industries such as silk weaving.

70 See Rebekah Clements, *A Cultural History of Translation in Early Modern Japan* (Cambridge, 2015), and Ruselle Meade, 'Translating Technology in Japan's Meiji Enlightenment, 1870–1879', *East Asian Science, Technology and Society*, IX/3 (September 2015), pp. 253–74.

71 Ibid., p. 43.

72 The full report is Kunitake Kume, Graham Healey, Marius B. Jansen and Martin Collcutt, trans., *The Iwakura Embassy, 1871–73: A True Account of the Ambassador Extraordinary and Plenipotentiary's Journey of Observation through the United States of America and Europe*, 5 vols (Chiba and Richmond, Surrey, 2002). A useful summary and assessment is F. G. Notehelfer, Igor R. Saveliev and W. F. Vande Walle, 'Review: An Extraordinary Odyssey: The Iwakura Embassy Translated', *Monumenta Nipponica*, LIX/1 (2004), pp. 83–119.

73 See Ishizuki Minoru, *Kindai Nihon no kaigai ryūgaku shi* (Kyoto, 1972), and Watanabe Minoru, *Kindai Nihon kaigai ryūgakusei shi*, 2 vols (Tokyo, 1977 and 1978). In English, see Hoi-eun Kim, *Doctors of Empire: Medical and Cultural Encounters between Imperial Germany and Meiji Japan* (Toronto, 2016). A useful English-language summary of Meiji study abroad is Japanese National Commission for UNESCO, *The Role of Education in the Social and Economic Development of Japan* (Tokyo, 1966), pp. 118–25.

74 On rail networks see Steven J. Ericson, *The Sound of the Whistle: Railroads and the State in Meiji Japan* (Cambridge, MA, 1996), and John P. Tang, 'Railroad Expansion and Industrialization: Evidence from Meiji Japan', *Journal of Economic History*, LXXIV/3 (2014), pp. 863–86. On the postal service, see Janet Hunter, 'People and Post Offices: Consumption and Postal Services in Japan from the 1870s to the 1970s', in *The Historical Consumer: Consumption and Everyday Life in Japan, 1850–2000*, ed. Penelope Francks and Janet Hunter (Basingstoke, 2012), pp. 235–58.

75 Martha Chaiklin, 'A Miracle of Industry: The Struggle to Produce Sheet Glass in Modernizing Japan', in *Building a Modern Japan: Science, Technology, and Medicine in the Meiji Era and Beyond*, ed. Morris Low (New York and Basingstoke, 2005), pp. 161–81, and Gregory Clancey, 'Modernity and Carpenters: Daiku Technique and Meiji Technocracy', in *Building a Modern Japan*, ed. Low, pp. 183–206.

76 Recent conservation science research suggests that synthetic dyes were not widely adopted as quickly as thought. See Anna Cesaratto, Yan-Bing Luo, Henry D. Smith and Marco Leona, 'A Timeline for the Introduction of Synthetic Dyestuffs in Japan during the Late Edo and Meiji Periods', *Heritage Science*, VI/1 (3 April 2018), doi.org/10.1186/s40494-018-0187-0. On Meiji prints see Julia Meech-Pekarik, *The World of the Meiji Print: Impressions of a New Civilization* (New York, 1986).

77 For a study of one *oyatoi gaikokujin* and his impact on the built environment in Meiji Japan, see Alice Y. Tseng, 'Styling Japan: The Case of Josiah Conder and the Museum at Ueno, Tokyo', *Journal of the Society of Architectural Historians*, LXIII/4 (1 December 2004), pp. 472–97. A useful discussion of interactions between *oyatoi gaikokujin* and Japanese colleagues is Kristin Meissner, 'Responsivity within the Context of Informal Imperialism', *Journal of Modern European History | Zeitschrift für moderne europäische Geschichte | Revue d'histoire européenne contemporaine*, XIV/2 (2016), pp. 268–89. On *oyatoi gaikokujin* overall, see the work of Umetani Noboru, including *Oyatoi gaikokujin: Meiji Nihon no wakiyaku tachi* (Tokyo, 2013).

78 On Wagener, see G. Waguneru [Gottfried Wagener], *Ishin sangyō kensetsu ronsaku shūsei*, ed. Takao Tsuchiya (Tokyo, 1944), a biography and compilation of Wagener's writings, and Gunhild Avitabile, 'Gottfried Wagener (1831–1892)', in *Meiji no takara – Treasures of Imperial Japan: Selected Essays*, ed. Oliver Impey and Malcolm Fairley (London, 1996), pp. 98–123. See also Dai-Nihon Tōgyō kyōkai, ed., *Nihon kinsei tōgyō-shi*, vol. III, pp. 1500–509.

79 See Richard J. Smethurst, *From Foot Soldier to Finance Minister: Takahashi Korekiyo, Japan's Keynes* (Cambridge, MA, 2009), pp. 79–95, for a succinct account of this debate.

80 Francks, *Japanese Economic Development*, pp. 56–7, and Kozo Yamamura, 'Entrepreneurship, Ownership and Management in Japan', in *The*

Economic Emergence of Modern Japan, ed. Kozo Yamamura (Cambridge, 1997), pp. 294–352.

81 On Alcock see Sano Mayuko, 'Banpaku no hito, Razafōdo Ōrukokku', in *Bankoku hakurankai to ningen no rekishi*, ed. Sano Mayuko (Kyoto, 2015), pp. 21–52.

82 Rutherford Alcock, *Catalogue of Works of Industry and Art, Sent from Japan* (London, 1862), and *International Exhibition 1862: Official Catalogue of the Industrial Department* (London, 1862).

83 Dresser, *Japan*, p. 174.

84 Tsunoyama Yukihiro, 'Sano Tsunetami to Tanaka Yoshio: Bakumatsu Meiji no aru kanryō no kōdō', *Kansai Daigaku keizai ronshū*, XLVIII/3 (December 1998), pp. 329–62, 331–2. Kuni Takeyuki, *Hakurankai to Meiji no Nihon* (Tokyo, 2010), analyses Japanese displays in several exhibitions, including Paris 1867.

85 Ibid., p. 117. Nakano Reishirō, ed., *Nabeshima Naomasa kōden* (Tokyo, 1921), vol. V, p. 574, summarizes all products selected for display. On the impact of Saga's and Satsuma's displays on European taste, see Teramoto Atsuko, *Pari bankoku hakurankai to japonizumu no tanjō* (Kyoto, 2017).

86 'Les Récompenses', in *L'Exposition Universelle de 1867: Publication internationale autorisée par la Commission impériale*, ed. François Ducuing, 2 vols (Paris, 1867), vol. I, p. 335. Kō Shimazu-ke Hensanjō, ed., *Sappan kaigun shi* (Tokyo, 1928), vol. II, pp. 574–630, is the Satsuma domain account of participation; a summary is in Tsunoyama, 'Sano Tsunetami to Tanaka Yoshio', pp. 340–41.

87 'Les Récompenses', p. 366. Ōtsuka Takematsu, ed., *Tokugawa Akitake taiō kiroku* (Tokyo, 1932), vol. II, lists the items acquired from domains for the *bakufu* display.

88 Livia Rezende, 'Of Coffee, Nature and Exclusion: Designing Brazilian National Identity at International Exhibitions, 1867 and 1904', in *Designing Worlds: National Design Histories in an Age of Globalization*, ed. Grace Lees-Maffei and Kjetil Fallan (Oxford, 2016), pp. 266–7. A comparison of Asian nations at the 1867 Exposition Universelle is Meredith Martin, 'Staging China, Japan, and Siam at the Paris Universal Exhibition of 1867', in *Beyond Chinoiserie: Artistic Exchange between China and the West during the Late Qing Dynasty (1796–1911)*, ed. Petra ten-Doesschate Chu and Jennifer Milam (Leiden, 2018), pp. 122–48.

89 Tsunoyama, 'Sano Tsunetami to Tanaka Yoshio', pp. 331–2.

90 Tanaka Yoshio and Hirayama Narinobu, eds, *Ōkoku hakurankai sandō kiyō* (Tokyo, 1897), vol. I, p. 11. This report, by two members of Japan's delegation to Vienna, recounts the Japanese display's genesis and delivery and assesses the impact of participation on Japanese industry in the subsequent 25 years.

91 Sano's biography is in Tsunoyama, 'Sano Tsunetami to Tanaka Yoshio, pp. 344–6. In English, a short biography is in Doshin Sato, *Modern Japanese Art and the Meiji State: The Politics of Beauty*, trans. Hiroshi Nara (Los Angeles, CA, 2011), p. 60. On Sano's involvement in the 1862 Paris exposition see Yoshida Midori, 'Keiō 3-nen Pari bankoku hakurankai de no Saga-han Sano Tsunetami o chūshin to shite', *Taishō Daigaku Daigakuin kenkyū ronshū*, 28 (2004), pp. 127–38; Mibuchi Hiroyuki, 'Bakumatsu Pari banpaku shisetsudan to Sano Tsunetami', *Kokugakuin Daigaku kiyō*, 50 (2012), pp. 181–93; and Fujita, 'Notomi Kaijiro', p. 19.

92 Tanaka and Hirayama, *Ōkoku hakurankai sandō kiyō*, Appendix, p. 11.

93 Yoshiaki Itō, 'Bankoku hakurankai to kōgei dezain: Tōji o chūshin ni', in *Nihon kindai dezain-shi*, ed. Nagata Kenichi, Hida Toyorō and Mori Hitoshi (Tokyo, 2006), pp. 48–9.

94 Tanaka and Hirayama, *Ōkoku hakurankai sandō kiyō*, Appendix, pp. 12–17.

95 Anna Jackson, 'Imagining Japan: The Victorian Perception and Acquisition of Japanese Culture', *Journal of Design History*, v/4 (1992), p. 245.

96 Tōkyō Kokuritsu Hakubutsukan, *Seiki no saiten bankoku hakurankai no bijutsu*, p. 61, illus. 49.

97 The most in-depth study of the Kiriū Kōshō Kaisha is Hida Toyojirō, *Nihon moyō zushō Meiji zuan no yushutsu kōgei zuan: Kiriū Kōshō Kaisha no rekishi* (Kyoto, 1998).

98 On painting culture in Tokugawa Japan, see Timon Screech, ed., *Obtaining Images: Art, Production and Display in Edo Japan* (London, 2012).

99 There is a growing literature in English and Japanese on the Japanese displays at both fairs. On the Japanese pavilion in Chicago see Ellen Conant, 'Japan "Abroad" at the Chicago Exposition, 1893', in *Challenging Past and Present*, ed. Conant, pp. 254–80. On the Japanese pavilion in St Louis see Carol Ann Christ, '"The Sole Guardians of the Art Inheritance of Asia": Japan and China at the 1904 St Louis Fair', *Positions*, VIII/3 (Winter 2000), pp. 675–709.

100 On Yamanaka see Yumiko Yamamori, 'Japanese Arts in America, 1895–1920, and the A. A. Vantine and Yamanaka Companies', *Studies in the Decorative Arts*, XV/2 (2008), pp. 96–126, and Constance J. S. Chen, 'Merchants of Asianness: Japanese Art Dealers in the United States in the Early Twentieth Century', *Journal of American Studies*, XLIV/1 (2010), pp. 19–46.

101 Yokomizo Hiroko, 'Meiji seifu to dentō kōgei: *Onchi zuroku* kara Meiji kyūden "senshu no ma tenjō-ga" e', in *Dentō kōgei saikō: Miyako no uchi soto*, ed. Inaga Shigemi (Kyoto, 2007), p. 152.

102 On Hirayama, see Yoshinori Amagai, 'Hirayama Eizo (1855–1915): The First Japanese Design Student in Vienna', in *Journal of the Asian Design International Conference* (Tsukuba, 2003), n.p.

103 On the *Onchi zuroku*, see Tōkyō Kokuritsu Hakubutsukan, ed., *Meiji dezain no tanjō: Chōsa kenkyū hōkokusho 'Onchi zuroku'* (Tokyo, 2004).

104 Yokomizo, 'Meiji seifu to dentō kōgei', pp. 153–4. Yokomizo points out that the Product Design Department continued to claim Chinese tradition as part of Japan's cultural heritage, at a time when artistic nationalism (*kokusui shugi*), looking to define a uniquely Japanese style and cultural heritage, was more common.

105 For these comparisons see Tōkyō Kokuritsu Kindai Bijutsukan, ed., *Nihon no āru nūvō 1900–1923: Kōgei to dezain no shinjidai*, exh. cat., Tokyo National Museum of Modern Art (Tokyo, 2005).

106 Sato, *Modern Japanese Art and the Meiji State*, p. 47. On concerns about the loss of artistic heritage, see Chelsea Foxwell, 'Japan as Museum? Encapsulating Change and Loss in Late-Nineteenth-Century Japan', *Getty Research Journal*, 1 (2009), pp. 39–52.

107 Yokomizo, 'Meiji seifu to dentō kōgei', p. 153. The society's journal has been reprinted as Ryūchikai, *Ryūchikai hōkoku* [1885] (Tokyo, 1991).

108 The new 'history' was promoted particularly overseas: in 1893, Japan's pavilion for the World's Columbian Exposition in Chicago featured

rooms in 'historical styles'. See also curator and writer Okakura Tenshin's French-language history of Japanese art, *L'histoire de l'art du Japon*, commissioned for the Paris Exposition Universelle of 1900.

109 The range of exhibited artefacts can be grasped from the jury's comments on each item. For 1877, see Naikoku Kangyō Hakurankai Jimukyoku, *Meiji jūnen naikoku kangyō hakurankai chōsa hyōgo*, 2 vols (Tokyo, 1877).

110 Ibid., p. 534.

111 For the Tokyo School of Fine Arts, see Victoria Louise Weston, *Japanese Painting and National Identity: Okakura Tenshin and His Circle* (Ann Arbor, MI, 2004), and Chelsea Foxwell, *Making Modern Japanese-Style Painting: Kano Hōgai and the Search for Images* (Chicago, IL, 2015).

112 Victoria Weston, 'Institutionalizing Talent and the Kano Legacy', in *Copying the Master*, ed. Jordan and Weston, p. 151.

113 On the factors affecting makers' working practices in the Meiji period see Tanimoto, ed., *The Role of Tradition in Japan's Industrialization*.

114 There is a large literature on distribution and retail in the Meiji period in Japanese. In English, see Francks and Hunter, eds, *The Historical Consumer*.

2 '100-yen cultured living': Design, Policy and Commerce in the Early Twentieth Century

1 On the *kazoku danran* see Jordan Sand, *House and Home in Modern Japan: Architecture, Domestic Space and Bourgeois Culture, 1880–1930* (Cambridge, MA, 2005), pp. 33–9. On the configuration of domestic space see Yuko Nishikawa, 'The Modern Family and Changing Forms of Dwellings in Japan: Male-Centered Houses, Female-Centered Houses, and Gender-Neutral Rooms', trans. Sarah Teasley, in *Gender and Japanese History*, vol. II: *The Self and Expression/Work and Life*, ed. Haruko Wakita, Anne Bouchy and Chizuko Ueno (Osaka, 1999), pp. 477–508.

2 On Kageyama Kōyō see *Nihon no shashinka 14: Kageyama Kōyō* (Tokyo, 1997), and Kōyō Kageyama, *Shashin Shōwa 50-nenshi: Aru kameraman no hanseiki* (Tokyo, 1975).

3 'Yōsaika 4kakan no keika hōkoku', *Ai shī ōru* (March 1934), p. 45 and Tsunemi Mikiko, 'Kōseigaku o kiban to shita fasshon dezain', *Dezaingaku kenkyū tokushūgō*, X/4 (2003), p. 54.

4 Samuel C. Morse, label text for museum record, Kageyama Kōyō, *Our Newly Married 'Cultured Life' in the Jingumae Apartments*, at museums. fivecolleges.edu, accessed 20 January 2020.

5 On consumption see Penelope Francks, *The Japanese Consumer: An Alternative Economic History of Modern Japan* (Cambridge, 2009), pp. 108–44, and Andrew Gordon, 'Consumption, Leisure and the Middle Class in Transwar Japan', *Social Science Japan Journal*, X/1 (1 April 2007), pp. 1–21.

6 The Patent Bureau replaced the Product Design Department. On the Ishō Jōrei see Amagai Yoshinori, 'Meiji nijūichinen Ishō Jōrei to ōyō bijutsu shisō ni tsuite', *Bigaku* LVIII/3 (2007), pp. 42–54, and Higuchi Takayuki and Miyazaki Kiyoshi, 'Nihon ni okeru kango "ishō" no juyō to kaishaku: Nihon ni okeru dezain shikō, kōi o arawasu gengo gainen no kenkyu (6)', *Dezaingaku kenkyū*, LIV/5 (2008), pp. 47–50.

7 See for example the Trade Bureau reports by Okonogi Tōshirō on textiles, *Nōshōmushō Shōkōkyoku rinji hōkoku: Shinkoku orimonogyō kansatsu fukumeish*, 5 vols (Tokyo, 1899), and Kitamura Yaichirō on ceramics, *Shinkoku yōgyō chōsa hōkoku* (Tokyo, 1908).

8 Nōshōmushō, ed., *Nōshōmushō shōhin chinretsukan annai* (Tokyo, 1900), pp. 1–2.

9 Fushimi Chūshichi, ed., *Shizuoka-shi Bussan Chinretsukan Nenpō*, 4 (Shizuoka, 1910), p. 2.

10 Nōshōmushō, ed., *Nōshōmushō shōhin chinretsukan annai*, pp. 12–13. On product exhibition halls see Miyake Takuya, *Kindai Nihon 'chinretsujo' kenkyū* (Kyoto, 2015).

11 Nōshōmushō, ed., *Nōshōmushō shōhin chinretsukan annai*, p. 11.

12 Kyōto Shōhin Chinretsujo, *Kyōto Shōhin Chinretsujo no shiori* (Kyoto, 1912), pp. 33–4.

13 Kōfu Shōgyō Kaigijo, ed., *Kōfu Shōgyō Kaigijo hōkoku* (Kōfu, 1912), vol. III, pp. 37–40.

14 See the case studies in Toshio Toyoda and Transformation Project on Technology Transfer and Development: The Japanese Experience (United Nations University), eds, *Vocational Education in the Industrialization of Japan* (Tokyo, 1987), pp. 73–184, particularly pp. 74–80 and 86–7.

15 Kyōto Shōhin Chinretsujo, *Kyōto Shōhin Chinretsujo no shiori*, p. 17.

16 Ibid., pp. 12–15.

17 Ibid., p. 19.

18 On the dual structure economy see Kōnosuke Odaka, 'The Dual Structure of the Japanese Economy', trans. Noah S. Brannen, in *Economic History of Japan 1914–1955*, vol. III: *A Dual Structure*, ed. Takafusa Nakamura and Kōnosuke Odaka (Oxford, 2003), p. 111.

19 Nōshōmushō, ed., *Nōshōmushō shōhin chinretsukan annai*, p. 3.

20 Shizuoka-shi Bussan Chinretsukan, ed., *Shizuoka-shi Bussan Chinretsukan Nenpō*, 7 (1913), p. 58.

21 Ibid., p. 61.

22 Kyōto Shōhin Chinretsujo, *Kyōto Shōhin Chinretsujo no shiori*, p. 20.

23 On Tejima see *Tejima Seiichi sensei den* (Tokyo, 1929), and Miyoshi Nobuhiro, *Tejima Seiichi to Nihon kōgyō kyōiku hattatsushi* (Tokyo, 1999). In English, see Benjamin C. Duke, *The History of Modern Japanese Education: Constructing the National School System, 1872–1890* (New Brunswick, NJ, 2008), pp. 222–7.

24 On the Tokyo Industrial School, later the Tokyo Higher Industrial School, see the school's 25-year history, *Tōkyō Kōtō Kōgyō Gakkō Nijūgonen shi* (Tokyo, 1906).

25 On Meiji debates about industrial education see Miyoshi Nobuhiro, *Nihon kōgyō kyōiku seiritsushi no kenkyū* (Tokyo, 2012).

26 On the divergence between skilled artisans (*shokunin*) and skilled workers (*shokkō*) see Odaka Kōnosuke, *Shokunin no sekai, kōjō no sekai*, new edn (Tokyo, 2000).

27 The Ministry of Education's official history summarizes vocational education laws and structures implemented in the Meiji period. See Monbushō, ed., *Sangyō kyōiku hyakunenshi*, pp. 27–73. On vocational education in late nineteenth- and early twentieth-century Japan see Toyoda Toshio, ed., *Wagakuni ririkuki no jitsugyō kyōiku* (Tokyo, 1982),

Designing Modern Japan

and Toyoda Toshio, ed., *Wagakuni sangyōka to jitsugyō kyōiku* (Tokyo, 1984). An abridged English version of both volumes is Toshio Toyoda, ed., *Vocational Education in the Industrialization of Japan* (Tokyo, 1987).

28 Monbushō, ed., *Sangyō kyōiku hyakunen-shi* (Tokyo, 1986), p. 67.

29 'Jitsugyō gakkō rei', in *Sangyō kyōiku hyakunenshi*, ed. Monbushō, p. 814.

30 Monbushō, ed., *Jitsugyō kyōiku hyakunen shi*, p. 31.

31 See for example the sections on industrial education in France in the 1888 report on commercial, industrial and agricultural promotion policies and mechanisms in Europe and the USA compiled by Ministry of Commerce and Agriculture officials Makino Kenzō, Seki Sumizō and Dōke Hitoshi, *Ōbei junkai torishirabesho* (Tokyo, 1888), vol. III, pp. 299–324.

32 Miyoshi, *Tejima Seiichi to Nihon kōgyō kyōiku hattatsushi*, p. 21.

33 With its required choice of pencil or brush, Japanese or Western-style paper, drawing education became part of larger debates about the direction of Japanese art and industry. See Raja Adal, 'Aesthetics and the End of the Mimetic Moment: The Introduction of Art Education in Modern Japanese and Egyptian Schools', *Comparative Studies in Society and History*, LVIII/4 (October 2016), pp. 993–4. On drawing education in Meiji Japan see Manrei Rin, *Kindai Nihon zuga kyōikuhō shi kenkyū: 'Hyōgen' no hakken to sono jissen* (Tokyo, 1989), and Raja Adal, *Beauty in the Age of Empire: Japan, Egypt, and the Global History of Aesthetic Education* (New York, 2019), pp. 120–79.

34 Uemura Yasutaro with Tejima Seiichi, *Jitsugyō fukushū kyōiku ron* (Tokyo, 1894), pp. 10 and 59. On handcraft education in Meiji Japan see Kano Kimiko, 'Meiji-ki ni okeru shukōka no keisei katei: Uehara, Okuyama, Gotō, Ichito no shukō kyōikukan o moto ni', *Nihon Daigaku Kyōiku Gakkai Kiyō*, 32 (1998), pp. 47–60, and Miyazaki Hiromichi, *Sōshiki no shukō kyōiku jissenshi* (Tokyo, 2003).

35 On Japanese drawing educators' attention to the UK South Kensington system see Adal, *Beauty in the Age of Empire*, and Amagai Yoshinori, *Ōyō bijutsu shisō dōnyū no rekishi: Uīn haku sandō yori Ishō Jōrei settei made* (Kyoto, 2010).

36 Yoshida Chizuko, 'Tōkyō Bijutsu Gakkō dezain kyōiku ryakushi', in *Kindai Nihon dezain shi*, ed. Nagata Kenichi, Hida Toyojirō and Mori Hitoshi (Tokyo, 2006), pp. 302 and 304.

37 Kyōto Kōtō Kōgei Gakkō, ed., *Kyōto Kōtō, Kōgei Gakkō ichiran* (Kyoto, 1902), pp. 10–17.

38 Miyajima Hisao, 'Kyōto Kōtō Kōgei Gakkō setsuritsu zenshi', *Kyōto Kōgei Seni Daigaku Kōgei Gakubu kenkyū hōkoku; Jinbun*, 43 (1994), pp. 111–20. On Nakazawa see *Nakazawa Iwata hakase no bijutsu kōgei monogatari (sutōrī): Tōkyō, Pari, Kyōto*, exh. cat., Museum and Archives, Kyoto Institute of Technology (Kyoto, 2016).

39 *Kyōto Kōtō Kōgei Gakkō shojūnen seiseki hōkoku* (Kyoto, 1913), pp. 63–96. On the design department curriculum see Miyajima Hisao, *Kansai modan dezain zenshi* (Tokyo, 2003). An illustrated overview is Namiki Seishi, Matsuo Yoshiki and Oka Tatsuya, *Zuan kara dezain e: Kindai Kyōto no zuan kyōiku* (Kyoto, 2016).

40 Yasuda Rokuzō, *Honpō kōgei no genzai oyobi shōrai* (Tokyo, 1917), p. 166. On the Industrial Design Department see Ogata Kōji, 'Meijiki no dezain

kyōiku: Tōkyō Kōtō Kōgyō Gakkō Zuanka no kenkyū', *Nihon kindai dezain-shi*, ed. Nagata Kenichi, Hida Toyorō and Mori Hitoshi (Tokyo, 2006), pp. 120–40, and Ogata Kōji, 'Tōkyō Kōtō Kōgyō Gakkō Zuan Gakka zuan no dezain keimō katsudō', in *Sōsho: Kindai Nihon no dezain*, vol. vii, ed. Mori Hitoshi (Tokyo, 2007), pp. 647–52.

41 Figures for graduate destinations by industry sector until 1906 are in *Tōkyō Kōtō Kōgyō Gakkō Nijūgonen shi*, p. 60. Figures for all graduates are in Tōkyō Kōtō Kōgyō Gakkō, ed., *Tōkyō Kōtō Kōgyō Gakkō yonjūnen-shi: Gakusei hanpu gojūnen kinen* (Tokyo, 1922), p. 84.

42 Monbushō, *Sangyō kyōiku hyakunenshi* (Tokyo, 1986), p. 68.

43 Yasuda, *Honpō kōgei no genzai oyobi shōrai*, pp. 121–7. See also Yoshida, 'Tōkyō Bijutsu Gakkō dezain kyōiku ryakushi', p. 313.

44 For the etymology of 'ishō', see Higuchi Takayuki and Miyazaki Kiyoshi, 'Nihon ni okeru kango "ishō" no juyō to kaishaku: Nihon ni okeru dezain shikō, kōi o arawasu gengo gainen no kenkyu (2)', *Dezaingaku kenkyū*, L/5 (January 2004), pp. 1–10; 'Meiji no jisho ni mirareru seiyōgo ni taiō shita [ishō] no goi: Nihon ni okeru dezain shikō, kōi o arawasu gengo gainen no kenkyū (3)', *Dezaingaku kenkyū*, L/5 (January 2004), pp. 11–20; 'Meiji shoki kara chōki no bijutsu kōgei fukkō undō ni arawareta "ishō" gainen: Nihon ni okeru dezain shikō, kōi o arawasu gengo gainen no kenkyū (4)', *Dezaingaku kenkyū*, LIV/1 (May 2007), pp. 87–96. In English, see Yoshinori Amagai, 'Japanese Industrial Design Concepts in the Transition from the Nineteenth to the Twentieth Century: With Special Reference to the Japanese Industrial Design Educators Hirayama Eizo (1855–1914) and Matsuoka Hisashi (1862–1944)', *Blucher Design Proceedings*, 1 (Aveiro, 2012), pp. 19–22.

45 Komuro Shinzō, *Ippan zuanhō* (Tokyo, 1909), p. 1.

46 *Seizu*, meaning to make an image but without the references to ideation, referred to the process of making engineering or fabrication drawings.

47 Komuro Shinzō, 'Zuan kyōjun ippan', in *Odamaki* (Tokyo, 1906), n.p. See also Ogata, 'Meijiki no dezain kyōiku', pp. 133–4.

48 Educators derived these standards from European design principles. See Sarah Teasley, 'The Gender of Beauty in Architectural and Interior Design Discourse in Modern Japan', in *Visualizing Beauty: Gender and Ideology in Modern East Asia*, ed. Aida Yuen Wong (Hong Kong, 2012), pp. 113–30.

49 Komuro, for example, referenced UK and Irish design educators' books, including Christopher Dresser's *Principles of Decorative Design* (London, 1873), James Ward's *The Principles of Ornament* (London, 1892), Frank G. Jackson's *Lessons on Decorative Design* (London, 1894) and Walter Crane's *The Bases of Design* (London, 1898), in his introduction to *Ippan zuan hō* (pp. 2–3). Historian Ogata Kōji has noted that Komuro builds on these principles but also diverges from them, to create locally appropriate aesthetics for Japanese makers. Ogata Kōji, 'Meiji to dezain: Komuro Shinzō (1)', *Dezain riron*, 19 (1980), pp. 656–8.

50 Ogata Kōji, 'Tōkyō Bijutsu Gakkō no zuan kyōiku: Shimada Yoshinari no baai', in *Sōsho: Kindai Nihon no dezain*, vol. vi, ed. Mori Hitoshi (Tokyo, 2007), p. 356.

51 Mori Hitoshi, 'Nihon no modan dezain o himotoku', in *Dezain no yōran jidai ten: Tōkyō Kōtō Kōgei Gakkō no ayumi* [1], ed. Matsudo Kyōiku Iinkai and Mori Hitoshi, exh. cat., Matsudo Museum (Matsudo, 1997), pp. 109–15. According to Mori, 683 Japanese travelled abroad on this scheme

Designing Modern Japan

between 1896 and 1923. For the scheme, see Nōshōmushō Shōkōkyoku, *Kaigai jitsugyō renshūsei ichiran* (Tokyo, 1914).

52 Namiki, Matsuo and Oka, *Zuan kara dezain e*, p. 35.

53 Asai travelled to Paris as a painter, not in preparation to teach in Kyoto; at the time he taught painting at the Tokyo School of Fine Arts. On Asai in Paris see Kurisutofu Maruke [Christophe Marquet], 'Pari no Asai Chū: "Zuan" no mezame', *Kindai kaisetsu*, 1 (1992), pp. 12–45.

54 Watanabe Minoru, *Kindai Nihon kaigai ryugakusei-shi* (Tokyo, 1977), vol. I, fig. 4, n.p.

55 On handcraft education for girls see Akiko Yamasaki, 'Handicrafts and Gender in Modern Japan', trans. Amelia Bonea, *Journal of Modern Craft*, V/3 (2012), pp. 259–74, an abridged translation of a section of Yamasaki Akiko, *Kindai Nihon no 'shugei' to jendā* (Yokohama, 2005).

56 On *ikebana* as women's creative labour, see Nancy Stalker, 'Flower Empowerment: Rethinking Japan's Traditional Arts as Women's Labor', in *Rethinking Japanese Feminisms*, ed. Julia C. Bullock, Ayako Kano and James Welker (Honolulu, HI, 2018), pp. 103–18.

57 While historians have explored women's creative practice in areas like embroidery, *ikebana* and social reform, most histories of 'modern Japanese design' present design as practised, taught and theorized in male-only environments, without naming or addressing the androcentric nature of these histories. See for example the bibliography of modern Japanese design history compiled by respected designer and researcher Hino Eiichi, 'Nihon kindai dezainshi: Sankō bunken shōkai', *Dezain shigaku kenkyū tokushūgō*, VI/2 (1998), pp. 52–64. While recording and celebrating the achievements and trajectory of male designers in modern Japan is crucial, adherence to categories set at a time when men dominated waged work in design excludes women's experiences. In Japanese, design historian Kashiwagi Hiroshi has directly addressed domestic economy and other aspects of 'women's work' as modern Japanese design history since the 1980s. See Kashiwagi Hiroshi, *Kaji no seijigaku* (Tokyo, 1995). A direct, critical attempt in English to address the gendered nature of modern Japanese design history and to write women into the story is Yasuko Suga, 'Modernism, Nationalism and Gender: Crafting "Modern" Japonisme', *Journal of Design History*, XXI/3 (2008), pp. 259–75.

58 Histories of the Girls' Art School are Joshi Bijutsu Daigaku Ryakushi Hensan Iinkai, ed., *Joshi Bijutsu Daigaku ryakushi: Sōritsu rokujūnen shunen kinen* (Tokyo, 1960), and Joshi Bijutsu Daigaku Rekishi Shirōshitsu, ed., *Joshi bijutsu kyōiku to Nihon no kindai: Joshibi 110nen no jinbutsushi* (Tokyo, 2010). Lively first-hand accounts of student experiences in the 1930s are compiled in Joshi Bijutsu Daigaku Rekishi Shiryō Chōsei Iinkai, ed., *Joshibi no rekishi*, vol. II: *Zoku Joshibi no hanashi* (Tokyo, 2003).

59 On *ryōsai kenbō* see Kumiko Fujimura-Fanselow, 'The Japanese Ideology of "Good Wives and Wise Mothers": Trends in Contemporary Research', *Gender and History*, III/3 (1991), pp. 345–9. On its roots in Tokugawa culture see Sumiko Sekiguchi, 'Confucian Morals and the Making of a "Good Wife and Wise Mother": From "Between Husband and Wife There Is Distinction" to "As Husbands and Wives Be Harmonious"', *Social Science Japan Journal*, XIII/1 (2010), pp. 95–113, and Rebecca

Corbett, *Cultivating Femininity: Women and Tea Culture in Edo and Meiji Japan* (Honolulu, HI, 2018), pp. 122–40.

60 See for example the designs offered by girls' and women's school teachers in *Doressumēkingu: Katei de dekiru kodomo oyobi fujinfuku* (Tokyo, 1922), vol. I.

61 Kyōto Kōtō Kōgei Gakkō, ed., *Kyōto Kōtō Kōgei Gakkō ichiran* (Kyoto, 1912), n.p.

62 'Kimiko Hashizume' (interview), in *Joshibi no rekishi*, vol. II, ed. Joshi Bijutsu Daigaku Rekishi Shiryō Chōsei Iinkai, p. 11. Girls in the Japanese painting course were required to wear navy blue kimono and were teased for looking like members of the Salvation Army. 'Morita Chie (Nakamura)', in *Joshibi no rekishi*, vol. II, p. 20. By the early 1930s, girls in the oil painting course could wear their own clothing after the first year, which they often preferred. 'Utomi Kinuko', in *Joshibi no rekishi*, vol. II, p. 13. On the Private Girls' Art School uniforms, see Ogura Fumiko, Kobayashi Rie and Oyamada Noriko, 'Joshi Bijutsu Gakkō seifku to Meiji no kairyōfuku', *Joshi Bijutsu Daigaku kenkyū kiyō*, 31 (2001), pp. 77–91.

63 On Shimada, see Ogata Kōji, 'Tōkyō Bijutsu Gakkō no zuan kyōiku: Shimada Yoshinari no bāi', in *Sōsho: Kindai Nihon no dezain*, vol. VI, ed. Hitoshi, pp. 355–61.

64 Ogata, 'Meiji to dezain: Komuro Shinzō (1)', pp. 656–7.

65 Similarly, the Ministry of Education contracted Shimada to deliver a nationwide series of lectures on mid-level drawing education, presumably to middle school teachers and normal school students, in 1906. Shimada's lectures too appeared as a book, with four printings between 1909 and 1922. Shimada Yoshinari, *Kōgei zuanhō kōgi* (Tokyo, 1909). An outline of the lectures is in Shimada Yoshinari, 'Kōgei zuan ni tsukite', in *Monbushō kōshōkai zuga-ka kōwashū*, ed. Shirahama Akira (Tokyo, 1917).

66 Teasley, 'The Gender of Beauty'.

67 Ibid., pp. 113–30. On Ōe Sumiko see Linda L. Johnson, 'Meiji Women's Educators as Public Intellectuals: Shimoda Utako and Tsuda Umeko', *U.S.-Japan Women's Journal*, 44 (2013), pp. 67–92.

68 Higa Akiko and Miyazaki Kiyoshi, 'Zuan shōreisaku to shite no Nōten Shōkōten no yōsō to sono igi: Nōten Shōkōten kenkyū (1)', *Dezaingaku kenkyū*, XLII/2 (1995), pp. 65–74.

69 An important exception was Seto, a ceramics production area, where industrial school design department professors taught and researched pattern design for Western-style ceramics. See *Zuan no henbō 1868–1945*, exh. cat., Tokyo National Museum of Modern Art Crafts Gallery (Tokyo, 1988), p. 13.

70 Yasuda, *Honpō kōgei no genzai oyobi shōrai*, pp. 15–16, see also p. 19.

71 Ibid., pp. 17–18.

72 Ibid., p. 148.

73 Ibid., p. 141.

74 Ibid., pp. 108–9.

75 Matsudo Kyōiku Iinkai and Mori, eds, *Dezain no yōran jidai ten*, pp. 112–13.

76 Ibid.

77 On the early history of the MCI see Chalmers A. Johnson, *MITI and the Japanese Miracle: The Growth of Industrial Policy, 1925–1975* (Stanford, CA, 1982), pp. 83–4 and 94–100.

78 Kashiwagi Hiroshi, *Kindai Nihon no dezain shisō* (Tokyo, 1979), pp. 157–60, and Lisbeth K. Brandt, *Kingdom of Beauty: Mingei and the Politics of Folk Art in Imperial Japan* (Durham, NC, 2007), pp. 86 and 129. See also Suga, 'Modernism, Nationalism and Gender', pp. 263–4.

79 Takeuchi Kakichi, 'Kōgei Shidōsho no sōsetsu o kataru', *Kōgei nyūsu*, XVII/2 (February 1949), p. 2.

80 Ibid., pp. 2–3, and Kunii Kitarō, 'Honpō kōgyō no kōgeiteki shinten o nozomu', *Kōgei nyūsu*, I/3 (August 1932), p. 1.

81 A summary is Kunii Kitarō, 'Kōgei Shidoshō no ayunde kita michi', pp. 4–6. For the history of the Institute see Kōgyō Gijutsuin Sangyō Kōgei Shikenjo, ed., *Kōgyō Gijutsuin Sangyō Kōgei Shikenjo 30-nenshi* (Tokyo, 1960).

82 Brandt, *Kingdom of Beauty*, pp. 131–5.

83 Uchikawa Yoshimi, ed., *Nihon kōkoku hattatsushi* (Tokyo, 1976), vol. I, p. 281, chart IV-17, compiled from industrial production data given in Tsūshōsangyōshō Daijin Kanbōkyoku Chōsa Tōkeibu, ed., *Kōkyō Tōkei 50-nenshi*, 3 vols (Tokyo, 1961).

84 The value of annual bicycle production grew from 860,000 yen in 1925 to over 41 million yen in 1935. Uchikawa, ed., *Nihon kōkoku hattatsushi*, vol. I, p. 280, chart IV-17.

85 Julia Sapin, 'Merchandising Art and Identity in Meiji Japan: Kyoto *Nihonga* Artists' Designs for Takashimaya Department Store, 1868–1912', *Journal of Design History*, XVII/4 (December 2004), p. 322. See also Hiroko T. McDermott, 'Meiji Kyoto Textile Art and Takashimaya', *Monumenta Nipponica*, LXV/1 (2010), pp. 37–88.

86 On painters' contracts with textile firms see also Ellen P. Conant, 'Cut from Kyoto Cloth: Takeuchi Seihō and His Artistic Milieu', *Impressions*, 33 (2012), pp. 70–93.

87 On Kyoto textiles *zuan* books see Hida Toyojirō and Yokomizo Hiroko, *Meiji Taishōki zuan no kenkyū* (Tokyo, 2004), and Scott Johnson, 'Zuan Pattern Books: The Glory Years', *Andon* 100 (2016), pp. 5–75. On Kamisaka Sekka see Ikeda Yūko and Donald A. Wood, eds, *Rinpa no keishō: Kindai dezain no sakigakesha Kamisaka Sekka*, exh. cat., Kyoto National Museum of Modern Art, and others (Tokyo, 2003), and Satō Keiji, 'Kindai no rinpa to shite no dezainā, Kamisaka Sekka: Dentō to dezain, shikki o chūshin ni', in *Dentō kōgei saikō: Miyako no uchi soto*, ed. Shigemi Inaga (Kyoto, 2007), pp. 283–317.

88 *Zuan* publisher Yamada Unsōdō published the winning entries as *Kōrin-shiki Meiji moyō: Mitsukoshi Gofukuten kenshō zuan*, 2 vols (Kyoto, 1909).

89 On Rinpa and modernism see Satō, 'Kindai no Rinpa to shite no dezainā Kamisaka Sekka', and Tamamushi Satoko, 'Rinpa no kindai to kokusaisei', in *Dentō kōgei saikō*, ed. Inaga, pp. 79–82.

90 Satō, 'Kindai no Rinpa to shite no dezaina Kamisaka Sekka', pp. 288–9.

91 Ibid. See also Gomi Hijiri, 'Kanzōhin ni miru zuanka Kishi Kōkei to Seikōsha no sakuhin ni tsuite', *Sannomaru Shōzōkan nenpō kiyō*, 11 (2004), pp. 55–64.

92 The classic study of department stores in early twentieth-century Japan is Hatsuda Tōru, *Hyakkaten no tanjō* (Tokyo, 1993).

93 Mitsukoshi has been well studied as an embodiment of modernity, transformation and luxury consumption in early twentieth-century Japan. Jinno Yūki, *Shumi no tanjō: Hyakkaten ga tsukutta teisuto* (Tokyo, 1996),

closely analyses graphic, interior and furniture design within the retailer's broader marketing strategy. In English see Tomoko Tamari, 'Rise of the Department Store and the Aestheticization of Everyday Life in Early 20th Century Japan', *International Journal of Japanese Sociology*, xv/1 (November 2006), pp. 99–119, and Noriko Aso, 'Mitsukoshi: Consuming Places', http://scalar.chass.ncsu.edu, accessed 4 November 2020.

94 This was not limited to Kyoto. In Tokyo, kimono merchant Matsuya hired Western-style artists such as Okada Saburōsuke to design billboards, flyers and other publicity materials. Sapin, 'Merchandising Art and Identity in Meiji Japan', pp. 318–19.

95 On Takashimaya's transformations during the Meiji period, see Takashimaya Honten, ed., *Takashimaya hyakunen-shi* (Kyoto, 1941).

96 Tamari, 'Rise of the Department Store and the Aestheticization of Everyday Life in Early 20th Century Japan', p. 111. On wealthy regional household purchasing see Satoru Nakanishi and Tomoko Futaya, 'Japanese Modernisation and the Changing Everyday Life of the Consumer: Evidence from Household Accounts', in *The Historical Consumer: Consumption and Everyday Life in Japan, 1850–2000*, ed. Penelope Francks and Janet Hunter (Basingstoke, 2012), pp. 107–26.

97 Jinno, *Shumi no tanjō*, p. 75.

98 Ibid., pp. 77–8.

99 'Moga Mobo no chōji: Sugiura fūfu', www.shiro1000.jp/tau-history/hisui/hisui.html, accessed 20 February 2020. In addition to this illustrated biography, see Sugiura Hisui, *Seitan 140-nen: Kaika suru modan dezain*, exh. cat., Ehime Museum of Art, Matsuyama (Matsuyama, 2017).

100 On the poster and the competition see Tajima Natsuko, 'Kindai Nihon posutā shi ni okeru Hashiguchi Goyō no "Kono bijin" to iu sonzai: Mitsukoshi Gofukuten ni yoru Dai-1-kai kōkoku zuan kenshō boshū no jissen to sono eikyō', *Meisei Daigaku Kenkyū Kiyō*, 23 (2015), pp. 52–65.

101 On the beautiful woman trope see Miya Elise Mizuta Lippit, *Aesthetic Life: Beauty and Art in Modern Japan* (Cambridge, MA, 2019).

102 Jinno, *Shumi no tanjō*, p. 87. See also Sand, *House and Home in Modern Japan*, pp. 118–30.

103 Sarah Teasley, 'Home-Builder or Home-Maker? Reader Presence in Articles on Home-Building in Commercial Women's Magazines in 1920s' Japan', *Journal of Design History*, xviii/1 (January 2005), pp. 81–97, and Teasley, 'The Gender of Beauty'.

104 Jinno, *Shumi no tanjō*, pp. 38–46. See also Noriko Aso, *Public Properties: Museums in Imperial Japan* (Durham, NC, 2014), pp. 172–7, and Tomoko Tamari, 'The Department Store in Early Twentieth-Century Japan: Luxury, Aestheticization and Modern Life', *Luxury*, iii/1–2 (October 2016), pp. 83–103.

105 Nōshōmushō Shōkōkyoku, *Kōgeihin ishō no enkaku* (Tokyo, 1900), p. 41.

106 Kida Takuya, 'Nihon no āru nūvō 1900–1923: "Atarashii geijutsu" to shite no shinjidai', in *Nihon no āru nūvō 1900–1923: Kōgei to dezain no shinjidai*, exh. cat., Tokyo National Museum of Modern Art Craft Gallery (Tokyo, 2005), p. 11 n. 5. Asai did not entirely like the style – a letter published in the journal *Hototogisu* in October 1910 described it as 'lines slithering around up and down and in circles-style' and 'slightly beastly'.

107 Kida, 'Nihon no āru nūvō 1900–1923', p. 34.

108 Ibid., pp. 12–13.

109 Tokyo passed a law in 1890 allowing advertisements to be attached to electrical posts. Uchikawa, ed., *Nihon kōkoku hattatsushi*, vol. I, p. 75.

110 Ibid., p. 88. Factors in the increase in newspaper publishing included public interest in the Sino-Japanese War of 1894–5, changes in postal delivery rates, increased newsprint production and printers' acquisitions of steam-driven rotary presses and movable metal type (most often cast at the Tsukiji Type Foundry in Tokyo, based on knowledge acquired from a Shanghai-based Presbyterian missionary in 1869–70).

111 Tōkeikyoku, ed., *Nihon teikoku tōkei nenkan* (1911, n.p. given), cited in Uchikawa, ed., *Nihon kōkoku hattatsushi*, vol. I, p. 90, chart II-3.

112 Dentsu was known by other names until 1907, when its founder merged two companies to form the Nippon Denpō Tsūshinsha (Japan Telegraphic Communication Co., Ltd.).

113 Kamitsukasa Shōten, *Sono hi sono hi: Shoken zuihitsu* (Tokyo, 1905), p. 38.

114 Uchikawa, ed., *Nihon kōkoku hattatsushi*, vol. I, p. 109. One 1909 analysis suggested that nationally circulated advertisements for pharmaceuticals, cosmetics and books comprised 92, 96 and 96 per cent respectively of their category totals. Nihon Denpō Tsushinsha, *Shinbun meikan* (Tokyo, 1909), cited in Uchikawa, ed., *Nihon kōkoku hattatsushi*, vol. I, p. 97, chart II-5. The majority of firms that advertised nationally were based in either Tokyo or Osaka.

115 Chihaya Masahiro, *Ōyō jizai gendai kōkoku monkū jirin* (Tokyo, 1919).

116 A lively description of Morinaga's design department is 'Imaizumi Takeji' in Tanaka Ikkō, ed., *Kikigaki dezain shi* (Tokyo, 2001), pp. 18–21. An English introduction is in *Zuan no henbō 1868–1945*, p. 19.

117 Ibid., p. 19.

118 Naikaku Tōkeikyoku, *Taishō jūyonen kokusei chōsa* (Tokyo, 1926), p. vi.

119 Ibid., p. 4.

120 Sugihara Kaoru, ed., *Taishō Ōsaka suramu* (Tokyo, 1986), p. 10.

121 On the concept of 'middle class' in 1920s and '30s Japan see Jordan Sand, '中流 Chūryū/Middling', *Review of Japanese Culture and Society*, xxv (2013), pp. 67–77.

122 On urban leisure see Andrew Gordon, 'Consumption, Leisure and the Middle Class in Transwar Japan', *Social Science Japan Journal*, x/1 (April 2007), pp. 1–21.

123 On regional cities see Louise Young, *Beyond the Metropolis: Second Cities and Modern Life in Interwar Japan* (Berkeley, CA, 2013).

124 Naimushō Keihōkyoku, ed., *Honpō eiga jigyo gaiyō* (Tokyo, 1940), cited in Uchikawa, ed., *Nihon kokoku hattatsu-shi*, vol. I, p. 273.

125 On design for children as a business strategy see Jinno Yūki, *Kodomo o meguru dezain to kindai: Kakudai suru shōhin sekai* (Kyoto, 2011), and in English, Yuki Jinno, 'Consumer Consumption for Children', trans. Emily B. Simpson, in *Child's Play: Multi-Sensory Histories of Children and Childhood in Japan*, ed. Sabine Frühstück and Anne Walthall (Berkeley, CA, 2017), pp. 83–101.

126 Yongkeun Chun, 'Displayed Modernity: Advertising and Commercial Art in Colonial Korea, 1920–1940', unpublished PhD thesis, Royal College of Art, London, 2019, pp. 120–21.

127 On *tanka* see Takeuchi Yukie, *Kindai kōkoku no tanjō: Posutā ga nyū media datta koro* (Tokyo, 2011), pp. 21–6, and Chun, 'Displayed Modernity', pp. 132–4.

128 On Shiseido, see Gennifer Weisenfeld, 'Selling Shiseido: Cosmetics Design and Advertising in Modern Japan', https://visualizingcultures.mit.edu, accessed 28 October 2020.

129 *Kōkokukai*, VII/1 (January 1930), quoted in Kawahata Naomichi, *Hara Hiromu to 'Bokutachi no shin kappanjutsu': Katsuji, shashin, insatsu no 1930 nendai* (Tokyo, 2002), p. 241.

130 On Kao see Gennifer Weisenfeld, '"From Baby's First Bath": Kaō Soap and Modern Japanese Commercial Design', *Art Bulletin*, LXXXVI/3 (2004), pp. 573–98. On Morinaga see Gennifer Weisenfeld, 'Japanese Typographic Design and the Art of Letterforms', in *Bridges to Heaven: Essays on East Asian Art in Honour of Professor Wen C. Fong* (Princeton, NJ, 2011), vol. I, pp. 845–6.

131 On lettering see Weisenfeld, 'Japanese Typographic Design'.

132 'Kenchiku suru', the phrase translated here as 'building', contains 'kenchiku', the Japanese word for architecture, suggesting rational design, aesthetics and construction techniques. Takashi Kōno, 'Fukuki riga kōkoku bijutsu o seisan shite mannerizumu o haigeki seyo', *Kokusai eiga shinbun*, XXXV (December 1929), in Kawahata, *Hara Hiromu to 'Bokutachi no shin kappanjutsu'*, p. 241.

133 On *Kōga*, see Tōkyō-to Shashin Bijutsukan, ed., *Kōga to shinkō shashin: Modanizumu no Nihon*, exh. cat., Tokyo Photographic Art Museum (Tokyo, 2018).

134 On left-wing political graphics see Christopher Gerteis, 'Political Protest in Interwar Japan, 1: Posters and Handbills from the Ohara Collection (1920s–1930s)', https://visualizingcultures.mit.edu, accessed 29 October 2020.

135 On designers' political work, see Gennifer Weisenfeld, *Mavo: Japanese Artists and the Avant-garde, 1905–1931* (Berkeley, CA, 2002), pp. 123–63, and Umemiya Hiromitsu, 'Tōmei na kinōshugi to hanbigaku: Kawakita Renshichirō no senkyūhakusanjū nendai', in *Modanizumu/nashonarizumu*, ed. Omuka Toshiharu and Mizusawa Tsutomu (Tokyo, 2003), pp. 102–30.

136 Annie Van Assche, 'Interweavings: Kimono Past and Present', in *Fashioning Kimono: Dress and Modernity in Early Twentieth Century Japan*, ed. Annie Van Assche (Milan, 2005), p. 21.

137 Penelope Francks, 'Kimono Fashion: The Consumer and the Growth of the Textile Industry in Modern Japan', in *The Historical Consumer*, ed. Francks and Hunter, p. 168.

138 Ibid., p. 169.

139 Ibid., pp. 164 and 167.

140 See Weisenfeld, *Mavo*, and Sarah Teasley, 'Travel-Writing the Design Industry in Modern Japan, 1910–25', in *Travel, Space, Architecture*, ed. Miodrag Mitrasinovic and Jilly Traganou (London, 2009), pp. 103–24.

141 Jinno, *Shumi no tanjō*, p. 84.

142 'Shinkan gaikoku zasshi shūyo kiji', *Kogei Nyusu*, II/3 (March 1933), p. 11.

143 Hara Hiromu, 'Atarashii shikakuteki keisei gijutsu e: Omo to shite insatsumen no keisei ni kanshite', in *Kōgei Bijutsu*, ed. Nishikawa Tomotake (Tokyo, 1936), p. 21.

144 *Zuan no henbō 1868–1945*, pp. 14–15, offers a useful summary of some of these groups. An engaging personal account of participation in groups in the Osaka–Kobe area is Tanaka, ed., 'Imatake Shichirō',

pp. 33–4 and 38–9. See also Yamana Ayao, *Taiken-teki dezainshi* (Tokyo, 1976), pp. 104–38.

145 On Hamada see Gennifer Weisenfeld, 'Japanese Modernism and Consumerism: Forging the New Artistic Field of Shōgyō Bijutsu', in *Being Modern in Japan*, ed. Elise Tipton and John Clark (Honolulu, HI, 2000), pp. 75–98.

146 Chun, 'Displayed Modernity', p. 125 n. 408. On *Kōkokukai* see Takeuchi, *Kindai kokoku no tanjo*, pp. 216–22. Takeuchi has published prolifically on advertising design in 1920s and '30s Japan, particularly on activities in the Osaka–Kyoto area.

147 Yamana, *Taikenteki dezain-shi*, pp. 166–7.

148 On this point see also the discussions in Hiroshi Kashiwagi, 'On Rationalization and the National Lifestyle: Japanese Design in the 1920s and 1930s', in *Being Modern in Japan*, ed. Tipton and Clark, pp. 61–4, and Sand, *House and Home in Modern Japan*, pp. 162–94.

149 On the lived experiences of the urban poor in Meiji Japan, including their experience of social reform movements, see James L. Huffman, *Down and Out in Meiji Japan* (Honolulu, HI, 2018).

150 Japan National Commission for UNESCO, ed., *The Role of Education in the Social and Economic Development of Japan* (Tokyo, 1966), pp. 75–6.

151 Kubouchi Kana, 'Taishōki Tōkyō Kyōiku Hakubutsukan ni okeru tokubetsu tenrankai: Senmon bunkaka to taishūka', *Seishōgakushū Shakaikyōikugaku kenkyū*, 20 (March 1996), p. 44.

152 Sand, *House and Home in Modern Japan*, p. 181. The roster of founding members is in Seikatsu Kaizen Dōmeikai, ed., *Seikatsu kaizen no shiori* (Tokyo, 1924), p. 5.

153 Seikatsu Kaizen Dōmeikai, ed., *Seikatsu kaizen no shiori*, p. 67.

154 Ibid., p. 68.

155 Seikatsu Kaizen Dōmeikai, ed., *Nōson seikatsu kaizen shishin* (Tokyo, 1931). On rural lifestyle improvement campaigns see Mariko Tamanoi, 'The City and the Countryside: Competing Taishō "Modernities" on Gender', in *Japan's Competing Modernities: Issues in Culture and Democracy, 1900–1930*, ed. Sharon Minichiello (Honolulu, HI, 1998), pp. 91–113; Simon Partner, 'Taming the Wilderness: The Lifestyle Improvement Movement in Rural Japan, 1925–1965', *Monumenta Nipponica*, LVI/ 4 (2001), pp. 487–520; and Masao Tsutsui, 'The Impact of the Local Improvement Movement on Farmers and Rural Communities', in *Farmers and Village Life in Japan*, ed. Yoshiaki Nishida and Ann Waswo (London, 2003), pp. 60–78. On the connection between housing design and rural lifestyle improvement campaigns see Izumi Kuroishi, 'Domesticating Others' Space: Surveys and Reforms of Housing in Chosen and Japan by Wajiro Kon', in *Constructing the Colonized Land: Entwined Perspectives of East Asia around WWII*, ed. Matthew Carmona and Izumi Kuroishi (Farnham, 2014), pp. 215–52.

156 Morimoto Kōkichi-den Kankōkai, ed., *Morimoto Kōkichi* (Tokyo, 1956), pp. 364–5. In other statements, Morimoto used the Japanese word commonly translated as 'rational' (*gōriteki*) interchangeably with the English word 'modern'. See Morimoto Kōkichi, *Apātomento hausu: Atarashii jūtaku no kenkyū* (Tokyo, 1926), p. 65, and English Appendix 2, 'Apartment House', n.p. On Morimoto see his biography and collected writings in Morimoto Kōkichi-den Kankōkai, ed., *Morimoto Kōkichi*. In

English, see Sand, *House and Home in Modern Japan*, pp. 194–8.

157 On maids in interwar Japan see Odaka, 'The Dual Structure of the Japanese Economy', pp. 112–17, and Koizumi Kazuko, ed., *Jochū ga ita Shōwa* (Tokyo, 2012).

158 Kokichi Morimoto, *The Standard of Living in Japan* (Baltimore, MD, 1918), p. 105.

159 Ibid.

160 Seikatsu Kaizen Dōmeikai, ed., *Fukusō kaizen no hōshin* (Tokyo, 1920), p. 7.

161 Ibid., p. 10.

162 For this argument, see Sand, *House and Home in Modern Japan*.

163 Dōjunkai, ed., *Dōjunkai jūnenshi* (Tokyo, 1934), pp. 3–24. On the Dōjunkai, including its legacy, see Uchida Seizō, *Dōjunkai ni manabe: Sumai no shisō to sono dezain* (Matsudo, 2004), and Dōjunkai Apātomento Kenkyūkai, ed., *Dōjunkai apāto seikatsushi: Edogawa Apāto Shinbun kara* (Tokyo, 1998).

164 On housing-related publishing see Sand, *House and Home in Modern Japan*, pp. 132–61 and 263–87, and Teasley, 'Home-Builder or Home-Maker?'

165 The League's propositions are in Seikatsu Kaizen Dōmeikai, ed., *Jūtaku kaizen no hōshin* (Tokyo, 1920), and Seikatsu Kaizen Dōmeikai, ed., *Jūtaku kagu no kaizen* (Tokyo, 1924). See also Sand, *House and Home in Modern Japan*, p. 187.

166 Of 588 houses inspected in 1925 in Asagaya, a new suburb in western Tokyo, 75 per cent were 'Japanese-style', 20 per cent 'culture-style' and 5 per cent hybrid 'Japanese and Western style'. Kon Wajirō and Yoshida Kenkichi, *Moderunorojii 'Kōgengaku'* (Tokyo, 1930), p. 115. See also Sand, *House and Home in Modern Japan*, pp. 258–9.

167 See Nakagawa Kiyoshi, *Nihon no toshi kasō* (Tokyo, 1985), pp. 185–91.

168 Naimushō, ed., *Saimin chōsa tōkei-hyo* (Tokyo, 1921), p. 40, cited ibid., p. 137.

169 On Keiji Kōbō, see Guruppe 5 and Katsuhei Toyoguchi, eds, *Keiji Kōbō kara: Toyoguchi Katsuhei to dezain no hanseiki* (Tokyo, 1987), and Anu Gosso [Anne Gossot] and Shikida Hiroko, 'Keiji Kōbō ni okeru tairyō seisan no hōhōron', *Kagu dōgu shitsunaishi*, 3 (2011), pp. 142–8.

170 On Moriya's ideas see Sarah Teasley, 'Furnishing the Modern Metropolitan: Moriya Nobuo's Designs for Domestic Interiors, 1922–1927', *Design Issues*, XIX/4 (2003), pp. 57–71, and Anne Gossot, 'L'Invention du mobilier domestique industriel normalisé: L'oeuvre de Moriya Nobuo, pionnier du design industriel dans le Japon des années vingt', *Ebisu – Études Japonaises*, 39 (Spring–Summer 2008), pp. 133–78.

171 Nishida Toraichi, *Saishin mokuzai kogei taisei* (Tokyo, 1935), epigram, n.p.

3 Coffee Sets and Militarism: Design in Empire, War and Occupation

1 Korea's emperor abdicated and Korean annexation became official in 1910. See Peter Duus, *The Abacus and the Sword: The Japanese Penetration of Korea, 1895–1910* [1995] (Berkeley, CA, 2009). There is an immense literature on Japanese imperial expansion. Louise Young, 'Rethinking Empire: Lessons from Imperial and Post-Imperial Japan', in *The Oxford Handbook of the Ends of Empire*, ed. Martin Thomas and Andrew S. Thompson (Oxford, 2018), pp. 155–207, offers an excellent introduction and bibliography.

2 Designers' accounts include Tagawa Seiichi, *Sensō no gurafizumu:* FRONT *o tsukutta hitobito* (Tokyo, 2000), and Tanaka Ikkō, ed., *Kikigaki dezain shi* (Tokyo, 2001).

3 Critical historians' work includes Dōjidai Kenchiku Kenkyūkai, ed., *Hikigeki 1930 nendai no kenchiku to bunka* (Tokyo, 1981); Kashiwagi Hiroshi, *Shōzō no naka no kenryoku: Kindai Nihon no gurafizumu o yomu* (Tokyo, 2000); and Inoue Shōichi, *Senjika Nihon no kenchikuka: Āto, kicchu, japanesuku* (Tokyo, 1995).

4 A substantial exception here is the research of Yuko Kikuchi, including the papers 'Visualising Oriental Crafts: Contested Notion of "Japaneseness" and the Crafts of the Japanese Empire', conference paper for 'Questioning Oriental Aesthetics and Thinking: Conflicting Visions of "Asia" under the Colonial Empires', International Research Center for Japanese Studies, Kyoto, 201, pp. 211–35, and '"Tōyō shumi" of Household Products Designed in Imperial Japan of Manchukuo and Taiwan', UEA Sainsbury Institute workshop '*Tôyô shumi* in Imperial Japan', 13–14 June 2013.

5 One exception is Hiroshi Kashiwagi, 'On Rationalization and the National Lifestyle: Japanese Design of the 1920s and 1930s', in *Being Modern in Japan: Culture and Society from the 1910s to the 1930s*, ed. Elise K. Tipton and John Clark (Honolulu, HI, 2000), pp. 69–73. On IARI activities to develop export products in the 1930s, see Kida Takuya, 'Kitarō Kunii's Discourse on Indigenous Industrial Arts: "Japaneseness" and Modern Design in 1930s Japan', *Design History*, 9 (2011), pp. 47–92.

6 See for example *Chōkyō suru Nihonjin: Kōgeika ga yume mita Ajia 1910s–1945*, exh. cat., Tokyo National Museum of Modern Art Craft Gallery (Tokyo, 2012).

7 On transnational and regional design history in East Asia, see Yuko Kikuchi and Yunah Lee, 'Transnational Modern Design Histories in East Asia: An Introduction', *Journal of Design History*, XXVII/4 (2014), pp. 323–34; Yuko Kikuchi, 'Transnationalism for Design History: Knowledge Production and Decolonization through East Asian Design History', in *A Companion to Contemporary Design (since 1945)*, ed. Anne Massey (London, 2019), pp. 75–90; and Haruhiko Fujita and Christine Guth, eds, *Encyclopedia of East Asian Design* (London, 2020).

8 On trans-war continuity, see Andrew Gordon, 'Consumption, Leisure and the Middle Class in Transwar Japan', *Social Science Japan Journal*, X/1 (April 2007), pp. 1–21. See also Kida, 'Kitarō Kunii's Discourse on Indigenous Industrial Arts', pp. 81–3.

9 Dai-gokai Naikoku Kangyō Hakurankai Jimukyoku, ed., *Dai-gokai Naikoku Kangyō Hakurankai shinsa hōkoku, Dai-rokubu-kan no san* (Tokyo, 1904), p. 405.

10 On *mingei* and colonialism see Nishihara Daisuke, 'Kindai Nihon kōgei to shokuminchi', in *Dentō kōgei saikō: Miyako no uchisoto*, ed. Inaga Shigemi (Kyoto, 2007), pp. 360–82; Yuko Kikuchi, *Japanese Modernization and Mingei Theory: Cultural Nationalism and Oriental Orientalism* (London, 2004); and Kim Brandt, *Kingdom of Beauty: Mingei and the Politics of Folk Art in Imperial Japan* (Durham, NC, 2007), pp. 7–37.

11 Brandt, *Kingdom of Beauty*, p. 7.

12 See Chia-Yu [Jiayu] Hu, 'Taiwanese Aboriginal Art and Artifacts: Entangled Images of Colonization and Modernization', in *Refracted*

Modernity: Visual Culture and Identity in Colonial Taiwan, ed. Yuko Kikuchi (Honolulu, HI, 2007), p. 215.

13 On the Japan Peasant Art Institute, see Yamaguchi Mari, Mitsuhashi Toshio and Miyazaki Kiyoshi, 'Yamamoto Kanae no Nihon nōmin bijutsu undō: Taishō Shōwa zenki ni okeru nōson kōgei fukkyō no naihatsusei ni kansuru kenkyū', *Dezaingaku kenkyū*, XLII/2 (1995), pp. 57–64, and Hoyt Long, *On Uneven Ground: Miyazawa Kenji and the Making of Place in Modern Japan* (Palo Alto, CA, 2011), pp. 162–3.

14 See Brandt, *Kingdom of Beauty*, pp. 83–123.

15 On 'Koreana' in Japan, see E. Taylor Atkins, *Primitive Selves: Koreana in the Japanese Colonial Gaze, 1910–1945* (Berkeley, CA, 2010), pp. 93–161. On Taiwanese goods in Japan see Jordan Sand, 'Tropical Furniture and Bodily Comportment in Colonial Asia', *Positions: East Asia Cultures Critique*, XXI/1 (Winter 2012), pp. 95–132.

16 On folklore studies see Marilyn Ivy, *Discourses of the Vanishing: Modernity, Phantasm, Japan* (Chicago, IL, 1995), pp. 66–97. On agricultural fundamentalism see Thomas R. H. Havens, *Farm and Nation in Modern Japan: Agrarian Nationalism, 1870–1940* (Princeton, NJ, 1974). A brief discussion is in Izumi Kuroishi, 'Domesticating Others' Space: Surveys and Reforms of Housing in Chosen and Japan', in *Constructing the Colonized Land: Entwined Perspectives of East Asia around WWII*, ed. Izumi Kuroishi (Farnham, 2014), pp. 223–5.

17 On Kūki, see Leslie Pincus, *Authenticating Culture in Imperial Japan: Kuki Shūzō and the Rise of National Aesthetics* (Berkeley, CA, 1996), and Hiroshi Nara, *The Structure of Detachment: The Aesthetic Vision of Kuki Shuzo* (Honolulu, HI, 2004).

18 There is an extensive literature on research as an aspect of Japanese colonialism. See Thomas David DuBois, 'Local Religion and the Imperial Imaginary: The Development of Japanese Ethnography in Occupied Manchuria', *American Historical Review*, CXI/1 (2006), pp. 52–74. See also Timothy Y. Tsu, 'Japanese Colonialism and the Investigation of Taiwanese "Old Customs"', in *Anthropology and Colonialism in Asia and Oceania*, ed. Jan van Bremen and Akitoshi Shimizu (Richmond, Surrey, 2000), pp. 197–218; Katsumi Nakao, 'Japanese Colonial Policy and Anthropology in Manchuria', in *Anthropology and Colonialism*, ed. van Bremen and Shimizu, pp. 245–65; Ying Xiong, *Representing Empire: Japanese Colonial Literature in Taiwan and Manchuria* (Leiden, 2014), pp. 237–64; Douglas R. Reynolds, 'Training Young China Hands: Tōa Dōbun Shoin and Its Precursors, 1886–1945', in *The Japanese Informal Empire in China, 1895–1937*, ed. Duus, Myers and Peattie, pp. 210–71; and Atkins, *Primitive Selves*, pp. 52–92.

19 On this argument see Yasuhiko Nishikawa, 'A Study of Japanese Colonial Architecture in East Asia', in *Constructing the Colonised Land*, ed. Kuroishi, pp. 11–41. On colonial urbanism in Seoul see Todd A. Henry, *Assimilating Seoul: The Politics of Public Space in Colonial Korea, 1910–45* (Berkeley and Los Angeles, CA, 2014), pp. 22–61.

20 Yongkeun Chun, 'Displayed Modernity: Advertising and Commercial Art in Colonial Korea, 1920–1940', unpublished PhD thesis, Royal College of Art, London, 2019, pp. 65–8.

21 On Japanese colonial ideology and practices see Ramon Hawley Myers and Mark R. Peattie, eds, *The Japanese Colonial Empire, 1895–1945*

(Princeton, NJ, 1984), and Tani E. Barlow, ed., *Formations of Colonial Modernity* (Durham, NC, 1997). On Japanese colonial rule in Korea see Andre Schmid, *Korea Between Empires, 1895–1919* (New York, 2002), and Mark E. Caprio, *Japanese Assimilation Policies in Colonial Korea, 1910–1945* [2009] (Seattle, WA, 2014). On Taiwan see Ping-Hui Liao and David Der-Wei Wang, eds, *Taiwan under Japanese Colonial Rule, 1895–1945: History, Culture, Memory* (New York, 2006).

22 Kyōto Kōtō Kōgei Gakkō, ed., *Kyōto Kōtō Kōgei Gakkō Ichiran* (Kyoto, 1913), pp. 110–28.

23 On commercial exhibitions in colonial period Korea, see Tae-woong Kim, 'Industrial Exhibitions ("Gonjinhoe") and the Political Propaganda of Japanese Imperialism in the 1910s', *International Journal of Korean History*, 3 (December 2002), pp. 179–223; Henry, *Assimilating Seoul*, pp. 92–129; and Hong Kal, *Aesthetic Constructions of Korean Nationalism: Spectacle, Politics and History* (London, 2011), pp. 34–52.

24 Zenra Hokudō, ed., *Zenra Hokudō yōran* (Zenshū [Jeonju], 1928), pp. 136–7.

25 Chōsen Sōtokufu Shōkō Shōreikan, *Chōsen no bussan* (Keijō [Seoul], 1935), pp. 107–8.

26 'Taipei ni shōhin chinretsujo', *Tōyō jihō*, 215 (August 1916), p. 61. On exhibitions in colonial Taiwan, see Lu Shao-Li, *Zhǎnshì Táiwān: Quánlì, kōngjiān yǔ zhímín tǒngzhì de xíngxiàng biǎo* (Taipei, 2011). See also Wen-Chi Chuang and Shang-Chia Chiou, 'Interior Design during Japanese Colonial Rule in Taiwan', conference proceedings, International Association of Societies of Design Research 2009, Seoul (Seoul, 2009), pp. 1997–2008, www.iasdr2009.or.kr, accessed 4 September 2020.

27 Kunii Kitarō, 'Yushutsu-muke kōgeihin tenjikai no seiseki ni kagamite', *Kōgei nyūsu*, I/5 (October 1932), p. 1.

28 'Kōgei shidōsho shohō', *Kōgei nyūsu*, II/3 (March 1933), p. 18.

29 They were to remain largely agricultural, supporting the Japanese mainland to industrialize by supplying rice, sugar and other food commodities. See Samuel Pao-San Ho, 'Colonialism and Development: Korea, Taiwan, and Kwantung', in *The Japanese Colonial Empire, 1895–1945*, ed. Myers and Peattie, pp. 349–50. This changed in the 1930s in Korea, as the Japanese government began encouraging Japanese conglomerates' investment in heavy industry; rapid urbanization and a shift from agriculture to factory, mining and construction work ensued. See Soo-Won Park, *Colonial Industrialization and Labor in Korea: The Onoda Cement Factory* (Cambridge, MA, 1999), and Soo-Won Park, 'Colonial Industrial Growth and the Working Class', in *Colonial Modernity in Korea*, ed. Gi-Wook Shin and Michael Robinson (Cambridge, MA, 1999), pp. 128–60.

30 Park Mijeong, 'Shokuminchi Chōsen no kōgei to Nihon: "sangyō seisaku" to "Ajia no kodai bunmei" e no kokoromi', in *Dentō kōgei saikō*, ed. Inaga, pp. 383–409.

31 On the industrial training centre in Seoul see ibid., pp. 384–5.

32 Yuko Kikuchi, 'Refracted Colonial Modernity: Vernacularism in the Development of Modern Taiwanese Crafts', in Kikuchi, *Refracted Modernity*, pp. 219–20 and 230. A summary of Japanese economic and industrial policy in colonial Taiwan is Ramon H. Myers and Tai-chun Kuo, *Taiwan's Economic Transformation: Leadership, Property Rights and Institutional Change, 1949–1965* (London, 2011), pp. 21–8.

33 Taiwan Sōtokufu Bunkyōkyoku, *Taiwan no kyōiku* (Taipei, 1933), p. 45. Striped cottons are in Dai-gokai Naikoku Kangyō Hakurankai Jimukyoku, ed., *Dai-gokai Naikoku Kangyō Hakurankai shinsa hōkoku, Dai-rokubu-kan no san* (VI/3), p. 405.

34 On Taiwanese bamboo and rattan see Kikuchi, *Japanese Modernisation and Mingei Theory*, pp. 163–89, and Sand, 'Tropical Furniture and Bodily Comportment', pp. 95–132. On *mingei* activists' promotion of Korean goods to Japanese consumers, see Brandt, *Kingdom of Beauty*, pp. 173–222.

35 Chuang and Chiou, 'Interior Design during Japanese Colonial Rule in Taiwan', p. 2006.

36 Kikuchi, 'Refracted Colonial Modernity', pp. 231 and 237–43. For craft design in Taiwan today see the work of the National Craft Research and Development Institute, www.ntcri.gov.tw, accessed 30 October 2020.

37 Moli Hou, Kenta Ono and Makoto Watanabe, 'Curriculum Contents of Higher Design Educations in Japan and Taiwan', *Dezaingaku kenkyū*, LVII/1 (2010), p. 17. Chuang and Chiou, 'Interior Design during Japanese Colonial Rule in Taiwan', suggest that this occurred in 1900 (p. 2003).

38 For the demographic breakdown of enrolled students and graduates at the Higher Industrial School in Taipei see *Taiwan no kyōiku*, p. 42. On design education in schools in colonial Korea see Jung Woosuk, 'Kankoku ni okeru Chōsen shokuminchiki zenki (1910–1922) no zuga kyōkasho ni mirareru dezainteki yōso', *Gakkō kyōikugaku kenkyū ronshū*, 6 (2002), pp. 117–30, and Jung Woosuk, 'Chōsen ni okeru Nikkan gappeiki chūki (1922–1938) no zuga kyōkasho ni mirareru dezainteki yōso', *Nihon bijutsu kyōiku kenkyū kiyō*, 35 (2002), pp. 11–22.

39 On status differences between Japanese citizens in colonies and colonial subjects see Jun Uchida, *Brokers of Empire: Japanese Settler Colonialism in Korea, 1876–1945* (Cambridge, MA, 2014).

40 Kyōto Kōtō Kōgei Gakkō, ed., *Kyōto Kōtō Kōgei Gakkō Ichiran*, pp. 104–5. On Chinese illustrators and book designers in Japan during the Republican era, see Iei Riku [Lu Weirong], *Chūgoku no kindai bijutsu to Nihon: 20-seiki nitchū kankei no ichi danmen* (Okayama, 2007), pp. 153–98.

41 Yue Wu, 'Chūka minkokuki ni okeru Nicchū kindai dezain no kōryū to hensen: Chen Zhifo ni itaru made', *Kyōto Seika Daigaku kiyō*, 53 (2000), pp. 266, 273. There is a growing literature in Chinese on Chen Zhifo's design work. In English, see Daniel Sze-Hin Ho, 'Graphic Design in Republican Shanghai: A Preliminary Study', unpublished PhD dissertation, McGill University, 2005, pp. 53–6. On Japanese design educators in Republican China, see Tomizawa Yoshia, 'Kindai Chūgoku ni okeru kōgyō kyōiku to bōshoku gijutsusha no yōsei', *Keizai-shi kenkyū*, XX (2017), p. 78.

42 Ibid., pp. 273–4. On students from other Asian countries at the Tokyo School of Fine Art, see Yoshida Chizuko, *Kindai higashi ajia bijutsu ryūgakusei no kenkyū: Tōkyō Bijutsu Gakkō ryūgakusei shiryō* (Tokyo, 2009).

43 For Chen's trajectory following his return to China in 1925, see Yue, 'Chūka minkokuki ni okeru Nicchū kindai dezain no kōryū to hensen', pp. 274–80, and Ho, *Graphic Design in Republican Shanghai*, pp. 56–62.

44 'Yi Changbong, *Joshibi no rekishi*, vol. II, p. 24. On Korean students at the Girls' Art School and Tokyo Women's Higher Normal School, see Park Soo-hyun, 'Joshi Bijutsu Gakkō ni okeru senzen no Chōsen ryūgakusei: Shishūka sotsugyōsei o chūshin ni', *Joshi Bijutsu Daigaku kenkyū kiyō*, 35

(2005), pp. 42–9. On Chinese students at the Girls' Art School, see Zhou Yichuan, 'Chūgokokujin joshi ryūgakusei o ukeireta watakushiritsu sankō ni tsuite: Minkoku shoki o chūshin ni', *Shigaku*, LXVIII/3–4 (1999), pp. 285–327.

45 'Honsho rokuji', *Kōgei nyūsu* (March 1932), p. 20.

46 Barlow, *Formations of Colonial Modernity*, and Giwook Shin and Michael Robinson, eds, *Colonial Modernity in Korea* (Cambridge, MA, 1997). For the historiography of colonial modernity, see Hyunjung Lee and Younghan Cho, 'Introduction: Colonial Modernity and Beyond in East Asian Contexts', *Cultural Studies*, XXVI/5 (September 2012), pp. 601–16.

47 Chuang and Chiou, 'Interior Design during Japanese Colonial Rule in Taiwan', p. 2004, and Chun, 'Displayed Modernity'.

48 For this argument, see Chun, 'Displayed Modernity'.

49 On contracts for visual promotion graphics in 1930s Taiwan see Lin Pin-Chang, 'Shisei yonjūshunen kinen Taiwan hakurankai: Taiwan shikaku dentatsu dezainshi kenkyū (4)', *Dezaingaku kenkyū*, XLVII/4 (2000), p. 85, and Lin Pin-Chang, 'Nihon tōji jiki no taikei gyōji ni miru shikaku dentatsu dezain: Taiwan shikaku dentatsu dezainshi kenkyū (5)', *Dezaingaku kenkyū*, XLVIII/1 (2001), pp. 93–102.

50 On Mantetsu's visual communication strategy, see Kishi Toshihiko, *Manshūkoku no bijuaru media: posutā, ehagaki, kitte* (Tokyo, 2010).

51 See Nakamura Shunichirō, 'Manshū fūzoku o egaita maboroshi no gaka: Itō Junzō to Mantetsu posutā', in *Chōkyō suru Nihonjin*, pp. 115–16.

52 Itō Junzō, *Teien no haru* [Spring in the Garden], colour on paper, hanging scroll, student work for the Tokyo School of Fine Art, 1913, The University Art Museum, Tokyo University of the Arts, accession number 298.

53 On Japanese male artists' and photographers' imagery of Manchurian women, see Ikeda Shinobu, 'Imperial Desire and Female Subjectivity: Umehara Ryūzaburō's Kunyan Series', trans. Ignacio Adriasola, *Ars Orientalis*, XLVII (2017), doi.org/10.3998/ars.13441566.0047.011.

54 See also Rika Hiro, 'Japan in the Age of Commercialism, Imperialism, and Modernism', online exh. cat., USC Libraries (University of Southern California), Los Angeles (2020), https://scalar.usc.edu, accessed 3 November 2020.

55 The Kwantung Army originated in 1906 as the security force for the Kwantung Leased Territory and South Manchurian Railway Zone. It was known for its senior leaders' embrace of fascist, expansionist ideology and actions. On Manchukuo see Louise Young, *Japan's Total Empire: Manchuria and the Culture of Wartime Imperialism* (Berkeley, CA, 1999), and Prasenjit Duara, *Sovereignty and Authenticity: Manchukuo and the East Asian Modern* (Lanham, MD, 2004). On Japanese imperialism in Manchuria until 1931, including the role of the SMRC, see Yoshihisa Tak Matsusaka, *The Making of Japanese Manchuria, 1904–1932* (Cambridge, MA, 2003).

56 There is a large literature on Mantetsu. See Y. Tak Matsusaka, 'Japan's South Manchuria Railway Company in Northeast China, 1906–34', in *Manchurian Railways and the Opening of China: An International History*, ed. Bruce A. Ellerman and Stephen Kotkin (Armonk, NY, 2010), pp. 37–58. and Ramon H. Myers, 'Japanese Imperialism in Manchuria: The South Manchuria Railway Company, 1906–1933', in *The Japanese Informal Empire in China*, ed. Duus, Myers and Peattie, pp. 101–13.

57 For this argument see Young, *Japan's Total Empire*, pp. 241–303, and Koshizawa Akira, *Manshūkoku no shuto keikaku: Tōkyō no genzai to shōrai o tou* (Tokyo, 1988).

58 Young, *Japan's Total Empire*, p. 245. On Japanese architecture and urban planning in Manchuria see also David Tucker, 'City Planning without Cities: Order and Chaos in Utopian Manchukuo', in *Crossed Histories: Manchuria in the Age of Empire*, ed. Mariko Tamanoi (Ann Arbor, MI, 2005), pp. 53–81; Anke Scherer, 'The Colonial Appropriaton of Public Space: Architecture and City Planning in Japanese-Dominated Manchuria', in *Urban Spaces in Japan: Cultural and Social Perspectives*, ed. Christoph Brumann and Evelyn Schulz (Abingdon, 2012), pp. 37–52; and Edward Denison and Guangyu Ren, *Ultra-Modernism: Architecture and Modernity in Manchuria* (Hong Kong, 2016).

59 Xiong, *Representing Empire*, pp. 246–53, shows how planning in Manchuria drew on Government-General experiences in Taiwan.

60 On tourism see Young, *Japan's Total Empire*, pp. 259–68, and Kenneth James Ruoff, *Imperial Japan at Its Zenith: The Wartime Celebration of the Empire's 2,600th Anniversary* (Ithaca, NY, 2010), pp. 82–147.

61 On the Ajia-gō see Amano Hiroyuki, *Mantetsu tokkyū 'Ajia' no tanjō: Kaihatsu zenya kara shūen made no zenbō* (Tokyo, 2012), and Young, *Japan's Total Empire*, pp. 246–7.

62 Several issues in 1935 of the popular science magazine *Kagaku to mokei* (Science and Models) included instructions for building models of the Asia Express. On the promotion of rail-based travel in Manchuria, see Yoshinobu Oikawa, Andrew Elliott and Daniel Milne, 'National Rail and Tourism from the Russo-Japanese War to the Asia-Pacific War: The Rise and Fall of a Business Approach to Rail Management', *Japan Review*, XXXIII (2019), pp. 87–116.

63 On avant-garde intellectuals' dissemination of images of Manchuria as modernist, see Annika A. Culver, *Glorify the Empire: Japanese Avant-Garde Propaganda in Manchukuo* (Vancouver, 2013), pp. 76–99.

64 Andrew Gordon, *A Modern History of Japan: From Tokugawa Times to the Present*, 4th edn (Oxford, 2003), p. 192, and Morris Low, 'Introduction', in *Building a Modern Japan: Science, Technology, and Medicine in the Meiji Era and Beyond*, ed. Morris Low (Farnham, 2005), p. 8.

65 On U.S. consumers' and manufacturers' attitudes towards Japanese silk in the 1930s see Lawrence B. Glickman, '"Make Lisle the Style": The Politics of Fashion in the Japanese Silk Boycott, 1937–1940', *Journal of Social History*, XXXVIII/3 (Spring 2005), pp. 573–608.

66 On the response of IARI head Kunii Kitarō to the fall in exports, see Kida, 'Kitaro Kunii's Discourse on Indigenous Industrial Arts', pp. 58–66.

67 'Atarashiku baishutsu subeki honpōhin no kōsatsu', *Kōgei nyūsu*, 1/4 (September 1932), p. 14.

68 There is a large literature on relationships between modernist architects in Japan, Europe and North America. See Ken Tadashi Oshima, *International Architecture in Interwar Japan: Constructing Kokusai Kenchiku* (Seattle, WA, 2009).

69 On NIPPON, see Shirayama Mari and Hori Yoshio, eds, *Natori Yōnosuke to Nippon Kōbō 1931–45* (Tokyo, 2006); Gennifer S. Weisenfeld, 'Touring "Japan-as-Museum": NIPPON and Other Japanese Imperialist Travelogues', *Positions: East Asia Cultures Critique*, VIII/3 (2000),

pp. 747–93; and Barak Kushner, *Japan's Thought War* (Honolulu, HI, 2006), pp. 75–6.

70 Tsuda Shingo, 'Nippon zuikan', NIPPON, Japanese edition (December 1936), cited in Shirayama and Hori, eds, *Natori Yōnosuke to Nippon Kōbō*, pp. 6 and 10.

71 On this point see also Kushner, *Japan's Thought War*, p. 11.

72 Shirayama and Hori, eds, *Natori Yōnosuke to Nippon Kōbō*, p. 13. See also Andrew Elliott, '"Orient Calls": Anglophone Travel Writing and Tourism as Propaganda during the Second Sino-Japanese War, 1937–1941', *Japan Review*, 33 (2019), pp. 117–42.

73 On images of health, industry, nature and culture in European modernism see Christopher Wilk, ed., *Modernism: Designing a New World, 1914–1939* (London, 2006).

74 Yamana Ayao, 'Kappan bijutsu zakkō', *Kōkokukai* (January 1936), cited in Shirayama and Hori, eds, *Natori Yōnosuke to Nippon Kōbō*, p. 18.

75 Gennifer Weisenfeld, 'Japanese Typographic Design and the Art of Letterforms', in *Bridges to Heaven: Essays on East Asian Art in Honour of Professor Wen C. Fong* (Princeton, NJ, 2011), pp. 827–48.

76 Natori's photographs are in Kokusai Bunka Shinkōkai, ed., *Japanische Gebrauchsgegenstaende* (Tokyo, 1938). Kida Takuya has noted that the selection of objects – historical items for Berlin, vs everyday objects made with local materials for Leipzig – prompted debate among organizers. See Kida, 'Kitaro Kunii's Discourse on Indigenous Industrial Arts', pp. 76–7.

77 On late 1930s exhibition design see Kawahata Naomichi, 'Kokusaku senden ni okeru datsu-shogyobijutsu no nagare', in *Shikaku no Shōwa: 1930–40-nendai*, exh. cat., Matsudo City Museum (Matsudo, 1998), pp. 143–9, and Gennifer Weisenfeld, 'Publicity and Propaganda in 1930s Japan: Modernism as Method', *Design Issues*, XXV/4 (2009), pp. 13–28.

78 Shirayama and Hori, eds, *Natori Yōnosuke to Nippon Kōbō*, p. 108.

79 Ibid., p. 68. On the photowall see Weisenfeld, 'Publicity and Propaganda in 1930s Japan', pp. 23–8, and Yamamoto Sae, '1940-nen Nyū Yōku banpaku ni shuppin sareta shashin hanga *Nihon sangyō* ni miru 'hōdō shashin no eikyō', *Dezaingaku kenkyū*, LVI/2 (2009), pp. 63–72.

80 'Imaizumi Takeji', in *Kikigaki dezain shi*, ed. Tanaka, p. 24.

81 On movement between commercial advertising and war propaganda work during and after the war, see also Kushner, *Japan's Thought War*, pp. 68–71 and 76–7, and the work of Gennifer Weisenfeld cited in this chapter.

82 Tōkyō Hyakunenshi Henshū Iinkai, ed., *Tōkyō hyakunenshi* (Tokyo, 1979), vol. V, p. 271, cited in Elise Tipton, 'The Café: Contested Space of Space of Modernity in Interwar Japan', in *Being Modern in Japan*, p. 122.

83 Chun, 'Displayed Modernity'.

84 Lin, 'Nihon tōji jiki no taikei gyōji ni miru shikaku dentatsu dezain', pp. 999–1000.

85 Lin, 'Shisei yonjūshunen kinen Taiwan hakurankai', p. 85.

86 A useful summary of colonial economic policy is Samuel Pao-San Ho, 'Colonialism and Development: Korea, Taiwan and Kwantung', in *The Japanese Colonial Empire*, ed. Myers, Peattie and Zhen, pp. 347–99.

87 On rural consumption in the 1930s, see Penelope Francks, *The Japanese Consumer: An Alternative Economic History of Modern Japan* (Cambridge,

2009), pp. 265–8. Two excellent accounts of rural life in the 1930s are Simon Partner, *Toshie: A Story of Village Life in Twentieth-Century Japan* (Berkeley, CA, 2004), pp. 35–63, and Kerry Smith, *A Time of Crisis: Japan, the Great Depression, and Rural Revitalization* (Cambridge, MA, 2001).

88 Partner, *Toshie*, p. 167.

89 On the Rural Economic Rehabilitation Campaign see Smith, *A Time of Crisis*, pp. 203–68.

90 On campaigns to encourage rural Japanese migration to Manchuria see Young, *Japan's Total Empire*, pp. 307–411; Sandra Wilson, 'Security, Prosperity and Serving the Nation: Japanese Famers and Manchuria, 1931–33', in *Farmers and Village Life in Twentieth-Century Japan*, ed. Ann Waswo and Yoshiaki Nishida (London, 2003), pp. 156–74; and Takemaro Mori, 'Colonies and Countryside in Wartime Japan', in *Farmers and Village Life in Twentieth-Century Japan*, ed. Nishiaki and Waswo, pp. 175–98.

91 On the rural reform housing-design project, see Kuroishi Izumi, *Kenchikugai no shisō: Kon Wajirō ron* (Tokyo, 2000), pp. 288–98.

92 'Sharurotto Perian [Charlotte Perriand] to Nihon' Kenkyūkai, ed., *Sharurotto Perian [Charlotte Perriand] to Nihon*, exh. cat., Museum of Modern Art, Kamakura and Hayama; Hiroshima City Museum of Contemporary Art; and Meguro Museum of Art, Tokyo (Tokyo, 2011), p. 82.

93 See Ōtomo Gisuke, *Sharurotto Perian [Charlotte Perriand] to Setsugai Chōsajo* (Shinjō, 2001).

94 The exhibition catalogue is Sharurotto Perian [Charlotte Perriand], *Sentaku, Dentō, Sōzō: Nihon geijutsu to no sesshoku*, trans. Sakakura Junzō (Tokyo, 1941). The exhibition has been extensively discussed. See Yuko Kikuchi, 'Modern Design and the Politics of Bamboo: Charlotte Perriand and Her Exhibition *Selection, Tradition, Creation* in Japan (1941)', in *Charlotte Perriand: Inventing a New World*, ed. Jacques Barsac, Sébastien Cherruet and Pernette Perriand, exh. cat., Fondation Louis Vuitton, Paris (Paris, 2019), pp. 273–307, and 'Sharurotto Perian to Nihon' Kenkyūkai, ed., *Sharurotto Perian to Nihon*, pp. 100–109 and 128. On Perriand in Japan, see also Tsuchida Maki, '1930 nendai no kōgei to "dentō": uchi kara to soto kara', in *Dentō kōgei saikō*, ed. Inaga, pp. 88–106.

95 Japanese designers' critiques of Perriand are in 'Kōgei zadankai ki: Perian [Perriand] joshi sōsakuhin-ten ni tsuite kiku 1', *Kōgei nyūsu*, X/5, pp. 11–17, and 'Kōgei zadankai ki: Perian [Perriand] joshi sōsakuhin-ten ni tsuite kiku 2', *Kōgei nyūsu*, X/6 (1941), pp. 34–6. In English, see Brandt, *Kingdom of Beauty*, p. 134, and Kida, 'Kitaro Kunii's Discourse on Indigenous Industrial Arts', pp. 70–74 and 78.

96 Gordon, *A Modern History of Japan*, p. 193.

97 Ibid., p. 212, Gordon's translations.

98 'Naigai kōgei sangyō jōhō', *Kōgei nyūsu*, VII/8 (August 1938), p. 41.

99 'Naigai kōgei sangyō jihō: Busshi chōsei', *Kōgei nyūsu*, VII/8 (August 1938), pp. 36–7, and 'Naigai kōgei sangyō jihō: Busshi tōsei', *Kōgei nyūsu*, VII/9 (September 1938), pp. 36–8.

100 'Kessenshita ni okeru kōgei gijutsu no tenkatsuyō: Aizu, Niigata, Takaoka o shisatsu shite', *Kōgei shidō*, XII/8 (September 1943), pp. 39–41.

101 On war work at Maruni Mokkō see the company history, Sōgyō 50 nenshi henshū iinkai, ed., *Sōgyō 50 nenshi: Yōkagu to tomo ni ayunda hanseiki* (Hiroshima, 1982).

102 'Kōgei shidōsho shohō: Mokusei kitai buhin shisakuhin shinsa kaigi', *Kōgei shidō*, XIII/5–6 (May–June 1944), p. 27, and '"Ikki demo ōku": Honjo ni okeru kita buhin mokuseika sokushin kyōgikai', *Kogei shidō*, XIII/2 (February 1944), p. 1. See also the official secondment of IARI employees to the government agency in charge of air force munitions in June 1944 in 'Kōgei shidōsho shohō: Jinji', *Kōgei shidō*, XIII/5–6 (May–June 1944), p. 28.

103 'Ecchu tokusan washi de hikaku daiyō o kenkyū', *Kōgei nyūsu*, VII/8 (August 1938), p. 40; 'Umihebi mo daiyō hikaku ni Shizuoka-ken de kenkyū-chū', *Kōgei nyūsu*, VII/8 (August 1938), p. 40. On shagreen's historic use in Japan see Christine Guth, 'The Aesthetics of Rayskin in Edo-Period Japan: Materials, Making and Meaning', *Impressions*, 37 (2016), pp. 88–105.

104 Suzuki Yaichi, 'Gunyō juhin ni tsuite', *Kogei nyūsu*, XI/4 (April 1942), pp. 16–18.

105 Kunii Kitarō, 'Jikyokuka ni okeru kōgeihin seisaku no mokuhyō', *Kōgei nyūsu*, VI/9 (September 1938), p. 1.

106 'Chūnanbei ni hōhin no juyō zōdai', *Kōgei nyūsu*, X/1 (January 1941), p. 36.

107 Kunii Kitarō, 'Zuan gijutsukan no sekimu', *Kōgei nyūsu*, VII/11–12 (November–December 1938), p. 1.

108 Kikuchi, 'Refracted Colonial Modernity', pp. 232–4.

109 'Dai nikai Chōsen yūshutsu kōgeihin tenrankai', *Kōgei nyūsu*, X/1, p. 24.

110 'Naigai kōgei sangyō jōhō', *Kōgei nyūsu*, VII/9 (September 1938), pp. 38–9.

111 Ibid.

112 'Shurēman [Schloemann] fujin no raichō to naichi shisatsu ryokō', *Kōgei nyūsu*, VIII/12 (December 1939), p. 8.

113 'Kōgei shidō nikki: Sendai Honjo', *Kōgei nyūsu*, X/1 (January 1941), p. 36.

114 'Tōsei: Nichiyōhin no kotei kakaku settei', *Kōgei nyūsu*, X/1 (January 1941), p. 37.

115 'Shōhin no tanjunka kikaku tōitsu ni hōteki kyōsei no hōshin', *Kogei nyusu*, VII/9 (September 1938), p. 38. One lasting effect was the expansion of Japanese Engineering Standards (JES), or 'Japan standardized standards' in Japanese (*Nihon hyojun kikaku*). The JES was the predecessor to the Japan Industrial Standards (JIS), enforced by law in 1949.

116 'Hyakkaten no shinseikatsu yōshiki kenkyū', *Kōgei nyūsu*, X/9 (September 1941), p. 42.

117 One critique of standardized new products as leading to wastefulness is 'Osaka ni okeru kokumin seikatsu sasshin to seikatsu yōhin kaizen zadankai', *Kōgei nyūsu*, XI/1 (January 1942), p. 27.

118 Kansai Shibu, 'Kansai chihō ippan jōhō', *Kōgei nyūsu*, X/1 (January 1941), p. 42.

119 Ibid.

120 See for example Kashiwagi, 'On Rationalization and the National Lifestyle'.

121 'Shōkōshō shūsai Dai Nikai Kokumin Seikatsu Yōhin Ten gaikyō', *Kōgei shidō*, XII/4 (May 1943), p. 12.

122 'Senji kikaku to gigeijutsu hōzon', *Kōgei nyūsu*, XII/2 (March 1943), p. 9.

123 The exhibition was supported by the Housing Association, the IARI, the central price control board and wartime industry associations for furniture, ceramics and lacquerware. See Nishiyama Uzō, 'Tenbō: Jūtaku Eidan kenkyū-bu', *Kenchiku zasshi*, LVI/10 (October 1942), p. 790, and

Ichiura Ken, 'Jūtaku Eidan no zenbō', *Kenchiku zasshi*, LVII/9 (September 1943), pp. 614–18.

124 One commentary on the changing status of *monpe* is Watanabe Tokutaro, 'Monpe', *Kōgei nyūsu*, XIII/1 (January 1944), pp. 33–6. On *monpe* as women's wartime wear see Murakami Masako, 'Takaga monpe, saredomo monpe – senjika fukusō ikkōsatsu', in *Sensō to josei zasshi*, ed. Kindai Josei Bunka Kenkyūkai (Tokyo, 2001), pp. 255–80.

125 Kawahata, 'Kokusaku senden ni okeru datsu-shogyobijutsu no nagare', p. 148.

126 Ibid., p. 146. See also Yamana Ayao, *Taikenteki dezain-shi* (Tokyo, 1976), pp. 138–45.

127 The organization originated as the All-Japan Commercial Art Alliance (Zen Nihon Shōgyō Bijutsu Renmei). It became the All-Japan Industrial Art Alliance (Zen Nihon Sangyō Bijutsu Renmei) in 1938.

128 'Imaizumi Takeji', in *Kikigaki dezainshi*, ed. Tanaka, pp. 21–2.

129 Kawahata, 'Kokusaku senden ni okeru datsu shōgyō bijutsu no nagare', p. 148 n. 2.

130 'Imaizumi Takeji', in *Kikigaki dezainshi*, ed. Tanaka, p. 22. See also Tagawa Seiichi, *Sensō no gurafizumu: 'Front' o tsukutta hitobito* (Tokyo, 2000), and, in English, the recollections of designer Nakai Kōichi in Kōichi Nakai, 'A Testimony from the Post-War Period (2008)', trans. Kim McNally, *Review of Japanese Culture and Society*, XXVIII (December 2016), pp. 118–19.

131 These are the standard English-language names for these groups, although they translate *hōdō* differently. On the Propaganda Art Association, see Kawahata, 'Kokusaku senden ni okeru datsu shōgyō bijutsu no nagare', p. 148 n. 2. On the Hōdō Gijutsu Kenkyūkai, see Yamana, *Taikenteki dezain-shi*, pp. 266–323, and Kushner, *Japan's Thought War*, pp. 68–73.

132 'Imaizumi Takeji', in *Kikigaki dezainshi*, ed. Tanaka, p. 24. On montage theory in Japanese cinema see Chika Kinoshita, 'The Edge of Montage: A Case of Modernism/*Modanizumu* in Japanese Cinema', in *The Oxford Handbook of Japanese Cinema*, ed. Daisuke Miyao (Oxford, 2013), pp. 124–51.

133 A summary history of *Kōkokukai* is Namba (Nanba) Kōji, 'Shōwa zenki no kōkokukai: Zasshi *Kōkokukai* ni miru hito to sangyō', *Ad Studies*, XXI (2007), pp. 25–9. On *Kōkokukai* and propaganda, see also Kushner, *Japan's Thought War*, p. 76.

134 This was known as *hōdō gijutsu* (reportage techniques) or *hōdō bijutsu* (reportage art). Tsukada Isamu, 'Hōdō bijutsu no honshitsu', *Kōkokukai*, XVIII/7 (July 1941), cited in Kawahata, 'Kokusaku senden ni okeru datsu shōgyō bijutsu no nagare', p. 145.

135 Kawahata, 'Kokusaku senden ni okeru datsu shōgyō bijutsu no nagare', pp. 144–5.

136 Imaizumi Takeji', in *Kikigaki dezainshi*, ed. Tanaka, p. 22.

137 Ibid., p. 25.

138 Akiko Moriyama, 'Shirīzu shōgen: Kōno Takashi', *Nikkei dezain* (October 1987), pp. 50–51. Kōno spent two years in a prisoner of war camp in Indonesia, returning to Japan in 1947. On the design work of the Propaganda Department in Indonesia, see Lintang Dewi Prasistiya and Donna Carollina, 'Tinjauan Makna Pada Label Korek Api Propaganda Jepang Di Indonesia Tahun 1942–1945', *Aksa: Jurnal Desain Komunikasi Visual*, 3 (2020), pp. 341–55. On the Propaganda Department more

generally, see Aiko Kurasawa, 'Propaganda Media on Java under the Japanese', *Indonesia*, 44 (1987), pp. 59–116.

139 'Ōhashi Tadashi', in *Kikigaki dezainshi*, ed. Tanaka, p. 102.

140 'Nanpō kōgei tokubetsu ten kan yori', *Kōgei nyūsu*, XI/4 (April 1942), pp. 24–5, and 'Naigai kōgei sangyō jōhō', *Kogei nyusu*, XII/8 (September 1943), pp. 46–8.

141 Osaka Kansai Shisho, 'Kansai chihō ippan jōhō', *Kōgei nyūsu*, XI/2 (February 1942), p. 39.

142 Koike's travel diary is in Koike Shinji, *Hanmi keikaku* (Tokyo, 1943), pp. 289–316.

143 Koike Shinji, 'Shina kōgei bunka no genjō', *Kōgei nyūsu*, XI/6 (June 1942), pp. 10–17.

144 Kikuchi, '*Tōyō shumi* of household products designed in Imperial Japan of Manchukuo and Taiwan', pp. 3–8, explores the motivations for Japanese designers' and craft promoters' engagement with China and Taiwan. See also Yasuko Suga, 'Crafting a Bridge between China and Japan: Jiyu Gakuen Beijing School 1938–1945', in *Translating and Writing Modern Design Histories in East Asia for the Global World* (Yunlin, 2013), n.p.

145 Shirayama and Hori, eds, *Natori Yōnosuke to Nippon Kōbō*, p. 127.

146 Tagawa, *Sensō no gurafizumu*, pp. 104–7 and 120.

147 The Chinese- and Burmese-language publications were hand-lettered, the others typeset, with the Mongolian type coming from a printer in Harbin, in Manchuria. Tagawa, *Sensō no gurafizumu*, pp. 131 and 317.

148 Ibid., pp. 104–7.

149 The paper, issued by the Imperial Navy, was 500 grams in weight and at A3 size inappropriate for distribution by air. Ibid., p. 116. Noted also in Kushner, *The Thought War*, p. 75.

150 Tagawa, *Sensō no gurafizumu*, pp. 63 and 94.

151 Ibid., p. 139.

152 Shirayama and Hori, eds, *Natori Yōnosuke to Nippon Kōbō*, p. 139.

153 Author interview with Takayabu Akira, December 2012. See also Tagawa, *Sensō no gurafizumu*, pp. 327–8.

154 Yamana, *Taikenteki dezain-shi*, p. 320.

155 'Ohashi Tadashi', in *Kikigaki dezainshi*, ed. Tanaka, pp. 105–6.

156 Lori Watt, *When Empire Comes Home: Repatriation and Reintegration in Postwar Japan* (Cambridge, MA, 2010), p. 2.

157 On life in the immediate post-war period, see John W. Dower, *Embracing Defeat: Japan in the Aftermath of World War II* (London and New York, 2000), pp. 87–120.

158 Koizumi Kazuko, Uchida Seizō and Takayabu Akira, *Teiryōgun jūgaku no kiroku jō: Nihon no seikatsu sutairu no genten to natta dependent hausu* (Tokyo, 1999), p. 120.

159 A. T. Steele, 'Packed Japan Grows Again Million a Year', *Washington Post*, 5 June 1947, p. 10.

160 'Nishijin saishō nenpyō', https://nishijin.or.jp, accessed 5 November 2020.

161 Herrymon Maurer, 'The U.S. Does a Job', *Fortune*, XXXV/3 (March 1947) pp. 179–80.

162 Toyota Jidōsha Kabushiki Kaisha, *Toyota: A History of the First 50 Years* (Toyota, 1988) p. 95.

163 Tendō Mokkō, *Kindai dezain nenpyō; Tendō Mokkō gojūnen-shi* (Tendō, 1993), pp. 143 and 147.

164 Tagawa, *Sensō no gurafizumu*, p. 292.

165 Iijima Minoru, '"Nippon Kobo" sōsetsu kara "Kokusai Hōdō Kōgei" kaisan made', in *Sakigake no seishun* (Tokyo, 1980), cited in Shirayama and Hori, eds, *Natori Yōnosuke to Nippon Kōbō*, p. 170.

166 Dower, *Embracing Defeat*, pp. 180–82.

167 Tagawa, *Sensō no gurafizumu*, p. 294.

168 Ibid., p. 295.

169 On export processes and protocols see *Kōgei nyūsu*, XV/2 (February–March 1947).

170 Gordon, *A Modern History of Japan*, pp. 240–41.

171 'Ōsaka no zakka', *Kōgei nyūsu*, XVII/7 (July 1949), p. 26.

172 Ibid., p. 25. Of the 125.2 million yen total export sales in electric fans, the top five markets were Thailand (37.3 million yen), Hong Kong (35.5 million yen), Iran (11.8 million yen), Ceylon (8.5 million yen) and Brazil (4.8 million yen).

173 Ray Cromley, 'Oriental Smugglers: Their Business Booms; Junks Ply Seven-Way Trade in Goods, People', *Wall Street Journal*, 20 June 1947, p. 2.

174 Shōkōshō Bōekichō and Shōkōshō Kōgei Shidōsho, eds, *Yushutsumuke kōgeihin sankō shiryō* (Tokyo, 1946), p. 49.

175 'Mibōjin ni yushutsu kōgeihin no naishoku', *Ehime Shimbun*, 14 October 1949, p. 2.

176 Shōkōshō Boekichō and Shōkōshō Kōgei Shidōsho, eds, *Yushutsumuke kōgeihin sankō shiryō*.

177 Joseph Alsop, 'Matter of Fact: Future of Japan', *Washington Post*, 23 October 1953, p. 25, and Philip Potter, 'Red Asian Trade Tempts Japanese', *Los Angeles Times*, 30 April 1952, p. 12.

178 Saitō Nobuharu, 'Sensaigo ichinenkan no kiroku', *Kōgei nyūsu*, XIV/1 (June 1946), p. 3.

179 'Zadankai: Yushutsu no kōgei ha dō suru ka 1', *Kōgei nyūsu*, XVII/6 (June 1949), p. 21.

180 Saitō, 'Sensaigo ichinenkan no kiroku', p. 3.

181 'Zadankai: Yushutsu no kōgei ha dō suru ka 1', p. 21.

182 Kōgei Shidōsho Sekkeibu, 'Yushutsu kōgeihin sekkei shiryō chōsa ni tsuite', *Kōgei nyūsu*, XIV/1 (June 1946), n.p.

183 Shōkōshō Bōekichō and Shōkōshō Kōgei Shidōsho, eds, *Yushutsumuke kōgeihin sankō shiryō*, pp. 1 and 50.

184 Toyoguchi Katsuhei, 'Yushutsu kōgeihin no sekkei kikaku', *Kōgei nyūsu*, XIV/1 (June 1946) pp. 7–8.

185 U.S. National Archives, Washington, DC, record group 331, box 5332, folder 7, 'Branch – Shinjuku – Reports'.

186 'Zadankai: Yushutsu no kōgei ha dō suru ka 2', *Kōgei nyūsu*, XVII/7 (July 1949), p. 30.

187 Toyoguchi, 'Yushutsu kōgeihin no sekkei kikaku', p. 7.

188 On visions of American affluence in post-war Japan, see Shunya Yoshimi, 'Consuming America, Producing Japan', in *The Ambivalent Consumer: Questioning Consumption in East Asia and the West*, ed. Sheldon Garon and Patricia Maclachlan (Ithaca, NY, 2006), pp. 63–84.

189 There is a parallel here with post-war corporate managers' and engineers' interest in the U.S. See Simon Partner, *Assembled in Japan: Electrical Goods and the Making of the Japanese Consumer* (Berkeley, CA, 1999).

Designing Modern Japan

190 'Ishō ha hanbai o sayu suru', *Nikkei Shimbun*, 19 April 1951, p. 8, cited in Wada Seiji and Ōtani Tsuyoshi, 'Dezain ni taisuru Matsushita Kōnosuke no keiei-teki senkensei ni suite: Kigyōnai detain bumon reimeiki no kenkyū (1)', *Dezaingaku kenkyū*, LI/5 (2005), p. 43. Loewy's comments on the trip are in Raymond Loewy, *Industrial Design* (Woodstock, NY, 1979), p. 35.

191 Koizumi, Uchida and Takayabu, *Teiryōgun jūgaku no kiroku jō*, p. 62. The number was later lowered to 10,000 dwellings, after shortages inflated the cost of construction materials.

192 On the Dependent Houses see the official IARI publication, Shōkōshō Kōgei Shidōsho, ed., *Dependento hausu: Rengōgun kazokuyō jūtakuku* (Tokyo, 1948), and the documentation and discussion in Koizumi, Uchida and Takayabu, *Teiryōgun jūgaku no kiroku jō*, and Koizumi Kazuko, Uchida Seizō and Takayabu Akira, *Teiryōgun jūtaku no kiroku ge: Dependento hausu ga nokoshita kenchiku kagu shiki* (Tokyo, 1999).

193 Noguchi Toshirō, 'Kagu . . . Sono shakai haikei no suii to', *Kōgei nyūsu*, XXXIX/4 (April 1970), p. 42. On Noguchi see Noguchi Asao and Kusumoto Atsushi, 'Sengo no hyakkaten kagu: Hyakkaten kagu dezainā Noguchi Toshirō', in *Nihon no seikatsu dezain*, exh. cat., Living Design Center Ozone, Tokyo, and International Design Center, Nagoya (Tokyo, 1999), pp. 78–9, and Higuchi Osamu and Nakamura Keisuke, 'Senzen no hyakkaten kagu: Shumi to seikatsu no shinboru', in *Nihon no seikatsu dezain*, pp. 74–5.

194 Dower, *Embracing Defeat*, pp. 240–41.

195 On Hamaguchi, see Kitagawa Keiko, *Dainingu kicchin ha kōshite tanjō shita: Josei kenchikuka daiichigō Hamaguchi Miho ga mezashita mono* (Tokyo, 2002), and Matsukawa Junko, 'Nihon ni okeru senzen sengo no sōsōki no josei kenchikuka gijutsuka', *Jūtaku Sōgō Kenkyū Zaidan kenkyū nenpyō*, XXX (2003), pp. 251–62.

196 One exception was the Jiyū Gakuen Institute for Art and Craft Studies, established by philanthropists and educators Hani Motoko and Hani Yoshikazu in 1932. See Yasuko Suga, 'Modernism, Nationalism and Gender: Crafting "Modern" Japonisme', *Journal of Design History*, XXI/3 (Autumn 2008), pp. 259–75.

197 Feminist historians in Japan have raised this point. See Yamasaki Akiko, *Kindai nihon no shugei to jendā* (Yokohama, 2005).

198 On women workers in textile mills, see E. Patricia Tsurumi, *Factory Girls: Women in the Thread Mills of Meiji Japan* (Princeton, NJ, 1990); Janet Hunter, *Women and the Labour Market in Japan's Industrialising Economy: The Textile Industry before the Pacific War* (London, 2003); and Elyssa Faison, *Managing Women: Disciplining Labor in Modern Japan* (Berkeley, CA, 2007).

199 On women's labour in silk thread and textile villages see Satoshi Matsumura, 'Dualism in the Silk-Reeling Industry in Suwa from the 1910s to the 1930s', in *The Role of Tradition in Japan's Industrialization*, ed. Masayuki Tanimoto (Oxford, 2006), pp. 93–120, and Jun Sasaki, 'Factory Girls in an Agrarian Setting circa 1910', in *The Role of Tradition in Japan's Industrialization*, ed. Tanimoto, pp. 140–56.

200 On women, sewing and sewing machines see Andrew Gordon, *Fabricating Consumers: The Sewing Machine in Modern Japan* (Berkeley, CA, 2012).

4 'A landscape like a picture book': Design, Society and Economic Growth in Post-War Japan

1 Andrew Gordon, *A Modern History of Japan: From Tokugawa Times to the Present* (Oxford, 2003), pp. 245–6.

2 Two important initiatives by designers to document their stories are Nihon Dezain Shōshi Henshū Dōjin, ed., *Nihon Dezain Shōshi* (Tokyo, 1970), and Tanaka Ikkō, ed., *Kikigaki dezain shi* (Tokyo, 2001). See also the work of the Ginza Graphic Gallery (ggg) and Kyoto ddd gallery, under curator Kitagawa Nagashi, documented at 'Exhibition Archive', www.dnpfcp.jp, accessed 9 November 2020. 21_21 DESIGN SIGHT in Tokyo programmes retrospectives as well as future-facing exhibitions. The Japan Graphic Designers Association (JAGDA) publishes prolifically. The Japan Industrial Designers' Association (JIDA)'s activities include a design museum in rural Nagano prefecture as well as exhibitions and publications to document members' activities, such as JIDA, ed., *Nippon Purodakuto: Dezaina no shogen, 50-nen!* (Tokyo, 2003). The Japan Interior Designers' Association's documentary projects include *Nihon no seikatsu dezain: 20 seiki no modanizumu o saguru*, exh. cat., Living Design Center Ozone, Tokyo, and International Design Center, Nagoya (Tokyo, 1999).

3 Industrial partners significant for the documentation and publicity of prominent narratives in post-war Japanese design activity include the Advertising Museum Tokyo, sponsored by Dentsu; the DNP Foundation for Cultural Promotion; Living Design Center Ozone, for furniture and interiors; and the Printing Museum, sponsored by Toppan. In addition to these Tokyo-based organizations, many regional manufacturers and governments document local design activity. With few exceptions however these narratives remain at the level of 'regional' activity, due not least to the dominance of Tokyo-based design organizations and their roles as the primary liaisons between Japanese designers and international organizations and audiences.

4 Katherine B. Hiesinger and Felice Fischer, *Japanese Design: A Survey since 1950*, exh. cat., Philadelphia Museum of Art (New York, 1995) provides a detailed historical narrative with many statements from male designers prominent in post-war Japan. This chapter overlaps with that narrative, particularly with curator Hiesinger's excellent essay, but places post-war design activities and developments within a longer trajectory. Exhibitions such as 'Kenmochi Isamu: Japanese Modern' (Akita Senshu Museum of Art; National Museum of Modern Art, Kyoto; Marugame Genichiro Inokuma Museum of Contemporary Art, Marugame; and Matsudo Museum (2004–5)), 'Riki Watanabe: Innovating in Modern Living' (Museum of Modern Art Tokyo, 2006), 'Hara Hiromu and the National Museum of Modern Art, Tokyo: What One Discovers through Design Work' (Museum of Modern Art Tokyo, 2011), and 'Ikko Tanaka and Future/Past/East/West of Design' (21_21 Design Sight, Tokyo, 2012) employed the format of the retrospective exhibition to tell larger, critical stories of design, social change and politics in twentieth-century Japan.

5 Documentation and publicity of Chiba University's educators and graduates includes the exhibition and accompanying catalogue 'Sengo Nihon dezain no kiseki 1953–2005: Chiba kara no chōsen' (Chiba

Art Museum, 2005). Musashino Art University has also extensively documented its educators and graduates' post-war activities in multiple exhibitions.

6 Akashi Kazuo, 'Jō', in *Indasutoriaru dezain III: Keikiki no dezain* 1, ed. Akashi Kazuo (Tokyo, 1956), p. 1.

7 'Export or die' remained a catchphrase for over a decade. See for example Robert Trumbull, 'Tight Money Puts Gloom over the Japanese Boom', *New York Times*, 7 January 1958, p. 49.

8 Jerome B. Cohen, 'Japan's Foreign Trade Problems', *Far Eastern Survey*, XXI/16 (19 November 1952), p. 167.

9 NHK Shuzaihan, *Sengo 50-nen sono toki Nihon ha Dai-1-kan (Kokusan jidōsha: zero kara no hasshin, 60-nen Anpo to Kishi Nobusuke: Hisomerareta kaizen kōsō) (NHK Supesharu)* (Tokyo, 1995), p. 39.

10 Cohen, 'Japan's Foreign Trade Problems', p. 167.

11 GATT countries accounted for 80 per cent of world trade at the time. Kotarō Suzumura, 'Japan's Industrial Policy and Accession to the GATT: A Teacher by Positive or Negative Examples?', *Hitotsubashi Journal of Economics*, XXXVIII/2 (December 1997), p. 106.

12 United States Congress House of Representatives Committee on Ways and Means, 'Administration of Operation of Customs and Tariff Laws and the Trade Agreements Program: Hearings Before a Subcommittee of the Committee on Ways and Means, House of Representatives, Eighty-fourth Congress, Second Session on Administration and Operation of Customs and Tariff Laws and the Trade Agreements Program', 'Part 4: Digests of Conferences Held in Europe, November 26 to December 13, 1956, and Japan, December 4 to 6, 1956, and Statements and Documents Received' (Washington, DC: United States Government Printing Office, 1957), p. 1987.

13 Ibid., pp. 2015–16.

14 Ibid., p. 2044.

15 For the IARI's post-war activities see *Modan ribingu e no yume: Sangyō kōgei shikenjo no katsudō kara*, exh. cat., Musashino Art University Museum and Library, Tokyo (Tokyo, 2017).

16 Akino Kōzō, 'Gōhan sukii no kōsaku', in *Dai 2 kai mokuzai kōgei gijutsu kenkyū happyōkai tekisuto* (Tokyo, 1954), pp. 38–58.

17 Shizuoka-ken Shizuoka Kōgyō Shikenjo, *Shizuoka-ken Shizuoka Kōgyō Shikenjo Nenpō, Shōwa 29-nendo – Shōwa 39-nendo* (Shizuoka, 1954–64).

18 Kōgyō Gijutsuin Sangyō Kōgei Shikenjo, *30+10* (Tokyo, 1975), pp. 93–4. On Gropius's trip, see Guropiusu-kai, ed., *Guropiusu to Nihon bunka* (Tokyo, 1956), particularly Isamu Kenmochi, 'Kōgei shikenjo de no ichinichi', pp. 59–70. *Kōgei nyūsu*, XXXIV/3 (March 1971), pp. 2–21, recalls the foreign designers hosted by the IAI as part of their IPI Design Seminar, 1955–70.

19 On design and the Cold War U.S.–Japan relationship, see Yuko Kikuchi, 'Russel Wright and Japan: Bridging Japonisme and Good Design through Craft', *Journal of Modern Craft*, I/3 (1 November 2008), pp. 357–82; Takuya Kida, 'Japanese Crafts and Cultural Exchange with the USA in the 1950s: Soft Power and John D. Rockefeller III during the Cold War', *Journal of Design History*, XXV/4 (November 2012), pp. 379–99; and Yuko Kikuchi, 'The Cold War Design Business of John D. Rockefeller 3rd', in *The Routledge Companion to Design Studies*, ed. Penny Sparke and Fiona Fisher (London, 2016), pp. 518–30.

20 'Seminā: Amerika no dezain', *Kōgei nyūsu*, XXIII/7 (July 1955), pp. 19–26.

21 Kenmochi reported prolifically on his travels and findings. See Kenmochi Isamu, 'Amerika tsūshin', serialized in *Kōgei nyūsu*, XX/7 (July 1952) to XX/11 (November 1952), and 'Amerika tsushin o musubu', *Kōgei nyūsu*, XXI/2 (February 1953), pp. 33–5.

22 On Japanese engineers' travel to the United States in this period, see Simon Partner, *Assembled in Japan: Electrical Goods and the Making of the Japanese Consumer* (Berkeley, CA, 1999), pp. 61–3, 113–16 and 120.

23 On cultural diplomacy in post-war Japanese–U.S. relations, see Christina Klein, *Cold War Orientalism: Asia in the Middlebrow Imagination, 1945–1961* (Berkeley, CA, 2003), and Barbara E. Thornbury, 'America's "Kabuki"-Japan, 1952–1960: Image Building, Myth Making, and Cultural Exchange', *Asian Theatre Journal*, XXV/2 (2008), pp. 193–230.

24 The Italian Foreign Ministry invited the Japanese government to participate in the Triennale di Milano in 1954, however the Japanese government decided not to fund the project.

25 'Sueden ni shinshutsu shita Nihon no dezain', *Kōgei nyūsu*, XXIII/7 (July 1955), pp. 40–42.

26 Kenmochi Isamu, 'Japaniizu modan ka, Japonika sutairu ka: yūshutsu kōgei no futatsu no michi', *Kōgei nyūsu*, XXII/9 (September 1954), pp. 2–7. An English translation is Kenmochi Isamu, 'Japanese Modern and Japonica Style: Two Routes for Exporting Japanese Industrial Design', trans. Eiko Sakai, in *Design: Isamu Noguchi and Isamu Kenmochi*, exh. cat., Isamu Noguchi Foundation and Garden Museum, Long Island City, New York (New York, 2007), pp. 139–43. See also Tetsuo Matsumoto, trans. Eiko Sakai and Wayne and Noriko Peet, 'Isamu Kenmochi and Japanese Modern Design', in *Design: Isamu Noguchi and Isamu Kenmochi*, pp. 111–15.

27 On this point see Ory Bartal, *Postmodern Advertising in Japan* (Hanover, NH, 2015), pp. 35–6.

28 'Guddo dezain no igi', *Kōgei nyūsu*, XXII/1, p. 1.

29 The JDC began in 1953 as the International Design Committee, to organize Japan's contribution to the 1954 Triennale di Milano, then became the JDC in 1955. On the IDC/JDC, see Sarah Teasley, 'Tange Kenzō and Industrial Design in Post-War Japan', in *Kenzō Tange: Architecture for the World*, ed. Seng Kuan and Yukio Lippit (Zurich, 2012), pp. 166–7.

30 Tadashi Takada, *Dezain no tōyō* (Tokyo, 1959), p. 97.

31 On licensing see Partner, *Assembled in Japan*, particularly pp. 110–21.

32 'Sony ni tsuite: dai 4-sho: Hajimete no raibei "turanjisuta no jisha seisan"', www.sony.co.jp, accessed 16 October 2020.

33 'Japanese Rivalry Troubles Britain', *New York Times*, 19 August 1954, p. 33; 'To Fight Design Piracy', *New York Times*, 8 December 1954, p. 56; and 'To Halt Design Piracy', *New York Times*, 17 June 1955, p. 36.

34 'Pottery Officials Attack Trade Act', *New York Times*, 27 January 1955, p. 9.

35 Takada, *Dezain tōyō*, p. 1.

36 On the G-Mark and Good Design Selection System, see *G-Maku taizen: Guddo Dezain Shō no 50-nen* (Tokyo, 2007), and *Minna no dezain: Guddo dezain to watashi-tachi no seikatsu*, exh. cat., Kawasaki Shimin Museum (Kawasaki, 2007).

37 Takada, *Dezain tōyō*, p. 101.

38 Joseph M. Lightman, 'Patent, Trademark, Industrial Design and Copyright Protection in Japan, Overseas Business Reports (U.S. Department of

Commerce)', *OBR*, LXV/54 (July 1965), pp. 7–8. An explanation for designers and the general public in Japan is 'Dezain jihō: dezain sentā no secchi', *Ribingu dezain*, 1 (January 1955), p. 89. For general merchandise see www.gmc.or.jp/gmc/enkaku.html, accessed 7 October 2020. For an example of how the new system worked for manufacturers in one area, scarves, see Monden Sonoko, trans. Shaikh Anika, 'The Awareness of Design in Yokohama Export Scarf Industry', *Design History*, 17 (2020), pp. 55–99.

39 Emerson Chapin, 'Japanese Patents Show a Sharp Rise', *New York Times*, 10 May 1964, p. F1.

40 George Melloan, 'Assault on Imitators: U.S. Firms Push Drive against Foreign Copies of American Products', *Wall Street Journal*, 1 March 1961, p. 1. On American company employees' responses to Japanese engineers observing U.S. factories, see Partner, *Assembled in Japan*, pp. 113–21.

41 Tsūshō Sangyōchō, ed., 'Nihon bōeki no shōhinbetsu kōzō no henka', in *Bōeki dōkō hakusho Shōwa 35-nen han* (Tokyo, 1960).

42 Tsūshō Sangyōchō, ed., 'Shuyō yushutsin no gyōshubetsu dōkō', in *Bōeki dōkō hakusho Showa 35-nen han*.

43 Tsūshō Sangyōchō, ed., 'Shōhin betsu no tokuchō', in *Bōeki dōkō hakusho Shōwa 36-nen han* (Tokyo, 1961).

44 Ajia Kyōkai, *The Smaller Industry in Japan* (Tokyo, 1957), pp. 1–2. The figure was an estimated 60 per cent of exports in 1956 (ibid.) and 54 per cent in 1962. See Toyoguchi Katsuhei, ed., *Dezain senjutsu: Chūken kigyō to kōgyō dezain* (Tokyo, 1965), p. 7.

45 Iwai Kazuyuki, 'Sangyō kōgei shikenjo no sankōhin shisakuhin ni tsuite', in *Modan ribingu e no yume*, p. 18.

46 Koike Iwatarō, Yoshitake Mōsuke, Yoshioka Michitaka, Akashi Kazuo, Hattori Shigeo and Chiku Atsushi, *Dezain ABC*, 2 vols (Tokyo, 1964).

47 Jane Fiske McCullough, 'More Impressions of Expo '58: Brussels World Exposition Part II', *Industrial Design*, V/8 (August 1958), p. 54.

48 Tadashi Wada, 'Japanese Attain Electronics Lead', *New York Times*, 13 January 1959, p. 76.

49 Kenmochi, 'GOOD DESIGN-ten to sono inshō', *Kōgei nyūsu*, XXII/1 (January 1954), p. 15. On perceptions of Mexican art in 1950s Japan, see Bert Winther-Tamaki, 'Six Episodes of Convergence Between Indian, Japanese, and Mexican Art from the Late Nineteenth Century to the Present', *Review of Japanese Culture and Society*, XXVI (2014), pp. 13–32. On craft design and export strategy in post-war Italy, see Penny Sparke, 'The Straw Donkey: Tourist Kitsch or Proto-Design? Craft and Design in Italy, 1945–1960', *Journal of Design History*, XI/1 (1998), pp. 59–69.

50 On the advantages of Swedish Modern as a design strategy in the American market, see Kenmochi, 'Japaniizu modan ka, Japonika sutairu ka'; 'Zadankai: Seihin no hinshutsu to dezain', *Kōgei nyusu*, XXII/1 (January 1954), pp. 2–7; and Suzuki Michitsugu, 'Hokuō: Northern Europe Finrando no Aalto. Swedish Modern to Suēden Kōgei Kyōkai', *Kōgei nyūsu*, XXI/1 (January 1953), p. 20.

51 Kida Takuya has made a similar argument for the IARI strategy of 'indigenous industrial arts' in the 1930s. See Kida Takuya, 'Kitarō Kunii's Discourse on Indigenous Industrial Arts: "Japaneseness" and Modern Design in 1930s Japan', *Design History*, 9 (2011), pp. 47–92.

52 'Nihon no kagu yushutsu to Denmāku kagu', *Kōgei nyūsu*, XXVI/2 (February 1958), p. 2.

53 On relationships connecting modernist design and craft in Japan and the Nordic countries see the work of Nagahisa Tomoko including Nagahisa Tomoko, '1950 nendai ni okeru Hokuō modanizumu to mingei undō, Sangyō Kōgei Shikenjo no shisōteki kōryū', *Aichi-ken Tōji Shiryōkan kenkyū kiyō*, XVIII (2013), pp. 35–76.

54 On the impact of changing consumer habits on manufacturing in the 1960s, see Sarah Teasley, 'Design Recycle Meets the Product Exhibition Hall: Craft, Locality and Agency in Northern Japan', in *Craft Economies*, ed. Susan Luckman and Nicola Thomas (London, 2018), pp. 162–72.

55 On *kōgei* and *kurafuto* in post-war Japan see Yuko Kikuchi, 'The Craft Debate at the Crossroads of Global Visual Culture: Re-Centring Craft in Postmodern and Postcolonial Histories', *World Art*, V/1 (2015), pp. 87–115.

56 Wada Seiji and Ōtani Tsuyoshi, 'Tōshiba no dezain bumon setsuritsu ni itaru keii: Senpūki o jirei to shite: Kigyōnai dezain bumon hanmeiki no kenkyū sono 3', *Dezaingaku kenkyū*, LI/6 (2005), pp. 53–60.

57 Ibid.

58 After visiting the USA in 1951, Matsushita is said to have disembarked from his return flight proclaiming, 'kore kara ha dezain da' (from now on it's design!). There is however no evidence for this myth. See Masunari Kazutoshi, 'Matsushita Kōnosuke no seihin dezain ni taisuru kangaekata to keiei: Shoki no Matsushita Denki ni okeru dezain katsudō ni kansuru kenkyū (1)', *Dezaingaku kenkyū*, LVIII/1 (2011), pp. 59–66.

59 'Kaku-sha dezain sekushon meguri: Gōrika o mezasu Tōshiba Isho-bu', *Kōgei nyūsu*, XXVIII/4 (1960), p. 13. On design within Toshiba's corporate organization, see Tōshiba Dezain Sentā, *Tōshiba dezain: 1953–2003* (Tokyo, 2004).

60 Wada Seiji and Ōtani Tsuyoshi, 'Mitsubishi Denki no dezain bumon setsuritsu ni itaru keii: Kigyōnai dezain bumon hanmeiki no kenkyū (2)', *Dezaingaku kenkyū*, LI/5 (2005), pp. 47–54. See also Mitsubishi Denki Dezainshi Henshūinkai, ed., *Mitsubishi Denki dezain shi* (Tokyo, 2004).

61 Wada Seiji and Ōtani Tsuyoshi, 'Dezain ni taisuru Matsushita Kōnosuke no keieiteki senkensei ni tsuite: Kigyōnai dezainbu hanmeiki no kenkyū (1)', *Dezaingaku kenkyū*, LI/5 (2005), p. 44.

62 Mano Zenichi, 'Tokushū: Nihon no kōgyō dezain 1945–1970 Matsushita Denki', *Kōgei nyūsu*, XXXIX/4 (April 1971), p. 10.

63 Wada and Ōtani, 'Dezain ni taisuru Matsushita Kōnosuke no keieiteki senkensei ni tsuite', p. 44.

64 Masunari Kazutoshi, 'Mano Zenichi ni yoru dezain manējimento: Shoki no Matsushita Denki ni okeru dezain katsudō ni kansuru kenkyū (4)', *Dezaingaku kenkyu*, LIX/5 (2013), pp. 51–60.

65 Matsushita's recognition for well-designed products paralleled its design divisions' expansion. When the G-Mark, the national standard for well-designed and original products, was established in 1957, Matsushita was the largest recipient of awards. Mano, 'Tokushū', p. 11. See also Toyoguchi Katsuhei, 'Mano Zenichi to Matsushita Denki Dezain Guruppu', *Libingu dezain*, 4 (Spring 1958), p. 16.

66 Kaku-sha dezain sekushon meguri: Gōrika o mezasu Tōshiba Ishō-bu', p. 13.

67 NHK Shuzaihan, *Sengo 50-nen sono toki Nihon ha Dai-1-kan*, p. 97.

68 Ibid., p. 71.

69 An excellent introduction to vehicle design in 1950s Japan is *Indasutoriaru dezain*, 3 (July 1957).

70 Yūge Makoto, interviewed in NHK Shuzaihan, *Sengo 50-nen sono toki Nihon ha Dai-1-kan*, p. 27.

71 Toyota Motor Company, *Toyota: A History of the First 50 Years* (Toyota, 1988), pp. 144 and 167.

72 Ibid., p. 176.

73 NHK Shuzaihan, *Sengo 50-nen sono toki Nihon ha Dai-1-kan*, p. 85.

74 Interview with Toyota engineer Kawahara Akira, ibid., p. 93.

75 Ibid.

76 Tsūshō Sangyō Shō, *Kokusan joyosha no rikai no tame ni* (Tokyo, 1952), quoted in NHK Shuzaihan, *Sengo 50-nen sono toki Nihon ha Dai-1-kan*, p. 96. On the MITI Automotive Division see also Yamazaki Shūji, 'Nihon no jōyōsha kōgyō ikuseisaku: Gaisha kumitate ni yoru gijutsu dōnyū, kokuminsha kōzō no tenkai katei', *Keizai ronshū*, CXLIV/5–6 (November 1989), p. 566.

77 NHK Shuzaihan, *Sengo 50-nen sono toki Nihon ha Dai-1-kan*, pp. 181–2.

78 See the discussion of Nissan versus Toyota in Satō Shōzō, 'Nissan Junia no baai', *Indasutoriaru dezain*, 3 (1957), pp. 9–10.

79 Toyota Motor Company, *Toyota*, p. 158. On the design process and the integration of design into the production workflow at Toyota in the late 1950s, see 'Kaku-sha dezain sekushon meguri (2): Toyota Jidōsha Kōgyō Dezain-ka', *Kōgei nyūsu*, XXVIII/5 (1960), pp. 10-19 and Hayashi Kōichi, Misono Hideichi and Watanabe Makoto, 'Toyota Jidōsha no dezain soshiki to dezain shuhō no hensen', *Dezaingaku kenkyū*, LXI/2 (2014), pp. 17–26.

80 On Kosugi Jirō see 'Indasutoriaru dezainā no shōkai (1): Kosugi Jirō no hito to sakuhin', *Kōgei nyūsu*, XX/8 (August 1952), pp. 34–5, and Koike Iwatarō, 'Kosugi Jiro', *Ribingu dezain*, 4 (March 1958), pp. 82–3. On the integration of wartime engineering experience into post-war manufacturing, see Takashi Nishiyama, *Engineering War and Peace in Modern Japan, 1868-1964* (Baltimore, MD, 2014).

81 NHK Shuzaihan, *Sengo 50-nen sono toki Nihon ha Dai-1-kan*, p. 77. Morimoto's recollections of his time at Toyota are in Morimoto Masao, *Toyota no dezain to tomo ni: 1940–1973* (Tokyo, 1984).

82 Ibid., p. 82.

83 Cadillac style was a straw man meant to dissuade reviewers who, the project's chief engineer felt, would realize upon seeing the models that a small car styled like a Cadillac would look like a toy car, and not appeal to Japanese consumers. Ibid., p. 79.

84 Ibid., pp. 159–60. By 1955, cab drivers surveyed by Toyota preferred doors that opened in one direction as more 'modern', but the design and production line technology had been set.

85 Ibid., pp. 162 and 164.

86 Satō Shōzō, 'Nissan Juniā no baai', *Indasutoriaru dezain*, 3 (1957), p. 13.

87 Satō, 'Nissan Juniā no baai', p. 14.

88 Tokyo Kokuritsu Kindai Bijutsukan, ed., *Tokyo Orinpikku 1964 dezain purojekuto*, exh. cat., National Museum of Modern Art, Tokyo (Tokyo, 2013), p. 72. On post-war magazines, see Insatsu Hakubutsukan, ed., *Dezainā tanjō: 1950 nendai Nihon no gurafikku*, exh. cat., Printing Museum, Tokyo (2008), and Insatsu Hakubutsukan, ed., *1960 nendai guraffizumu*, exh. cat., Printing Museum, Tokyo (2002). In English, see Martyn David Smith, *Mass Media, Consumerism and National Identity in Post-War Japan* (London, 2018).

89 Tokyo Kokuritsu Kindai Bijutsukan, ed., *Tokyo Orinpikku 1964 dezain purojekuto*, p. 76. On *Ie no hikari*, see Amy Bliss Marshall, *Magazines and the Making of Mass Culture in Japan* (Toronto, 2019).

90 On GK Design, see GK Design Group, *GK Design: 50 years, 1952–2002/ Dezain sekai tankyū* (Tokyo, 2002).

91 Masaru Katsumie, 'Koike Iwatarō to GK', *Kōgei nyūsu*, XXVI/3 (March–April 1958), pp. 32–7.

92 Ekuan Kenji, *Indasutoriaru dezain: Dōgu sekai no genkei to mirai* (Tokyo, 1971), p. 38.

93 Arai Seiichirō, *Amerika kōkoku tsūshin* (Tokyo, 1952), and Arai Seiichirō, 'Kaigai no āto direkutā (taidan)', *Shimbun rajio kōkoku*, VII/9 (September 1952), pp. 8–13.

94 On the ADC, see Bartal, *Postmodern Advertising in Japan*, pp. 46–56. On the establishment of the ADC, see Nakai Kōichi, 'Jidai no shōgen: Nakai Kōichi', in *Dezainā tanjō*, ed. Insatsu Hakubutsukan, in English as Kōichi Nakai, 'A Testimony from the Post-War Period', trans. Kim McNally, *Review of Japanese Culture and Society*, XXVIII (December 2016), p. 122.

95 See Partner, *Assembled in Japan*, pp. 121–32.

96 See for example Shōgyō Dezain Zenshū Henshū Iinkai, ed., *Shōgyō dezain zenshū* (Tokyo, 1954), published by business publisher Daviddosha.

97 On the Shinseisaku Art Association, see Teasley, 'Tange Kenzō and Industrial Design in Post-War Japan', pp. 159–65.

98 On this point, see also Yamana Ayao, *Taikenteki dezain-shi* (Tokyo, 1976), pp. 322 and 347–9.

99 On the transition from wartime propaganda research groups to post-war graphics groups, see Nakai, 'A Testimony from the Post-War Period', pp. 118–19.

100 On Nissenbi, see Segi Shinichi, ed., JAAC = *Nissenbi 20-nen* (Tokyo, 1971), and Segi Shinichi, Tanaka Ikkō and Sano Hiroshi, eds, *Nissenbi no jidai: Nihon no gurafikku dezain 1951–70* (Tokyo, 2000). Other major organizations included the Tokyo Commercial Artists' Association (Toshōbi) and the Nika Association Commercial Art Section (Nikakai). In English-language reports and histories, Nissenbi has received more attention, not least due to the effective communication and networking of its founding members and because prominent Nissenbi members favoured the Swiss typography style then popular with influential designers and publishers in the United States and Europe and looked down on Nika and Toshōbi work as overly decorative and insufficiently modernist. See Nakahara Yūsuke, 'Nikaten Shōgyō Bijutsubu hyō', IDEA, 33 (February 1959), pp. 48–9, and IDEA, 64 (December 1964), pp. 65–84, and Nakai, 'A Testimony from the Post-War Period', p. 119.

101 In 1948, some of the founding members of JIDA organized IDA, the Industrial Designers' Association. IDA was short-lived due to lack of enthusiasm and a difference of opinion among members as to whether it should function primarily as a cultural or a professional organization. *Ribingu dezain*, XVIII (May 1956), p. 10.

102 Toyoguchi Katsuhei, 'Nihon kōgyō dezain-kai no genjō', *Industrial Art News*, XXI/6 (June 1953), p. 7.

103 Kenmochi Isamu, 'Amerika tsūshin', *Kōgei nyūsu*, XX/9 (September 1952), p. 33.

Designing Modern Japan

104 The account of design education in this chapter draws on reports of student work published in period journals, most importantly *Kōgei nyūsu* and *IDEA*. An excellent overview of 'key' design universities is Takao Miyashita, *Dezain handobukku* (Tokyo, 1958), pp. 417–29.

105 For the history of *Idea* see *Idea: International Graphic Art*, 300 (September 2003).

106 Kazumasa Nagai, 'My Involvement with Posters', *IDEA*, 300 (March 2003), p. 191.

107 Japanese National Commission for UNESCO, *The Role of Education in the Social and Economic Development of Japan* (Tokyo, 1966), p. 93.

108 Ministry of Education, *Higher Education in Post-War Japan: The Ministry of Education's 1964 White Paper*, trans. John Edward Blewett (Tokyo, 1965), p. 54.

109 Kon Wajirō, 'Zadankai: wakai josei dezainā ha kataru', *Ribingu dezain*, 1 (January 1955), pp. 31–8, trans. Haley Blum as 'Roundtable: Young Women Designers Speak (1956)', *Review of Japanese Culture and Society*, 28 (2016), pp. 128–43.

110 Ibid.

111 On KDS, see Tsunemi Mikiko, *Kuwasawa Yōko to modan dezain undō* (Tokyo, 2007).

112 Keizai Kikakucho, *Shōwa 29-nen Nenji keizai hōkoku: Jigatame no toki* (Tokyo, 1954), www5.cao.go.jp, accessed 25 April 2021. Data is in Fuhyō 88 'Rōdōsha setai shūnyū no suii', www5.cao.go.jp, accessed 25 April 2021. Monthly household income in this annual economic report were drawn from Sōri-fu tōkei chōsa, 'Katei chōsa (Tōkyo-to)' (Tokyo, 1952–4), a survey of Tokyo household income only.

113 An overview of winners and trends in the first six competitions is 'Shin Nihon Kōgyō Dezain nyūshō sakuhin dai 1-kai – dai 6-kai', *Ribingu dezain*, 4 (Spring 1958), pp. 116–24.

114 'Dai 4-kai Shin Nihon Kōgyō Dezain nyūshō sakuhin', *Kōgei nyūsu*, XXIV/3 (March 1956), p. 19.

115 See for example 'Kōgyō Dezainā Meibō', *Ribingu dezain*, 4 (Spring 1958), pp. 146–9. Of the 101 designers listed in this national directory, all were male.

116 'Kimura Tsunehisa', in *Kikigaki dezain shi*, ed. Tanaka, p. 253.

117 'Dezain kankei gakkō no sotsugyōsei no yukue', *Kōgei nyūsu*, XXIV/2 (February 1956), p. 26.

118 Kōno Takashi, 'Shōgyō bijutsu no ayumi to ugoki', *Dentsu geppo: Shinbun, rajio, kōkoku* (February 1952), reprinted in *Dezainā tanjō*, ed. Insatsu Hakubutsukan, p. 173.

119 'Kimura Tsunehisa', in *Kikigaki dezain shi*, ed. Tanaka, p. 256.

120 Ekuan, *Indasutoriaru dezain*, p. 39.

121 Matsuzaki Fukasaburō, 'Nozomitai kōgei no ninshiki to rikai', *Kōgei nyūsu*, XX/1 (January 1952), p. 5.

122 Katagata Zenji, *Denka seikatsu annai: Hyūzu kara kūrā made* (Tokyo, 1962). On manuals for living with electrical appliances see Partner, *Assembled in Japan*, pp. 156–62.

123 For an extended explanation of the growth of post-war Japan's electrical appliance industries see Partner, *Assembled in Japan*.

124 '35-nendo shōhi seikatsu no tokuchō', in *Shōwa 36-nen nenji keizai hōkoku: Seichō keizai no kadai* (Tokyo, 1962), www5.cao.go.jp, accessed 25 April 2021.

125 There is an extensive literature in Japanese on rural lifestyle improvement initiatives in post-war Japan. Within the design history literature, see Tsunemi, *Kuwasawa Yōko to modan dezain undō*, p. 77. In English, see Simon Partner, 'Taming the Wilderness: The Lifestyle Improvement Movement in Rural Japan, 1925–1965', *Monumenta Nipponica*, LVI/4 (2001), pp. 487–520.

126 Tsunemi, *Kuwasawa Yōko to modan dezain undō*, pp. 78–81.

127 Keizai Kikakuchō, *Shōwa 31-nendo keizai hakusho* (Tokyo, 1956).

128 The dimensions of tatami mats vary between western, central and eastern Japan. A 4.5-tatami-mat room occupies between 6.96 and 8.21 m².

129 On the Jūtaku Eidan see Nishiyama Uzō Kinen Sumai Machidukuri Bunkō Jūtaku Eidan Kenkyūkai, ed., *Senji Sengo fukkōki jūtaku seisaku shiryō: Jūtaku Eidan*, 6 vols (Tokyo, 2001). On Kōdan, see Nihon Jūtaku Kōdan-shi Kankō Iinkai, ed., *Nihon Jūtaku Kōdan-shi* (Tokyo, 1981). In English, see Ann Waswo, *Housing in Post-War Japan, a Social History: A Social History* (London, 2002), pp. 56 8 and 74–84.

130 On the 51-c standardized unit, see Waswo, *Housing in Post-War Japan*, pp. 71–3.

131 On Nishiyama and the Jūtaku Eidan see Morimoto Nobuaki, 'Nishiyama Uzō no Jūtaku Eidan jidai to mochiya shugi hihan', in *Nishiyama Uzō to sono jidai*, ed. NPO Hōjin Nishiyama Uzō Kinen Sumai Machidukuri Bunkō (Kyoto, 2000), pp. 170–73.

132 Waswo, *Housing in Post-war Japan*, p. 57.

133 Shimofusa Kaoru, 'Tokyo tonai ni okeru kōei jūtaku, kōkō chintai jūtaku, kōdan chintai jūtaku nyūkyosha no kakei no keikō ni tsuite', *Nihon Kenchiku Gakkai ronbun hōhokushū*, 64 (1960), p. 121.

134 Sasaki Kyōko, 'Experiencing the Housing Crisis', trans. Ann Waswo, in Waswo, *Housing in Post-War Japan*, p. 22.

135 See Inge Daniels, 'The "Social Death" of Unused Gifts: Surplus and Value in Contemporary Japan', *Journal of Material Culture*, XIV/3 (2009), pp. 385–408, and Fabio Gygi, 'The Metamorphosis of Excess: "Rubbish Houses" and the Imagined Trajectory of Things in Post-Bubble Japan', in *Consuming Life in Post-Bubble Japan: A Transdisciplinary Perspective*, ed. Katarzyna J. Cwiertka and Ewa Machotka (Amsterdam, 2018), pp. 129–51.

136 'Depāto', *Ribingu dezain*, 1 (January 1955), p. 68.

137 On furniture manufacturing, distribution and retail in post-war Japan, see Arai Ryūji, *Sengo Nihon no mokusei kagu* (Tokyo, 2014).

138 Sarah Teasley, 'Why Furniture Is a Global Concern: Local Industry and Global Networks, through the Lens of Shizuoka Furniture-Making', *Current Issues in Global Furniture: Proceedings of the 8th Biennial Furniture Research Group Conference. Missenden Abbey. Buckinghamshire New University 20 November 2013* (High Wycombe, 2014), pp. 41–64.

139 Tendō Mokkō Kagu Dezain Konkūru Jimukyoku, 'Nyūshō sakuhin shūkei', corporate archives of Tendo Co., Ltd. See also Mitsunobu Sugasawa, *Tendō Mokkō* (Tokyo, 2008), p. 74.

140 Ibid., p. 77.

141 On economic aspects of changes in women's dress and the fashion industry in post-war Japan see Penelope Francks, 'Was Fashion a European Invention? The Kimono and Economic Development in Japan', *Fashion Theory*, XIX/3 (1 June 2015), pp. 331–61, and Tamura Hitoshi,

Fasshon no shakai keizaishi: Zairai orimonogyō no gijutsu kakushin to ryūkō shijō (Tokyo, 2004).

142 On Western-style fashion and sewing in twentieth-century Japan see Inoue Masahito, *Yōsai bunka to Nihon no fasshon* (Tokyo, 2017).

143 Andrew Gordon, *Fabricating Consumers: The Sewing Machine in Modern Japan* (Berkeley, CA, 2012), p. 197.

144 On fashion and sewing machines in post-war Japan, see Iwamoto Shinichi, *Mishin to ifuku no keizaishi: Chikyū kibō keizai to kanai seisan* (Kyoto, 2014).

145 Gordon, *Fabricating Consumers*, p. 195.

146 On local made-to-measure shops within the post-war fashion industry see Iwamoto Shinichi, *Kindai Nihon no fukusō sangyō: Himeji-shi Fujimoto Shitate-ten ni miru tenkai* (Kyoto, 2019).

147 Gordon, *Fabricating Consumers*, p. 194.

148 On the apparel system in post-war Japan, see Pierre-Yves Donzé and Rika Fujioka, 'The Formation of a Technology-Based Fashion System, 1945–1990: The Sources of the Lost Competitiveness of Japanese Apparel Companies', *Enterprise and Society*, 19 March 2020, pp. 1–37.

149 On the post-war kimono industry, see Francks, 'Was Fashion a European Invention?', pp. 352–4.

150 For examples of how different textile firms adapted to changing conditions in postwar Japan, see Ronald Dore, *Flexible Rigidities: Industrial Policy and Structural Adjustment in the Japanese Economy, 1970–1980* (London, 1986), pp. 159–76, and Motoshige Itoh and Masayuki Tanimoto, 'Rural Entrepreneurs in the Cotton-Weaving Industry of Japan', in *Toward the Rural-Based Development of Commerce and Industry*, ed. Yūjiro Hayami (Washington, DC, 1998), pp. 47–68.

151 Dentsu Advertising, Ltd, *Marketing Activities in Japan 1962* (Tokyo, 1962), p. 75.

152 Sōmushō Tōkeikyoku, '10-10, Fuel Consumption for Household Use', www.stat.go.jp, accessed 25 June 2013.

153 On appliance marketing see Partner, *Assembled in Japan*, p. 137.

154 On the JDC, see Nippon Dezain Sentā Sōritsu 30shunen Kinen Sakuhinshū Henshū Iinkai, ed., *Nippon Dezain Sentā no 30-nen* (Tokyo, 1990), and Nippon Dezain Sentā, ed., *Dezain no porirōgu: Nippon Dezain Sentā no 50-nen* (Tokyo, 2010).

155 Dentsū Shashi Henshū Iinkai, ed., *Dentsū 66-nen* (Tokyo, 1968), p. 233.

156 The magazines *Insatsukai* (Printing World) and *Insatsu Zasshi* (Printing Magazine, or Japan Printer) and industry annual *Nihon Insatsu Nenkan* provide a granular sense of technical change in the printing industry, as do printed materials from the period. For printing processes in the 1960s, see Kōno Tōru, '1960 nendai no insatsu bunka: insatsu media no kakuchō', in *1960 nendai guraffizumu*, ed. Insatsu Hakubutsukan, pp. 256–7, 'Yōichi Michihata, '1960 nendai no insatsu bunka: Shashin seihan no reberu appu', in *1960 nendai guraffizumu*, ed. Insatsu Hakubutsukan, pp. 258–9, and Zaidan Hōjin Insatsu Toshokan Nihon Insatsu Bunkazai Hozonkai, ed., *Nihon insatsu gijutsushi nenpyō* (Tokyo, 1984).

157 On neon sign design and technology, see Ōhira Keiichi, *Neon sain: Dezain kara sekō made* (Tokyo, 1964).

158 On Persona 65 see *Dezain*, 79 (December 1965).

159 Mizuo Hiroshi, *Dezainā no tanjō* (Tokyo, 1962).

160 Ibid., p. 232.

161 In September 1959 Koike Iwatarō, Ekuan Kenji, Iwata Yoshiharu (Toshiba), and Yaegashi Mamoru (Toyota) travelled to Venice to attend the ICSID conference. *Dezain*, 31 (April 1962), pp. 17–19.

162 The conference was followed by a three-day trip to the Osaka-Kyoto-Nara area.

163 The conference record is *World Design Conference 1960*, ed. World Design Conference Organization (Tokyo, 1961). See also *IDEA*, 42 (August 1960). An overview is Toshino Iguchi, 'Reconsideration of the World Design Conference 1960 in Tokyo and the World Industrial Design Conference 1973 in Kyoto: Transformation of design theory', IASDR 2013, available at http://design-cu.jp, accessed 21 October 2020.

164 On Yokoo, see Minami Yūsuke, Fujii Aki and Dehara Hitoshi, eds, *Yokoo Tadanori: Mandarazō*, exh. cat., Museum of Contemporary Art Tokyo and Hiroshima City Museum of Contemporary Art (Tokyo, 2002). On poster design by Yokoo, Uno Aquirax, Awazu Kiyoshi and others for the Art Theatre Guild see Tokyo Kokuritsu Kindai Bijutsukan Firumu Sentā, ed., *Nihon no eiga posutā geijutsu*, exh. cat., National Film Center, Tokyo, and Kyoto National Museum of Modern Art (Tokyo, 2012). On countercultural theatre and film and the cultural politics of 1960s Japan, see Miryam Sas, *Experimental Arts in Postwar Japan: Moments of Encounter, Engagement, and Imagined Return* (Cambridge, MA, 2011).

165 On art and cultural politics in 1960s Japan, see Charles Merewether and Rika Iezumi Hiro, eds, *Art, Anti-Art, Non-Art: Experimentations in the Public Sphere in Postwar Japan, 1950–1970*, exh. cat., J. Paul Getty Museum, Los Angeles (Los Angeles, CA, 2007), and Doryun Chong, ed., *Tokyo 1955–1970: A New Avant-Garde*, exh. cat., Museum of Modern Art, New York (New York, 2012).

166 On Shinkansen design, see 'Tokaidō Shinkansen', *Kōgei Nyūsu*, XXXII/3 (Autumn 1964), pp. 21–40.

167 On design for the 1964 Summer Olympics see Takuya Kida, 'Japanese-ness in Designs for the 1964 Tokyo Olympic Games', in *Tokyo Orinpikku 1964 dezain purojekuto*, ed. Tokyo Kokuritsu Kindai Bijutsukan, pp. 120–27, and Jilly Traganou, *Designing the Olympics: Representation, Participation, Contestation* (London, 2017), pp. 47–106. On the 1964 Summer Olympics as cultural diplomacy, see Jessamyn R. Abel, 'Japan's Sporting Diplomacy: The 1964 Tokyo Olympiad', *International History Review*, XXXIV/2 (2012), pp. 203–20.

168 Tokyo Kokuritsu Kindai Bijutsukan, ed., *Tokyo Orinpikku 1964 dezain purojekuto*, p. 88.

169 'Zadankai: Katsumi Masaru, Kamekura Yūsaku, Takeda Tsuneyoshi, Tange Kenzō Tokyo Orinpikku o dō enshutsu sure ka: Sōgōteki na dezain keikaku no kakuritsu o', *Asahi jānaru*, 13 (October 1963), reprinted in *Tokyo Orinpikku 1964 dezain purojekuto*, ed. Tokyo Kokuritsu Kindai Bijutsukan, pp. 132–9: p. 138.

170 Nagai Kazumasa, 'Nekki ni afureta hibi', Tokyo Kokuritsu Kindai Bijutsukan, ed., *Tokyo Orinpikku 1964 dezain purojekuto*, p. 114.

171 For an extended argument on this point, see Ory Bartal, *Critical Design in Japan: Material Culture, Luxury, and the Avant-Garde* (Manchester, 2020).

5 'Generosity and tolerance': Design and the Information Industries in Late Twentieth-Century Japan

1   Hamano Yasuhiro, 'Dezain no jidai ni atarashii akushisu o . . . .', AXIS, 1 (September 1981), p. 1.
2   The planned shift and its rationale are apparent in the annual Economic White Papers published by the national Economic Planning Agency. See Keizai Kikaku-chō, *Shōwa 45-nen nenji keizai hōkoku: Nihon keizai no atarashii jigen* (Tokyo, 1970), with its subtitle 'The New Dimensions of the Japanese Economy', and Keizai Kikaku-chō, *Shōwa 46-nen nenji keizai hōkoku: Naigai kinkō tassei e no michi* (Tokyo, 1971), subtitled 'The Road to Achieving Internal and External Equilibrium'.
3   Kashiwagi Hiroshi makes this argument as well. See Kashiwagi Hiroshi, 'Sengo Nihon no posuta – 1960 nendai irai/Japanese Posters in the Post-war Era – The 1960s and Onward', in DNP *Gurafikku Dezain Akaibu Setsuritsu=ten: Posuta gurafikkusu 1950–2000 / DNP Archives of Graphic Design Inaugural Exhibition: Poster Graphics, 1950–2000*, ed. Center for Contemporary Graphic Art and Tyler Graphics Archive Collection (Sukagawa-shi, 2000), pp. 11–13.
4   Pieter Wesemael, *Architecture of Instruction and Delight: A Socio-Historical Analysis of World Exhibitions as a Didactic Phenomenon (1798–1851–1970)* (Rotterdam, 2001), p. 820.
5   The official report is Nihon Bankoku Hakurankai Kyōkai (Commemorative Association for the Japan World Exposition), *Japan World Exposition, Osaka, 1970: Official Report*, 3 vols (Osaka, 1970). Oruta Bukkusu Henshūbu and Jun Matsuhisa Jun, EXPO 70 densetsu: *Nihon Bankoku Hakurankai anofisharu gaidobukku* (Tokyo, 1999), offers an effective visual overview. Architectural overviews include *Shinkenchiku* (May 1970), JA (Japan Architect) (May–June 1970) and JA, 113 (Spring 2019).
6   *Asahi Shinbun*, 9 September 1966, reprinted in Guruppu Chekku no kai, 'Bankokuhaku ga yatte kuru', *Dezain*, 79 (September 1966), p. 9.
7   Zadankai Datsu jidai no keiei to māketingu 4: EXPO'70 Kigyō pabirion o kiru! Shutten kigyō ha soko ni nani o motome, nani o eta ka', *Senden Kaigi*, XVII/6 (June 1970), pp. 98–100.
8   On the design process for the Japan Pavilion and several Japanese corporate pavilions, see 'EXPO '70 no dezain (IV): disupurē', *Kōgei nyūsu*, XXXVIII/2 (February 1970), pp. 14–41.
9   On Expo 70 as entertainment and as part of consumer society, see Shunya Yoshimi, *Hakurankai no seijigaku* (Tokyo, 1992), pp. 219–40, and Shunya Yoshimi, *Banpaku gensō: Sengo seiji no jūbaku* (Tokyo, 2005), pp. 35–100.
10 On music and performance practice at Osaka Expo 70 see Ikegami, Hiroko, '"World Without Boundaries"? E.A.T. and the Pepsi Pavilion at Expo '70, Osaka', *Review of Japanese Culture and Society*, XXIII (2011), pp. 174–90; *E.A.T.*, exh. cat., NTT intercommunication center, Tokyo (Tokyo, 2003). On Yokoo Tadanori at Expo 70, see Midori Yoshimoto, 'Textiles Pavilion: An Anomaly and Critique of Expo '70', *Review of Japanese Culture and Society*, 23 (2011), pp. 113–31.
11 Marie Anchordoguy, *Computers, Inc.: Japan's Challenge to IBM* (Cambridge, MA, 1989), pp. 3 and 15–16.

12 On the shift towards knowledge-intensive industries in 1970s Japanese industrial policy see Ronald Dore, *Flexible Rigidities: Industrial Policy and Structural Adjustment in the Japanese Economy, 1970–1980* (London, 1986), and Mikiyo Sumiya, *A History of Japanese Trade and Industry Policy* (Oxford, 2000).

13 Japan's national pavilion at Expo 67 also displayed new IT products from Japanese firms, but as display items, not control systems integrated into the exhibition environment. Toyoguchi Dezain Kenkyūjō, 'Nihonkan no disupurei', *Kōgei nyūsu*, xxxv/2 (February 1967), pp. 25–31.

14 Japan Information Service, Consulate General of Japan, New York, 'Japan World Exposition 1970, Osaka (Part II): Review in Detail', *Japan Report*, xiv/6 (31 March 1968), p. 2.

15 On control systems at Osaka Expo 70, see Tsukio Yoshio, 'Seigyo kikō', *Bijutsu techo*, 330 (July 1970), pp. 121–6.

16 Nihon Bankoku Hakurankai Kyōkai, *Japan World Exposition, Osaka, 1970*, vol. II, p. 478: 'Proposal for the Computerization of the Exposition and Development of the Information Industry'. See also the description in Wesemael, *Architecture of Instruction and Delight*, p. 816.

17 Hasegawa Aiko, ed., *Dezain dengon: GK 30-nen no ayumi* (Tokyo, 1988), pp. 150–51.

18 *Bijutsu techō* (July 1970).

19 On Tange's masterplan, see Kenzō Tange, 'The EXPO '70 Master Plan and Master Design', *Japan Architect*, xliv/4 (April 1969), pp. 18–20, and the discussions in Zhongjie Lin, *Kenzo Tange and the Metabolist Movement: Urban Utopias of Modern Japan* (London, 2010), pp. 200–232. Angus Lockyer, 'The Logic of Spectacle *c.* 1970', *Art History*, xxx/4 (September 2007), pp. 582–6, and Hyunjung Cho, 'Expo '70: The Model City of an Information Society', *Review of Japanese Culture and Society*, xxiii (2011), pp. 57–71.

20 Keiichirō Fujimori, 'Osaka Banpaku sutorīto fānichā to sain keikaku [1970 nen]', p. 77.

21 Zadankai Datsu jidai no keiei to māketingu 4: EXPO '70 Kigyō pabirion o kiru! Shutten kigyō ha soko ni nani o motome, nani o eta ka', *Senden Kaigi*, xvii/6 (June 1970), pp. 98–100.

22 Ekuan drew on Metabolist ideas for the GK Design modular furniture experiments. See for example GK Indasutorial Dezain Kenkyūjo, 'Sosei suru kagu', *Dezain*, 84 (May 1966), pp. 8–19. There is a large literature on Metabolism as an architectural movement. In English, see Lin, *Kenzo Tange and the Metabolist Movement*; Rem Koolhaas, Hans Ulrich Obrist and Kayoko Ota, *Project Japan* (Cologne, 2011); Agnes Nyilas, *Beyond Utopia: Japanese Metabolism Architecture and the Birth of Mythopia* (London, 2018); and William O. Gardner, *The Metabolist Imagination: Visions of the City in Postwar Japanese Architecture and Science Fiction* (Minneapolis, MN, 2020).

23 J. Kurisutofā Jōnuzu [J. Christopher Jones], 'Dezain hōhōron seminā', *Kōgei nyūsu*, xxxviii/2 (February 1970), pp. 56–72.

24 L. Burūsu Āchā [L. Bruce Archer], 'Dezain purosesu no kōzō (I)', *Kōgei nyūsu*, xxxviii/4 (April 1970), pp. 53–71, and L. Burūsu Āchā, 'Dezain purosesu no kōzō (II)', *Kōgei nyūsu*, xxxviii/5 (May 1970), pp. 53–69.

25 A summary of this collaborative project is in Tsukio Yoshio, 'Dōnyū katsuyō no kokoromi: Kenchiku doboku sekkei', *Kōgei nyūsu*, xxxvi/5

Designing Modern Japan

(May 1968), pp. 44–5. The project's references included research by L. Bruce Archer, Christopher Alexander and the American transport planner Marvin L. Manheim.

26 Minato Yukie, 'Dōnyū katsuyō no kokoromi: Saiteki sekkei', *Kōgei nyūsu*, XXXVI/5 (January 1968), pp. 39–43.

27 See for example Kōhei Sugiura, 'Dōnyū katsuyō no kokoromi: Gurafikku dezain', *Kōgei nyūsu*, XXXVI/5 (January 1968), pp. 51–3 and Akira Kamoi, 'Konpyūtā ni yoru ukei jōhō shori to nyūshutsuryoku sōchi', *Kōgei nyūsu*, XXXVI/5 (January 1968), pp. 54–61. Kamoi was a researcher at Hitachi's Central Research Institute, one of the lead organizations for computing research in the public-private arrangements agreed. On the early development of CAD at MIT see Molly W. Steenson, *Architectural Intelligence: How Designers, Tinkerers, and Architects Created the Digital Landscape* (Cambridge, MA, 2017). On the Cybernetic Serendipity exhibition, see Jasia Reichardt, *Cybernetic Serendipity: The Computer and the Arts* [special issue of *Studio International*] (London and New York, 1968).

28 Ginya Yasunaga, 'Conpyūta gurafikku dezain kara konpyūta āto e', *Kogei nyūsu*, XL/4 (February 1973), pp. 60–63.

29 Mukai Shūtarō, 'Dezainteki shikō e no teian: Denshi keisanki jidai ni taiō shite', *Kōgei nyūsu*, XXXVI/5 (January 1968), pp. 70–73.

30 'Hongō tokushū ni tsuite', *Kōgei nyūsu*, XXXV/4 (May 1968), p. 74.

31 Yaegashi Mamoru and Iwata Dai, 'Dōnyū katsuyō no kokoromi: Jidōsha dezain', *Kōgei nyūsu*, XXXVI/5 (January 1968), pp. 35–8.

32 Research on environmental activism in post-war Japan is extensive. For an effective summary, see Simon Avenell, *Transnational Japan in the Global Environmental Movement* (Honolulu, HI, 2017), pp. 24–51.

33 On protests in 1968, see William Marotti, '1968: The Performance of Violence and the Theater of Protest', *American Historical Review*, MCXIV/1 (2009), pp. 97–135. On student activism, see Hiroe Saruya, 'Protests and Democracy in Japan: The Development of Movement Fields and the 1960 Anpo Protest', unpublished PhD dissertation, University of Michigan, Ann Arbor, 2012.

34 On artists' critiques and anti-Expo activism, see Midori Yoshimoto, 'Expo '70 and Japanese Art: Dissonant Voices, an Introduction and Commentary', *Review of Japanese Culture and Society*, XXIII (2011), pp. 2–3, and Kuro DalaiJee, 'Performance Art and/as Activism: Expo '70 Destruction Joint-Struggle Group', *Review of Japanese Culture and Society*, XXIII (2011), pp. 154–73.

35 Haryū Ichirō, quoted in 'Rensai: Gurafiumu e no shiten – sono 1: Nihon Senden Bijutsu Kyōkai kaihō', *Dezain*, 135 (July 1970), p. 30. On Hariu's critique of Osaka Expo 70 see also Haryū Ichirō, 'Expo '70 as the Ruins of Culture (1970)', trans. Ignacio Adriasola, *Review of Japanese Culture and Society*, XXIII (2011), pp. 44–56, and Yasufumi Nakamori, 'Criticism of Expo '70 in Print: Journals *Ken*, *Bijutsu Techō*, and *Dezain Hihyō*', *Review of Japanese Culture and Society*, XXIII (2011), pp. 132–44.

36 There is also an extensive literature on critical responses to the post-war political and economic settlement within art, cinema and performance. See Sas, *Experimental Arts in Postwar Japan*, and William A. Marotti, *Money, Trains, and Guillotines: Art and Revolution in 1960s Japan* (Durham, NC, 2013).

37 On *Dezain hihyō*, see Toshino Iguchi, 'Standing at the Crossroads: Post-War Design in Japan and the Japanese Journal *Design Hihyo* (The Design Review)', 7th Conference of International Committee of Design History and Design Studies, Brussels, October 2010, pp. 212–15.

38 See for example Ekuan Kenji, trans. Frank Feltens, 'An Introduction to the World of Tools (1969)', *Review of Japanese Culture and Society*, 28 (2016), pp. 169–76.

39 This dual positioning – actions and stances as both specific to particular conditions in Japan and part of a wider transnational network or response to a common or similar set of conditions – is discussed in many of the secondary histories cited in this chapter. See for example Avenell, *Transnational Japan in the Global Environmental Movement*.

40 Kanda Akio, quoted in 'Rensai: Gurafiumu he no shiten – sono 1: Nihon Senden Bijutsukai kaiho', p. 23. For a glimpse of the rawness and lingering effects of the JAAC conflict, see Yusaku Kamekura, 'Graphics', in Katherine B. Hiesinger and Felice Fischer, *Japanese Design: A Survey since 1950*, exh. cat., Philadelphia Museum of Art (New York, 1995), p. 41.

41 Moriyama Akiko, 'Shirīzu shōgen: Kōno Takashi', *Nikkei dezain* (October 1987), p. 52.

42 Mutsuo Takahashi, 'Gurafikku: Yokoo Tadanori zenshū-ten', *Dezain*, 135 (July 1970), p. 14. On Yokoo see Minami Yūsuke, Fujii Aki and Dehara Hitoshi, eds, *Yokoo Tadanori shinra banshō*, exh. cat., Museum of Contemporary Art, Tokyo (Tokyo, 2002), and Minami Yūsuke and Fujii Aki, eds, *Genkyo Yokoo Tadanori: A Visual Story: Genkyō kara genkyō e soshite genkyō ha. 1*, exh. cat., Museum of Contemporary Art, Tokyo (Tokyo, 2021).

43 Nishijima Isao, quoted in 'Rensai: Gurafiumu he no shiten – sono 1', p. 30.

44 On Ishioka see *Ishioka Eiko fūshi kaden* (Tokyo, 1983), Ishioka Eiko, *Eiko by Eiko* (San Francisco, CA, 1990), and Kawajiri Kōichi, TIMELESS: *Ishioka Eiko to sono jidai* (Tokyo, 2020).

45 On feminist activism in 1970s Japan, see Setsu Shigematsu, *Scream from the Shadows: The Women's Liberation Movement in Japan* (Minneapolis, MN, 2012).

46 Kimura Tsunehisa, quoted in 'Rensai: Gurafiumu he no shiten – sono 1', p. 29.

47 'Ikushiizu: Nijūdai no quoritī raifu o enshutsu suru', *Bijutsu techō bessatsu: From Designers' Workshop part 2*, II/6 (Autumn 1983), p. 21.

48 Dore, *Flexible Rigidities*, p. 20.

49 On changes in the kimono market after 1970 see Julie Valk, 'From Duty to Fashion: The Changing Role of the Kimono in the Twenty-First Century', *Fashion Theory*, XXII/3 (2018), pp. 309–40. On the structural adjustments made within the textile industry in 1970s Japan see Dore, *Flexible Rigidities*, pp. 205–43.

50 Tosaka Yasuji, *Genroku kosode kara minisukato made* (Tokyo, 1972), p. 246.

51 Hirakawa Takeji, 'Media to tomo ni imēji o shōhinka', *Nikkei dezain* (October 1995), pp. 44–50.

52 Thomas R. H. Havens, *Architects of Affluence: The Tsutsumi Family and the Seibu-Saison Enterprises in Twentieth-Century Japan* (Cambridge, MA, 1994), pp. 104–7.

Designing Modern Japan

53 Takeji, 'Media to tomo ni imēji o shōhinka', p. 45.

54 Shimokawa Kazuya, 'Tensō kara dezain e to shōka', *Nikkei dezain* (October 1995), pp. 51–3. On the interior design of Japanese fashion boutiques in the 1980s, see also Penny Sparke, *Modern Japanese Design* (New York, 1987), p. 129.

55 'Chronology of Inax', www.lixil.co.jp, accessed 10 December 2020.

56 'Hakurai dezain kōsei o kangaeru', *Kōgei nyūsu*, XL/3 (1972), p. 18, Table II.

57 Toyoguchi Kyō, 'Kagu tokushū: Saikin no kagu interia no keikō', *Kōgei nyūsu*, XL/3 (1972), p. 40 and p. 42.

58 'Hakurai dezain kōsei o kangaeru', p. 18, Table I. The value of furniture imported from other countries in Asia rose as well, as Japanese manufacturers offshored production, in response to rising labour costs in Japan.

59 One list of high-end furniture shops in 1975 is 'Tokyo Yokohama Kobe Osaka omo na kagu shōrūmu', *Modan ribingu*, 93 (February 1975), pp. 132–40.

60 'FROM THE EDITORS', *Casa Brutus* (Spring 1984), p. 299.

61 Sarah Teasley, 'Why Furniture Is a Global Concern: Local Industry and Global Networks, through the Lens of Shizuoka Furniture-Making', *Current Issues in Global Furniture: Proceedings of the 8th biennial Furniture Research Group Conference. Missenden Abbey. Buckinghamshire New University 20 November 2013* (High Wycombe, 2014), p. 42.

62 On the Law for the Promotion of Traditional Craft Industries of 1974, see Sarah Teasley, 'Design Recycle meets the Product Introduction Hall: Craft, Locality and Agency in Northern Japan', in *Craft Economies: Cultural Economies of the Handmade*, ed. Susan Luckman and Nicola Thomas (London, 2018), pp. 165–6.

63 There is continuity or a looping back, here, with *mingei* in the 1930s. See Lisbeth K. Brandt, *Kingdom of Beauty* (Durham, NC, 2007).

64 Penelope Francks, *The Japanese Consumer: An Alternative Economic History of Modern Japan* (Cambridge, 2009), pp. 161–2, points out that because women shopped in small local shops, there was less need to advertise these products.

65 On flexible specialization, see also Sparke, *Modern Japanese Design*, pp. 37, 47 and 63.

66 There is a large business and management literature on productivity and efficiency techniques implemented in 1970s and '80s Japan. A critical historical contextualization is in William Tsutsui, *Manufacturing Ideology: Scientific Management in Twentieth-Century Japan* (Princeton, NJ, 1998).

67 Sparke, *Modern Japanese Design*, pp. 56–8.

68 On lifestyle research in Japan, see John McCreery, *Japanese Consumer Behaviour: From Worker Bees to Wary Shoppers* (Honolulu, HI, 2000).

69 'Kigyō senryaku Sanyō Denki: Raifu Kurietibu shitsu wo kaku ni kikaku kara hanbai made porishī tsuku', *Nikkei dezain* (July 1989), p. 27.

70 Japan Information Service, Consulate General of Japan, New York, 'News in Brief: Spending Pattern of Unmarried Workers in Japan', *Japan Report*, XIV/7 (15 April 1968), p. 6.

71 Sōrifu Tōkeikyoku, *Zenkoku shōhi jittai chōsa hōkoku* (Tokyo, 1980), reported in 'Dēta de miru "anmarizoku" no seitai', *Senden kaigi* (June 1983), p. 49.

72 'Dēta de miru "anmarizoku" no seitai', pp. 44–52. On advertisers' targeting of young women as consumers, see Lise Skov and Brian Moeran, 'Introduction: Hiding in the Light: From Oshin to Yoshimoto Banana', in *Women, Media and Consumption in Japan*, ed. Lise Skov and Brian Moeran (Honolulu, HI, 1995), pp. 27–8, and Chizuko Ueno, 'Seibu Department Store and Image Marketing: Japanese Consumerism in the Post-War Period', in *Asian Department Stores*, ed. Kerrie L. MacPherson (Honolulu, HI, 1998), pp. 182–4.

73 Ōhashi Terue, 'Josei shinguru shijō no yukue', *Senden kaigi* (June 1983), pp. 38–43.

74 On the Sony Walkman, see Paul du Gay, Stuart Hall, Linda Janes et al., *Doing Cultural Studies: The Story of the Sony Walkman* (London, 1997). Sony's history is 'Chapter 5 Promoting Compact Cassettes Worldwide', www.sony.com/en/SonyInfo/CorporateInfo/History/SonyHistory/2-05.html, accessed 5 August 2021 and 'Chapter 6 Just Try It', www.sony.com/en/SonyInfo/CorporateInfo/History/SonyHistory/2-05.html, accessed 5 August 2021.

75 'PP' stood for Product Planning, Product Proposal and Product Presentation. See ibid., p. 63.

76 Kanō Akihiro, 'Sonī Uōkuman to Kuroki Yasuo', *AXIS*, 3 (April 1982), pp. 30–31, and du Gay et al., *Doing Cultural Studies*, p. 58.

77 On Seibu's strategy see Ueno Chizuko and Masuda Tsūji, *Paruko no senden senryaku: kyanpēn obu Paruko* (Tokyo, 1984). On Ishioka's graphics for Seibu, see Jonathan Reynolds, *Allegories of Time and Space: Japanese Identity in Photography and Architecture* (Honolulu, HI, 2015), pp. 197–204, and Ory Bartal, *Critical Design in Japan: Material Culture, Luxury, and the Avant-Garde* (Manchester, 2020), p. 76.

78 On the development of the Mujirushi Ryōhin brand see Nishikawa Hidehiko, 'Mujirushi Ryōhin no keieigaku 1: Mujirushi Ryōhin no tanjō', *Hitotsubashi bijinesu rebyū*, LXIII/1 (2015), pp. 148–53, and Bartal, *Critical Design in Japan*, pp. 126–35.

79 Bartal, *Critical Design in Japan*, pp. 132–3.

80 On overseas perceptions of MUJI as minimalist and 'Japanese', see ibid., pp. 124–5 and 138–45.

81 On Matsushita's marketing activities in 1950s and '60s Japan see Simon Partner, *Assembled in Japan: Electrical Goods and the Making of the Japanese Consumer* (Berkeley, CA, 1999), pp. 125–32 and 153–68.

82 Dore, *Flexible Rigidities*, p. 34.

83 'Shiryō Dezain purodakushon, sengo no dōkō', *Tategumi Yokogumi*, 15 (Winter 1987), pp. Y8–Y9. Advertising spending doubled between 1960 and 1964, then more than doubled, again, by 1970, for a 400 per cent rise in the 1960s alone.

84 'Chōsa dezain jimusho keiei sōran Tonai-hen: CI būmu o irokoku hanei, gyōmu takakuka no keikō mo medatsu', *Nikkei dezain* (July 1989), p. 52.

85 Sparke, *Modern Japanese Design*, p. 47.

86 '10: Progressing Hand in Hand with Graphic Design', www.jagda.or.jp/en, accessed 6 December 2020. On members' motivations and hopes for JAGDA see 'Tokushū: Arukidashita kuriētā tachi: JAGDA Nihon Gurafikku Dezainā Kyōkai tanjō', *Senden kaigi*, XXV/14 (November 1978), pp. 15–40.

87 'Tokushū: Arukidashita kuriētā tachi', pp. 30–34.

88 Moriyama Akiko, 'ᴅᴏ kanpanī Matsushita Denki Sangyō: Jōhō sangyō bunka de hakki sareru seikatsu mitsumeru dezain no sōgōryoku', *Nikkei dezain* (May 1989), p. 107.

89 'Dezainā no jittai ishiki chōsa: Dezain bijinesu e kigyō yōsei no takamari mazamaza to', *Nikkei dezain* (July 1987), p. 83.

90 Hirobashi Keiko, 'Pakkēji dezain', *Tategumi Yokogumi*, 7 (Winter 1985), p. ʏ22.

91 'ᴄɪ shōshi', *Nikkei dezain* (October 1995), p. 63.

92 On waste and wastefulness in 1970s and '80s Japan, see Eiko Maruko Siniawer, *Waste: Consuming Postwar Japan* (Ithaca, ɴʏ, 2018).

93 Maurice Cooper, 'Shoe Box', *Blueprint*, 47 (May 1988), p. 32.

94 The 'Tsutsumu' exhibition developed from Hideyuki Oka, *How to Wrap Five Eggs* (New York, 1967). For an example of the response, see Norma Shurka, 'Design: An Art in Packaging', *New York Times*, 9 February 1975, p. 227. For another significant exhibition, 'Space-Time in Japan: ᴍᴀ', see Arata Isozaki, *Space-Time in Japan: ᴍᴀ*, exh. cat., Cooper-Hewitt Museum, New York (New York, 1978).

95 See *Visions of Japan*, exh. cat., Victoria and Albert Museum, London (London, 1991).

96 'Kōporēto dezain shōshi', *Nikkei dezain* (October 1995), p. 81.

97 Kunio Okina, Masaaki Shirakawa and Shigenori Shiratsuka, 'The Asset Price Bubble and Monetary Policy: Japan's Experience in the Late 1980s and the Lessons', *Monetary and Economic Studies*, special edition (February 2001), pp. 395–450, p. 408.

98 Ibid., p. 399.

99 Kei Takeuchi, 'Home Electric Appliance Industry', trans. Lora Sharnoff, in *Made in Japan: Revitalizing Japanese Manufacturing for Economic Growth*, ed. Japanese Commission on Industrial Performance (Cambridge, ᴍᴀ, 1997), p. 57, translation of Takeuchi Kei, *Meido in Japan: Nihon seizōgyō henkaku e no hōshin* (Tokyo, 1994).

100 'Kigyō senryaku Sanyō Denki', p. 26.

101 Dentsu, *1989 Hit Products in Japan, Dentsu Information Series* (Tokyo, 1989), p. 4. For profiles of Japanese consumers in the 1980s see McCreery, *Japanese Consumer Behaviour*.

102 Takeuchi, 'Home Electric Appliance Industry', p. 66.

103 Kigyō senryaku Sanyō Denki', p. 26.

104 Ibid., p. 24.

105 The Communications White Paper of 1973 flagged Japan's transformation into an information society (rendered as 'informationized society', or *jōhōka shakai*): 'The fact that recently many people are using the phrase "informationized society" is because we can recognize the value of information and our dependence on information close to home, in our contemporary daily lives.' *Tsūshin hakusho* (1973), www.soumu.go.jp, accessed 29 March 2020.

106 *Mono* (May 1986), cover.

107 Dentsu, *1989 Hit Products in Japan*, p. 1.

108 On marketers' concerns around *monobanare* see Nihon Dēta Sentā, *Shin shōhi kanren shijō no jittai chōsa repōto: 'Monobanare' keikō no tsuyomaru naka* (Ichikawa, 1983), and Tsutsumi Emi, *Onna ga jidai o kaeru! Monobanare sedai no māketingu* (Tokyo, 1983).

109 Dentsu Dezaininzu Kenkyūkai, ed., 'Atogaki', *Dezaininzu: Atarashii hassō to hōhōron* (Tokyo, 1986), p. 331. On this point see also Ory Bartal, *Postmodern Advertising in Japan* (Hanover, NH, 2015).

110 Hirobashi Keiko, 'Pakkēji dezain', *Yokogumi Tategumi*, 7 (Winter 1985), p. Y22.

111 See Bartal, *Postmodern Advertising in Japan*, pp. 140–41.

112 For the history of Seibu's retail strategy see Havens, *Architects of Affluence*; Chizuko Ueno et al., eds, *Sezon no hassō* (Tokyo, 1991); and Yui Tsunehiko, ed., *Sezon no rekishi: Henkaku no dainamizumu,* 2 vols (Tokyo, 1991).

113 'DO kanpanī Seibu Hyakkaten', p. 87.

114 'Dezainā no jittai ishiki chōsa: Dezain bijinesu e kigyō yōsei no takamari mazamaza to', *Nikkei dezain* (July 1987), p. 92.

115 'Kigyō toppu ga motomeru dezain to ha, motormeru dezainā to ha', *Nikkei dezain* (Spring 1987), p. 27.

116 Saji Keizō, 'Seikatsu bunka o uru: Santorī', *Senden kaigi*, 397 (January 1984), pp. 15–24.

117 'Bunkamura no rekishi', www.bunkamura.co.jp, accessed 7 December 2020.

118 On the image of contemporary Japanese architecture internationally, see Christophe Polarier and Erez Golani Solomon, 'Japanese Architecture as Export', in *Exporting Japanese Aesthetics: Evolution from Tradition to Cool Japan,* ed. Tets Kimura and Jennifer A. Harris (Brighton, 2020), pp. 105–36.

119 An introduction to the AXIS building in the 1980s, in English, is Terry Trucco, 'Shopper's World: Axis: Sleek and Chic in Tokyo', *New York Times*, 10 July 1983.

120 Kashiwagi Hiroshi, trans. Lynsey Clark, 'The "Information City" as Management Apparatus', *Japan Forum*, 23 (2011), pp. 263–71, a translation of Kashiwagi's essay 'Kanri sōchi to shite no jōhō toshi', in *Dōgu to media no seijigaku* (Tokyo, 1989).

121 On Shibuya as mediatized, commodified space see Kitada Akihiro, *Zōhō Kōkoku toshi Tokyo: Sono tanjō to shi* [2002] (Tokyo, 2011). Miura Atsushi, *'Fujiyū na jidai' no 'fuan na jibun': Shōhi shakai no datsu-shinwa ka* (Tokyo, 2006), offers a counter-argument.

122 Yoshimi Shunya, *Toshi no doramaturugii* (Tokyo, 1987). In English, see Shunya Yoshimi, trans. Miriam Chusid, 'The Market of Ruins, or the Destruction of the Cultural City', *Japan Forum*, XXIII (2011), pp. 287–300, a translation of Yoshimi's 'Haikyo no shijō, arui wa bunka toshi no hōkai', in *Onna no 70 nendai: Paruko posutā ten: 1969–1986*, ed. Masuda Tsūji (Tokyo, 2001), reprinted in Shunya Yoshimi, *Karuchuraru tān, bunka no seijigaku e* (Tokyo, 2003).

123 *Tategumi Yokogumi* was sponsored and published by type foundry Morisawa, as one of Morisawa's own cultural projects. As Japan's most prominent type foundry, Morisawa would benefit, of course, from any printing activity, whether for cultural publications or corporate annual reports.

124 Nakanishi Motoo, 'Cōporēto aidentiti', *Tategumi Yokogumi*, 7 (Winter 1985), pp. Y26–Y27.

125 On this point see also Francks, *The Japanese Consumer*, p. 191.

126 'Chōsa dezain jimusho keiei sōran Tonai-hen', p. 52, and 'Kōporēto dezain shōshi', *Nikkei dezain* (October 1995), p. 81.

127 Ibid.

128 'Chōsa dezain jimusho keiei sōran Tonai-hen', p. 54.

129 'Dezainā no jittai ishiki chōsa', p. 85.

130 Ibid., p. 86.

131 Shiseido was one exception to this rule; into the 1990s, Shiseido's design department was known informally among female design graduates as one of the best places to begin one's career, thanks to a culture more encouraging of female employees. Ishioka Eiko also began her career at Shiseido.

132 Ōnishi Chizuko, quoted in 'Dezainā no jittai ishiki chōsa', pp. 88–9.

133 Maeda Masahito, 'Shirīzu teidan: Shōhin kaihatsu to josei pawā: Ishitsu na mono o kyōzon saseru junzairyoku o hikidasu', *Nikkei dezain* (July 1989), p. 130.

134 Ibid.

135 Dentsu Dezainingu Kenkyūkai, ed., 'Atogaki', p. 330.

136 'Kēsu sutadī DO kanpanī Dentsū: Henshin suru sekai saidai no kōkoku gaisha ni "dezain shinjidai" ga kage o utsusu', *Nikkei dezain* (July 1987), p. 49.

137 Murakami Masaaki, '"Dezain no jidai" ga motomeru habahiroku, kanōsei yutaka na jōhō', *Nikkei dezain* (Spring 1987), p. 2.

138 See for example the discussion of the process and context for designing telephone handsets in 'Shirīzu kandan: Ima, dezain no chikara o tou, Denwaki dezain no miseijuku bubun', *Nikkei dezain* (Spring 1987), pp. 38–45.

139 See for example the survey of design integration at leading companies, 'Ichiryū jōba kigyō toppu ankēto chōsa: Anata no kigyō ha DO kanpanī ka', *Nikkei dezain* (Spring 1987), pp. 18–29.

140 On the IdcN and public design promotion activities in Nagoya and Aichi see Kazuo Kimura, 'A New Era for Design Centers', *Design Management Journal*, IV/3 (1993), pp. 68–71. A useful timeline is 'Significant History', www.idcn.jp/en, accessed 11 December 2020.

141 Manufacturing in Aichi has eroded since the 1980s, with the decline of the Seto ceramics industry and Toyota's offshoring of manufacturing.

142 'Shiryō Dezain purodakushon, sengo no dōkō', *Tategumi Yokogumi*, 15 (Winter 1987), pp. Y8–Y9.

143 Ibid.

144 'Chōsa dezain jimusho keiei sōran Tonai-hen', p. 51.

145 'Shiryō Dezain prodakushhon', pp. Y8–Y9.

146 See for example 'Tokushū: Nippori Shinzō no dezain purodakushon tatemichi yokomichi', *Tategumi Yokogumi*, 15 (Winter 1987), pp. Y1–Y23.

147 Taketomo Masanobu, 'Zenkoku no shōkigyō ni mo supotto o', *Nikkei dezain*, 1 (July 1987), p. 7.

148 Araki Hironobu, 'Dezain to ha tokubetsu na mono de ha nai', *Nikkei dezain*, 1 (July, 1987), p. 7.

149 Murakami Katsunari, 'Nihon kigyō ni yoru gurōbaru dezain to chikyū kibō de hassō sareru māketingu ni tsuite', *AXIS*, 13 (Autumn 1984), p. 18.

150 Takeuchi, 'Home Electric Appliance Industry', p. 54.

151 Ibid., p. 53.

152 'Ikushīzu: Nijūdai no kuoritī raifu o enshutsu suru', *Bessatsu Bijutsu Techo Aki Dezain no genba kara part 2*, II/6 (Autumn 1983), p. 26.

153 Davina Jackson, 'Open the Pod Door', *Blueprint*, LXIV (February 1990), pp. 28–9.

154 On early 1980s Chinese exposure to Japanese design, see Yun Wang, 'The History of Contemporary Chinese Graphic Design in the Context of Globalisation', unpublished PhD dissertation, Royal College of Art, London, 2020, pp. 35, 43 and 63–7.

155 On Japan's economic downturn in the 1990s see Gary R. Saxonhouse and Robert M. Stern, eds, *Japan's Lost Decade: Origins, Consequences and Prospects for Recovery* (Malden, MA, 2004).

156 Okina, Shirakawa and Shiratsuka, 'The Asset Price Bubble and Monetary Policy', p. 399.

157 Ibid., p. 401.

158 Takeuchi, 'Home Electric Appliance Industry', p. 52.

159 On designers' experiences of recession in the 1990s, see Sarah Teasley, 'Contemporary Design History', in *A Companion to Contemporary Design (since 1945)*, ed. Anne Massey (London, 2019), pp. 9–31.

160 Nobumitsu Ōseko, 'Gurafikku dezain kono 10-nen', unpublished lecture given as part of the Nihon Dezain no Genjō lecture series, Maison Franco-Japonaise, Tokyo, 10 December 2007.

161 A useful overview of computer use in graphic and product design firms in the early 1990s is *Dezain no genba*, X/62 (June 1993), a special issue on 'Design in the Computer Age'. JAGDA's own report on industry digitalization is JAGDA no mirai o kangaeru kai (JAMIRA), *Gurafikku dezain no kinmirai ni kansuru repōto* (Tokyo, 1997).

162 On the history of game design in Japan, see Nikkei BP-sha Gēmu Sangyō Shuzai-han, *Nihon gēmu sofuto no sangyō-shi: Gēmu sofuto no kyojin-tachi* (Tokyo, 2016). There is a large literature on the history of anime. In English, see Jonathan Clements, *Anime: A History* (London, 2013).

163 For one account, see Teasley, 'Contemporary Design History', pp. 9–11.

164 Ogawa Shunji, 'GUI no 90 nendai', *Dezain nyūsu*, XXV/2 (Winter 2000), p. 55.

165 Ōseko, 'Gurafikku dezain kono 10-nen'.

Epilogue

1 On Japan in the 1990s, see Tomiko Yoda and Harry D. Harootunian, eds, *Japan after Japan: Social and Cultural Life from the Recessionary 1990s to the Present* (Durham, NC, 2006).

2 On the experience of changing labour market and employment structures in Japan since 1990, see Anne Allison, *Precarious Japan* (Durham, NC, 2013).

3 On consumption and society since the 1990s in Japan, see Katarzyna J. Cwiertka and Ewa Machotka, eds, *Consuming Life in Post-Bubble Japan: A Transdisciplinary Perspective* (Amsterdam, 2018).

4 Useful sources for mapping changes in product design in 1990s and 2000s Japan are the magazines AXIS, *Nikkei dezain* (Nikkei design) and some issues of *Casa Brutus*.

5 On PostPet, see Machiko Kusahara, 'Bridging Art, Technology and Pop Culture: Some Aspects of Japanese New Media Art Today', in *Routledge Handbook of New Media in Asia*, ed. Larissa Hjorth and Olivia Khoo (London, 2015), pp. 70 and 77 n17.

6 On population decline and ageing in Japan in the 1990s and early 2000s, see Florian Coulmas, *Population Decline and Ageing in Japan: The Social Consequences* (London, 2007).

7 On fiscal and administrative decentralization in the 1990s and early 2000s, see Carola Hein and Philippe Pelletier, eds, *Cities, Autonomy, and Decentralization in Japan* (London, 2006) and Brendan Barrett, 'Decentralization in Japan: Negotiating the Transfer of Authority', *Japanese Studies*, xx/1 (2000), pp. 33–48.

8 See Sarah Teasley, 'Why Furniture Is a Global Concern: Local Industry and Global Networks, through the Lens of Shizuoka Furniture-Making', *Current Issues in Global Furniture: Proceedings of the 8th biennial Furniture Research Group Conference. Missenden Abbey. Buckinghamshire New University 20 November 2013* (High Wycombe, 2014), pp. 41–64.

9 On depopulation, sustainability and rural revitalization, see Peter Matanle, 'Organic Sources for the Revitalization of Rural Japan', *Japanstudien*, xviii/1 (2007), pp. 149–80; Peter Matanle and Anthony Rausch, with the Shrinking Regions Research Group, *Japan's Shrinking Regions in the Twenty-First Century* (Amherst, NY, 2011); and Stephanie Assmann, ed., *Sustainability in Contemporary Rural Japan: Challenges and Opportunities* (London, 2015).

10 On Benesse Art Site Naoshima, see Adrian Favell, 'Islands for Life: Artistic Responses to Remote Social Polarization and Population Decline in Japan', in *Sustainability and Contemporary Development in Rural Japan*, ed. Assmann, pp. 109–24, and 'Benesse Art Site Naoshima', https://benesse-artsite.jp/en, accessed 27 April 2021. On the Echigo-Tsumari Art Triennale, see Susanne Klien, 'Contemporary Art and Regional Revitalisation: Selected Artworks in the Echigo-Tsumari Art Triennial 2000–6', *Japan Forum*, xxii/3–4 (2010), pp. 513–43; Ewa Machotka, 'Consuming Eco-Art: Satoyama at the Echigo-Tsumari Art Triennale 2012', in Cwitertka and Machotka, *Consuming Life in Post-Bubble Japan*, pp. 215–36; and 'Echigo-Trumari Art Field', www.echigo-tsumari.jp, accessed 27 April 2021.

11 On Nagaoka Kenmei and d design travel, see the D&DEPARTMENT website, www.d-department.com, accessed 27 April 2021. For discussions of D&DEPARTMENT projects including d design travel, see Sarah Teasley, 'Design Recycle Meets the Product Introduction Hall: Craft, Locality and Agency in Northern Japan', in *Craft Economies: Cultural Economies of the Handmade*, ed. Susan Luckman and Nicola Thomas (London, 2018), pp. 162–72, and Toby Slade, 'Decolonizing Luxury Fashion in Japan', *Fashion Theory*, xxiv/6 (2020), pp. 837–57.

12 On regional branding see Bridget Love, 'Fraught Fieldsites: Studying Community Decline and Heritage Food Revival in Rural Japan', *Critical Asian Studies*, xxxix/4 (2007), pp. 541–59, and Anthony Rausch, 'Japanese Rural Revitalization: The Reality and Potential of Cultural Commodities as Local Brands', *Japanstudien*, xx/1 (2009), pp. 223–45.

13 See Teasley, 'Design Recycle Meets the Product Introduction Hall'; Slade, 'Decolonizing Luxury Fashion in Japan'; and Liliana Morais, 'Spicing Up a 150-Year-Old Porcelain Factory: Art, Localism and Transnationalism in Arita's Happy Lucky Kiln', *International Journal of Japanese Sociology*, xxix (2019), pp. 52–73.

14 On *komyuniti dezain*, see Yamaguchi Ryo, *Komyuniti dezain: Hito ga tsunagaru shikumi o tsukuru* (Kyoto, 2011). An excellent analysis in English is Christian Dimmer, 'Place-Making Before and After 3.11: The Emergence of Social Design in Post-Disaster, Post-Growth Japan', *Review of Japanese Culture and Society*, xxviii (2016), pp. 196–226.

15 On *komyuniti dezain* and the 3.11 disaster, see Dimmer, 'Place-Making Before and After 3.11'.

16 A careful description of one design response to the 3.11 disaster is Yoko Akama, 'Ba of Emptiness: A Place of Potential for Designing Social Innovation', *Review of Japanese Culture and Society*, XXVIII (2016), pp. 227–46.

17 The Good Design Award website illustrates how categories have expanded since 2000, as well as providing an archive of categories and past winners since 1995. See 'Good Design Award', www.g-mark.org, accessed 27 April 2021.

18 On Cool Japan, see Michal Daliot-Bul, 'Japan Brand Strategy: The Taming of "Cool Japan" and the Challenges of Cultural Planning in a Postmodern Age', *Social Science Japan Journal*, XII/2 (2009), pp. 247–66, and Takeshi Matsui, 'Nation Branding through Stigmatized Popular Culture: The "Cool Japan" Craze among Central Ministries in Japan', *Hitotsubashi Journal of Commerce and Management*, XLVIII/1 (2014), pp. 81–79.

19 See for example *Modan ribingu e no yume: Sangyō kōgei shikenjo no katsudō kara*, exh. cat., Musashino Art University Museum and Library, Tokyo (Tokyo, 2017), the catalogue for an exhibition of prototypes and other materials from the Industrial Arts Institute (IAI). The exhibition and catalogue were major public outcomes of a large research grant from the Japanese Ministry of Education, Culture, Sports, Science and Technology which aimed to identify and catalogue important cultural heritage, including the materials of the former IAI now dispersed between multiple organizations.

20 On collaborative efforts to establish a design museum in Japan in the late 2000s, see *Dezaingaku kenkyū*, XIV/3, special issue: 'Dezain to myūjiamu: Aratana chi no bunka riron o motomete' (2007), and Nihon Dezain Dantai Kyōgikai (D8), 'Japan Dezain Myūjiamu Kōsō', unpublished workshop material, Tokyo, *c.* 2008. See also the archiving project conducted by NPO PLAT, 'Nihon no dezain ākaibu no jittai chōsa', npo-plat.org/archive.html, accessed 19 August 2021.

21 For the revisions to the Design Law (2020), see 'Reiwa Gannen Ishō-hō kaisei tokusetsu saito', sub-section 'Ishō-hō kaisei', www.jpo.go.jp, accessed 27 April 2021. A useful summary with English content is 'Ishō Seido no gaiyō', www.jpo.go.jp, accessed 27 April 2021.

22 See for example Ogawa Nobuko and Tanaka Atsuko, *Biggu ritoru Nobu: Raito [Wright] no deshi josei kenchikuka Tsuchiura Nobuko* (Tokyo, 2001); Mikiko Tsunemi, *Kuwasawa Yōko to modan dezain undō* (Tokyo, 2007); and Yasuko Suga, 'Modernism, Nationalism and Gender: Crafting "Modern" Japonisme', *Journal of Design History*, XXI/3 (2008), pp. 259–75.

23 See for example Akiko Yamasaki, *Kindai Nihon no shugei to jendā* (Yokohama, 2005); Sarah Teasley, 'Home-Builder or Home-Maker? Reader Presence in Articles on Home-Building in Commercial Women's Magazines in 1920s' Japan', *Journal of Design History*, XVIII/1 (2005), pp. 81–97; and Sarah Teasley, 'The Gender of Beauty in Architectural and Interior Design Discourse in Modern Japan', in *Visualizing Beauty: Gender and Ideology in Modern East Asia*, ed. Aida Yuen Wong (Hong Kong, 2012), pp. 113–30.

24 For a similar argument, see Nancy Stalker, 'Flower Empowerment', in *Rethinking Japanese Feminisms*, ed. Julia C. Bullock, Ayako Kano and James Welker (Honolulu, HI, 2018), pp. 103–18.

25 Penelope Francks, *The Japanese Consumer: An Alternate Economic History of Modern Japan* (Cambridge, 2009), pp. 179–80.

26 The interplay between overseas perceptions of Japan, images of Japan presented to international audiences and images of Japan held domestically has been the subject of extensive research in multiple disciplines. On this point in design specifically, see Ignacio Adriasola, Sarah Teasley and Jilly Traganou, 'Design and Society in Modern Japan: An Introduction', *Review of Japanese Culture and Society*, XXVIII (2016), pp. 1–3.

27 On Uniqlo see Stephanie Assmann, 'Consumption of Fast Fashion in Japan Local Brands and Global Environment', in Cwiertka and Ewa Machotka, eds, *Consuming Life in Post-Bubble Japan*, pp. 49–68.

28 There is an extensive body of work on contemporary Japanese fashion. An overview of avant-garde fashion from Japan, 1980–2010, is Akiko Fukai, Catherine Ince and Rie Nii, *Future Beauty: 30 Years of Japanese Fashion*, exh. cat., Barbican Art Gallery, London (London, 2010).

29 For a critical, historical contextualization of Japanese popular culture, see E. Taylor Atkins, *A History of Popular Culture in Japan: From the Seventeenth Century to the Present* (London, 2017).

30 On the minimalist craft aesthetic as luxury consumption, see Slade, 'Decolonizing Luxury Fashion in Japan'.

31 On participatory planning and *machi-zukuri*, see André Sorensen and Carolin Funck, eds, *Living Cities in Japan: Citizens' Movements, Machizukuri and Local Environments* (London, 2007), and Shigeru Satoh, *Japanese Machizukuri and Community Engagement: History, Method and Practice* (London, 2020). On activism, see Noriko Manabe, *The Revolution Will Not Be Televised: Protest Music After Fukushima* (Oxford, 2016).

Bibliography

1950 nendai Nihon no gurafikku dezain: Dezainā tanjō, exh. cat., Printing Museum, Tokyo (Tokyo, 2008)

1960 nendai gurafizumu, exh. cat., Printing Museum, Tokyo (Tokyo, 2002)

Adriasola, Ignacio, Sarah Teasley and Jilly Traganou, eds, *Review of Japanese Culture and Society*, xxviii, special issue: 'Design and Society in Japan' (December 2016)

Atkins, E. Taylor, *A History of Popular Culture in Japan: From the Seventeenth Century to the Present* (London, 2017)

Bartal, Ory, *Critical Design in Japan: Material, Luxury, and the Avant-Garde* (Manchester, 2020)

——, *Postmodern Advertising in Japan: Seduction, Visual Culture, and the Tokyo Art Directors Club* (Hanover, NH, 2015)

Brandt, Lisbeth K., *Kingdom of Beauty: Mingei and the Politics of Folk Art in Imperial Japan* (Durham, NC, 2007)

CCGA Gendai Gurafikku Āto Sentā, ed., *DNP Gurafikku dezain ākaibu setsuritsuten: Posutā gurafikkusu 1950–2000*, exh. cat., DNP Graphic Design Archive, Tokyo (Tokyo, 2000)

Cwiertka, Katarzyna J., and Ewa Machotka, eds, *Consuming Life in Post-Bubble Japan: A Transdisciplinary Perspective* (Amsterdam, 2018)

Donze, Pierre-Yves, 'Le Design industriel et l'intégration du Japon à l'économie globale (1900–1937)', *Histoire, économie et société*, xxxiv/4 (2015), pp. 93–109

——, and Rika Fujioka, 'The Formation of a Technology-Based Fashion System, 1945–1990: The Sources of the Lost Competitiveness of Japanese Apparel Companies', *Enterprise and Society* (19 March 2020), pp. 1–37

Dresser, Christopher, *Japan: Its Architecture, Art and Art Manufactures* [1882] (Cambridge, 2015)

Fischer, Felice, and Katherine B. Hiesinger, *Japanese Design: A Survey since 1950* (New York, 1995)

Francks, Penelope, *The Japanese Consumer: An Alternative Economic History of Modern Japan* (New York and Cambridge, 2009)

——, and Janet Hunter, eds, *The Historical Consumer: Consumption and Everyday Life in Japan, 1850–2000* (Basingstoke and New York, 2012)

Fujita, Haruhiko, *Gendai dezain-ron* (Kyoto, 1999)

——, and Christine Guth, eds, *Encyclopedia of East Asian Design* (London, 2020)

Geijutsu Kōgakukai Chiiki Dezainshi Tokusetsu Iinkai, ed., *Nihon chiiki dezain shi 1* (Kokubunji, 2013)

Graham, Patricia, *Japanese Design: Art, Aesthetics and Culture* (North Clarendon, VT, 2014)

Guth, Christine M. E., *Craft Culture in Early Modern Japan: Materials, Makers, and Mastery* (Berkeley, CA, 2021)

Hirano, Keiko, ed., *Jidai no aikon: 1950–2004: Nihon no gurafikku dezain 50-nen* (Tokyo, 2004)

Idea, 300 (September 2003), 50th anniversary special issue idea scrapbook

Inaga Shigemi, ed., *Dentō kōgei saikō: Miyako no uchisoto* (Kyoto, 2007)

Ihara Eiichi, *Nihon no dezain undō: Indasutoriaru dezain no keitō*, expanded edn (Tokyo, 1992)

Jinno Yūki, *Shumi no tanjō: Hyakkaten ga tsukutta teisuto* (Tokyo, 1996)

Kashiwagi Hiroshi, *Kindai Nihon no sangyō dezain shisōshi* (Tokyo, 1979)

Kawahata Naomichi, *Hara Hiromu to 'bokutachi no shin kappan jutsu': Katsuji shashin insatsu no 1930 nendai* (Tokyo, 2002)

Kikuchi, Yuko, *Japanese Modernisation and Mingei Theory* (London and New York, 2004)

——, 'Transnationalism for Design History: Knowledge Production and Decolonization through East Asian Design History', in *A Companion to Contemporary Design (since 1945)*, ed. Anne Massey (London, 2019), pp. 75–90

——, ed., *Refracted Modernity: Visual Culture and Identity in Colonial Taiwan* (Honolulu, HI, 2007)

Kōgei Zaidan, ed., *Nihon no kindai dezain undōshi: 1940 nendai kara 1980 nendai* (Tokyo, 1990)

Kōgyō Gijutsuin Sangyō Kōgei Shikenjo, ed., *Sangyō Kōgei Shikenjo 30 nenshi* (Tokyo, 1960)

Kōgyō Gijutsuin Seihin Kagaku Kenkyūjo, ed., *Sangyō Kōgei Shikenjo yonjū nenshi* (Tokyo, 1976)

Low, Morris, ed., *Building a Modern Japan: Science, Technology, and Medicine in the Meiji Era and Beyond* (Basingstoke and New York, 2005)

Matsudo-shi Kyōiku Iinkai Bijutsukan Junbishitsu, ed., *Dezain Nippon no suimyaku: Tōkyō Kōtō Kōgei Gakkō no ayumi 3*, exh. cat., Matsudo Municipal Museum (Matsudo, 2000)

——, *Dezain no yōran jidai: Tōkyō Kōtō Kōgei Gakkō no ayumi 1*, exh. cat., Matsudo Municipal Museum (Matsudo, 1996)

——, *Shikaku no Shōwa: 1930–40 nendai Tōkyō Kōtō Kōgei Gakkō no ayumi 2*, exh. cat., Matsudo Municipal Museum (Matsudo, 1998)

Modan ribingu e no yume: Sangyō Kōgei Shikenjo no katsudō kara, exh. cat., Musashino Art University Museum and Library, Kodaira (Kodaira, 2017)

Mori Hitoshi, *Nihon 'kōgei' no kindai; Bijutsu to dezain no botai to shite* (Tokyo, 2009)

——, ed., *Japanīzu modan: Kenmochi Isamu to sono sekai* (Tokyo, 2005)

——, ed., *Sōsho: Kindai Nihon no dezain*, 67 vols (Tokyo, 2007–15)

——, and Gifu-ken Gendai Tōgei Bijutsukan, eds, *Seramikkusu Japan: Tōjiki de tadoru Nihon no modan*, exh. cat., Museum of Modern Ceramic Art, Gifu, Tajimi (Tajimi, 2016)

Nagata Kenichi, Hida Toyorō and Mori Hitoshi, eds, *Kindai Nihon Dezain shi* (Kokubunji, 2006)

Namiki Seishi, Matsuo Yoshiki and Oka Tatsuya, *Zuan kara dezain e: Kindai Kyōto no zuan kyōiku* (Kyoto, 2016)

Nihon Dezain Shōshi Henshū Dōjin, eds, *Nihon dezain shōshi* (Tokyo, 1970)

Nihon Indasutoriaru Dezainā Kyōkai, *Nihon purodakuto dezainā no shōgen, 50 nen!* (Tokyo, 2006)

Nihon Interia Dezainā Kyōkai, eds, *Nihon no seikatsu dezain: 20 seiki no modanizumu o saguru*, exh. cat., Ozone Living Design Center, Tokyo, and International Design Center Nagoya (Tokyo, 1999)

Nihon Interia Dezainā Kyōkai Sōritsu 50 Shūnen Kinen Jigyō Jikkō Iinkai, ed., *Nihon dezain 50-nen* (Tokyo, 2008)

Nihon Sangyō Dezain Fukkōkai, ed., *Jidai o tsukutta Guddo Dezain: G-māku 40-nen sūpā korekushon: Shōhin katarogu + G-māku 40-nenshi* (Tokyo, 1996)

Partner, Simon, *Assembled in Japan: Electrical Goods and the Making of the Japanese Consumer* (Berkeley, CA, 2009)

——, *Toshié: A Story of Village Life in Modern Japan* (Berkeley, CA, 2004)

Pollard, Clare, *Master Potter of Meiji Japan: Makuzu Kôzan (1842–1916) and His Workshop* (Oxford, 2002)

Sand, Jordan, *House and Home in Modern Japan: Architecture, Domestic Space, and Bourgeois Culture* (Cambridge, MA, 2005)

——, 'Tropical Furniture and Bodily Comportment in Colonial Asia', *Positions: East Asia Cultures Critique*, XXI/1 (Winter 2012), pp. 95–132

Segi Shinichi, Tanaka Ikkō and Sano Hiroshi, eds, *Nissenbi no jidai: Nihon no gurafikku dezain 1951–70* (Tokyo, 2000)

Sengo Nihon dezain no kiseki 1953–2005: Chiba kara no chosen, exh. cat., Chiba Art Museum (Chiba, 2005)

Sparke, Penny, *Modern Japanese Design* (New York, 1987)

Suga, Yasuko, 'Modernism, Nationalism and Gender: Crafting "Modern" Japonisme', *Journal of Design History*, XXI/3 (2008), pp. 259–75

Takehara Akiko and Moriyama Akiko, eds, *Nihon dezain shi: karā-han* (Tokyo, 2003)

Takeuchi Yukie, *Kindai kōkoku no tanjō: Posutā ga nyū media datta koro* (Tokyo, 2011)

Tamari, Tomoko, 'The Department Store in Early Twentieth-Century Japan: Luxury, Aestheticization and Modern Life', *Luxury*, III/1–2 (October 2016), pp. 83–103

Tanaka Ikkō, ed., *Kikigaki dezain shi* (Tokyo, 2001)

Tanimoto, Masayuki, ed., *The Role of Tradition in Japan's Industrialization* (Oxford, 2006)

Teasley, Sarah, 'Design Recycle Meets the Product Exhibition Hall: Craft, Locality and Agency in Northern Japan', in *Craft Economies*, ed. Susan Luckman and Nicola Thomas (London, 2018), pp. 162–72

——, 'Tange Kenzō and Industrial Design in Postwar Japan', in *Kenzō Tange: Architecture for the World*, ed. Seng Kuan and Yukio Lippit (Zurich, 2012), pp. 157–75

Tipton, Elise K., and John Clark, eds, *Being Modern in Japan: Culture and Society from the 1910s to the 1930s* (Honolulu, HI, 2000)

Tōkyō Kokuritsu Hakubutsukan, ed., *Seiki no saiten bankoku hakurankai no bijutsu: Pari Uīn Shikago banpaku ni miru tōzai no meihin*, exh. cat., Tokyo

National Museum, and Osaka City Museum of Fine Arts, Osaka (Tokyo, 2004)

Tōkyō Kokuritsu Kindai Bijutsukan, ed., *Nihon no āru nūvō 1900–1923: Kōgei to dezain no shinjidai*, exh. cat., Tokyo National Museum of Modern Art (Tokyo, 2005)

——, ed., *Zuan no henbō 1868–1945*, exh. cat., Tokyo National Museum of Modern Art (Tokyo, 1988)

Waswo, Ann, *Housing in Postwar Japan: A Social History* (London, 2002)

Weisenfeld, Gennifer, '"From Baby's First Bath": Kao Soap and Modern Japanese Commercial Design', *Art Bulletin*, LXXXVI/3 (September 2004), pp. 573–98

——, 'Publicity and Propaganda in 1930s Japan: Modernism as Method', *Design Issues*, XXV/4 (October 2009), pp. 13–28

——, 'Selling Shiseido: Cosmetics Design and Advertising in Modern Japan', MIT Visualizing Cultures, http://visualizingcultures.mit.edu, accessed 10 March 2020

——, 'Touring Japan-as-Museum: NIPPON and Other Japanese Imperialist Travelogues', *Positions: East Asia Cultures Critique*, VIII/3 (December 2000), pp. 747–93

Yamasaki, Akiko, 'Handicrafts and Gender in Modern Japan', trans. Amelia Bonea, *Journal of Modern Craft*, V/3 (2012), pp. 259–74

Young, Louise, *Beyond the Metropolis: Second Cities and Modern Life in Interwar Japan* (Berkeley, CA, 2013)

Acknowledgements

The support and generosity of many people underpin this book. Grants and fellowships that facilitated the research and writing include: an Association for Asian Studies Northeast Asia Council Japan Studies Grant (2009); a Design History Society Research Grant (2009); Royal College of Art (RCA) internal research funding (2009); a Foreign Professional Development Research Fellowship at Musashino Art University (2009); a UK Arts and Humanities Research Council Early Career Fellowship (AH/I027088/1, 2012); a British Academy International Partnership and Mobility Award (175504, 2013–14); a Visiting Research Fellowship at Tokyo Zokei University (2013–14); an Ishibashi Foundation Visiting Professorship in Japanese Art History at a Heidelberg University (2018); a Japan Society for the Promotion of Science Grant-in-Aid for Scientific Research (A) (23242056, 2011–16); and the Program for the Strategic Research Foundation at Private Universities from the Ministry of Education, Culture, Sports, Science and Technology in Japan (S0801040, 2013–17). I am grateful to Sekine Yasumasa and to Kashiwagi Hiroshi and colleagues at Musashino Art University, respectively, for including me on the two latter projects. The College of Design and Social Context and School of Design at RMIT University generously supported publication.

Among individuals and companies who generously shared time, archives and insights, I thank Sugasawa Mitsumasa, Takayabu Akira, the late Meg Torbert, Maruni Wood Industry, Muroga Kiyonori and colleagues at Seibundo Shinkosha, Sano Yoshikazu and colleagues at the Industrial Research Institute of Shizuoka Prefecture, Zushi Masayuki of Shizuoka City, and Okuyama Takayoshi and colleagues at Tendo Co., Ltd. I am also indebted to the many individuals and organizations who facilitated image access and permissions for the book.

Several chapters were workshopped in 2018 at the Institute of East Asian Art History, Heidelberg and the School of Design at the Central Academy of Fine Arts (CAFA). I am grateful to Melanie Trede, Mio Wakita, Song Xiewei, Zhou Bo, Wang Naiyi and colleagues and students for the warm welcome and generous feedback. Presenting earlier versions of chapters at the 11th Symposium of the Design History Workshop Japan (2013), the Seattle Art Museum event 'Deco Japan: Shaping Art and Culture, 1920–1945' (2014), the University of Washington (2014), the Meiji Jingu-SISJAC Lectures (2016), the École des Hautes Études en Sciences Sociales (2016), the Design History Workshop Japan the 7th China Design Study Forum of Young Scholars at Nanjing University of the Arts (2017) and meetings of the International Committee on Design History and Studies (2018) and the Design History Society (2015, 2019) allowed me to hone the narrative and arguments.

Teaching with collections of the Victoria and Albert Museum (v&a), through my roles on the v&a/rca postgraduate programme in History of Design, allowed insights from artefact analysis to underpin the arguments, alongside work with archives, oral histories and secondary scholarship. I deeply appreciate this privilege. I thank Josephine Rout, Masami Yamada, Rupert Faulkner, Anna Jackson and colleagues in the v&a Asia Department, and Dorothy Armstrong and our students on the Material Histories of Asia course.

Situating design policy and practice in modern Japan within the regional context of northeast Asia was essential. I am indebted to my PhD students Yongkeun Chun and Wang Yun, both of whose theses are cited, to Jennifer Altehenger and Denise Y. Ho, and to colleagues at cafa, Nanjing University of the Arts and Tsinghua University Academy of Arts and Design for sharing their research into design in twentieth-century China.

My understanding of design in Japan has been forged by years of interchange with designers and design historians, journalists, editors and curators in Tokyo, London, the u.s. and now Melbourne. In Tokyo, heartfelt thanks go to professors, *senpai* and classmates at Musashino Art University and the University of Tokyo, particularly Kashiwagi Hiroshi, Hasegawa Gyō, the late Shimada Atsushi and Tanaka Jun, and to Mori Hitoshi and Uchida Seizō. I thank Watabe Chiharu for introductions, friendship, accommodation and embarking on projects together, and colleagues and friends at *Designers' Workshop*, idea and Nendo. Working with colleagues and students in the Schools of Design at the rca and rmit University has shaped my understanding of design's capacities. Colleagues and students in the v&a/rca History of Design postgraduate programme, the soas University of London Japan Research Centre, the Northwestern University Department of Art History and the University of Massachusetts Dartmouth Department of Art History helped me to situate the project in a wider temporal and transnational context.

Friends and colleagues provided constructive criticism and moral support. Members of the Japan Design History Workshop, including Suga Yasuko, Iguchi Toshino and Endō Ritsuko, provided a lively, supportive environment in the early stages of the project. Elizabeth Guffey, Angus Lockyer and Christine Guth commented on chapter drafts, measurably improving the book. Other friends and colleagues whose insights, questions and faith strengthened the project include Yuko Kikuchi, Jilly Traganou, Micah Auerback, Christina Laffin, Tanaka Atsuko, Laura Hein, Victor Margolin, Scott Johnson, Aleksandra Kobilijski, Yoko Akama, Aric Chen, Sunnie Chan and Sarah Cheang. Conversations with Hagishita Michiyo, Hagishita Katsuhisa, Hatakeyama Tomoko, the late Hatakeyama Yūji and Sahori Takeko helped me consider the significance of the project in very immediate ways. Thank you for your belief in me and in the book.

At Reaktion, editor Vivian Constantinopoulos offered patience, encouragement and keen suggestions. Managing editor Martha Jay, copy-editor Aimee Selby and designers Simon McFadden and Oliver Keen smoothly handled production and created a beautiful book.

My deepest gratitude is to the Teasley and Osborne families for their love and support, particularly to Cameron and Astrid. Astrid's contributions to image selection made completing this book significantly more fun.

Photo Acknowledgements

The author and publishers wish to express their thanks to the below sources of illustrative material and/or permission to reproduce it. Every effort has been made to contact copyright holders; should there be any we have been unable to reach or to whom inaccurate acknowledgements have been made please contact the publishers, and full adjustments will be made to any subsequent printings.

21_21 DESIGN SIGHT: p. 335; AIST (National Institute of Advanced Industrial Science and Technology)/private collection: pp. 207 (from *Kōgei nyūsu*, XVI/12, December 1948), 208 (from *Kōgei nyūsu*, XXV/2, February 1957), 271 (from *Kōgei nyusu*, XXXVI/5, January 1969); AIST/Sakakura Associates Inc./private collection (from *Kōgei nyūsu*, XXVIII/4, July 1960): p. 218; AIST/Sugiura Kōhei: p. 274 (from *Kōgei nyūsu*, XXXVI/5, January 1969); AIST/ Toshiba Science Museum/private collection: p. 223 (from *Kōgei nyūsu*, XXVIII/4, July 1960); Alamy: pp. 257 (Universal Art Archive); 285 (ZUMA Press, Inc.); Bijutsu Shuppan Sha/Nissan Motor Co. Ltd./private collection: pp. 224 (from *Ribingu Dezain*, IV, August 1958), 268 (from *Bijutsu Techo*, July 1970, pp. 34-35), 283 (from *Bijutsu techo bessatsu: Dezain no genba kara*, II-6, Autumn 1983); The Trustees of the British Museum (from *Front*, no. 1–2, Tokyo, 1942): p. 178; Canon Inc.: p. 331; D&DEPARTMENT PROJECT: p. 337 top; DNP Foundation for Cultural Promotion, Tokyo: p. 229; DNP Foundation for Cultural Promotion, Tokyo/family of Hayakawa Yoshio: p. 240; Free Library of Philadelphia: p. 22; m-louis/Flickr: p. 264 (Creative Commons Attribution-ShareAlike 2.0); GK Design Group, Tokyo: p. 265; Information Processing Society of Japan: p. 266; Hara Design Institute/Ryohin Keikaku: p. 334; Japan Design Committee: p. 213; collection of Scott Johnson: pp. 106, 120; JVCKENWOOD/Bijutsu Shuppan Sha/private collection: p. 294 (from *Bijutsu techo bessatsu: Dezain no genba kara*, II-7, Winter 1983); Kuwasawa Gakuen Educational Foundation/Bijutsu Shuppan Sha/private collection: p. 237 (from *Ribingu dezain*, 3, January 1955); Lafayette College, Easton, PA: pp. 118, 149 (Lin Chia-Feng Family Postcard Collection); The Mainichi Newspapers Co., Ltd.: pp. 216, 269, 279, 287, 293, 296; Maruni Wood Industry Inc.: pp. 289, 290; Mead Art Museum, Amherst College, Amherst, MA: pp. 76, 165 (Kageyama Tomohiro and Museum purchase with gift of funds from Scott H. Nagle (Class of 1985) in honor of Samuel C. Morse, Howard M. and Martha P. Mitchell Professor of the History of Art and Asian Languages and Civilizations, and the Richard Templeton (Class of 1931) Photography Fund); Meguro Museum of Art, Tokyo: p. 308; The Metropolitan Museum of Art, New York: pp. 37, 39; Museum of Applied Arts & Sciences, Sydney: p. 152 (Purchased 1998, Photo Marinco Kojdanovski); National Diet Library, Japan: pp. 28 (from *Dai Nippon bussan zue*, vol. I, publisher Ōgura Magobei, Tokyo, 1877), 30 (from *Nihon sankai meibutsu zue*, vol. III, publisher Kawachiya Morimoto Tasuke, Naniwa [Osaka], 1797), 32 (from *Dai Nippon bussan zue*, vol. I, publisher Ōgura Magobei, Tokyo, 1877), 33 (from *Hinagata miyako fūzoku*, vol. II, published by Tanimura Seibei et al., Kyoto, 1716), 34 (from *Sanyō zue ehon takara no itosuji*, publisher Maekawa Rokuzaemon, Edo [Tokyo], 1786), 36 (from *Tsukimi hakkei*, publisher Matsumura Tatsuemon), 38 (from *Kowatari sarasa fu*), 56 (from *Tokyo meisho zue*), 68–9 (from *Dai Sankai Naikoku Kangyō Hakurankai zue*, publisher Kodama Matashichi, 1890), 80 (from Nōshōmushō Shōkōkyoku, *Shinkoku kōgeihin ishō chōsa hōkokusho*, Tokyo, 1908), 82 (from *Tokyo fūkei*, publisher Ogawa Kazumasa, Tokyo, 1911), 86 and 88 (from *Tokyo fūkei*, publisher Ogawa Kazumasa, Tokyo, 1911), 104 (from *Azuma fūzoku fukuzukushi – Fukudoku*, publisher Takekawa Unokichi, 1889), 112 (from *Tokyo fūkei*, publisher Ogawa Kazumasa, Tokyo, 1911), 114 (from Nōshōmushō Sanrinkyoku ed., *Kokuyūrin to mokuzai*, Tokyo, 1907), 115 top (from Kansai Fuken Sōgō Kyōshinkai Aichi-ken Kyōsankai, *Kansai fuken sōgō kyōshinkai kinen shashinchō, daijūkai*, Nagoya, 1910), 130 (from Seikatsu Kaizen Dōmeikai ed. *Nōson seikatsu kaizen shishin*, Tokyo, 1931), 146 (from Chōsen Sangyō Ginkō, ed., *Chōsen shokusan ginkō to Chōsen no sangyō*, Keijō [Seoul], 1924), 153 (from Gaimushō Tsūshōkokyu, ed., *Zai Chōshun Nihon Ryōjikan kannai yōran*, Tokyo, 1929), 154 and 155 (from Matsumura Kōbundō, ed., *Zen Manshū meishō shashinchō*, Tokyo, 1937), 160 (from Pari Bankoku Hakurankai Kyōkai, ed., *1937-nen 'Kindai seikatsu ni okeru bijutsu to kōgei' Pari Bankoku Hakurankai Kyōkai jimu hōkoku*, Tokyo, 1939), 163 (from Taichū-shi, ed., *Taichū-shi gaikyō*, Taichū [Taichung], 1936); National Gallery of Victoria, Melbourne: pp. 119, 122, 144, 162; Nippon Design Center, Inc., Tokyo: p. 253; Nissan Motor Co., Ltd./Gihōdō/Private collection: p. 227 (from *Indasutoriaru dezain*, March 1957); Panasonic Corporation: p. 211; Panasonic Corporation/Bijutsu Shuppan Sha/ private collection: p. 317 (from *Bijutsu techo bessatsu: Dezain no genba kara*, II-6, Autumn 1983); PARCO CO., LTD/family of Ishioka Eiko/The Miyake Issey Foundation: p. 299; Printing Museum, Tokyo: p. 109; Printing Museum, Tokyo/family of Fushikida Takeshi/family of Uematsu Kuniomi/Asahi Kasei Corp./Studio Coba: p. 252; private collection: pp. 55 (from *Tejima Seiichi sensei den*, Tokyo, 1929), 90–91 (from Yasuda Rokuzō, *Shinshiki Nihon zuan no ōyō*, Tokyo, 1913), 99, 108, 111 (from *Mokkō to sōshoku* 2, April 1919), 115 bottom (from *Mokkō to sōshoku* 8, October 1919), 116 (from Atorie-sha, ed., *Gendai shōgyō bijutsu zenshū*, XIII: *Shimbun zasshi kōkoku sakurei shū*, Tokyo, 1929), 131 (from Kogure Joichi, *Wagaya o kairyō shite*, Tokyo, 1930), 134 (from Nishida Toraichi, *Saishin mokuzai kōgei taisei*, Tokyo, 1935), 136 (from *Kōgei nyūsu*, XIV/3, March 1946), 156 (from Minami Manshū Tetsudō Gaisha, ed., *Manshū ryokō no shiori*, Dairen [Dalian], 1935), 171 (from *Asahi kōkū*, February 1944), 172 (from Nihon Denken Kabushiki Gaisha Shuppanbu, ed., *Katei de dekiru kantan kagu to tsukuritsuke kagu*, 1942), 186 (from *Kōgei nyūsu*, XIV/3, March 1946), 187 (from Shōkōshō Bōekichō and Shōkōshō Kōgei Shidōsho, eds, *Yushutsu-muke kōgeihin sankō shiryō*, Tokyo, 1946), 192 and 195 (from *Kōgei nyūsu*, XV/7, October 1947), 196 (from *Kurashi no techō*, I, 1948), 233 (from Segi Shinichi, ed., *JAAC=Nissenbi 20-nen*, Tokyo, 1971), p. 243 (from Katagata Zenji, *Denka seikatsu annai*, Tokyo, 1962), 250 and 251 (from *Natsu no kateigi to gaishutsufuku*, July 1954), 260; Ryohin Keikaku/ family of Tanaka Ikkō/DNP Art Communications Co., Ltd: p. 300; Seibundo Shinkosha Publishing Co., Ltd: p. 232 (from *IDEA Magazine* 3 (November 1953); SOAS Library, SOAS University of London: pp. 204, 205, 217 (from Ajia Kyokai, *The Smaller Industry in Japan*, 1957); Sony Corporation: p. 297; Sony Network

Communications Inc.: p. 330; Sputniko!: p. 341; Suntory Holdings: p. 295; Super Potato/Shiratori Yoshio (Zoom): p. 288; Tadanori Yokoo/albertz benda, New York: p. 255; Tama Art University/ Bijutsu Shuppan Sha/private collection: p. 326 (from *Dezain no genba*, x/62, June 1993); photo Sarah Teasley: p. 337 bottom; Tendo Co., Ltd.: pp. 8, 16, 193, 249; Tokyo Institute of Technology Museum (from *Tokyo Kōtō Kōgyō Gakkō Nijūgonenshi*, Tokyo, 1906): p. 94; The University Art Museum, Tokyo University of the Arts and DNP Art Communications Co., Ltd: p. 92; University of Hawai'i at Mānoa Library, Honolulu: pp. 174, 182; Victoria and Albert Museum, London: pp. 23, 29, 44, 45, 46, 48, 49, 50–51 (from Murakami Takeji ed., *Kokon moyōshū: Musō kōeki monchō kanshu*, publisher Maekawa Zenbei, Osaka, 1885), 123, 141, 170; Waseda University Library: pp. 61–2; Yomiuri Photo Data Base: p. 278; Yusaku Kamekura Archive/Bijutsu Shuppan Sha (from *Ribingu dezain* 17 (May 1956): p. 199.

Designing Modern Japan

Index

Page numbers in *italics* indicate illustrations

Designing Modern Japan